THE NATURE
OF COMPUTERS

Second Edition

The Nature
of Computers

Second Edition

James A. O'Brien
Northern Arizona University

The Dryden Press
Harcourt Brace College Publishers

Fort Worth   Philadelphia   San Diego   New York   Orlando   Austin   San Antonio
Toronto   Montreal   London   Sydney   Tokyo

Executive Editor	Richard J. Bonacci
Developmental Editor	Elizabeth Hayes
Project Editor	Michele Tomiak
Art Director	Jeanette Barber
Production Manager	Erin Gregg
Director of Editing, Design, and Production	Diane Southworth

Copy Editor	John Dycus
Photo Researcher	Steven Lunetta/Page to Page
Indexer	Cheri Throop
Compositor	York Graphic Services, Inc.
Text Type	10.5/12 Clearface

Cover photos	Stuart Cummings, Florida

Address for orders:
The Dryden Press
6277 Sea Harbor Drive
Orlando, FL 32887-6777
1-800-782-4479 or 1-800-433-0001 (in Florida)

Address for editorial correspondence:
The Dryden Press
301 Commerce Street, Suite 3700
Fort Worth, TX 76102

ISBN: 0-03-006922-X

Photo and literary credits appear on pages 448 and 449, which constitute a continuation of the copyright page.

Printed in the United States of America

4 5 6 7 8 9 0 1 2 3 048 9 8 7 6 5 4 3 2 1

The Dryden Press
Harcourt Brace College Publishers

*To those who learn
and those who teach
about the
nature of computers
and to Erika
with love and light*

The Dryden Press Series in Information Systems

Arthur Andersen & Co./Flaatten, McCubbrey,
O'Riordan, and Burgess
Foundations of Business Systems
Second Edition

Arthur Andersen & Co./Boynton and Shank
Foundations of Business Systems: Projects and Cases

Anderson
*Structured Programming Using Turbo Pascal: A Brief
Introduction*
Second Edition

Brown and McKeown
Structured Programming with Microsoft BASIC

Coburn
Beginning Structured COBOL

Coburn
Advanced Structured COBOL

Dean and Effinger
*Commonsense BASIC: Structured Programming with
Microsoft QuickBASIC*

Federico
WordPerfect 5.1 Primer

Forcht
Management Information Systems: A Casebook

Goldstein Software, Inc.
Joe Spreadsheet, Macintosh Version

Goldstein Software, Inc.
Joe Spreadsheet, Statistical

Gray, King, McLean, and Watson
Management of Information Systems
Second Edition

Harrington
*Database Management for Microcomputers: Design
and Implementation*
Second Edition

Harris
Systems Analysis and Design: A Project Approach

Head
Introduction to Programming with QuickBASIC

Janossy
COBOL: An Introduction to Software Engineering

Laudon and Laudon
Information Systems: A Problem-Solving Approach
Third Edition

Laudon and Laudon
Information Systems: A Problem-Solving Approach
(A CD-ROM interactive version)

Laudon, Laudon, and Weill
The Integrated Solution

Lawlor
Computer Information Systems
Third Edition

Liebowitz
*The Dynamics of Decision Support Systems and Expert
Systems*

McKeown
Living with Computers
Fifth Edition

McKeown
Working with Computers
Second Edition

McKeown
Working with Computers with Software Tutorials
Second Edition

McKeown and Badarinathi
*Applications Software Tutorials: A Computer Lab Manual Using WordPerfect 5.1, Lotus 1-2-3, dBASE III
PLUS and dBASE IV*

McKeown and Leitch
*Management Information Systems: Managing with
Computers*

McLeod
*Systems Analysis and Design: An Organizational
Approach*

Martin
QBASIC: A Short Course in Structured Programming

Martin and Burstein
Computer Systems Fundamentals

Mason
*Using IBM Microcomputers in Business: Decision
Making with Lotus 1-2-3 and dBASE III PLUS/dBASE
IV*

Millspaugh
Business Programming in C for DOS-Based Systems

O'Brien
The Nature of Computers
Second Edition

Parker
Computers and Their Applications
Fourth Edition

Parker
Understanding Computers & Information Processing: Today and Tomorrow
Fifth Edition

Parker
Understanding Computers & Information Processing: Today and Tomorrow with BASIC
Fifth Edition

Robertson and Robertson
Microcomputer Applications and Programming: A Complete Computer Course with DOS, WordPerfect 5.1, Lotus 1-2-3, dBASE III PLUS (or dBASE IV) and BASIC

Robertson and Robertson
Using Microcomputer Applications (A Series of Computer Lab Manuals)

Simpson and Tesch
Introductory COBOL: A Transaction-Oriented Approach

Sullivan
The New Computer User

Swafford and Haff
dBASE III PLUS

Thommes and Carey
An Introduction to CASE Tools with Visible Analyst (DOS)
Using CASE Tools with Visible Analyst (Windows

Electronic Learning Facilitators, Inc.
    The DOS Book
    The Lotus 1-2-3 Book
    Stepping Through Excel 4.0 for Windows
    Stepping Through Windows 3.1
    Stepping Through Word 2.0 for Windows

Up and Running with Harvard Graphics 1.03 for Windows
Up and Running with PageMaker 5.0 for Windows
Up and Running with WordPerfect 5.2 for Windows
Up and Running with Quattro Pro 1.0 for Windows
Up and Running with Microsoft Works 2.0 for Windows
Up and Running with Lotus 1-2-3 Release 4 for Windows
Up and Running with Paradox 4.5 for Windows
Up and Running with DOS 6.0
Up and Running with Paradox 4.0 for DOS
Up and Running with Microsoft Works 3.0 for DOS
Up and Running with Excel 4.0 for the Macintosh
Up and Running with Word 5.1 for the Macintosh
Up and Running with PageMaker 5.0 for the Macintosh
Up and Running with Windows 4.0
Up and Running with WordPerfect 6.0 for Windows
Up and Running with Access 2.0 for Windows
Up and Running with Microsoft Works 3.0 for Windows
Up and Running with Excel 5.0 for Windows
Working Smarter with DOS 5.0
Working with WordPerfect 5.0
Working with WordPerfect 5.1

Martin and Parker
Mastering Today's Software Series
Texts available in any combination of the following:
    Microcomputer Concepts
    Extended Microcomputer Concepts
    Disk Operating System 5.0 (DOS 5.0)
    Disk Operating System 6.0 (DOS 6.0)
    Windows 3.1
    Word Processing with WordPerfect 5.1
    Word Processing with WordPerfect 5.2 for Windows
    Word Processing with WordPerfect 6.0 for DOS
    Word Processing with WordPerfect 6.0 for Windows
    Spreadsheets with Lotus 1-2-3 (2.2/2.3)
    Spreadsheets with Lotus 1-2-3 (2.4)
    Spreadsheets with Lotus 1-2-3 for Windows (4.01)
    Spreadsheets with Quattro Pro 4.0
    Spreadsheets with Quattro Pro 6.0 for Windows
    Database Management with dBASE III PLUS
    Database Management with dBASE IV (1.5/2.0)
    Database Management with Paradox 4.0

*Database Management with Paradox 5.0 for
    Windows*

Martin, Series Editor
*Productivity Software Guide Lab Manual Series
    Disk Operating System (DOS)
    Windows 3.1
    Word Processing with WordPerfect 5.1
    Word Processing with WordPerfect 5.2 for Windows
    Word Processing with WordPerfect 6.0 for Windows
    Spreadsheets with Lotus 1-2-3
    Spreadsheets with Lotus 1-2-3 for Windows (4.01)
    Spreadsheets with Quattro Pro 4.0
    Spreadsheets with Quattro Pro 6.0 for Windows
    Database Management with dBASE III PLUS
    Database Management with dBASE IV*

*Database Management with Paradox 4.0
Database Management with Paradox 5.0 for
    Windows
A Beginner's Guide to BASIC*

The Harcourt Brace College Outline Series

Kreitzberg
Introduction to BASIC

Kreitzberg
Introduction to FORTRAN

Pierson
Introduction to Business Information Systems

Veklerov and Pekelny
Computer Language C

Preface

The nature of computer literacy and the courses designed to teach it continue to change. Dynamic developments in computer technology and applications have required us to rethink and retool the content and pedagogy of introductory computer education. The content, organization, and teaching methodology of just a few years ago no longer meet current student and industry needs. Today it is not enough to teach students about the most current software and hardware. Students must learn how problem-solving principles are enhanced by harnessing the power of the computer. Part of this instruction must prepare students to understand that change is a constant in the world of computers. It is not enough for students to learn the keystrokes of a spreadsheet program, they must also learn the principles of how spreadsheet programs can solve business problems. It is not sufficient for students to learn a finite set of definitions and protocol, they must learn to think as end users of computer tools that change as quickly as do current events. This is the premise on which both the first and second editions of *The Nature of Computers* were written.

So many current textbooks are simply updated "introduction to data processing" texts, enhanced with coverage of microcomputer technology, productivity software, and other recent technological advancements. Many textbooks include far too many chapters on the details of computer hardware, programming languages, file and database processing, traditional systems development, and BASIC programming. Others resemble updated "computers and society" texts overflowing with so many topical items that it is difficult for students to read and comprehend the fundamental conceptual content of each chapter. Still others are simply enhanced software lab manuals whose conceptual content is replaced by their cookbook, hands-on content. Few of these approaches meet the educational needs of the majority of today's students. Most students will be end users in the workplace and in society—no matter what their majors are or what their careers will be.

A New Generation

Today's students need a new generation of computer literacy textbooks. The goal of the many instructors and Dryden Press specialists who have worked with me to produce this book has been to meet this growing need. I think we have succeeded in *The Nature of Computers*—we have developed a textbook that

- Truly uses an end user orientation in its organization and presentation.
- Effectively and personally introduces students to computing concepts and applications.
- Uses simple models and examples to illustrate the components of computer systems and information systems.
- Organizes its content into twelve nontraditional chapters that reflect changing technology and end user computing needs.
- Integrates coverage of the major functions of both system and application software packages.

The Nature of Computers represents an innovative, flexible, and "right-sized" new generation of computer literacy textbooks. It can be used as a stand-alone concepts text, or it can be paired with one or more of the many software-specific lab manuals available through the Dryden Press's EXACT custom publishing program. The text is written for the general end user of any academic major; it features up-to-date coverage of technical developments and examples of real-world end user applications, and it stresses ethical issues in each chapter that are directly related to the chapter's contents.

Modular Organization

The twelve chapters of this book are organized into four parts. After covering the material in "Part I: Foundations" the other three parts ("Part II: Software," "Part III: Hardware," and "Part IV: Applications and Issues") can be covered in any order, depending on the teaching preferences of the instructor.

The text also contains a Viewpoints section at the end of each part. Viewpoints use photo essays and text to dramatize "Computers in the Real World," "The World of Computer Graphics," "An End User's Guide to Computer Selection," and "Computers Past and Future." An appendix entitled "Computer Codes and Number Systems," a glossary, and an in-depth index complete the book.

Chapter Components

Each chapter begins with an outline and learning objectives; and each ends with an end note; a summary; key terms and concepts; a review quiz of true/false, multiple-choice, and fill-in questions; questions for thought and discussion; and review quiz answers. Each chapter also contains three brief Real-World Examples that illustrate how the chapter's topics apply to real people and organizations in today's workplace. Finally, each chapter features a section entitled Ethics that challenges students to think about ethical issues related to the chapter's contents.

Part I: Foundations   The first two chapters of the text serve as a *core module* of foundation concepts on computer hardware, software, and information systems. This enables instructors to cover the chapters of the remaining modules in any order that supports their instructional preferences. Chapter 1 introduces students to basic concepts of computers, their hardware, software, and capabilities, and a few key issues that affect end users working in a global information society. Chapter 2 introduces students to the basic components and types of information systems in the real world and discusses the importance of career and ethical issues in information systems.

Part II: Software   The four chapters of Part II cover software and its use in a variety of important end user applications such as office automation, desktop publishing, electronic spreadsheets, expert systems, and database management. This approach differs from others, which cover major types of software packages with only brief generic descriptions or detailed hands-on tutorials. This module is also placed early in the text to provide chapters on software concepts and applications, which supports early hands-on instruction and assignments using software-specific tutorial lab manuals.

Chapter 3 covers operating systems and other system software concepts and issues important to end users. Chapter 4 focuses on office automation software and applications, especially their use for word processing, desktop publishing, computer graphics, electronic mail, and office management. Chapter 5 focuses on decision-support software and applications, including electronic spreadsheets, what-if analysis, integrated packages, and expert systems. Finally, Chapter 6 covers database management software and its use for database development, information retrieval, and report generation. Personal information managers, text and image databases, and hypertext and hypermedia applications are also discussed in this chapter.

Part III: Hardware   The three chapters of Part III cover computer systems, peripherals, and telecommunications topics in more detail but from an end user perspective. Part III can be assigned before Part II if instructors prefer to discuss hardware concepts before covering software topics. Chapter 7 stresses the importance of major types of computer systems and also covers other computer concepts such as how computers execute instructions and represent data. Chapter 8 surveys the many types of peripheral devices used for input, output, and storage by end users. Chapter 9 discusses telecommunications network resources as well as many other important telecommunications topics end users should know.

Part IV: Applications and Issues   The three chapters of Part IV cover topics in application development by end users, computer applications in the workplace, and security and societal issues. Chapter 10 introduces students to application development from an end user perspective and covers related topics such as computer-aided development, prototyping, programming, and programming languages. Chapter 11 introduces a variety of computer applications in the workplace including applications in business, management, manufacturing, engineering and design, health care, and government. Chapter 11 includes a discussion of issues involved in managing end user and organizational computing in the workplace. Finally, Chapter 12 presents a lively discussion of computer crime and security, the impact of computers on society, and privacy, health, and ethical issues in computing.

New to the Second Edition

Software Coverage   New and expanded coverage in Part II, "Software," includes sections on Windows and Windows NT, planning for word processing, designing spreadsheet applications, and using database management packages.

Hardware Coverage   Chapter 7, "Computer Systems: Machines for End User and Organizational Computing," has been reorganized for better flow. The chapter now includes a Technical Note on how computers work that gives an explanation of how computers execute instructions. This material is optional for those instructors who do not wish to cover it.

Telecommunications Coverage   A new section on the Internet and the Information Superhighway has been added to Chapter 9, "Telecommunications Networks: Sharing Information and Computing Resources." This chapter has also been reorganized and includes a Technical Note on communications alternatives, covering such topics as transmission speeds, single versus multiple transmissions of data, and switching and access methods.

Quick Quizzes   Each chapter now has three self-test quizzes appearing after major sections within the chapter to help students check their reading comprehension. Answers are provided at the end of each quiz.

What Do You Think? Questions   These thought-provoking questions at the end of each Ethics box give students the opportunity to apply the material on ethics to their own lives.

Currency   Many of the Real-World Examples, photos, and technical material have been replaced with new, up-to-date examples.

Support Materials

The Nature of Computers is accompanied by an impressive supplement package worthy of a new-generation computer textbook. The various components utilize current software technology and new learning techniques, which together provide an integrated, innovative set of teaching tools.

Instructor's Manual   The *Instructor's Manual*, by Harvey Kaye of the City College of CUNY, utilizes an innovative learning methodology called *Integrated Skills Reinforcement*. Each chapter of the *Instructor's Manual* not only includes detailed lecture notes, a list of key terms, and teaching suggestions, but also includes exercises that enhance students' basic reading, writing, listening, and speaking skills while reinforcing the text's contents. Also included is a section on how to assign and evaluate student writing and collaborative activities.

Study Guide   The *Study Guide*, by Denis Titchenell of Los Angeles Community College, provides chapter summaries that include definitions of all key terms, additional questions for students to use in quizzing themselves on the text material, and numerous experiential exercises to enhance their learning experiences.

Information Systems Interactive Tutorial   This tutorial software, available for IBM-compatible computers on 3.5-inch diskettes, helps students review important concepts presented in classroom lectures. The program addresses the four major components of computers: hardware, software, systems, and computers in society. Each learning module has three parts: a content section, a practice section that includes a brief review of the concepts followed by multiple-choice questions, and a Flash Card Review that allows the student to make a "flash card" of any particular content screen for easy review. The flash card section lets the student review all the flash cards created for the module.

Other features include a notepad function, allowing students to take notes that they can print as hard copy, "hot" words that when double-clicked give a definition, and a pretest and final test that can be used by the instructor for tracking purposes.

LectureActive Software with Laserdisc   This package, featuring a laserdisc and software, is notable for its ease of use and time savings in creating vivid classroom presentations. The laserdisc includes video segments from CBS News and CSTV, hundreds of full-color electronic transparencies, and bulleted lecture outlines of the text for display in the classroom.

The laserdisc is driven by LectureActive, a user-friendly software program that lets the instructor create custom lectures swiftly and simply. A browse function helps the instructor search through the hundreds of stills and nearly 58 minutes of motion-video entries on the laserdisc. Once any video segment or still has been selected, the instructor can choose to attach the visual material to a lecture notecard on the computer screen. Instructors can use existing notecard prompts, editing or revising as needed, or create their own. Lecture notes from other sources can be brought over to the notecard lectures, so previous work is not lost. LectureActive is available for both Microsoft Windows and Macintosh platforms.

Transparencies and Testbook   More than 100 four-color overhead *Transparencies* are also available. A *Testbook* by Charles Beard of Blinn College includes more than 2,500 true/false, multiple-choice, and fill-in questions that are rated by type and difficulty. *Computerized Testbanks* by EXAMASTER are available in both 3.5-inch and 5.25-inch DOS, Windows, and Macintosh formats.

Videos   The 1995 Information Systems Video Series is currently available to adopters. This series, produced by Beverly Amer of Northern Arizona University, has been custom-developed specifically for classroom use. The series includes 14 videos ranging from 8 to 14 minutes in length. This informative, thought-provoking new series contains segments on the use of information technology in a variety of businesses such as United Parcel Service, Dell Computer Corporation, Alamo Rent A Car, and The Seagram Company. Accompanying the series is a detailed instructor's guide. Ask your Dryden Press sales representative for details on adoption criteria.

Acknowledgments

First of all, I wish to acknowledge the contributions of the following reviewers, whose constructive criticism and suggestions were invaluable in refining the content and form of both editions of *The Nature of Computers:*

Eve Austin
South Puget Sound Community College

Robert Anson
Boise State University

Anthony Q. Baxter
University of Kentucky

David Alan Bozak
State University of New York at Oswego

Carl M. Briggs
Indiana University

Warren G. Briggs
Suffolk University

Jack D. Cundiff
Horry-Georgetown Technical College

Mohammad B. Dadfar
Bowling Green State University

Joyce M. Farrell
McHenry County College

Shirley A. Hudson
Southern Illinois University at Carbondale

Peter L. Irwin
Richland College of the Dallas County Community College District

Taj-ui Islam
State University of New York at Brockport

Robert Jenkins
Utah Valley Community College

Brenda L. Killingsworth
East Carolina University

Marilyn G. Kletke
Oklahoma State University

Gene W. Lewis
Colorado State University

Dan Maguire
Northeast Texas Community College

M. Khris McAlister
University of Alabama at Birmingham

James N. Morgan
Northern Arizona University

Kay V. Nelson
North Idaho College

George Novotny
Ferris State University

Carl M. Penziul
Corning Community College

William Rayburn
Austin Peay State University

Richard St. Andre
Central Michigan University

Denis K. Titchenell
Los Angeles Community College

Karen L. Watterson
Watterson Database Group

John D. Witherspoon
Monroe Community College

In addition, I wish to recognize the following for their valuable contributions to the development of the textbook: Gerry Bedore of the University of Phoenix, who contributed the ideas and material for the text's "Viewpoint: An End User's Guide to Computer Selection;" Craig VanLengen of Northern Arizona University, who contributed many valuable ideas and material for sections on end user development, prototyping, and programming; and Gene W. Lewis of Colorado State University, who provided invaluable advice on the organization of the software section. I also wish to thank the authors of the support materials, which make this text a complete teaching/learning package:

Harvey Kaye
City College of CUNY
Instructor's Manual

Denis Titchenell
Los Angeles Community College
Study Guide

Charles Beard
Blinn College
Testbook

A special acknowledgment is owed to the editorial, production, and marketing team at The Dryden Press, who helped make this book a reality. I would especially like to thank executive editor Richard J. Bonacci for strongly supporting and encouraging this project and contributing invaluable advice and ideas for the book. I wish to thank developmental editor Elizabeth Hayes for steering this project through its review and revision stages and project editor

Michele Tomiak for her editing and coordination of the many pieces of this project as it wound its way through the complex production process. Jeanette Barber, our book designer, produced a design worthy of a new generation of textbooks. Photo/permissions editor Steven Lunetta researched and acquired the many photographs to accompany the text. Production manager Erin Gregg deserves praise for her careful monitoring of the production process. High praise is certainly deserved by Scott Timian, product manager, and Kathleen Sharp, Scott's assistant, for their hard work in marketing this project. Thanks also go to Michele Allen, whose word-processing skills helped me meet several manuscript deadlines.

The contributions of many authors, periodicals, and firms in the computer industry who provided ideas, illustrations, and photographs used in this text are also thankfully acknowledged.

James A. O'Brien

About the Author

James A. O'Brien is a professor of computer information systems at Northern Arizona University. He completed his undergraduate studies at the University of Hawaii and Gonzaga University and earned an M.S. and Ph.D. in business administration from the University of Oregon. He has been coordinator of the computer information systems area at Northern Arizona University, professor of finance and management information systems and chairman of the department of management at Eastern Washington University, and a visiting professor at the University of Alberta and the University of Hawaii.

Dr. O'Brien's business experience includes the Marketing Management Program of the IBM Corporation and General Electric's Financial Management Program. He spent several years as a financial analyst for the General Electric Company. He has also served as an information systems consultant to several banks and computer services firms.

Dr. O'Brien has written eight books, including several that have been translated into Dutch, French, and Japanese. He has contributed to a wide variety of business and academic journals and participates actively in academic and industry associations in information systems.

Contents in Brief

Contents

The Nature of Computers

Second Edition

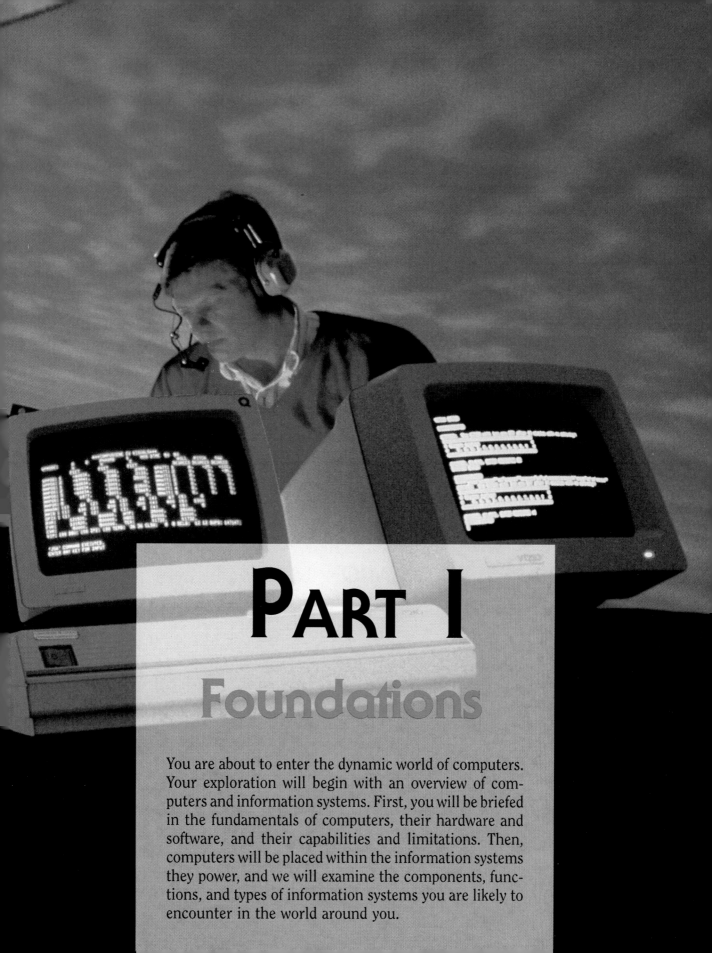

PART I

Foundations

You are about to enter the dynamic world of computers. Your exploration will begin with an overview of computers and information systems. First, you will be briefed in the fundamentals of computers, their hardware and software, and their capabilities and limitations. Then, computers will be placed within the information systems they power, and we will examine the components, functions, and types of information systems you are likely to encounter in the world around you.

CHAPTER

1

COMPUTERS: ENGINES FOR OUR INFORMATION SOCIETY

OUTLINE

You and Computers

End User Computing

Overview of Computer Hardware

Overview of Computer Software

What Computers Can and Can't Do

The Global Information Society

Ethics: Computer Crime and Ethics

End Note: End Users and
  Computers

LEARNING OBJECTIVES

After reading and studying this chapter, you should be able to

Explain why you need both conceptual and functional computer literacy.

Describe the basic functions of computer systems and their hardware components.

Describe the basic functions and types of system and application software.

Identify commonly used terms for computer time elements and storage capacity.

Identify key benefits and limitations of computers.

Discuss your responsibilities in the ethical use of computers.

You and Computers

Do you really have to learn about how computers are used by people and organizations in society, and how you can personally use them? That is, do you need to achieve **computer literacy**? The answer is no if you don't really care whether you succeed in the workplace of today or tomorrow. The answer is yes if you want to be a successful professional, executive, or entrepreneur in a society where computers are vital but commonplace tools. So whether you want to rise to the top of your profession, be a manager in a large organization, or just be your own boss, you will need to know about computers and how they can help you get the information you will need to be successful.

computer literacy
Learning the fundamentals of how computers are used in society and how you can personally use them.

Computer Literacy

The first thing you need to know are some basic facts about computers, their benefits and limitations, and how they help people working in many types of organizations. That's what we call **conceptual computer literacy**. A common misconception is that you just need to know how computers can help accomplish specific jobs you may need to perform. While this view may enable you to survive in society, it does not really help you succeed. Some people who use computers at work or play may just be feeding data to a computer, responding to its requests, or accepting the output that it produces. They may not have a clear idea of how people use computers to become more effective and productive. So having a basic conceptual knowledge of computers and their use in business and society is an important achievement. Without it, "you can't see the forest for the trees."

conceptual computer literacy
Knowledge of the technology and uses of computers and their benefits and limitations.

The second thing you need to know is how to actually use a computer. You really should acquire a "hands-on" knowledge or **functional computer literacy**. That is, you need to attain *competency* in your use of computer systems. This will make you a valuable **end user**, someone who effectively uses computers or the information they produce.

functional computer literacy
Knowing how to actually use a computer.

end user
Anyone who uses an information system or the information it produces.

The days of relying on computer professionals—such as systems analysts or programmers—to meet most of our information-processing needs are over. That's because many organizations can't keep up with the information demands of their end users. More and more people must learn to use microcomputers as *end user workstations* in order to get the information they need to accomplish their jobs. Thus, a conceptual knowledge of computers and their uses is important, but not good enough. As a computer-literate end user, you also need firsthand experience in using computers to help you get things done. That is, you need to experience *end user computing*.

End User Computing

What is **end user computing**? It's the direct, hands-on use of computers by end users, instead of the indirect use provided by the hardware, software, and personnel resources of an organization's computer services or *information systems* (IS) department. This does not mean that people don't rely on such resources. However, in end user computing, an IS department plays only a supportive role to an end user's own computing resources and efforts.

end user computing
The direct, hands-on use of computers by end users, instead of the indirect use provided by the hardware, software, and personnel resources of an organization's information systems department.

REAL-WORLD EXAMPLE

PED Manufacturing: End User Computing

PED Manufacturing in Oregon City, Oregon, is typical of a company facing the challenges of end user computing. The 100-employee firm, which manufactures casings for the aerospace and medical industries, had strong business motivations for spending nearly $100,000 to switch its 45 computer users to microcomputer-based end user applications. "We are bringing in lots of new employees, and we wanted them to get up to speed quickly on several applications," says Information Systems Manager Dave Howell.

At first, most users at PED were Johnny-one-notes who used a single application, either Lotus 1-2-3 or WordPerfect, and rarely experimented with other programs. Today, PED feels the invest-

ment has paid off. Training time has been cut by 40 percent, and almost everyone now uses five applications—Word for Windows for word processing, Excel for spreadsheet analysis, Mail for telecommunications, PackRat for contact information, and Superbase for data management. "By cross-training on several programs, people can easily move among departments and contribute more to the entire organization," says President Richard Day.

1. Is computer literacy a job requirement at PED Manufacturing? Explain.
2. What benefits do you think PED Manufacturing gains from end user computing?

End user computing has grown because of dramatic improvements in the cost and capabilities of computer hardware and software. The development of personal computers (microcomputers) has brought computing power to individual end users. Also, software packages for all types of applications have proliferated and improved in their cost, power, and ease of use. The improvements have made hardware and software affordable and attractive. These developments are reinforced by the growing familiarity of many people with computers, caused by their long-time and widespread use in schools, businesses, and other organizations. Thus, end users can turn to the direct use of computers to solve their information processing problems.

For instance, end users can create and edit letters and reports (*word processing*), use an electronic worksheet for analysis and planning (*electronic spreadsheets*), create files of data and produce reports based on that data (*database management*), use graphics displays to present their results (*graphics*), and use telecommunications networks to access and communicate with other end users and computer systems (*telecommunications*). As a computer-literate end user, your goal should be to acquire a similar ability to effectively use computers as productivity tools to help you achieve your career goals.

Overview of Computer Hardware

Let's start our discussion of computers by defining what a computer is. Then we will see how a computer's hardware components work together to perform information processing chores for you and other end users.

Note: This chapter will give a brief overview of computer hardware and software so you can then move to later software topics (Chapters 3, 4, 5, and 6) or hardware topics (Chapters 7, 8, and 9) at your instructor's discretion.

Computers come in all sizes. These examples show a micro-computer chip (top left), a typical desktop microcomputer (top right), and a large mainframe computer (bottom).

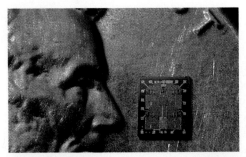

What Is a Computer?

computer
A device that has the ability to accept data, internally store and automatically execute a program of instructions, perform mathematical and other operations on data, and report the results.

Generically, a **computer** is *a device that has the ability to accept data, internally store and automatically execute a program of instructions, perform mathematical and other operations on data, and report the results.* Most computers use microelectronic *chips* that place the circuitry to process or store data on tiny pieces (about 1/4-inch square) of silicon or other materials. There are many varieties of computers, including tiny *microprocessors* that can fit a computer's processing components on a microelectronic chip, small *microcomputers*, midsize *minicomputers*, and large *mainframe* computers.

This computer system consists of a keyboard for input, microprocessors and other circuitry in its main system unit for processing and control, a video monitor and printer for output, and memory chips, floppy disk drive, and hard magnetic disk for storage.

The physical devices of a computer are known as **hardware.** Examples include the central processing unit, or CPU, and *peripheral* devices such as keyboards, video monitors, disk drives, and printers. The operating instructions for a computer are called **software.** Most of the time, this means the *programs* or sets of instructions that computers need to operate. But, generically, software can also include the *procedures,* or instructions, for people who operate computers and do information processing chores.

A Computer System

Most computers consist of interconnected hardware components that form a **computer system.** For example, a typical microcomputer system might include a keyboard and electronic mouse for *input* of data and commands, a main *processing* unit, a video monitor and printer for *output* of results, and magnetic disk drives for *storage* of data and programs.

It is important for you to realize that any computer is more than an electronic "black box" or a collection of electronic devices. A computer is a **system**—*an interrelated combination of components that work together to achieve a common goal.* That goal is to provide a powerful information processing tool. Understanding a computer as a computer system is an important step in attaining computer literacy. You should be able to visualize any computer this way, from a microcomputer to a large computer system whose components are interconnected by a telecommunications network and spread throughout a large geographic area. Figure 1-1 illustrates that a computer is a system of hardware devices organized to perform five basic functions: input, processing, output, storage, and control.

Input

Input devices enter your data and commands into a computer system. Examples include keyboards, touchscreens, electronic "mice," and optical scanners. These input devices convert data and instructions into electronic pulses for entry directly or through telecommunications links into a computer system. For example, you may use a keyboard and mouse to communicate with your microcomputer, while a supermarket depends on optical scanners to "read" the bar codes on food packages.

Processing

The **central processing unit (CPU)** is the main information processing component of a computer system. (In microcomputers, it is called the main **microprocessor.**) The electronic circuits of the *arithmetic–logic unit (ALU),* one of the CPU's major components, perform the arithmetic and logic functions required by computer instructions. For example, when you are ready to graduate, the ALU of your university's computer will perform the *arithmetic* functions needed to compute your grade point average (GPA). Then it will do *logic* functions that compare your GPA with the minimum GPA needed to graduate at your college or university to determine your graduation status.

---

hardware
The physical devices of a computer, including its central processing unit (CPU), and peripheral devices such as keyboards, video monitors, and printers.

software
Computer programs and end user procedures concerned with the operation of an information system.

computer system
A computer is a system of input, processing, output, storage, and control components. Thus a computer system consists of input and output peripheral devices, primary and secondary storage devices, and a central processing unit (CPU).

system
A group of interrelated components working together to achieve a common goal.

central processing unit (CPU)
The unit of a computer system that includes the circuits that control the interpretation and execution of instructions. In many computer systems, the CPU includes an arithmetic-logic unit and a control unit, and other processing and control circuitry.

microprocessor
A central processing unit on a chip.

Output

The output devices of a computer system enable it to communicate with you. Examples include video monitors, printers, and voice response units. Thus, output devices convert electronic information produced by the computer system into a *human-intelligible* form for presentation to you and other end users. For example, you will typically receive output in the form of video displays, paper reports, and voice responses from many computer systems.

Storage

A computer stores data and programs temporarily during processing in the microelectronic circuit chips of its *primary storage unit,* popularly called its *memory.* Data and programs stored in memory are lost when most computers are turned off. So, a computer also stores data and programs in more permanent form on *secondary storage* devices such as magnetic disks, magnetic tape, and optical disks. These devices provide large storage capacities for data and programs until the next time they need to be used.

Control

Computers need to control their input, processing, output, and storage activities. That's why they have a *control unit,* which is part of the CPU. The electronic circuitry in the control unit interprets the instructions of the computer programs you are using, and transmits directions on what to do to other components in the system.

Figure 1-1
A computer is a system of hardware components.

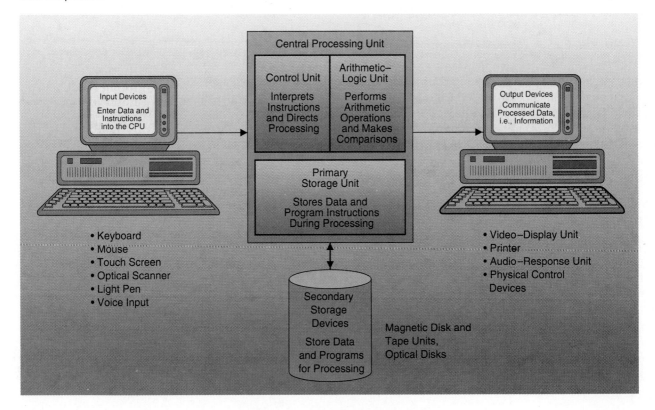

The three most common categories of computer systems are the microcomputer, minicomputer, and mainframe computer.

Types of Computer Systems

There are several types of computer systems, as the photographs above show. Traditionally, small personal computers (PCs) have been classified as *microcomputers,* and small to midsize computers used for departmental or small organization computing have been known as *minicomputers.* Larger computers that can handle the computing needs of large organizations are typically called *mainframe* computers, or simply *mainframes.*

However, these classifications do overlap each other. That's why classifications such as *supermini* computers, which are more powerful than some mainframe computers, exist in the computer industry. In addition, computers are frequently classified by their primary use or *application.* For example, computers that help control telecommunications networks of other computers may be called *host* computers or network *servers,* while some microcomputers with extensive computing power and graphics capabilities may be called *technical workstations.*

Storage media used in computer peripherals may include silicon chips, optical disks, hard magnetic disks, and floppy disks.

Computer Peripherals

Peripherals is the name given to computer system devices for input, output, and secondary storage. Popular input peripherals include keyboards, electronic mice, trackballs, touchscreens, and optical scanning devices. Video monitors and printers are the most widely used output devices; voice response units and plotters are other examples. Storage peripherals include magnetic disks in the form of floppy disks and hard disk drives, magnetic tape, and optical disks such as CD-ROM (compact disk read-only memory).

Peripheral devices depend on direct connections or telecommunications links to the CPU. Thus, all peripherals are **online** devices; that is, they are separate from, but can be electronically connected to and controlled by, the central processing unit. (This is the opposite of **offline** devices, such as typewriters or calculators, that are not under CPU control.) Many peripheral devices use a variety of *media* to help process or store data. Examples include magnetic disks, magnetic tapes, optical disks, and, of course, paper documents such as paychecks or sales forms.

peripherals
In a computer system, any equipment distinct from the central processing unit that may provide the system with input, output, or secondary storage capabilities.

online
Pertaining to devices under control of the central processing unit.

offline
Pertaining to devices not under control of the central processing unit.

Computer Networks

Many computer systems are interconnected by communications links so end users can communicate electronically and share the use of hardware, software, and data resources. **Telecommunications** is the use of *networks* of

telecommunications
The use of networks of interconnected computers and other devices to communicate electronically and share computing resources.

interconnected computers and other devices to electronically exchange data and information and share computing resources.

Telecommunications networks may cover a wide geographic area (a *wide area network* or *WAN*) or interconnect computers in an office or other work site (*a local area network or LAN*). Telecommunications networks use a variety of hardware devices and software packages to support electronic communication of data, text, voice, and images among end users. For example, your microcomputer may have to be outfitted with a communications circuit board and use a telecommunications package so you can communicate over a worldwide communications satellite network to other computer users. Or your microcomputer may just be part of an office local area network that allows you to share data and programs and communicate with your colleagues as you work together on projects.

Quick Quiz

1. A computer is a system of _____ devices.
2. The physical devices of computers are called _____.
3. Computer _____ are a computer system's input, output, and secondary storage devices.
4. The _____ is the main processing and control component of a computer system.
5. The three most common categories of computer systems are _____, _____, and _____.

Answers: 1. input, processing, output, storage and control
2. hardware 3. peripherals 4. central processing unit (CPU)
5. microcomputers, minicomputers, mainframes

A local area network (LAN) helps office workers share hardware, software, and data resources.

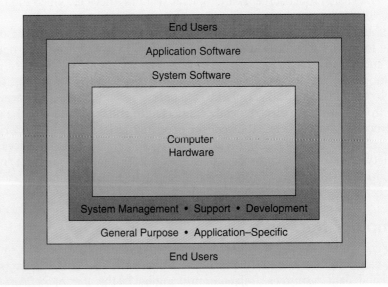

Figure 1-2
System and applications programs provide a software interface or layer between end users and computer hardware.

Overview of Computer Software

You will depend on several major types of software as you work with computers. Software "gives life" to hardware. For example, most computers can do nothing when you turn them on until you load programs stored on magnetic or optical disks into their main memory. That's why you should know the characteristics and purposes of major types of *software packages*, that is, computer programs. Computer software is typically classified as *system software* and *application software*. Figure 1-2 shows that such programs form a vital *software interface*, or software layer, between computer hardware and the computing efforts of end users.

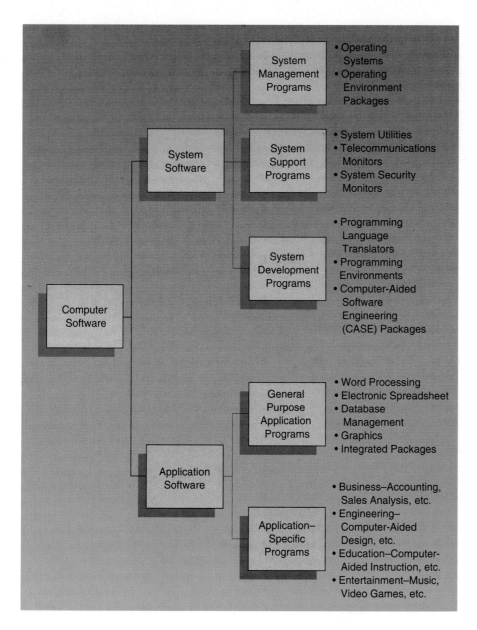

Figure 1-3
Computer software can be divided into a variety of system and application software packages.

REAL-WORLD EXAMPLE

Hyundai Motor America:
Laptop Dependency

Hyundai Motor America, headquartered in Fountain Valley, California, had a problem. Its sales reps carried reams of paper records in case they had to look up information on their sales calls to Hyundai dealers. A big percentage of their time was spent making telephone calls back to their regional offices. Reps also spent a lot of their time doing administrative paperwork. Hyundai's solution involved outfitting all of its 60 dealer sales reps with Compaq laptops. Each notebook-size computer is installed with a variety of software packages to increase sales rep productiity. These including Lotus 1-2-3 for spreadsheets and graphics, Displaywrite for word processing, Rbase for database management, and the PS/PC package for electronic mail and other telecommunications.

Several months later, Hyundai's four regions reported a reduction in work load for their administrative staffs, less need to fly in sales reps for meetings, and a significant reduction in phone bills due to the use of electronic mail. The sales reps also save time in meetings because they can pinpoint required sales data in spreadsheets instead of searching through extensive paper records. They also are more prepared and have more time to spend with the car dealers they call on. The laptops were such a hit that the central region's general manager told Hyundai Motor America's executive committee, "If you try to take away these PCs from my people, I'd have complete mutiny. You cannot take these away; we are dependent on them; that's how they do their jobs."

1. Why have the sales reps at Hyundai become so dependent on their laptop computers?
2. What other types of occupations could also benefit from the use of laptop computers?

Figure 1-3 presents an overview of these major types of software. It summarizes the major categories of system and application programs developed for end users by computer professionals called *programmers*. Of course, this is a conceptual illustration. The type of software you will encounter depends to a great extent on the manufacturer and the model of computer you use. More importantly, it depends on what additional software is acquired to increase your computer's performance or to accomplish specific tasks for you and other end users.

System Software

system software
Programs that manage and support a computer system as it executes the application programs of end users. The operating system is the most important system software package.

operating system
The main control program of a computer system. It controls a computer by communicating with end users, managing hardware resources and files, supervising the accomplishment of tasks, and providing other support services.

System software forms a layer of programs that manage and support your computer system as it uses other software packages to do whatever you have asked it to do, whether it's word processing or running a video game. As Figure 1-3 shows, there are many types of system programs. Notice that system software can be grouped into the three major categories of *system management, system support,* and *system development* programs.

System management programs manage the hardware, software, and data resources of a computer system during its execution of the application programs jobs of end users. Major system management programs are operating systems (like Microsoft's DOS, IBM's OS/2, or Apple's System 7) and operating environment packages like Microsoft's Windows. The **operating system** is one of the most important software packages for any computer. That's because

REAL-WORLD EXAMPLE

Mrs. Fields Cookies: Software for Cookie Stores

There really is a Mrs. Fields. She's Debbie Fields, CEO and president of Mrs. Fields Cookies Inc. of Park City, Utah. Her 600 cookie stores are a familiar sight in shopping malls and other retail centers in the United States, Canada, and several other countries. How does she run her cookie empire? With computers, of course. Each store has a personal computer (PC) connected by telephone links to a central microcomputer in Park City. In addition, Debbie Fields uses her PC to communicate with store managers at each location and keep track of their performance. Here's what she says: "I use Lotus 1-2-3 [a spreadsheet software package] to rank people and their performance. I look at people by all of the food group categories. Who sells the most cookies and muffins? I rank those people from top to bottom and post the results on the system . . . Agenda [a personal information manager package] has helped me because it pops up what I consider to be the priorities. What I love about this system is that it balances my thinking style. I love detail, but I don't want to get bogged down in it."

1. Why does Debbie Fields use the Lotus 1-2-3 and Agenda software packages?
2. Would you like to be a store manager at Mrs. Fields? Why or why not?

---

it manages the input, processing, output, and storage operations of the computer system. For example, do you realize that the operating system of a computer must be loaded into memory and activated before you can accomplish any other task with your computer?

System support programs refers to software that provide a computer system with a variety of support services. Examples are system utilities, telecommunications monitors, and security monitors. *Utility* programs frequently do chores such as copying disks or sorting data. Telecommunications and security monitors help manage telecommunications and protect computer system resources. For example, *telecommunications monitors* may control and support your use of telecommunications to access a computer network, while *security monitors* may control your access to sensitive data resources.

System development programs help computer specialists and end users develop programs and procedures for end user applications. Examples include programming language translators and CASE (computer-aided software engineering) packages. For example, if you want to develop or use a program in a programming language like BASIC, you need to use a BASIC *language translator program*. CASE packages provide helpful features and programs that automate many of the software-development activities of computer professionals.

Application Software

Application software makes it possible for computers to do a particular job, or *application,* that you want accomplished. Thousands of *application packages* are available because there are thousands of jobs end users want computers to do. The widespread use of personal computers has accelerated the growth of application programs.

application software
Programs that direct the performance of a particular use or *application* of computers for end users. Examples are word processing and spreadsheet programs, business, engineering, or educational programs, and so on.

Popular microcomputer application software may be purchased off-the-shelf or through catalogs.

This photo has been enhanced on a computer to show the chemical variations in the rings surrounding the planet Saturn.

Figure 1-4 showed that application software includes a variety of programs that can be subdivided into *general-purpose* and *application-specific* categories. General-purpose application programs perform common information processing jobs for end users. For example, word processing programs like WordPerfect or Microsoft Word, spreadsheet programs like Lotus 1-2-3 or Excel, database management programs like dBase IV and Paradox, integrated packages like Microsoft Works, and graphics programs like Lotus Freelance are popular with microcomputer users for home, education, business, scientific, and many other purposes. Because they significantly increase end user productivity, they are also known as *productivity packages.*

Numerous packages are also available to support specific applications of end users in business, science, and other fields. Business application programs help accomplish important business activities. Examples of such business functions and their corresponding applications are accounting (payroll), marketing (sales analysis), finance (cash budgeting), manufacturing (production scheduling), operations management (inventory control), and human resource management (employee benefits analysis).

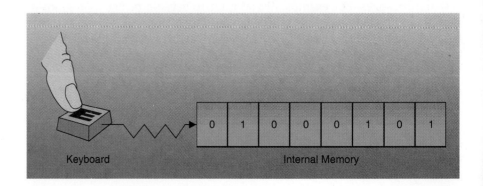

Figure 1-4
Pushing the letter **E** on the keyboard transmits its binary code into the computer's memory.

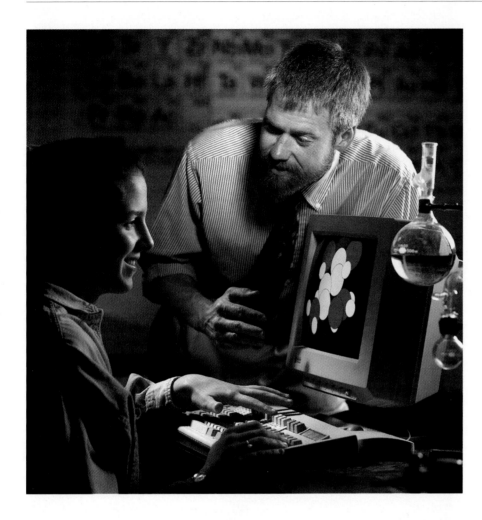

Software packages are available for performing educational experiments with a computer.

Scientific application programs perform information processing tasks for the natural, physical, social, and behavioral sciences and for mathematics, engineering, and all other areas involved in scientific research, experimentation, and development. Broad application categories include scientific analysis, engineering design, and monitoring of experiments. The computer enhancement of data transmitted by spacecraft on journeys into outer space is an example of the use of scientific application software.

There are so many other application areas of computers that we can only mention a few examples here. For instance, we can talk of application packages in edu-cation, entertainment, music, art, law enforcement, and medicine. Some specific examples are computer-assisted instruction programs in education, medical diagnostics programs in health care, and computer-generated music and art packages.

Quick Quiz

1. The operating instructions for computers are called _____.
2. Computer software is typically classified as _____ and _____ software.

3. System software forms a software _____ or _____ of programs that manage and support your computer system as it uses application software packages.
4. An operating system is an important example of _____ software.
5. A video game package is an example of _____ software.

Answers: 1. software   2. system and application   3. interface or layer   4. system   5. application

What Computers Can and Can't Do

Computers can do some amazing things. The popular media—TV, movies, books, and magazines—glamorize the speed, power, and accuracy of computers in everything from art and music, business and medicine, to military and spacecraft systems. You yourself have probably experienced the excitement of the speed and power computers bring to video games and other everyday activities that depend on computers. However, you should remember that computers are just electronic tools, not the *electronic brains* of science fiction. In fact, computers can do nothing without humans to conceive, design, and implement how they can be used. Let's take a closer look at what computers can and can't do.

Computers and Humans

Computers compute, humans think. Computers can do complex calculations and other data manipulations faster, more accurately, and more dependably

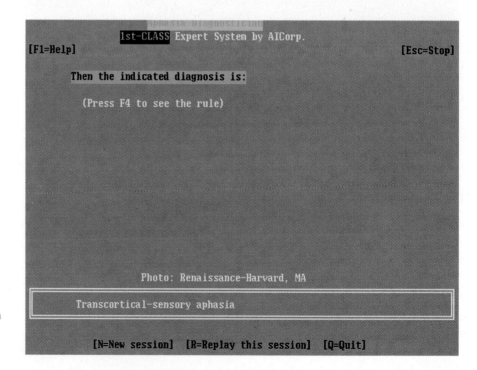

This 1st-Class expert system software package was used to develop an expert system program to help doctors diagnose the condition of patients suffering from aphasia.

than humans. But humans have to develop the detailed instructions computers need, or they can't do anything. Computers can't weigh alternatives and make decisions without following instructions provided by humans. Computers can't remember anything that wasn't fed to them as data or hasn't resulted from the processing of that data according to instructions from humans. Therefore, computers can't dream up creative ways to do things differently like we can. Instead, they will always follow their programmed instructions consistently, even if they are sometimes dangerous, nonsensical, or incorrect!

What about **artificial intelligence?** That's the name for efforts to develop computers that *think,* as well as see, hear, feel, talk, and walk. Two examples are *robots* and *expert systems.* But even robots—computers with humanlike physical capabilities—follow programmed instructions from humans. Likewise, expert systems—software that gives expert advice on how to accomplish difficult chores—consist of programmed rules and knowledge initially provided by human experts. For example, American Express uses an expert system called *Authorizer's Assistant.* It helps credit authorizers decide on telephoned requests for more credit in 90 seconds or less, while still protecting the firm from bad-credit losses. *Authorizer's Assistant* contains a *knowledge base* of facts and rules extracted from the combined expertise of many experienced human credit authorizers.

artificial intelligence
A science and technology whose goal is to develop computers that can think as well as see, hear, walk, talk, and feel. Examples include intelligent robots and *expert systems* that can give end users expert advice in a specific area.

Accuracy and Errors

Computers are accurate. They can accurately process large volumes of data according to complex and repetitive procedures. This contrasts with human computing, where the constant repetition of the same tasks becomes a cumbersome and tedious chore, and is extremely susceptible to errors. This is not to say that computers always produce accurate information. However, most errors blamed on computers are minimal compared with the volume of data being processed and are frequently the result of human error.

For example, errors in management reports or customer statements are usually the result of incorrect data supplied by humans or errors in a computer program developed by a programmer. Thus the phrase "garbage in, garbage out" (GIGO) is frequently used by information systems professionals. GIGO emphasizes that incorrect data entry will result in incorrect results as computers blindly follow their instructions. It also emphasizes the importance of having control procedures to ensure the accuracy of such systems.

Speed and Timeliness

Computers are fast. Computers are capable of executing *millions of instructions per second (MIPS).* Thus, it takes a computer only seconds to perform millions of functions that human beings would take years to complete. Of course, the human brain, with its billions of neuron circuits, is a lot faster at other tasks than any computer. For example, you can instantly recognize the face or voice of a person you haven't seen in years—something no computer can do. However, the computational processing speed of computers means that they can provide split-second control of computerized devices and provide information in a *timely* manner to managers and other end users.

Computer operating speeds formerly measured in **milliseconds** (thousandths of a second) are now being measured in **microseconds** (millionths of

millisecond
One-thousandth of a second.

microsecond
One-millionth of a second.

This Cray Y-MP C90 supercomputer is so fast that if you charged a dollar for every calculation it performs, you could pay off the national debt in one hour. Research is underway on a system that, in the same scenario, would pay off the national debt in four seconds.

nanosecond
One-billionth of a second.

picosecond
One-trillionth of a second.

a second) and **nanoseconds** (billionths of a second), with **picoseconds** (trillionths of a second) speed being attained by some supercomputers. Such speeds seem almost incomprehensible. For example, an average person taking one step each nanosecond would circle Earth about 20 times in one second! Even tiny microprocessors can process millions of instructions per second, while some supercomputers have been clocked at more than 1,000 MIPS. The photograph on this page illustrates how much a computer operating at such speeds can do.

However, we are all aware of how slow and unresponsive some computer-based information systems are. No matter how fast their computer processing speed, such systems can still be slowed down by poorly designed programs and procedures, hardware operated beyond its capacity, and ill-trained operators. So, once again, computer-based systems are only as good as their human designers and end users.

Memory and Volatility

RAM (random-access memory)
One of the basic types of memory chips, used for temporary storage of data or programs during processing. The contents of RAM can be instantly changed to store new data or programs.

ROM (read-only memory)
A more permanent type of memory chip, typically used to permanently store parts of the computer's operating system and other selected programs.

volatility
A characteristic of memory chips describing how easily they lose their contents when electrical power is interrupted.

Computers remember. As we said earlier, a computer remembers by storing data and programs in its primary storage circuits and on secondary storage devices such as magnetic disks. More specifically, a computer's *memory* consists of microelectronic circuit chips in its primary storage unit. Most of these *memory chips* are known as **RAM** (random-access memory). Their contents can be instantly changed to store new data and programs. Other, more permanent memory chips are known as **ROM** (read-only memory), which permanently store parts of the computer's operating system and other programs that need to be instantly available when your computer is turned on.

One major shortcoming of much of a computer's memory is its **volatility.** That is, RAM will lose its contents if electrical power is disconnected. That's why the memory contents of anything you want to keep must be saved on a floppy disk or hard disk before turning off your microcomputer. That's also

Bit–a 1 or a 0	Megabyte–roughly 1 million bytes	**Table 1-1**
Byte–typically 8 bits	Gigabyte–roughly 1 billion bytes	**Examples of Storage**
Kilobyte–roughly1,024 bytes	Terabyte–roughly 1 trillion bytes	**Elements**

why standby electrical power from battery packs or emergency generators is a common security feature of many computer centers.

Bits and Bytes

"Computers store byte-size bits of data." That is, a computer's memory and storage capacity are usually expressed in *bits* and *bytes.* The simplest way to think of a **byte** is that it's a storage capacity that can hold one *character* of data. For example, Suppose you have a floppy disk with a capacity of 1.44 million bytes. This means it can hold 1,440,000 alphabetic, numeric, and other characters of data. This is equivalent to about 800 double-spaced typewritten pages.

In Chapter 7 and in the Appendix, we discuss in more detail how each byte of storage can typically hold eight *bits* to represent a character of data. A **bit** is a contraction of the term *binary digit,* that is, a 0 or a 1, the only digits in the base 2 or *binary number system.* Microelectronic circuits and other computer storage media only need to show an "on" or "off" condition to represent a 1 or a 0. That's all computers need to form binary codes that can represent the numbers, letters, and other characters we normally use to communicate. So each time you press a key on your computer's keyboard, you send an electronic signal representing the binary code of a character to your computer's memory. Figure 1-4 shows how the letter *E* is transmitted using the ASCII code, a popular code for microcomputers.

Computer storage capacities are typically measured in **kilobytes** (abbreviated KB or K), **megabytes** (abbreviated MB or M), or **gigabytes** (abbreviated GB or G). Although kilo means 1,000 in the metric system, the computer industry uses K to represent 1,024 (2^{10}) storage positions. Therefore, a computer memory size of 640 kilobytes, or 640K, for example, is really 655,360 storage positions, rather than 640,000 positions. However, such differences are frequently disregarded in order to simplify descriptions of storage capacity. Thus, a megabyte is roughly 1 million bytes (1,048,576, or 2^{20} bytes), a gigabyte is more than 1 billion bytes (1,073,741,824, or 2^{30} bytes), while a **terabyte** exceeds 1 trillion bytes of storage. See Table 1-1.

Typically, memory capacities might range from 640K bytes (655,360 bytes) to 32 megabytes for many microcomputer memories. Memory capacities up to 10 GB (10 gigabytes, or approximately 10 billion bytes) might be found in a large mainframe computer. Magnetic disk capacities can range from several hundred bytes to several megabytes for floppy disks, more than 300 megabytes for hard magnetic disk drives, and more than 500 megabytes for optical disks. Large mainframe magnetic disk units can supply many gigabytes of secondary storage capacity.

byte
In many computer systems, a grouping of eight bits that can represent one numeric, alphabetic, or other character.

bit
A contraction of "binary digit." It can be either 0 or 1.

kilobyte
Roughly 1 thousand bytes, or 1,024 (2^{10}).

megabyte
Roughly 1 million bytes, or 1,048,576 (2^{20}).

gigabyte
Roughly 1 billion bytes, or 1,073,741,824 (2^{30}).

terabyte
Roughly 1 trillion bytes, or 1,009,511,627,776 (2^{40}).

These 32-megabyte memory boards may be "snapped in" to a microcomputer's main system unit to increase its processing speed.

Reliability and Failure

Computers are reliable. The accuracy of computer-based information systems is directly related to the reliability of computers and their electronic circuitry. Computers consistently and accurately operate for long periods without failure. Their circuitry is amazingly reliable and includes self-checking features that ensure accuracy and automatically diagnose failure conditions. Such built-in "diagnostics" and regular preventive maintenance checks help guarantee reliability.

Computers do "crash" (stop working) due to component failures or software errors. We all know how frustrating this can be, especially if we are in a hurry. However, such *downtime* is usually only a fraction of a percent of the operating time of most systems. Backup systems and protective measures can also minimize the effects of such failures.

Economy and Cost

Computers are economical. You would not be able to enjoy their speed, accuracy, and reliability if it were not for their very real economy. Except for very simple and low-volume tasks, computerized information processing is more economical than human processing. This cost advantage continues to increase as competition and the fast pace of developments in technology continue to drive down the cost of computer hardware and software.

Microcomputers are the most common medium for end user computing.

REAL-WORLD EXAMPLE

Jones Day Reavis & Pogue:
E-Mail for Attorneys

What do 1,200 attorneys spread out over 11 offices in the United States and nine offices overseas depend on? Computers of course. Computers have helped build Jones Day Reavis & Pogue into one of the world's largest law firms. Its managing partner, Richard Pogue, wants to transform the Cleveland, Ohio-based company from a regional to a worldwide law firm. Besides using computers for office productivity and legal research, Pogue and the firm's attorneys rely heavily on computers to send and receive electronic mail (E-mail) messages to help them communicate with each other on legal cases and developments. Says Pogue: "The E-mail really encourages communication. There's a lot of stuff that people shoot to me on E-mail that I don't think they would bother with otherwise. . . . There is a more personal character that comes through electronic mail than one that comes on a piece of paper, and it's a more interactive medium. When I am typing out a message to somebody on the system, I feel more directly in contact with them than I do when I dictate a letter or a memorandum and my secretary takes it away for half an hour."

1. How dependent on computers are law firms such as Jones Day Reavis & Pogue? Explain.
2. Is such dependency unique to the legal profession? Explain.

Of course, the costs of computing can go out of control. For example, adding features and options to a microcomputer you want will drive up its cost significantly. Also, organizations frequently find their computing costs (hardware, software, telecommunication networks, computer specialists, end user training) rising faster than increases in their productivity. That's why managers have to develop procedures to control such costs.

Quick Quiz

1. (True/False) Computers can think like humans, but they never make mistakes.
2. Many current computers can compute at one-trillionth of a second or _____ speeds. *nanos*
3. Most of the main memory capacity of computers consists of _____ chips. *RAM*
4. A computer's memory and storage capacity is usually expressed in _____. *byte*
5. A byte of storage typically uses eight _____ to represent a character of data. *bits*

Answers: 1. False   2. nanosecond   3. RAM (random access memory)
4. bytes   5. bits

The Global Information Society

The real-world example of computers in the legal profession emphasizes the dramatic growth in the widespread use of computers in the last few decades.

E T H I C S

Computer Crime and Ethics

Unfortunately, a few end users and IS professionals use computers irresponsibly, even to the point of committing crimes. Examples of such criminal or irresponsible behavior include the theft of money, data, and software, unauthorized access to computer systems and data files, and unauthorized copying of software. Another notorious example is the destruction of data and programs by *computer viruses,* destructive programs that replicate themselves and spread to other computer systems. We will discuss such examples of computer crime in more detail later.

Do you have a *responsibility* to do something about computer crime and other abuses of computer power? More positively, how can you be a *responsible end user* or IS professional? That's what **computer ethics** is all about. In later chapters, we examine what computer crime laws and codes of conduct by professional IS organizations can tell us about computer ethics. For now, let's just say that having good computer ethics means being a responsible end user or IS professional by

• Acting with personal integrity in your access and use of computer resources.
• Striving to increase your computer competency.
• Setting high standards of job performance with computers.
• Accepting responsibility for the results of using computers in your work.
• Acting to advance the health, privacy, and general welfare of your colleagues and the public when using computers.

If you do this, you will be demonstrating ethical conduct, avoiding computer crime, and increasing the security and benefits of any computer-based information systems you develop or use.

What Do You Think?

Are most students at your college or university responsible end users? How about other computer users you know? What do you think?

computer ethics
Issues concerning the legal, professional, social, and moral responsibilities of computer specialists and end users.

computer revolution
The dramatic growth in the widespread use of computers in the last few decades.

This development is frequently called the **computer revolution.** Technological breakthroughs continue to cause rapid increases in the speed, power, and ease of use of computers, and significantly decrease their size and cost. Thus computers are now commonplace in many homes, schools, businesses, and other organizations. In particular, microcomputer hardware and software finally have made it possible for millions of end users to do their own computing.

The computer revolution has created an *information society.* That's a society whose economy is heavily dependent on the creation, management, and

Knowledge workers depend on computer technology to input, process, store, access, and output information pertinent to their jobs.

distribution of information resources. People in many developed countries no longer live in *agricultural societies,* composed primarily of farmers, or even *industrial societies,* where most in the work force are factory workers. Instead, the work force consists mainly of workers in service occupations and **knowledge workers,** or people who spend most of their workday creating, using, and distributing information. Knowledge workers include executives, managers, and supervisors; professionals such as accountants, doctors, engineers, lawyers, scientists, social workers, stockbrokers, and teachers; and staff personnel such as secretaries and clerical office personnel. So you probably will be a knowledge worker.

Most knowledge workers are computer end users. They make their living using computers to create, distribute, manage, and use information resources. Computers thus help them manage the human, financial, material, energy, and other resources involved in their work responsibilities. And since many computers are interconnected by local, regional, and global telecommunications networks, knowledge workers can access and distribute information and manage resources all over the world. As an example, in our information society, retailers can electronically communicate with product suppliers from all over the globe; engineering firms can supervise international construction projects; securities dealers can make instant trades on foreign securities exchanges; accounting firms can audit the worldwide operations of multinational corporations.

knowledge workers
People whose primary work activities include creating, using, and distributing information.

End Note: End Users and Computers

The examples of computer use in the real-world examples in this chapter should emphasize how important computer literacy is in today's global information society. We should also stress that computers can do nothing without computer-literate humans to conceive, design, and implement how they should be used. Remember, this role is not only for computer professionals. The computing revolution has placed end users like you directly into the development and use of computers in the workplace.

Your knowledge of how to use computer hardware and software will help you succeed in whatever career you choose to follow. For example, your ability to use computers as flexible systems of hardware devices and computer software packages as electronic tools to help you accomplish your work activities are your keys to this success. However, remember that tools are only as good as the person who uses them. Responsible end users acting with competence and integrity are the indispensable element for success in our information society.

Summary

You and Computers   You need to be computer literate to succeed in today's information society. That is, you need both a conceptual knowledge of computers and their uses, benefits, and limitations (conceptual computer literacy) and a "hands-on" knowledge of how to use computers (functional computer literacy).

End User Computing   Technological breakthroughs have dramatically increased the performance and decreased the cost of computer hardware and software. Microcomputer use has spread rapidly and allows end users to do their own computing, such as word processing, electronic spreadsheets, database management, graphics, and telecommunications.

Computer Hardware Overview   A computer is a system of interconnected hardware components that includes a central processing unit (CPU) composed of an arithmetic-logic unit and control unit, a primary storage unit or memory, and peripheral devices such as keyboards for input, video monitors for output, and magnetic disks for secondary storage. Several varieties of systems meet the computing needs of organizations and end users. These include small microcomputers, midsize minicomputers, and large mainframe computers. Many systems are interconnected by telecommunications links to form wide area or local area networks. These computer networks help end users communicate with each other and share hardware, software, and data resources.

System Software   System software manages and supports the use of a computer system. It can be subdivided into system management, system support, and system development programs. System management programs manage the hardware, software, and data resources of a computer system. Examples include operating systems and operating environments. System support programs, such as utilities and telecommunications monitors, support the operations and management of computer systems by providing a variety of services. System development programs help IS professionals and end users develop programs and procedures for computer-based systems. Examples include language translator programs and CASE packages.

Application Software   Application programs direct computers to perform information-processing tasks for specific applications of end users. Application software can be subdivided into general-purpose, business, scientific, and other application-specific categories. General-purpose application programs perform common information processing tasks for end users. Examples of such productivity packages are word processing, electronic spreadsheet, and database management programs. Some application-specific packages accomplish information processing tasks for business functions such as accounting or marketing, while others support scientific research and experimentation and other areas such as art, education, and entertainment.

Computer Speed and Capacity   Computers are capable of executing millions of instructions per second (MIPS). Computer hardware speeds are typically measured in milliseconds (thousandths of a second), microseconds (millionths of a second), nanoseconds (billionths of a second), or picoseconds (trillionths of a second). Computers process and store data as binary digits (bits), typically in groups of eight bits (a byte) to represent one character of data. Computer-memory storage capacities may be measured in kilobytes (1,024 bytes), megabytes (roughly 1 million bytes), gigabytes (roughly 1 billion bytes), and terabytes (roughly 1 trillion bytes).

What Computers Can and Can't Do   Computers are electronic tools that can compute faster, more accurately, and more dependably and economically than humans. But unlike computers, humans are flexible and creative thinkers. Computers can do nothing without a human to conceive, design, and implement how they can be used. However, this means that many problems blamed on computers are the results of errors in hardware, programs, or data designed or supplied by humans.

The Global Information Society   We live in an information society heavily dependent on the use of computers and telecommunications networks by knowledge workers to create, use, and distribute information around the globe.

Computer Crime and Ethics   A few end users and IS professionals use computers to commit crimes such as theft of money, data, and software. Responsible end users and IS professionals can demonstrate ethical computing behavior by acting with integrity and competency and by advancing the health, privacy, and welfare of their colleagues and the public.

Key Terms and Concepts

application software	computer literacy
bit	computer program
byte	computer system
central processing unit	end user
computer	end user computing
computer applications	gigabyte
computer benefits and limitations	global information society
computer crime	hardware
computer ethics	input devices

kilobyte
knowledge workers
mainframe computer
megabyte
memory
microcomputer
microprocessor
microsecond
millisecond
minicomputer
nanosecond
online

operating system
output devices
peripherals
picosecond
primary storage
RAM
ROM
secondary storage
software
system software
telecommunications networks
volatility

Review Quiz

True/False

___T___ 1. A computer is a device that can accept data, store and automatically execute a program of instructions, and report the results.

___F___ 2. Software includes all the physical devices of computers.

___F___ 3. Hardware includes any operating instructions for computers.

___T___ 4. A computer system is a group of interconnected computer hardware components performing input, processing, output, storage, and control activities.

___T___ 5. The theft of money, data, and software are examples of computer crime.

___F___ 6. A computer specialist is anyone who uses a computer system or the information it produces.

___T___ 7. The central processing unit is the main processing component of a computer system.

___T___ 8. Peripherals are input, output, and secondary storage devices connected to a CPU.

___F___ 9. Secondary storage includes the memory circuits of a computer system.

___F___ 10. Primary storage devices provide additional storage capacity for a computer system.

Multiple Choice

___C___ 1. One-billionth of a second is a
    a. millisecond.
    b. microsecond.
    c. nanosecond.
___C___   d. picosecond.

_____ 2. One billion characters of storage is a
    a. kilobyte.
    b. megabyte.

c. gigabyte.

d. terabyte.

_b_ 3. Computers and end users interconnected by communications links form

a. computer systems.

b. telecommunications networks.

c. offline systems.

d. knowledge networks.

_a_ 4. Programs that manage and support the operations of computers are called

a. system software.

b. applications software.

c. programmed software.

d. operations software.

_b_ 5. Programs that direct the performance of a specific use of computers are called

a. system software.

b. applications software.

c. programmed software.

d. operations software.

_c_ 6. A CPU on a microelectronic chip is called a

a. CPU chip.

b. microcomputer.

c. microprocessor.

d. miniprocessor.

_d_ 7. The direct, hands-on use of computers by end users is called

a. computer application.

b. computer usage.

c. manual computing.

d. end user computing.

_c_ 8. A society whose economy is heavily dependent on the global flow of information is

a. an agricultural society.

b. an industrial society.

c. an information society.

d. a modern society.

_a_ 9. People who spend most of their workday creating, using, and distributing information are called

a. knowledge workers.

b. end users.

c. information analysts.

d. authors.

_d_ 10. The property that determines whether data in memory is lost when power fails is called
   a. power loss.
   b. data loss.
   c. data retention.
   d. volatility.

Fill-in

1. Examples of _input_ devices include keyboard and optical scanners.
2. Examples of _output_ devices include printers and video monitors.
3. Examples of _secondary storage_ devices include magnetic disk and tape units.
4. An _operating system_ is an important program that manages the operations and resources of a computer system.
5. Operating systems, telecommunications monitors, and programming language translator programs are examples of _system software_
6. Word processing, electronic spreadsheet, and graphics programs are examples of _application software_
7. Computer memory consists of _RAM/ROM_ and _____.
8. Peripherals are _online_ devices controlled by a CPU.
9. A _program_ is a set of computer processing instructions.
10. Computers typically are categorized as microcomputers, minicomputers, and _mainframe_ computers.

Questions for Thought and Discussion

1. In what specific ways might knowing how to use computers affect your career expectations?
2. Refer to the Real-World Example of Hyundai in the chapter. Why do you think the performance of the salespeople improved after they received portable computers with preinstalled software?
3. How are computers better than humans? How are humans better than computers?
4. What does the phrase "garbage in, garbage out" (GIGO) tell you about some of the errors made by computers?
5. Can computers think? Explain your answer in light of developments in artificial intelligence such as robots and expert systems.
6. Why is it important to think of a computer as a system instead of as a computing device?
7. Are you already a computer end user? A knowledge worker? Explain.
8. Refer to the Real-World Example of Mrs. Fields Cookies. Would you like to be an information systems specialist or manager for Mrs. Fields Cookies? Why or why not?

9. How can you practice computer ethics as a college student? As an employee or manager?

10. Learn more about how computers are used in one of the following: (a) offices, (b) factories, (c) finance, (d) retailing, (e) products, (f) science and engineering, (g) medicine, (h) government, (i) education, or (j) arts and entertainment. Briefly report your findings to the class.

Review Quiz Answers

True/False: **1.** T **2.** F **3.** F **4.** T **5.** T **6.** F **7.** T **8.** T. **9.** F **10.** F

Multiple Choice: **1.** c **2.** c **3.** b **4.** a **5.** b **6.** c **7.** d **8.** c **9.** a **10.** d

Fill-in: 1. input **2.** output **3.** secondary storage **4.** operating system **5.** system software **6.** application software **7.** RAM/ROM **8.** online **9.** program **10.** mainframe

2

INFORMATION SYSTEMS: TRANSFORMING DATA INTO INFORMATION

LEARNING OBJECTIVES

After reading and studying this
chapter, you should be able to

Discuss the role of end users in
information systems.

Identify the generic components of
a system.

Explain how information systems in
the real world (1) use people,
hardware, software, and data as
resources, (2) to perform input,
processing, output, storage, and
control activities, (3) that transform
data resources into information
products.

Identify several types of information
systems.

Identify several career opportunities
in the information systems field.

Information Systems and You

Chapter 1 introduced some basic facts about computers. However, a computer is just one of the components of the *information systems* that people use in most organizations. Generically, an **information system (IS)** is a set of people, procedures, and resources that collects, transforms, and disseminates information in an organization.

Many information systems are *computer-based*—they rely heavily on computers to accomplish their activities. Thus, to be truly computer literate, you must understand how computer-based information systems provide the information that people need to be productive. This requires a knowledge of the basic components and functions of such systems. As a computer-literate end user, you will be able to apply such concepts to information systems you encounter in the real world.

In this chapter we will first cover basic concepts applicable to all types of information systems. End users and their organizations rely on several types of information systems to collect, transform, and disseminate information. These include simple *manual* (paper and pencil) information systems and *informal* (word of mouth) information systems.

We will concentrate on *computer-based* information systems that use computers to help end users accomplish their information processing activities. We will also discuss several major categories of such information systems and how you can recognize them in the real world. Finally, we will discuss some of the careers available in the information systems field, and several ethical implications of information systems for end users.

Information System Fundamentals

In this chapter, we will emphasize that information systems consist of people, hardware, software, and data components that transform an organization's data resources into a variety of information products. But first, we need a better understanding of several concepts that apply to information systems. Then we will examine in more detail the basic components and activities present in the information systems encountered in the real world.

System Concepts

System is such an overused term today that its meaning needs to be clarified. What is a system? A **system** can be very simply defined as *a group of interrelated or interacting elements forming a unified whole*. Many examples of systems can be found in the physical and biological sciences, in modern technology, and in human society. For instance, we can talk of the physical system of the sun and its planets, the biological system of the human body, the technological system of an automobile, and the socioeconomic system of a business or other organization.

However, as a computer-literate end user, you need to understand a more specific, yet generic concept of a system that underlies the design and use of computers and information systems. That is, *a system is a group of interrelated components working together toward a common goal by accepting inputs and producing outputs in an organized transformation process*. This important concept of a system has five basic components as illustrated in Figure 2-1:

---

information system
A system that uses the resources of people, hardware, software, and data to perform input, processing, output, storage, and control activities that transform data resources into information products.

system
A group of interrelated components working together toward a common goal by accepting input and producing output in an organized transformation process.

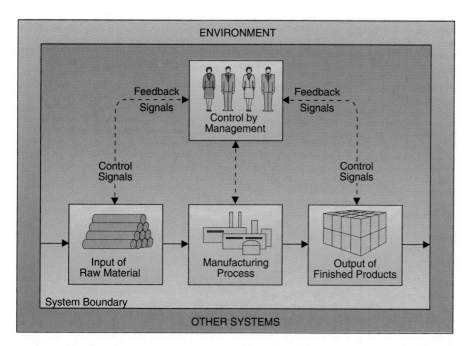

- **Input** is capturing and assembling resources that enter the system for processing. For example, raw materials, energy, and data must be secured and organized for processing in a manufacturing system.
- **Processing** is activities that transform input into output. For example, a manufacturing process converts a variety of raw material inputs into finished products.
- **Output** is transferring processed resources to their ultimate destination. For example, finished products must be moved out of the factory to warehouses and retail stores.
- **Feedback** is data concerning the performance of a system. For example, a car manufacturer may collect data about how many cars were produced and sold this month.
- **Control** is monitoring and evaluating feedback and making adjustments to a system to help it reach its goals. For example, a car manufacturer may evaluate car sales and then increase its TV advertising to help meet its sales goals.

input
Capturing and assembling resources that enter a system for processing.

processing
Activities that transform input into output.

output
Transferring processed resources, or finished products, to their ultimate destination.

feedback
Data concerning the performance of a system.

control
Monitoring and evaluating feedback and making adjustments to a system to help it reach its goals.

Figure 2-1 is an example of a manufacturing system that emphasizes the roles feedback and control play to ensure that inputs are properly processed into outputs and the goals of a system are achieved. It also illustrates how a system can exchange inputs and outputs with other systems across the *boundary* that separates a system from its *environment*.

Components of an Information System

The system concept emphasizes that we can view an information system as a system that accepts data resources as input and processes them into information products as output. But how does an information system accomplish

Figure 2-2
Information systems use people, hardware, software, and data to perform input, processing, output, storage, and control activities that transform data into information products.

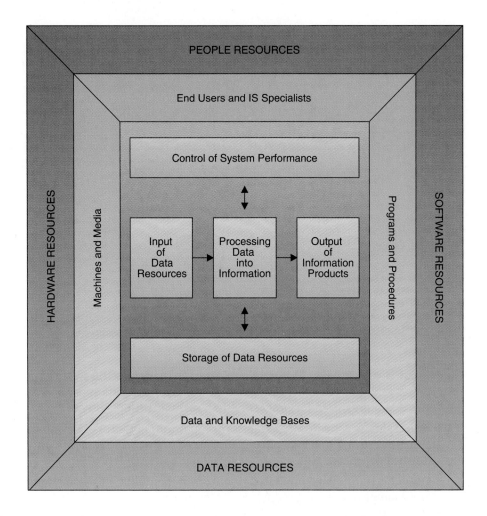

this? What resources and activities make this happen? To answer these questions, we need a more specific understanding of the components of an information system.

Figure 2-2 illustrates that an information system *uses the resources of people (specialists and end users), hardware (machines and media), software (programs and procedures), and data to perform input, processing, output, storage, and control activities that transform data resources into information products.* This information system concept provides a framework that emphasizes three major ideas that can be applied to all types of information systems:

- People (end users and IS specialists), hardware (machines and media), software (programs and procedures), and data are the four basic resources of information systems.

- Data resources are transformed by information processing activities into a variety of information products for end users.

- Information processing consists of input, processing, output, storage, and control activities.

REAL-WORLD EXAMPLE

Toyota Motor Sales: Computers and Customer Service

A computer-based information network was part of Toyota's master plan when it began developing its Lexus luxury car line. So each Lexus dealership uses PCs and an IBM AS/400 minicomputer linked by satellite to an IBM mainframe at Toyota's Torrance, California, headquarters. Each dealer may also use more than 2,000 AS/400 programs, including software for finance, insurance, inventory control, customer service, parts ordering, and repair diagnostics.

For example, a Lexus dealer can have information instantly about each customer's service history. John Dunn, vice-president of Lexus of Brookfield, Wisconsin, explains: "Let's say you're in transit. You live in California, and while driving through Wisconsin, you have a problem. We can instantly, via the system, retrieve your service history for the last place your car was repaired."

Lexus service personnel can also use their computers to access parts information from an electronic catalog and even order parts electronically from Torrance. Lexus car mechanics can get advice on service problems from the Torrance mainframe within minutes using the satellite link.

1. Is Toyota's computer-based Lexus dealer network a system? An information system? Explain.

2. What IS components do you recognize in the Lexus dealer network?

Information System Resources

We just said that an information system uses four types of resources: people, hardware, software, and data. Let's briefly discuss the role these resources play in information systems. Table 2-1 provides examples of information system resources and products.

People Resources

People are required for the operation of all information systems. These **people resources** include *end users* and *IS specialists*. **IS specialists** are the information systems professionals and technicians who develop and operate computer-based information systems. **End users** (also called *users* or *clients*) are the many people who use an information system or the information it produces. They can be accountants, salespeople, engineers, clerks, customers, managers, or people like you and the authors. We are all important resources in the successful operation of the information systems we use each day.

Hardware Resources

Hardware resources include *all physical devices and materials* used in information processing. Specifically, this should include not only **machines,** such as computers or calculators, but also all data **media,** that is, *all tangible objects on which data are recorded,* whether a sheet of paper or a magnetic disk.

Large *mainframe* computers, midsize *minicomputers,* and personal *microcomputer* systems are obvious examples of hardware in computer-based information systems. *Computer peripherals* such as a keyboard or electronic mouse for input of data, a video screen or printer for output of information,

people resources
Persons required for the operation of all information systems. These people include *IS specialists* and *end users.*

IS specialists
Professionals and technicians who develop and operate computer-based information systems.

end user
Anyone who uses an information system or the information it produces.

hardware resources
Includes all physical devices and materials used in information processing.

machines
Devices, such as computers or calculators, that perform tasks at the direction of human beings.

media
All tangible objects on which data are recorded, such as paper forms or magnetic disks.

Table 2-1
Examples of Information System Resources and Products

Hardware Resources	Machines—computers, optical scanners, video monitors, magnetic disk drives, printers Media—floppy disks, magnetic tape, optical disks, plastic cards, paper forms
Software Resources	Programs—operating system programs, spreadsheet programs, word processing programs, graphics programs Procedures—data entry procedures, error correction procedures, registration procedures
People Resources	Specialists—systems analysts, programmers, computer operators End users—anyone else who uses information systems
Data Resources	Course descriptions, student records, instructor files, department databases
Information Products	Management reports and registration documents using text and graphics displays, audio responses, and paper forms

and magnetic or optical disks for storage are other common examples of hardware resources. So are *telecommunications networks* of computers, computer terminals, communications processors, and other devices interconnected by a variety of media to provide information and computing power throughout an organization.

Software Resources

software resources
Includes all sets of information processing instructions.

programs
Sets of instructions that cause a computer to perform particular tasks.

procedures
Sets of instructions used by people to complete a task.

Software resources include *all sets of information processing instructions*. This generic concept of software can thus be applied to all instructions needed to operate manual, mechanical, or computer-based information systems. Typically, we think of software as the sets of operating instructions or **programs** that direct and control computer hardware. However, generically, software also includes the sets of information processing instructions needed by people, called **procedures**.

Examples of software include *operating system* programs that manage and support the operations of a computer system, and *application software* packages that accomplish the applications of end users. Specific examples include word processing and spreadsheet programs, inventory and payroll programs, engineering design and medical diagnostic programs, and so on. Instructions on how to fill out a paper form, use a bank's automated teller machine (ATM), or use a microcomputer software package are examples of common *procedures* for end users.

Data Resources

data resources
A concept emphasizing that data are valuable end user and organizational resources that we must manage effectively in our use of information systems.

data
Facts or observations about physical phenomena or business transactions. Specifically, data are observations about the *attributes* (characteristics) of *entities* such as people, places, things, and events.

Data are the raw material resources of information systems. The concept of **data resources** emphasizes that data are valuable end user and organizational resources that we must manage effectively.

The word *data* is the plural of *datum*, though data is commonly used to represent both singular and plural forms. **Data** is commonly defined as *raw facts* or *observations,* typically about physical phenomena or business transactions. For example, a spacecraft launch or the sale of an automobile would generate a lot of data describing those events. More specifically, data are observations about the *attributes* (the characteristics) of *entities* (such as people, places, things, and events).

Data can take many forms. Examples include traditional *alphanumeric data,* composed of numeric and alphabetic characters and other symbols that describe business transactions and other events and entities. *Text data,* consisting of sentences and paragraphs used in written communications, *image data,* such as graphic shapes and figures, and *audio data,* that is, the human voice and other sounds, are also important forms of data.

The data resources of an organization are typically stored by information systems in the following basic forms:

- **Databases,** which store detailed processed and organized data needed by organizations and end users.

- **Knowledge bases,** which store knowledge about a specific subject in a variety of forms such as facts and rules.

For example, data about students can be accumulated and stored in a database of student statistics, which is processed to produce reports needed by professors and administrators. Information systems known as *expert systems* use knowledge bases to help end users with expert advice in business, engineering, medicine, and many other fields. We will discuss these forms of information systems in more detail later in the chapter.

Data resources are typically recorded and stored on several types of *data media,* including paper, magnetic, optical, film, or electronic media. Examples are paper documents, magnetic disks, magnetic tape, optical disks, microfilm, and electronic circuit chips.

Data versus Information

You often hear the terms *data* and *information* used interchangeably. However, it is helpful to view data as raw material *resources* that are processed into finished information *products.* **Information** can then be defined as data that has been transformed into a meaningful and useful context for specific end users by *information processing* or *data processing* activities. Stated another way, information is *processed data* placed in its proper context to give it value for specific end users. See Figure 2-3.

Let's look at a typical example. Names, quantities, and dollar amounts recorded on sales forms represent data about daily sales results. However, a sales manager may consider them to be data, not information. Only when such

database
A collection of processed and organized data needed by organizations and end users.

knowledge base
A collection of knowledge about various subjects in a variety of forms such as facts and rules.

information
Data placed in a meaningful and useful context for an end user.

Data		Information
$ 42,000　10 units		Salesperson: S. Mills
$ 16,000　S. Mills	Data Processing	Sales Territory:
Northwest Region		Northwest Region
$120,000　100 units		Current Sales:
26 units		136 units = $178,000

Figure 2-3
Data about sales must be processed into information to give it value for a sales manager.

facts are properly organized and manipulated can meaningful information about sales be provided to the sales manager. Examples of such information might be the amount of sales by product type, sales territory, salesperson, type of product, and so on.

Quick Quiz

1. The five basic components in many kinds of systems are input, processing, output, feedback, and _____.
2. People, hardware, software, and _____ are the four basic resources of information systems.
3. The people resources of an information system include _____ and IS specialists, while its hardware resources include machines and data _____.
4. Software resources include all sets of information processing _____, including computer programs and _____ for people.
5. Data resources include both _____ bases and _____ bases.

Answers: 1. control   2. data   3. end users, media   4. instructions, procedures   5. data, knowledge

Information System Activities

Let's take a closer look now at each of the basic information processing activities that occur in information systems. We can define **information processing** (or *data processing*) as the transformation of data resources into information products by input, processing, output, storage, and control activities. Table 2-2 lists examples that illustrate each of these basic activities of information systems.

Input of Data Resources

Information processing starts with activities for the **input of data**. *Data entry* activities capture and prepare data about business transactions and other events for processing. End users typically *record* data about transactions on some type of physical medium, such as a paper form (a *source document*), or enter it directly into a computer system. This usually includes a variety of *editing* activities to ensure that data has been recorded correctly. Once entered, data may be transferred onto *machine-readable media,* such as magnetic disk or tape, until needed for processing.

---

information processing
Transformation of data resources into information products by input, processing, output, storage, and control activities.

input of data
Capturing and preparing data for processing by recording, editing, and conversion activities.

Table 2-2
Some Basic Activities of Information Systems

Input	Optical scanning of student exam answer sheets
Processing	Calculating student grades and grade point averages
Output	Producing reports and displays about student performance
Storage	Maintaining records on students, instructors, and courses
Control	Generating audible signals to indicate proper scanning of exam data

For example, data about department store sales can be recorded on paper sales-order forms. Alternatively, sales data can be captured by clerks using computer keyboards or optical scanning devices. They may be visually prompted to enter data correctly by video displays. Thus, methods such as optical scanning of merchandise tags and displays of menus, graphic symbols, and fill-in-the-blank formats make it easier for sales clerks to enter data correctly into a computer-based information system.

Data-entry displays support the input of data resources.

processing of data
Transforming data into information by calculating, comparing, sorting, classifying, summarizing, and other activities.

Processing of Data into Information

Processing of data involves mathematical and other manipulations. Data are typically manipulated by activities such as calculating, comparing, sorting, classifying, and summarizing. These activities organize, analyze, and transform data, thus converting it into information products for end users. The quality of any data stored in an information system must also be *maintained* by a continual process of correcting and updating activities.

For example, data received about a purchase you made can be (1) *added* to a running total of sales results, (2) *compared* to a standard to determine eligibility for a sales discount, (3) *sorted* by arranging the data in a numerical order based upon a product identification number, (4) *classified* into product categories (such as food and nonfood items), and (5) *summarized* to provide a store manager with information about sales summarized by various product categories, and (6) used to update sales records to reflect new sales transactions.

Output of Information Products

output of information
Delivering processed data to end users in a variety of information products.

information products
Forms of information produced by an information system. Common information products include video displays, paper documents, and audio responses that provide us with messages, forms, reports, and graphics displays.

Activities for the **output of information** deliver information in a variety of forms. The goal of any information system is the production of appropriate **information products** for end users. Common information products are *video displays, paper documents,* and *audio responses* that provide us with *messages, forms, reports, graphics displays,* and so on. We depend on the information provided by these products as we work in organizations and live in society. For example, you may check a computer display of flight information at an airport, receive a computer-produced customer statement, or be told your bank balance over the telephone by a computer voice response unit.

Storage of Data Resources

storage of data
Retaining data resources in an organized manner for easy access.

Storage of data is an additional system component of information systems. Information systems use storage activities to retain data resources in an organized manner for easy access. Just as written text material is organized into words, sentences, paragraphs, and documents, stored data are commonly organized into *fields, records, files,* and *databases*. This makes it easier to use stored data when processing transactions, updating data files, and producing information products.

For example, a retail store may store data about your latest credit purchases in a *sales transaction file*. Other more permanent information about you—such as your name, address, and previous account balance—may be stored as a *customer record* with the records for all of the other customers of the store in a *customer database*. At the end of each month, this stored data is used to update the balance you owe the store, and to prepare monthly statements (bills) to mail to you and other customers. Figure 2-4 gives other examples of these commonly used data elements.

A sales-analysis display is the result of processing sales data into information needed by a sales manager.

Control of System Performance

The performance of an information system must be maintained by control activities. For example, an information system should produce adequate feedback about its input, processing, output, and storage activities. Feedback must

US Air: Flying into the Future

What do you think the "terminal of the future" should be like? US Air wanted to create the terminal of the future at Pittsburgh International Airport. What they meant was a place where lines would be shorter, baggage handling would be quicker and more dependable, and everything from check-in to take-off would be easier and less confusing for air travelers, and where information would be more readily available to employees, so they could be more responsive to customers.

US Air hired IBM to develop a system that would integrate a wide range of different computer manufacturers' equipment and would maximize the computing power of personal computers. The new system uses a mainframe computer to distribute information to over 650 PS/2 microcomputer workstations that are networked to hundreds of ticket printers, touchscreens, credit card readers and other devices. US Air employees now get immediate and reliable updates of pertinent information. Skycaps use touchscreens and bag-tag printers to streamline curb-side check-in of passengers. Even tower operators can make better decisions about managing gate traffic, resulting in fewer flight delays. That's US Air's terminal of the future.

1. What IS resources and activities do you recognize in the example of a computer-based information system?
2. What else do you think computers could do to create a terminal of the future?

be monitored and evaluated to determine if a system is meeting established performance standards. Then various system activities may have to be adjusted so that proper information products are produced for end users.

For example, suppose you noticed that your receipts for purchases this month from a retail store did not add up to the total amount you had been billed. This might mean that your store's procedures for sales data entry or

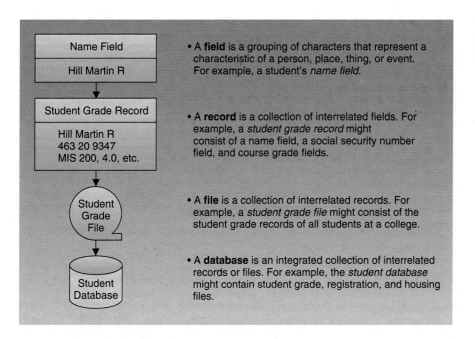

Figure 2-4
Several basic data elements help organize the storage of data in information systems.

REAL-WORLD EXAMPLE

Au Bon Pain: Restaurants and Information Systems

Imagine a chain of 100 quick-service restaurants and bakeries in Boston, New York, and Washington, D.C. How would you manage them all? Answer: Put a PC in each store and connect them by telecommunications lines to computers at the Boston headquarters. That's what top managers of the Au Bon Pain restaurant chain did. They can monitor food costs and other facts from detailed information entered by store managers into their PCs and transmitted at the end of the day. Each restaurant's daily data are processed and stored in sales inventory and payroll databases for reporting and access by corporate management. Regional managers also use laptop computers to view displays of management reports before visiting stores in their territories.

Au Bon Pain's store management software not only tracks sales and adjusts prices of menu items at each store, it also monitors the inventory of more than 200 food items and compares it to reports of sales, waste, and unsold items. Au Bon Pain's software also helps manage human resources. For example, employee work schedules are entered into each restaurant PC. Each store's time clock is also connected to its PC. Therefore, an employee can only clock in when he or she is scheduled to work. This feature alone saves Au Bon Pain thousands of dollars annually in wages that might have been paid for unauthorized work time.

1. What are the people, hardware, software, data resources, and information products produced by Au Bon Pain's information system?

2. What are some of the input, processing, output, storage, and control activities that you recognize in this information system?

processing need to be corrected. Correcting such procedures would ensure that all customer sales transactions would be properly captured and processed by their sales processing information system.

Quick Quiz

1. The five basic activities of information systems are input, processing, _____, storage, and control.
2. Information processing starts with _____ of data, and its _____ into information.
3. The goal of any information system is the production of appropriate _____ for end users.
4. Information systems use _____ activities to retain data resources for access by end users.
5. System performance is maintained by appropriate _____ activities.

Answers: 1. output 2. input, processing 3. information products
4. storage 5. control

Recognizing Information Systems

As a computer-literate end user, you should be able to recognize what resources and activities are used in the computer-based information systems that you encounter in the real world. Let's see if we can do this right now by analyzing a real-life example of a computer-based information system.

Analyzing Au Bon Pain's Information System

We can learn a lot about computers and information systems from the Real-World Example of Au Bon Pain. Installing PCs at each restaurant tied to the Boston headquarters, and using a comprehensive restaurant management package changes turned what could be a nightmare to manage into an efficiently and effectively run business. Au Bon Pain's computer-based information system greatly reduces the amount of time restaurant managers must spend in daily reporting, inventory control, and other restaurant management activities. It allows the restaurant chain's management to fully account for all food items and work activity in each restaurant, to quickly set and adjust prices for all menu items, and to see at a glance what foods are most popular with their customers.

Figure 2-5 illustrates some of the components you might see in a micro-computer-based information system for an end user like the manager of an Au Bon Pain restaurant. Hardware resources include machines—like the microcomputer and its keyboard, video monitor, printer, and magnetic disk drives—as well as the PC-connected time clock, and media consisting of magnetic disks and printer paper. Software resources include restaurant management programs executed by the PC and procedures followed by the restaurant manager. People resources include the restaurant manager and the employees who use the system.

Data resources (sales, inventory, and work activity data) and various commands and inquiries are entered into the system as input through the keyboard by the restaurant manager and employees. Processing is accomplished

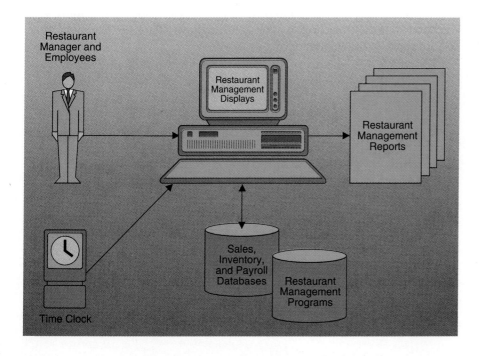

Figure 2-5
These are the components of the computer-based information system at an Au Bon Pain restaurant.

by the *microprocessor*, or CPU of the microcomputer, under the control of the restaurant management program and the procedures followed by the employees and the restaurant manager. Output of information products needed for restaurant management is accomplished by a variety of video displays and printed management reports. Storage of data and software resources is provided by magnetic disks on which are stored databases of sales, inventory, and payroll records. Finally, the fact that employees cannot clock in early emphasizes the control features built into the system.

Overview of Information Systems

There are many kinds of information systems in the real world. All of them use hardware, software, and people resources to transform data resources into information products. Some are simple *manual* information systems, where people use simple tools such as pencils and paper, or even machines such as calculators and typewriters. Others are **computer-based information systems** that rely on a variety of computer systems to accomplish their information processing activities.

It is also important not to confuse our discussion of *information systems* with the concept of *computer systems*. As we said in Chapter 1, a computer system is a group of interconnected hardware components that may take the form of a *microcomputer, minicomputer*, or large *mainframe* computer system. However, whether it sits on a desk or is one of many computers in a telecommunications network, a computer system still represents only the *hardware resources* component of a computer-based information system. As we have just seen, an information system also consists of people, software, and data resources.

The Roles of Information Systems

Another important fact about information systems is shown in Figure 2-6. No matter how they may be classified, information systems perform only three basic roles in an organization:

computer-based information system
An information system that uses computer hardware and software to perform its information processing activities.

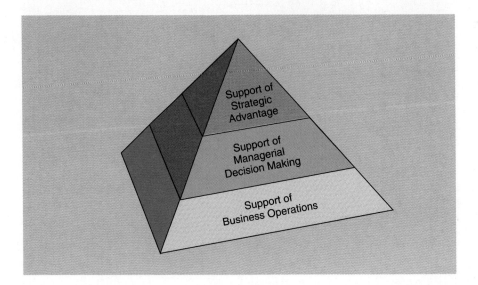

Figure 2-6
Information systems have three basic roles.

Universities and colleges use information systems for business operations, managerial decision making, and strategic advantage. Students at Glendale Community College have access to an impressive computer lab to learn computer skills and access resources provided by the college.

- Support of business operations.
- Support of managerial decision making.
- Support of strategic organizational advantage.

Let's take a university as an example to illustrate this important point. As a student, you have to deal regularly with information systems used to support business operations at your university. For example, most universities use computer-based information systems to help them schedule classes, register students, plan meals, provide housing, record grades, and bill students for tuition and fees. University operations would grind to a halt without the support of such information systems.

Information systems also help university administrators make better decisions and attempt to gain a strategic organizational advantage. For example, decisions on which academic programs or services need to be added or discontinued, or which kind of funding they deserve, are typically made after an analysis provided by computer-based information systems. This not only supports the decision making of administrators, but also helps them look for ways to gain an advantage over other universities in the competition for students. For example, administrators might make a decision to invest in a touch-tone telephone registration system as a strategic information system.

Table 2-3
Some Major Categories of Information Systems

Transaction Processing Systems	Record and process data resulting from business transactions
Process Control Systems	Monitor and control industrial processes
Office Automation Systems	Enhance office communications Provide information in the form of reports and displays to managers
Decision Support Systems	Give direct computer support to managers during a decision-making process
Executive Information Systems	Provide critical information in easy-to-use displays to top management
Strategic Information Systems	Provide products and services that give an organization a strategic advantage over its competitors

This might attract higher student enrollments based on the ease of registering for classes provided by such a computer-based information system.

Types of Information Systems

Conceptually, information systems in the real world can be classified in many ways. For example, some information systems process data resulting from business *transactions* such as sales to customers, purchases from suppliers, wages paid to employees, and so on. These information systems are commonly called *transaction processing systems*. Other information systems provide reports and displays that help managers make more informed decisions. These are typically called *management information systems*. Table 2-3 summarizes these and other categories of information systems. Let's look briefly at some examples.

- *Transaction processing systems* record and process data resulting from business transactions. They process transactions in two basic ways. In *batch processing*, transactions data are accumulated over a period of time and processed periodically. In *realtime* (or *online*) *processing*, data are processed immediately after a transaction occurs. For example, point-of-sale (POS) systems at retail stores use electronic cash register terminals to electronically capture and transmit sales data over telecommunications links to regional computer centers for immediate (realtime) or nightly (batch) processing.

- *Process control systems* monitor and control physical processes. For example, a chemical refinery uses electronic sensors linked to computers to continually monitor a chemical process and make instant (realtime) adjustments that control the refining process.

- *Office automation systems* enhance office communications and productivity. For example, a government agency may use word processing for office correspondence, electronic mail to send and receive electronic messages, and teleconferencing to hold electronic meetings.

- *Management information systems* provide information in the form of reports and displays to managers. For example, sales managers may us their computer workstations to get instantaneous displays about the sales of a particular product and also receive weekly sales analysis reports that evaluate sales made by each salesperson.

- *Decision support systems* give direct computer support to managers during the decision-making process. For example, advertising managers may use an electronic spreadsheet package to do "what-if" analysis as they test the impact of alternative advertising budgets on the forecasted sales of a new product.

- *Executive information systems* provide critical information in easy-to-use displays to top management. For example, top executives may use touchscreen terminals to instantly view text and graphics displays about key areas of organizational and competitive performance.

- *Strategic information systems* help provide strategic products and/or services that give an organization a comparative advantage over its competitors. For example, a manufacturing company may use telecommunications networks to link its computers to those of its customers and

Retail sales information systems can combine features of both transaction processing and management information systems.

suppliers in order to make it easier for them to do business with the company than with its competitors.

Table 2-3 summarized some of the many ways to classify information systems. However, it is important to realize that, typically, information systems in the real world are combinations of these conceptual classifications. For example, most retail stores have information systems that process customer sales transactions and also produce reports that analyze sales performance for store management. So these systems really combine features of both transaction processing systems and management information systems into one *retail sales* information system.

Careers in Information Systems

Computers and their use in information systems have created interesting, highly paid, and challenging career opportunities for millions of men and women. Employment opportunities in the field of computers and information systems are excellent, as organizations continue to expand their use of computers. National employment surveys continually forecast shortages of qualified information systems personnel in many job categories. For these reasons, learning more about computers may help you decide if you want to pursue a computer-related career.

Job opportunities in computers and information systems are continually changing due to dynamic developments in information technology (IT), including computer hardware, software, telecommunications, and other technologies. One major source of jobs is the computer industry itself. Thousands of companies develop, manufacture, market, and service computer hardware and software, or provide related services such as computer training or data communications networks. Many of the more technical jobs in the computer industry are held by graduates of *computer science* programs. Their education helps prepare them for careers in the research and development of computer hardware, system software, and application software packages.

Millions of other jobs are held by graduates of college and university programs in information systems (IS), management information systems (MIS) or computer information systems (CIS). The focus of these programs is training students to be information systems specialists. That's because the biggest source of jobs is the hundreds of thousands of businesses, government agencies, and other organizations that use computers. They need many types of IS managers and specialists to help them support the work activities and supply the information needs of their end users.

Information system specialists are IS professionals who develop, implement, and operate computer-based information systems. Typical examples include systems analysts, programmers, and computer operators. Basically, *systems analysts* design information systems based on the information requirements of end users; *programmers* prepare computer programs based on the specifications of systems analysts; and *computer operators* operate large computer systems.

Many other managerial, technical, and clerical IS personnel are also needed. For example, the top IS management job in many organizations belongs to the *chief information officer (CIO)*. This executive oversees the use of information technology throughout an organization, concentrating especially on IS planning and strategy. The growth of end user computing has also

Information systems specialists support the work activities and information needs of end users.

information systems specialist
A professional who develops, implements, or operates computer-based information systems; for example, a systems analyst, programmer, or computer operator.

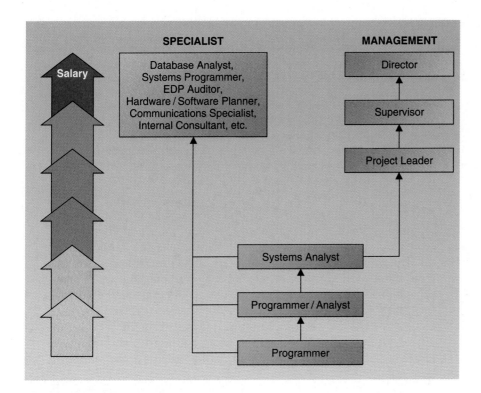

Figure 2-7
Career paths for IS professionals
can lead to a variety of specialist
or managerial positions.

created additional IS career opportunities. Examples of jobs in *end user ser-vices* include positions as user consultants, user trainers, and user liaisons. These IS specialists support efforts by employees to use computers to accomplish their work activities more easily and productively.

Figure 2-7 gives valuable insight into the variety of job types and *career paths* for IS professionals, showing how they can move upward into management or specialist positions.

Quick Quiz

1. Computer systems are part of the hardware resources of an _____.
2. The three basic roles of information systems are the support of business operations, _____ , and strategic advantage.
3. _____ systems record and process data resulting from the occurrence of business transactions.
4. _____ information systems produce reports and displays for managers.
5. Examples of information systems specialists include computer programmers, computer operators, and _____.

Answers: 1. information system   2. managerial decision making
3. transaction processing   4. management   5. systems analysts

End Note: End Users and Information Systems

The example of information systems at Au Bon Pain Restaurants mentioned earlier should tell you much about the role of end users in information sys-

E·T·H·I·C·S

Ethical Issues in Information Systems

Information systems professionals have to deal with many ethical issues that are similar to those in other professions. So do end users, as we mentioned in Chapter 1, when we briefly talked about computer crime by end users and IS specialists. National organizations of IS professionals have responded to the ethical issues faced by their members by devising codes of professional conduct. Most of these codes deal with the professional obligations or responsibilities of their members to their employees, to their profession, and to society. One good example is the code of conduct of the Data Processing Management Association (DPMA), one of the top organizations of IS professionals.

The DPMA code, parts of which are shown in Table 2-4, summarizes the ethical considerations and major responsibilities of many professionals in the computer industry. It provides general guidelines for ethical conduct by IS specialists when developing and operating computer-based information systems. However, it should also give you a good idea of your responsibilities as an end user to your employer and to society as you work with information systems in the real world.

What Do You Think?

What are your responsibilities as an end user to your college or university? To your employer and society? What do you think?

In recognition of my obligation to my employer I shall:
- Avoid conflict of interest and ensure that my employer is aware of any potential conflicts.
- Protect the proper interests of my employer at all times.
- Protect the privacy and confidentiality of all information entrusted to me.
- Not misrepresent or withhold information that is germane to the situation.
- Not attempt to use the resources of my employer for personal gain or for any purpose without proper approval.

In recognition of my obligation to society I shall:
- Protect the privacy and confidentiality of all information entrusted to me.
- To the best of my ability, ensure that the products of my work are used in a socially responsible way.
- Support, respect, and abide by the appropriate local, state, provincial, and federal laws.
- Never misrepresent or withhold information that is germane to a problem or a situation of public concern, nor will I allow any such known information to remain unchallenged.
- Not use information of a confidential or personal nature to achieve personal gain.

Table 2-4
Part of the DPMA Code of Professional Conduct

tems. First of all, the chain's management in Boston told IS professionals what they expected from the system. Top executives thus played a major role in the development of the store management system. Second, store managers are the primary users of the system in each store. They not only enter daily sales and inventory data, but they also receive reports that help them manage their stores. So managers throughout a company typically play a major role in the development and use of its information systems.

In many cases, you as an end user also act as your own IS specialist. The availability of microcomputers and useful software packages makes this possible. Of course, first you have to attain conceptual and functional computer literacy. This will allow you to evaluate and suggest improvements for software and data resources, information products, and input, processing, output, storage, and control activities of the information systems you encounter in your work. Even then, you probably will need the assistance of the IS specialists who work with end users at your organization. Or you may have to rely on external IS consultants to help you. Your challenge is to become computer literate and also knowledgeable in the field you wish to make your career. Then you can help develop and use information systems successfully.

Summary

Information Systems and You   To be truly computer literate, you must understand how computer-based information systems provide the information people need to be productive and successful. This requires a knowledge of the basic components and functions of information systems. Then you will be able to apply such concepts to information systems you encounter in the real world.

System Concepts   Information systems are based on the concept of a system as a group of interrelated components working toward a common goal. A system accepts input and produces output in an organized transformation process. Its control component monitors and evaluates feedback about the performance of the system and makes any adjustments needed to help the system meet its goals.

Information System Components   An information system uses people, hardware, software, and data to perform input, processing, output, storage, and control activities that transform data resources into information products. Data are collected for processing (input), manipulated and converted into information (processing), and then stored for future use (storage) or communicated to the ultimate user (output) according to processing procedures (control).

IS Resources and Products   People resources consist of information systems specialists and end users. Hardware resources include machines and media used in information processing. Software resources can include computerized instructions (programs) and instructions for people (procedures). Data resources include alphanumeric, text, image, and audio data. Information products can take a variety of forms, including paper reports, graphics displays, and audio responses.

Overview of Information Systems   Information systems can be classified in many ways. Examples include transaction processing systems, office automation systems, management information systems, and decision support systems. Information systems in the real world actually are combinations of these conceptual classifications. In addition, information systems perform support roles in an organization's business operations, managerial decision making, and attainment of strategic advantage.

Computer Careers Computers and their use in information systems have created career opportunities for millions of men and women in the computer industry and in computer-using organizations. This includes information systems specialists like systems analysts, programmers, and end user consultants.

Key Terms and Concepts

batch versus realtime processing	management information
careers in information systems	system
computer-based information systems	media
control	people resources
data elements	procedures
data or information processing	processing
data versus information	programs
decision support system	office automation system
ethical issues in information	output
systems	process control system
executive information system	roles of information systems
feedback	software resources
hardware resources	source document
information products	storage
information system	strategic information system
IS (information system) specialist	system
input	transaction processing system

Review Quiz

True/False

_____T_____ 1. An information system uses people, hardware, software, and data to perform information processing that transforms data resources into information products.

_____F_____ 2. A manual information system uses computers and their hardware and software.

_____T_____ 3. Information systems can be classified as transaction processing systems, office automation systems, management information systems, and so on.

_____T_____ 4. A system is a group of interrelated components working together toward a common goal.

_____F_____ 5. Control is data about a system's performance.

_____F_____ 6. Feedback is making adjustments to a system's performance so that it operates properly.

_____T_____ 7. Information is data placed into a meaningful context for an end user.

F   8. Converting data into information is called conversion processing.

T   9. Software resources include programs and procedures.

T   10. Hardware resources include machines and media.

Multiple Choice

a   1. The people resources of an information system are composed of

    a. information systems specialists and end users.
    b. the programmers who programmed it.
    c. the systems analysts who designed it.
    d. computer operators at the computer center.

d   2. Stored data are typically organized into

    a. records.
    b. files.
    c. databases.
    d. all of the above.

b   3. Transaction processing systems that process data immediately do

    a. batch processing.
    b. realtime processing.
    c. offline processing.
    d. multiprocessing.

a   4. Transaction processing systems that process data periodically do

    a. batch processing.
    b. realtime processing.
    c. offline processing.
    d. multiprocessing.

d   5. Systems analysts, programmers, and user consultants are examples of

    a. end users.
    b. knowledge engineers.
    c. systems engineers.
    d. IS specialists.

b   6. An information system that provides reports and displays to management is

    a. an office automation system.
    b. a management information system.
    c. a decision support system.
    d. a process control system.

a   7. An information system that enhances office communications and productivity is

    a. an office automation system.
    b. a management information system.
    c. a decision support system.
    d. an executive information system.

c   8. An information system that gives direct computer support during decision making is

    a. an office automation system.

b. a management information system.
c. a decision support system.
d. an executive information system.

___d___ 9. An information system that provides critical information to top management is

a. an office automation system.
b. a management information system.
c. a decision support system.
d. an executive information system.

___b___ 10. An information system that gives an organization an advantage over its competitors is

a. a management information system.
b. a strategic information system.
c. a decision support system.
d. an executive information system.

Fill-in

1. Using a computer keyboard to enter data is an _input_ activity.
2. Doing loan payment calculations is an _processing_ activity.
3. Printing a letter using a computer is an _output_ activity.
4. Saving a copy of the letter on a disk is an _storage_ activity.
5. Having a sales receipt to document a purchase is an example of a _control_ method.
6. Magnetic disks, magnetic tape, plastic cards, and paper forms are examples of _data media_
7. Messages, documents, reports, and graphics displays are examples of _information products_
8. Sets of instructions for a computer are _programs_
9. Sets of instructions for people are _procedures_
10. Categories of _information systems_ include transaction processing systems, office automation systems, and management information systems.

Questions for Thought and Discussion

1. Are computer systems a necessary component of information systems? Explain.
2. Refer to the Real-World Example of Toyota Motor Sales in the chapter. Do other car dealers use a system like Lexus? Should they? Explain.
3. Why are there several types of information systems? What roles do they play in an organization?
4. Refer to the Real-World Example of US Air in the chapter. Have you been to an airport lately? What computer-based information systems did you encounter? Which were most useful? Most frustrating?
5. Identify several uses of the term "system" in this chapter. Why is this term so useful in the study of computers and information systems?

6. Refer to the Real-World Example of Au Bon Pain in the chapter. If you were a restaurant manager, what other features would you like in a restaurant management system?

7. Identify several types of data resources and information products mentioned in the chapter. Give other examples.

8. Refer to the Real-World Example of Au Bon Pain in the chapter. Is its restaurant management system a transaction processing system or a management information system? Explain.

9. A student uses a microcomputer and a word processing program to prepare a report. When the report is edited and formatted to an instructor's specifications, the student saves it on the computer's magnetic disk and prints a copy on its printer. If the student tries to save the report using a file name previously used for saving another document, the program displays a warning and waits until it receives an additional command. What information system resources, activities, and products can you identify in this example?

10. Describe the components of an information system that you use regularly, such as a department store POS system, a supermarket checkout system, a university registration system, or a bank ATM system. What resources, activities, and products of computer-based information systems can you identify? Make a brief report to the class.

Review Quiz Answers
True/False   1. T 2. F 3. T 4. T 5. F 6. F 7. T 8. F 9. T 10. T
Multiple Choice   1. a 2. d 3. b 4. a 5. d 6. b 7. a 8. c 9. d 10. b
Fill-in   1. input 2. processing 3. output 4. storage 5. control 6. data media
7. information products 8. programs 9. procedures 10. information systems

VIEWPOINT

COMPUTERS IN THE REAL WORLD

Many books could be written on the countless uses or **applications** of computers in business, government, and the rest of society. We have already mentioned some of them in our discussion of end user computing and knowledge work. You already use computers in many ways yourself—from the tiny microprocessors that help control your automobile or wristwatch to the large mainframe computers that may have recently checked the status of your account at a bank or retail store or processed your registration for this class. Instead of detailing their many uses in a lot of words, this photo essay gives you a visual overview of some of the many applications of computers in the real world.

Computer-aided manufacturing (CAM) systems help increase the efficiency and quality of manufacturing operations by controlling many manufacturing processes. For example, industrial robots such as these welding robots on an assembly line use computer intelligence and computer-controlled physical capabilities to perform production activities in automated factories.

Computers have revolutionized how the banking, credit, and securities industries operate by making *electronic funds transfer* (EFT) possible. For example, you can transfer funds electronically by using convenient automated teller machines (ATMs), buy or sell securities electronically on computerized stock exchanges, and use credit cards to make purchases that are instantly authorized by computers.

Computers have become an integral part of the modern office. They make possible a variety of *office automation* applications, like word processing and electronic mail, that dramatically improve the efficiency and effectiveness of office activities and communications.

Computers have automated the capture of sales transaction data with point-of-sale (POS) terminals that use optical scanning wands to read merchandise tags.

Computers make *smart products* possible. Built-in microprocessors are really *special-purpose computers* that significantly improve the performance and capabilities of products ranging from automobiles to microwave ovens, toys to wristwatches, cameras to credit cards, and a host of other consumer, commercial, and industrial products.

Computers have become indispensable tools for scientific analysis, experiment monitoring, and engineering design. Computer graphics play a major role in scientific analysis and computer-aided design (CAD).

Computers are used in advance diagnostic and treatment devices and in hospital information systems that automate patient monitoring and medical records processing. Shown are computerized patient monitoring and medical imaging systems.

Artists can electronically draw and paint whatever they can visualize, from simple graphics images to elaborate and realistic pictures in TV, movies, video games, books, and magazines.

Computers process tax returns, produce social security checks, count votes, control spacecraft and military weapons systems, keep track of wanted criminals, and perform many other chores faced by national, state, and local government agencies.

Computers have become common educational tools as students and teachers rely on them for computer-assisted instruction (CAI) and computer-managed instruction (CMI).

PART II

SOFTWARE

Software is the bridge that brings the power of computers to you, the end user. In the following chapters, we delve into the basic functions of the software that manages your computer resources, primarily operating systems and end user applications. Word processing, desktop publishing, computer graphics, electronic mail, and office management software are all discussed within the context of office automation. Electronic spreadsheets, integrated packages, and expert systems are covered as decision support software. Database development and information retrieval and reporting are discussed in the context of using database management software.

CHAPTER

3

SYSTEM SOFTWARE: MANAGING YOUR COMPUTER RESOURCES

OUTLINE

LEARNING OBJECTIVES

After reading and studying this chapter, you should be able to

Identify three major types of system software.

Describe the five basic functions of an operating system.

Identify the advantages and disadvantages of the three types of software user interfaces.

Identify the functions of operating environments, system utilities, and performance and security monitors.

You and System Software

system software
Programs that manage and support a computer system.

System software consists of programs that manage and support your use of a computer system. As noted in Chapter 1, system programs serve as a *software interface* between the hardware of your computer system and the application programs you are using. So no matter what type of jobs you are doing with your computer, you are being assisted by three major types of system software, as shown in Figure 3-1.

- *System management programs* manage hardware, software, and data resources while the computer system executes the information processing jobs you want accomplished. Operating systems and operating environment packages are examples of such software.

- *System support programs* provide a variety of support services. System utilities and security monitors are examples.

- *System development programs* help end users and IS professionals develop and prepare software for computer processing. Programming language translators and computer-aided software engineering (CASE) packages are examples of such programs.

Let's look first at operating systems and operating environments. Then we will discuss examples of several system support and development programs.

What Is an Operating System?

operating system
The main control program of a computer system. It controls the operations of a computer by communicating with end users, managing hardware resources and files, supervising the accomplishment of tasks, and providing other support services.

The most important system software package for your computer is its **operating system**. Why is it called an *operating system*? Because it is an integrated *system* of various programs that manage the *operations* of your computer. Operating systems like Microsoft DOS, or IBM's OS/2 control your

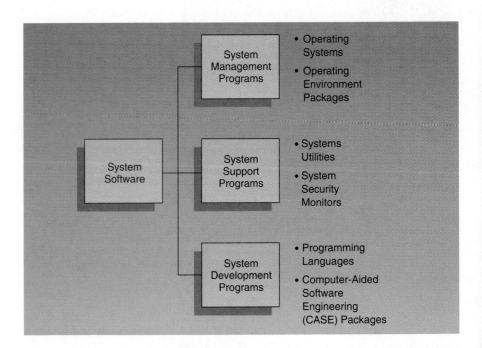

Figure 3-1.
These are examples of three categories of system software that help you use your computer system.

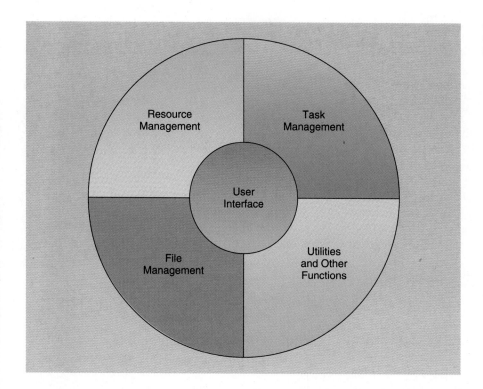

Figure 3-2
Operating systems perform five
basic functions.

computer's activities as the computer executes your application programs and also provide a variety of support services. For example, your operating system is involved every time you press a key, click a mouse, access a file on disk, display a result, or print a document.

Thus, an operating system maximizes your productivity by operating your computer efficiently. An operating system also minimizes the work you and other end users have to do. Its programs help your application software packages perform common input, processing, output, and storage operations, such as entering data into a spreadsheet, saving and retrieving database files, and printing or displaying word processing documents. If you have any hands-on experience with a computer, you know that the operating system must be loaded and activated before you can accomplish other tasks. This emphasizes that an operating system is the most indispensable component of the software interface between you and your computer system.

Functions of an Operating System

Operating systems perform many jobs to help make using a computer system easier. We can group what an operating system does into five categories as shown in Figure 3-2.

- The *user interface* communicates between the operating system and end users.
- *Resource management* manages the hardware resources of a computer system.
- *File management* manages files of data and programs.

Häagen-Dazs: Windows on Ice Cream

Suppose you're a sales manager for the Häagen-Dazs Company in Teaneck, New Jersey. How do you get the latest information on ice cream sales quickly displayed on your PC screen? You couldn't a few years ago. Sales reports from 19 distribution centers in the United States and overseas were faxed to corporate headquarters in Teaneck each week. Then the sales data was manually entered into an HP minicomputer system so managers could view columns of sales figures on their video terminals.

All that's changed now that Häagen-Dazs has switched to PCs running the Microsoft DOS operating system and Windows operating environment. Now, every company executive and sales manager, as well as marketing and financial analysts, has a microcomputer workstation. A telecommunications network allows them to ac-

cess sales databases updated electronically from all company locations. So to get the latest sales figures on ice cream sales, all you have to do is use your PC's mouse to click on an icon displayed by Windows on your video screen. Then DOS would connect you to the Häagen-Dazs Corporate Sales Reporting (CSR) program, which would give you the sales figures you want in dazzling color. And guess what icon you use to access ice cream sales? Why, one shaped like a pint of Häagen-Dazs of course!

1. Why did Häagen-Dazs change to a DOS/Windows operating system on PCs from it's previous sales reporting system?

2. Which of the five basic functions of an operating system do you see in the Häagen-Dazs example?

- *Task management* manages tasks the computer must accomplish.
- *Utilities and other functions* provide support services.

The User Interface

user interface
The part of the operating system that allows you to communicate with it.

The part of the operating system that you see is called its **user interface** or *shell*. It allows you to communicate with the operating system to get things done. User interface programs interpret your requests or *commands* and transfer them to other programs in the operating system to be accomplished. Thus user interface programs are sometimes known as *command interpreters* or *processors*.

There are three main types of user interfaces for operating systems and many other types of software: *command-driven, menu-driven,* and *graphical-user interfaces*. The trend in user interfaces has been away from stark command-driven interfaces toward easier-to-use menu-driven interfaces, but now has shifted dramatically toward the more intuitive and "user friendly" graphical-user interface (GUI). Let's briefly take a look at how they are implemented in operating systems and other types of software packages.

Command-Driven Interfaces

command-driven interface
The oldest form of user interface. In this method, you enter a command by typing a few codes or words and then execute it by pressing the Enter or Return key.

The oldest form of user interface is the **command-driven interface**. In this method, you enter a command by typing in a few codes or words and then press the Enter or Return key to issue the command. If you enter your command in-

```
C:\>dir a: /w/p

Volume in drive A has no label
Directory of A:\

MEM            CLOSE         HEUF(C).MEM      HUEFWP.TOC      HEUFCMEM.DUP
DAVIS.LET      LOOKY         DAVIS.MEM        HUEFWPTC.DUP    SCHY.ADD
SMBIZCOV.S-H   RONJIMLT.001  ROBWNGRM.(C)     LEEPIE.LET      BOBPIE.LET
JOEPIE.LET     SCHY.LET      LARGAYLT.001
      18 file(s)      60420 bytes
                     291840 bytes free


C:\>
```

Command-driven interfaces like MS-DOS require the user to type combinations of keystrokes, words, and codes to initiate commands.

correctly, the operating system will display an error message so you can try again. Many times, you enter commands in response to **prompts** displayed by the operating system that indicate it is ready to receive commands. The prompt is followed by a blinking **cursor** (a movable point of light or other shape). The photograph above shows a typical command-driven interface.

Typically the codes and words in command-driven interfaces are part of a *command language* that an end user must learn in order to use the operating system. (In mainframes, it's called the JCL, or *Job Control Language*.) For example, in command-driven versions of the DOS operating system, a DIR command asks for a directory listing of files on a disk. Or the command COPY A: STUDENT B: directs the operating system to copy the STUDENT file from the disk in drive A to the disk in drive B.

The advantage of the command-driven interface is that commands are brief and quick to use. However, it requires that you memorize many of the commands in the operating system's command language. Also, the prompts of a command-driven interface are frequently too brief for inexperienced end users to understand and respond to correctly.

prompts
Messages that guide (prompt) an end user when using a computer.

cursor
A movable point of light displayed on video display screens to assist users in data input.

Natural Language Interfaces

One way to improve the command-driven interface is to use *natural language* commands. A **natural language interface** allows you to use simple English-like phrases to direct the computer to accomplish your requests. However, entering long natural language commands is slower than using a more traditional command-driven interface or other alternatives. So natural language interfaces are not expected to come into widespread use until conversational voice-input technology is perfected.

Natural language interfaces are available in several types of software packages. For example, some database management packages allow you to use natural language commands such as:

SHOW ME SALES BY SALESREPS IN THE NORTHWEST REGION

natural language interface
Allows you to use conversational phrases to direct the computer to accomplish your requests.

This command would cause a computer to display a list of the sales (in dollars) made by each of the salespersons in the company's Northwest sales region.

Menu-Driven Interfaces

menu-driven interface
Allows the end user to select from a menu or list of choices of things the computer can do.

menu
A displayed list of options from which an end user makes a selection.

A **menu-driven interface** allows you to select from a **menu** or list of choices or options of things you want the computer to do. The process is *menu driven* because you typically select from a series of menus until you accomplish a particular task. For example, many software packages display a *menu bar* of choices at the top of the screen. Each menu bar selection can lead to one or more *pull-down menus* of additional choices. Selections from each of these menus can generate additional menus, some of them in *pop-up windows* that appear on the screen.

A menu-driven interface is easier to learn and use than command-driven interfaces, especially for inexperienced users. However, it is usually slower and less flexible than other interfaces. For instance, it may require you to work your way through a long series of menus to accomplish a task that could be done by entering a few commands. Nevertheless, menu-driven interfaces, such as the one below continue to be a popular method of computer interaction for end users.

Graphical-User Interfaces

graphical-user interface
Using graphics images (icons, bars, buttons) to represent tasks you want to perform, choices you want to make, files you want to access, and devices or programs you want to use.

The **graphical-user interface** (**GUI**, pronounced *gooey*) has become the most popular user interface method for operating systems and environments like Microsoft Windows for DOS and many other types of software packages. Graphics images (such as *icons,* bars, and buttons) are used to represent tasks you

Menu-driven interfaces contain menus that often require mouse support to pull down, point, and click to initiate commands.

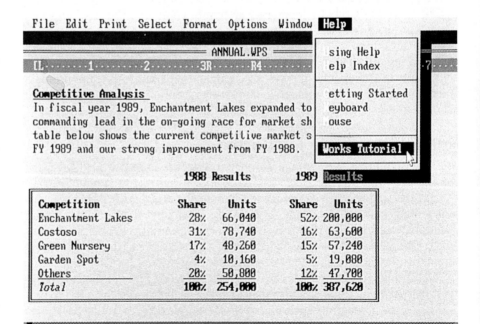

Graphical-user interfaces (GUI), popularized by Macintosh, are now available for most other operating systems. Here is an example of Microsoft Windows for DOS-based systems.

want to perform, choices you want to make, files you want to access, and devices or programs you want to use. **Icons** are small, easily recognizable, pictorial figures. Examples include a file folder (to represent a data file), a trash can (to delete a file), and a filing cabinet (to load a file manager program). **Windows**, which divide the screen into individual displays, or other graphics devices may be used to organize the screen into a *desktop* display or other familiar images. The photograph above shows a graphical-user interface.

Typically, graphical-user displays enable you to use *pointing devices* such as an electronic mouse to move an arrow or other cursor figure to an icon or other image on the screen. You select what you want to do by pressing buttons on the mouse to complete "point and click" or "point and drag" operations. For example, you can delete an unwanted file by pointing to a file folder and "dragging" it to the trash can icon. Clicking buttons on the mouse completes the job.

Thus the graphical-user interface is easier and faster for many applications. Selecting a single icon can help you do a task that otherwise would have taken several commands or navigating a series of menus to accomplish. However, using a mouse does require more eye–hand coordination and is not appropriate for data entry and other tasks. So many software packages use a combination of command-driven, menu-driven, and graphical-user interfaces.

Operating Environments

Many operating systems are enhanced with **operating environment** programs such as OS/2's Workplace Shell, or by add-on packages such as Microsoft Windows and DESQview for the DOS operating system. Operating environments enhance the user interface by adding a layer of software between the operating system and your application programs. They offer a graphical user

icons
Small pictorial figures that are easy for end users to recognize; they represent tasks, files, or programs.

windows
Sections of a computer's display screen, each of which can have a different display.

operating environment
Software packages that add a graphics-based interface between end users, the operating system, and their application programs; they may also provide a multitasking capability.

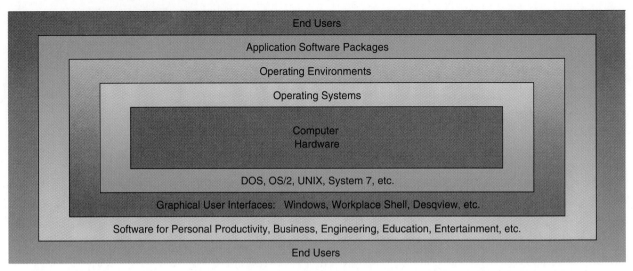

End Users
Application Software Packages
Operating Environments
Operating Systems
Computer Hardware
DOS, OS/2, UNIX, System 7, etc.
Graphical User Interfaces: Windows, Workplace Shell, Desqview, etc.
Software for Personal Productivity, Business, Engineering, Education, Entertainment, etc.
End Users

Figure 3-3
Operating environments add a layer of software between the operating system and your application software packages.

interface similar to those provided by the Apple Macintosh operating system. Operating environments thus serve as a *shell* around your operating system and application packages, so you can switch among them easily and they can share common data files. See Figure 3–3.

Operating environment packages use icon and other graphic displays that give you an attractive, easy-to-use graphical interface. They also support the use of electronic mice and other pointing devices. Typically, operating environments allow the output of several programs to be displayed at the same time in multiple windows. Finally, many of these packages support some type of multitasking, so your computer can work on several tasks from one or more programs at the same time.

 ## Quick Quiz

1. You need _____ software to manage and support your computer system.
2. The most important system software program is the _____.
3. The _____ is the part of an operating system that you see when you use it.
4. Command-driven and menu-driven user interfaces have been replaced by _____ in many software packages.
5. An _____ program provides a graphical-user interface for an operating system.

Answers: 1. system software   2. operating system   3. user interface   4. graphical-user interfaces   5. operating environment

Managing Computer Resources

An operating system manages the demands made on your computer's resources by the software packages you use. A computer system's resources include its CPU, memory, secondary storage devices, and input/output pe-

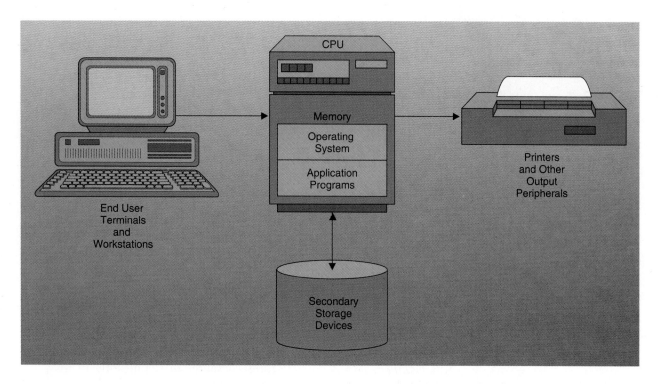

CPU

Memory

Operating
System

Application
Programs

End User
Terminals
and
Workstations

Printers
and Other
Output
Peripherals

Secondary
Storage
Devices

Figure 3-4
An operating system manages
your computer's resources.

ripherals, as shown in Figure 3-4. For example, if you are using software for word processing, the operating system will interrupt the CPU when you enter a command to print or save a document. Then it will select the appropriate printer or magnetic disk and notify the CPU to begin executing the instructions in the *device driver* programs that control the operations of individual peripheral devices. The operating system will also monitor the printing or disk storage process and tell the CPU when to resume its other computing assignments.

The resource management programs of mainframe operating systems that control input, output, and secondary storage devices are sometimes called the IOCS (input/output control system). Similar programs for microcomputer operating systems are known as BIOS (basic input/output system). BIOS is usually permanently stored on ROM chips and thus is instantly available when your microcomputer is turned on to load or *boot* parts of the operating system into main memory (RAM) from the magnetic disk drive where they are stored. These *memory-resident* parts of the operating system remain in memory while other parts stay on disk until they are needed.

Memory Management

A computer's memory is another valuable resource that must be managed. Operating systems contain **memory management** programs that divide memory into a number of *partitions* and keep track of where programs and data are stored. Memory management programs also monitor the transfer or *swapping* of programs and data between memory and secondary storage devices. Memory management may also allow some operating systems to have a **virtual memory** capability. This means that the operating system can expand a

memory management
Dividing a computer's memory into sections and keeping track of where programs and data are stored. Also monitoring the transfer or swapping of programs and data between memory and secondary storage devices.

virtual memory
The use of secondary storage devices as an extension of the primary storage of a computer, thus enabling a computer to act as if it had a larger main memory than it actually does.

Figure 3-5
Some operating systems let secondary storage devices provide additional *virtual memory* capacity to a computer system.

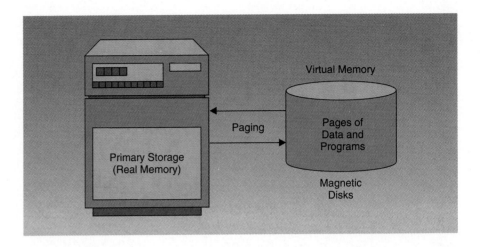

computer's capacity by swapping pieces of programs and data (called *pages* or *segments*) between memory and magnetic disks, as Figure 3-5 illustrates.

With virtual memory, unneeded portions of programs and data are temporarily moved from memory to magnetic disk storage. They are replaced with pages of programs and data retrieved from the disks for processing by the CPU. This *paging* makes it possible for a computer to significantly increase the number of programs and amount of data its memory can handle. That's why a computer can have *virtual memory* capacity that is substantially larger than its actual RAM or *real memory* capacity. For example, some microcomputers with a real memory capacity of 32 megabytes can act as if they had a memory of 4 gigabytes by using virtual memory operating systems.

Managing Files

file management
Enables the operating system to control the creation, deletion, location, and retrieval of data and programs.

Most operating systems view everything stored on magnetic disks and other secondary storage devices as files. So an operating system has to do **file management**. That is, it must control the creation, deletion, location, and retrieval of files of data and programs. A file in this context is simply a *named collection of data or instructions*. For example, an operating system needs to be able to locate and access the document files you create when you do word processing, the spreadsheet files you develop when using a spreadsheet program, and the database files you create when using a database management package.

When you save a file you give it a filename, so the operating system can find the file. The software package you are using then adds a three-character *file extension*. For example, a Lotus 1-2-3 spreadsheet for sales analysis might be called SALES.WK1 and a Microsoft Word document for a form letter might be called LETTER2.DOC, while a dBASE IV data file of student information might be called STUDENT.DBF.

Most operating systems have file management or *data management* programs responsible for the creation, deletion, and access of files. *File access* activities include locating, opening, reading, writing, closing, and copying files in response to instructions from an application program.

```
E:\>tree
Directory PATH for Volume STACVOL_DSK
E:.
    ┌──ADDRBOOK
    ├──ANYUCI
    │      ├──DOC
    │      └──MM
    ├──EDITOR
    ├──INSTALL
    │      ├──EXAMPLES
    │      │      └──INSTALL.NEW
    │      ├──SOURCE
    │      └──UTIL
    ├──TEMP
    ├──TEST2
    │      └──PDQ2.17
    ├──TYPESET
    │      ├──HRW
    │      │   INSTALL
    │      └──PCTYPE
    └──VENTURA
           └──DICT

E:\>
```

Directory trees illustrate the organization of files into subdirectories on the system's hard drive.

File management also involves determining the physical arrangement of files on magnetic disks and other secondary storage devices. An operating system keeps track of the location of files by maintaining *directories* or catalogs of information about the files in your computer system. These directories typically contain the name and location of a file, as well as other information such as the type of file, its size in bytes, and the date it was created.

Typically, directories on hard disk drives are organized as a series of *subdirectories*, each containing related files. Grouping files in subdirectories makes them easier to find. For example, spreadsheet files could be contained in a WKSHEET subdirectory, correspondence files in a LETTERS subdirectory, report files in a REPORTS subdirectory, and so on. The photograph above shows one example of a directory tree.

Task Management

How can some computers do many things at once for many users? Their speed and **task management** is the answer. We know that the CPUs of many computers can execute millions of instructions per second, but most CPUs still execute only one instruction at a time. Therefore, computers need operating systems that use task management programs that help them process many competing tasks at the same time.

A *task* is an operation like calculating, printing, or accepting keyboard input. Task management involves giving each task a slice (a fraction of a second) of a CPU's time. This process of *time slicing* can occur on a first-come, first-served basis, a round-robin fashion, or according to a schedule that gives some tasks a higher priority than others. When a task's time slice is over, or if higher priority tasks need to be accomplished, the operating system's *interrupt handler* program will *interrupt* the CPU and substitute another task for processing.

task management
Enables a computer to process many competing tasks at the same time. This typically involves giving each task a fraction of a second of a CPU's time. When a task's time slice is over, or if higher priority tasks need to be accomplished, the operating system will interrupt the CPU and substitute another task for processing.

Multitasking operating systems allow the user to operate several applications at once. In this case, a word processing program, a database, and a spreadsheet are operable.

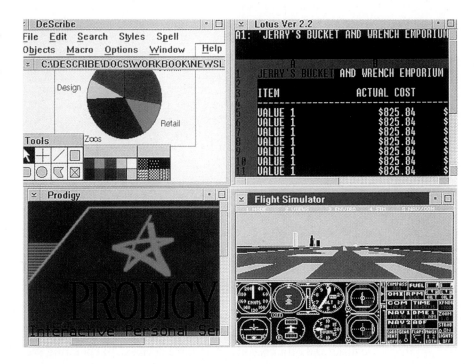

Task management (also called *process* or *job management*) takes advantage of the fact that many computing tasks are relatively slow compared to the speed of the CPU. For example, in the time it takes you to enter responses on a keyboard or a printer to print a line of output, a CPU could do millions of other operations. Therefore, an operating system can assign the CPU many high-speed tasks that take only a few nanoseconds to do (such as calculations or memory transfers) while it is waiting for slower operations to occur.

Multitasking

Many current microcomputers can only do one thing at a time for one user at a time. Their microprocessors and operating systems can only perform basic activities of task management. Some operating systems or add-on packages allow microcomputers to do *task switching* or *task swapping* operations. For instance, they allow you to switch from a word processing package to a spreadsheet package and back at the touch of a key. Thus, you can work on several projects alternately without having to exit one program and load a new one.

Mainframe and minicomputer operating systems and some microcomputer operating systems can use task management to provide a **multitasking** capability. Multitasking is the capability that allows you to do two or more operations (for example, printing and keyboarding) *concurrently,* that is, at the same time on the same computer. Multitasking can also take the form of *multiprogramming*, where a CPU can process the tasks of several programs (for example, word processing and spreadsheet packages) concurrently. Multitasking is essential for *multiuser* computer systems, where several end users share the same computer at the same time in a process known as **time sharing.**

multitasking
Allows the end user to do two or more operations (for example, printing and keyboarding) at the same time.

time sharing
A process by which several end users share the same computer at the same time.

Multitasking on microcomputers has been made possible by the development of advanced operating systems and more powerful microprocessors (like the Intel Pentium) and their ability to work with much larger memory capacities (up to 4 gigabytes). This allows an operating system to divide primary storage into several large *partitions,* each usable by a different application program. In effect, a computer with a single CPU can act as if it were several computers, or *virtual machines,* since each application program is running independently at the same time. So you don't need a *multiprocessor* computer (which may have several or many CPUs) to do multitasking. Multiprocessor computers can do *multiprocessing,* that is, they can execute several instructions at the same time.

In multitasking, the number of programs that you can run concurrently depends on the CPU's processing power, the amount of memory your computer has, and the amount of processing each job demands. That's because a CPU or main microprocessor can become overloaded with too many jobs and provide unacceptably slow response times. However, if memory and processing capacities are adequate, multitasking allows a CPU to switch easily from one application to another, share data files among applications, and process some applications in a *background* mode. Typically, while you do *foreground* tasks like data entry, a CPU can be doing background tasks like printing, extensive mathematical computation, or unattended telecommunications sessions.

Quick Quiz

1. Managing the use of the hardware devices of a computer system is an operating system function called _____.
2. Managing the files of data and programs of a computer system is _____.
3. Managing the processing of the jobs being accomplished by a computer system is an operating system _____ function.
4. Some operating systems provide a _____ capability so a computer can do more than one operation at the same time.
5. Several end users sharing the processing power of a computer at the same time is known as _____.

Answers: 1. resource management 2. file management 3. task management 4. multitasking 5. time sharing

Popular Operating Systems

Let's take a look now at several popular operating systems and operating environments—MS-DOS, Windows and Windows NT, OS/2, UNIX, and Macintosh System 7. All are microcomputer operating systems or environments, except for UNIX, which also has versions for mainframes and minicomputer systems. Other popular mainframe and minicomputer operating systems, such as VM or MVS for IBM mainframes and VMS for Digital VAX minicomputers, are beyond the scope of this text. Several versions of most popular microcomputer operating systems are available. Which version you use depends pri-

Figure 3-6
The MS-DOS operating system
has these basic components.

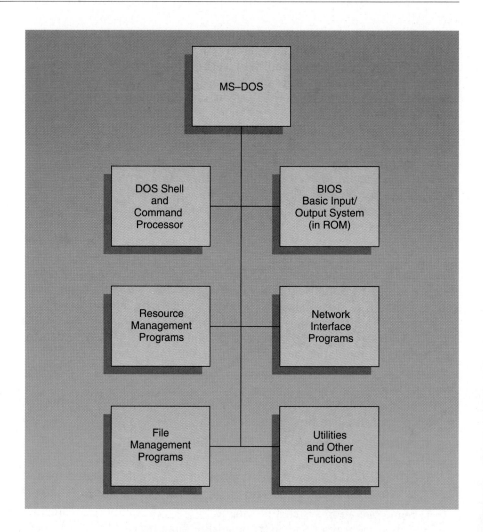

marily on your computing needs and the main microprocessor and memory capacity of your microcomputer system.

MS-DOS

The most widely used operating system today is MS-DOS (Microsoft Disk Operating System) by the Microsoft Corporation. Developed for the IBM Personal Computer in 1981 as PC-DOS, it soon became the dominant operating system in the microcomputer world, as manufacturers began producing millions of microcomputers compatible with the IBM PC and software developers churned out thousands of programs that could work with MS-DOS.

MS-DOS is a single-tasking, single-user operating system consisting of a variety of programs known as DOS *commands*. Many are utility programs that do jobs such as copy files (COPY), prepare disks to receive files (FORMAT), and list files on a disk (DIR). Others are important programs such as COMMAND.COM, which is the DOS command processor. Some of these programs are used so often that they load into your computer's memory from a floppy or hard disk when you turn on the machine, so they can be accessed quickly. These programs are called "resident" or "internal" commands. Other DOS commands are left on disk, ready to be called up when you need them. See Figure 3-6.

Microsoft releases new versions of DOS every few years. For example, versions 3.0 to 3.3 added support for local area networks and hard disk drives, while version 4.0 added a menu-driven interface or *shell* and other improvements to MS-DOS, which had always been command driven. Version 5.0 added a graphics-based shell, the ability to do task switching between programs, help displays, and other features. Version 6.0 added virus detection and other utility programs to DOS. Still, DOS remains a single-user, single-tasking operating system that can only manage 640 kilobytes of memory, unless it is supplemented with add-on packages that extend its capabilities. As an end user, you should know which DOS version you have. Any application software package you buy should state that it is compatible with that version.

Windows and Windows NT

If you want a true graphical-user interface and multitasking capabilities, you can add *Microsoft Windows* or other operating environment packages like DESQview to recent versions of MS-DOS. However, for best results, you will need a PC with a main microprocessor at least as powerful as the Intel 80386 chip, several megabytes of memory, and a hard disk drive. Many application software packages designed to use MS-DOS along with Microsoft Windows are

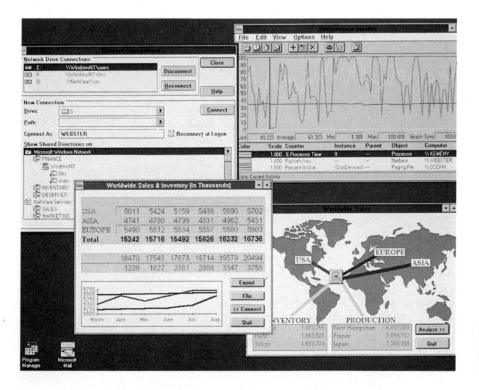

Microsoft hopes that Windows NT will compete effectively as one of the "next generation" of operating systems.

available, so millions of users now use DOS with Windows to add the ease of a graphical-user interface to their PCs.

In July 1993, Microsoft Corporation introduced *Windows NT* (New Technology), billed as an operating system/operating environment successor to DOS and Windows and as a competitor to IBM's OS/2 and other operating systems. Windows NT requires a minimum of 12 megabytes of RAM, 75 megabytes of magnetic disk drive capacity, and at least the equivalent of an Intel 80386 microprocessor (Microsoft recommends 16 megabytes of RAM, and independent testers recommend the equivalent of an Intel 80486 as a minimum microprocessor requirement). Windows NT is designed to be a more powerful and capable operating system and GUI for networked PCs than Windows/DOS or its competitors. However, tests of early versions of Windows NT indicate that more development work is needed to improve its processing speed and overall performance. Thus, Microsoft continues to improve Windows NT so it can compete effectively as one of the "next generation" of operating systems.

OS/2

Microsoft and IBM introduced OS/2 (Operating System/2) in 1988 as a successor to MS-DOS. It was designed to capitalize on the capabilities of more powerful microprocessors from Intel, manage up to 16 megabytes of real memory and 4 megabytes of virtual memory, support true multitasking operations, and provide a graphical-user interface called Presentation Manager. IBM took over development of OS/2 in 1990 and introduced substantially improved versions beginning in 1992. Figure 3-7 illustrates the OS/2 components. Notice that OS/2 consists of a main *kernel* and program modules for the user inter-

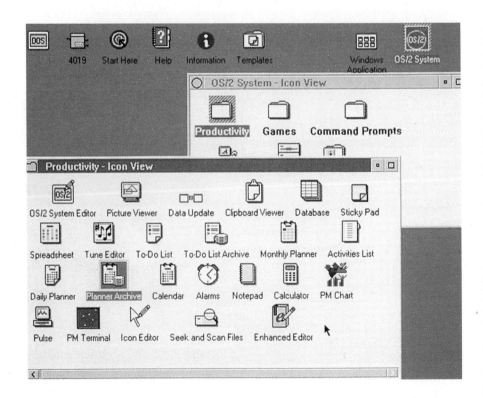

The operating system OS/2 provides a friendly interface called Workplace Shell.

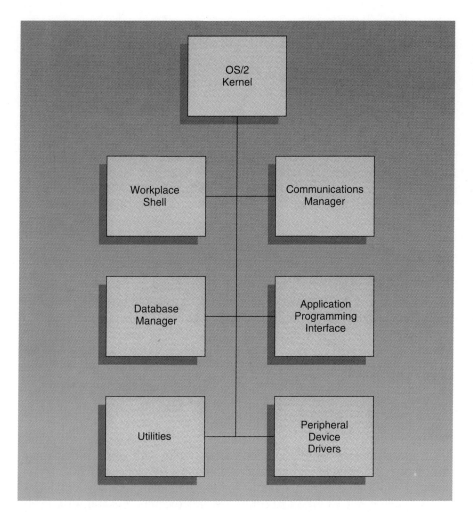

Figure 3-7
The components of OS/2 help manage the user interface, telecommunications, databases, programming, and peripheral devices.

face (Workplace Shell), the programmer interface (Applications Programming Interface), telecommunications control (Communications Manager), database management (Database Manager), the interface with peripheral devices (device drivers), and various utilities.

OS/2's Workplace Shell provides an attractive GUI operating environment with icons, windows, and other graphics images designed for use with a mouse or other pointing devices. MS-DOS and Windows can even run as applications within OS/2. OS/2 is large and complex, as well as powerful and easy to use. It can take up to 1.5 megabytes of memory, though more compact versions are available. For best results, many consultants recommend a PC with at least an Intel 80386 main microprocessor, 4 megabytes of memory, and 60 megabytes of hard disk capacity.

These resource requirements, as well as the greater variety of application software packages available for users of MS-DOS and Windows, have hurt OS/2's acceptance by end users. For now, an improved OS/2 remains as a more powerful but less popular alternative to MS-DOS and Windows for IBM and IBM-compatible microcomputers.

REAL-WORLD EXAMPLE

Chicago Tribune:
The News on OS/2

Does a big-city newspaper need a multitasking operating system for its PCs? You bet it does, says the *Chicago Tribune*. That's why it installed the OS/2 operating system on more than 400 Compaq microcomputers for reporters, editors, and other staff members who must write copy for the daily newspaper. Each PC has at least 6 megabytes of memory and is networked to four Tandem CLX minicomputers that control the network and its databases.

But why OS/2 and not a Microsoft DOS/Windows combination? Software Services Manager Jim Joyce explains that the true multitasking capability of OS/2 allows reporters to run several jobs at once in separate windows displayed on their PC screens. For example, a reporter can be writing a story in one window, looking at news coming from The Associated Press in another window, and checking facts on the story by interrogating the newspaper's databases in a third window, all at the same time! Even editing functions like hyphenation and formatting can be going on in the background as a reporter is working on a story.

1. Are the capabilities of the OS/2 operating system important for newspaper reporters to have? Explain.

2. What other occupations could benefit from the multitasking capabilities of operating systems like OS/2?

UNIX

UNIX is a multiuser, multitasking operating system with versions that run on mainframes, minicomputers, and microcomputers. Developed by AT&T, it is now licensed and available from several vendors. Microcomputer versions include Zenix by Microsoft for IBM and compatible microcomputers and A/UX for the Apple Macintosh. Minicomputer and mainframe versions include Solaris by Sun Microsystems, AT&T's own UNIX System V and IBM's AIX. Thus, one of the keys to UNIX's popularity is its *portability*. That is, UNIX is an *open system* that can be easily modified and used on many types and brands of computers.

However, unlike MS-DOS and OS/2, UNIX's main appeal is that it is a powerful multiuser operating system designed for networks of many computers and end users. UNIX allows a computer network to handle the computing needs of many end users doing a variety of tasks simultaneously. Thus, UNIX demonstrates advanced multitasking, virtual memory, and time-sharing capabilities. It can even run other operating systems, such as MS-DOS, as separate jobs, thus allowing it to process application programs written for MS-DOS. Figure 3-8 illustrates the variety of programs that make up UNIX.

UNIX also has a cost advantage because it can support a network of end users at inexpensive *video display terminals (VDTs)*. These keyboard/video screen devices can be connected to a minicomputer or powerful microcomputer, instead of a network of more expensive microcomputers. UNIX's main disadvantages have been its inadequate network security features, incompatibility among its different versions, and the difficulty of using its *shell,* or command-driven interface. However, these limitations are being addressed by improvements to UNIX, including easy-to-use graphical-user interfaces such

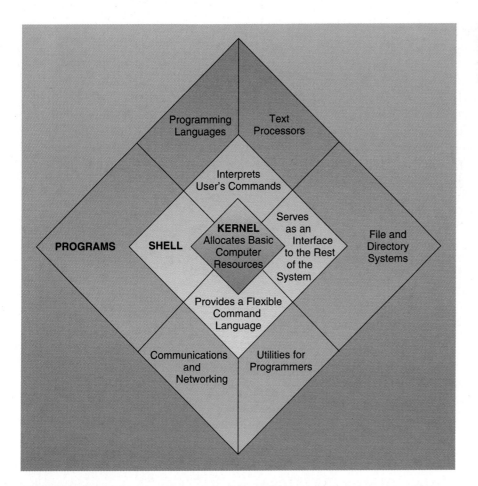

Figure 3-8
UNIX includes a kernel to manage resources, a shell for a user interface, and a variety of other programs.

Programming Languages

Text Processors

Interprets User's Commands

KERNEL Allocates Basic Computer Resources

Serves as an Interface to the Rest of the System

PROGRAMS   **SHELL**

File and Directory Systems

Provides a Flexible Command Language

Communications and Networking

Utilities for Programmers

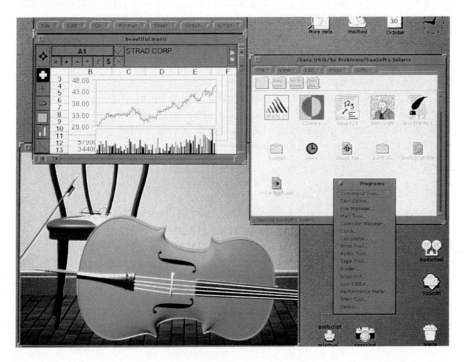

The UNIX operating system supports the OpenLook graphical-user interface. Here the program Solaris Deskset is open.

REAL-WORLD EXAMPLE

Garber Travel Services:
Is DOS Dead?

"DOS is dead. I love DOS and hate Windows as it exists today, but the reality is that all our new application development work is being done in Windows and OS/2," said Rock Blanco, director of information systems at Garber Travel Services in Boston. In general, IS managers report that they have moved to Windows because doing so makes it easier and less costly to support end users. Blanco, for example, said his staff spends considerably less time training end users how to run applications on Windows and OS/2 because of their easy to use graphical user interfaces.

Thus the PC software industry appears to be lining up to put the final nails in the DOS coffin as major suppliers begin to downgrade the relative importance of DOS as a platform for new application software packages. As Windows expands its dominance of the PC industry, both WordPerfect Corp. and Borland International are relegating DOS to secondary status behind future Windows, OS/2, Windows NT, Macintosh and Unix versions of their software. And Lotus Development Corp. said it is currently evaluating what course its future commitments to DOS will take. All its major software products, except Lotus 1-2-3 for DOS and CC:Mail for DOS are focused on graphical user environments. Thus, Lotus plans to evaluate what the future market demand for DOS will be, said Jeff Anderholm, director of marketing for spreadsheets.

1. Why do you think someone like Rock Blanco would say he "loves DOS and hates Windows as it exists today"?

2. Why is the software industry moving away from DOS and towards Windows-based software packages?

as OpenLook, Motif, and NextStep. The photograph on page 83 shows the OpenLook graphical-user interface running on the UNIX operating system.

Unix has long been used at colleges and universities, especially on minicomputers made by Digital Equipment Corporation (DEC). Its applications were primarily in engineering, computer science, and scientific research at universities, government agencies, and in industry. Its powerful utilities make it a favorite of scientific programmers and users of high-powered engineering workstations. Now that it is available on many types of computers, its applications are expanding into business and other areas. Thus, many popular application software packages for microcomputers are now available for users of UNIX.

The Macintosh System

The latest version of the operating system for the Apple Macintosh line of microcomputers is called System 7. For many years, the System, with its graphical-user interface and support of the mouse as an input device, made the Mac a popular, easy-to-use microcomputer. Based on earlier computers such as the Xerox Star and the Apple Lisa, many of the System's features can be found in other GUIs, including Microsoft Windows and OS/2's Workplace Shell. The photograph on page 85 shows the graphical-user interface of a paint program for the Macintosh.

The graphical-user interface of this sophisticated paint program for the Macintosh simulates a painter's tools, palette, and canvas.

The Macintosh System was designed as a single-user operating system to run on the Motorola 68000 series of microprocessors that power Macintosh computers. Unlike many computers, the entire system is stored on ROM chips and thus is instantly available when the Macintosh is turned on. Application software for the Macintosh usually cannot run on IBM and other computers that use Intel microprocessors (or vice versa). However, special circuit boards and software can be added to a Mac to let it run MS-DOS and OS/2 software. Some recent models now come with this as a built-in feature.

Macintosh System 7 is designed for the powerful Motorola 68030 and 68040 microprocessors, and the Power PC microprocessor, and thus supports multi-tasking and virtual memory. System 7 includes an efficient file manager called the Finder and a program manager called Multifinder, which manages its task-switching and multitasking operations. Many popular application software packages are designed to use the Macintosh System. Programs that support commercial art, engineering design, and desktop publishing are highly popular because of the Macintosh's extensive graphics capabilities. Apple and software developers are also making a concerted effort to develop packages that use the capabilities of the Macintosh and System 7 for business applications.

Quick Quiz

1. The most widely used microcomputer operating system is _____.
2. The most widely used microcomputer operating environment is _____.
3. Microsoft's planned successor to DOS/Windows is _____.
4. IBM's competing operating system to DOS/Windows is _____.
5. A popular operating system that has versions that can be run on microcomputers, minicomputers, and mainframes is _____.

Answers: 1. MS-DOS 2. Microsoft Windows 3. Windows NT
4. OS/2 5. UNIX

Other System Software

As mentioned earlier, system support programs and system development programs are other major types of system software. They can be used to support

Figure 3-9
Programs written in high-level programming languages like BASIC must be translated into a computer's own machine language of binary codes.

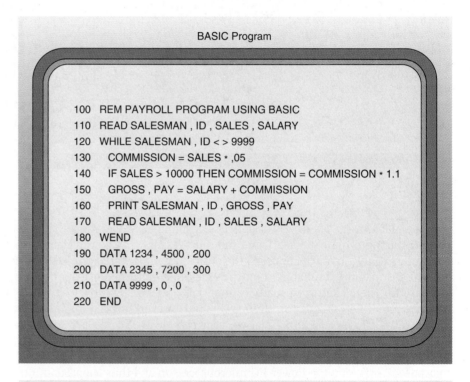

BASIC Program

```
100  REM PAYROLL PROGRAM USING BASIC
110  READ SALESMAN , ID , SALES , SALARY
120  WHILE SALESMAN , ID < > 9999
130    COMMISSION = SALES * ,05
140    IF SALES > 10000 THEN COMMISSION = COMMISSION * 1.1
150    GROSS , PAY = SALARY + COMMISSION
160    PRINT SALESMAN , ID , GROSS , PAY
170    READ SALESMAN , ID , SALES , SALARY
180  WEND
190  DATA 1234 , 4500 , 200
200  DATA 2345 , 7200 , 300
210  DATA 9999 , 0 , 0
220  END
```

Machine Language Program

Operation Code	Operand
1010	11001
1011	11010
1100	11011

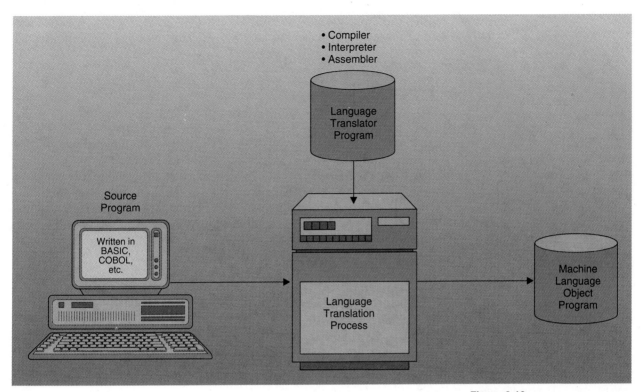

Figure 3-10
A program must be translated into machine language instructions before it can be executed.

the operations or develop software for your computer system. Sometimes they may be included as programs within your operating system, though most can be purchased as separate software packages. We will discuss some types of system software, such as mainframe database management systems and telecommunications monitors, in later chapters. Others, like programming language translators, and system utilities, we can discuss now.

Programming Language Translators

Language translators (or *language processors*) are systems development programs that translate the instructions of other programs into binary codes a computer can execute. They also allow you to write your own programs by providing helpful features for creating and editing programs. Remember that all computer programs consist of sets of computing instructions. They are written in *programming languages*, such as BASIC, Pascal, or COBOL. Then they must be *translated* into a computer's own binary codes (called its *machine language*) before they can be processed, or *executed*. We will discuss programming and programming languages in more detail in Chapter 10. See Figure 3-9.

Programming language translator programs are known by a variety of names. An **assembler** translates the symbolic instruction codes of programs written in an assembler language, while a **compiler** translates high-level language statements. An **interpreter** is a special type of compiler that translates and executes each program statement one at a time, instead of first producing a complete machine language program, like compilers and assemblers do. Figure 3-10 illustrates the typical language translation process. A program

language translators
Programs that translate the instructions of other programs into binary codes a computer can execute.

assembler
A computer program that translates a program written in an assembler language into a computer's machine language.

compiler
A program that translates a program written in a high-level programming language into a computer's machine language.

interpreter
A computer program that translates and executes each program instruction before translating and executing the next one.

written in a language such as BASIC is called a *source program*. A source program translated into machine language is called an *object program,* which can then be executed by a computer.

Utilities

utilities
Specialized programs that help perform routine computing functions, such as sorting data, loading programs, and copying files of data.

Utilities are system support programs provided by an operating system or add-on package that help you perform routine computing jobs. Many utility programs perform a variety of *housekeeping* and file conversion functions. For example, utility programs do jobs such as sorting data, loading programs, clearing and recording the contents of memory, and copying files of data from one storage medium to another, such as from disk to tape or from floppy disk to hard drive. Many of the operating system commands used with microcomputers and other computer systems provide utility programs and routines for a variety of chores. See Figure 3-11.

Performance Monitors

performance monitor
A software package that monitors the processing of computer system jobs and the use of system resources; produces statistics that can be used to improve the efficiency of a computer system.

Most operating systems monitor a computer system's performance. For example, they display messages concerning the status of processing or the availability of hardware resources. Specialized **performance monitor** programs can also be used to monitor the processing activities of individual or networked mainframes, minicomputers, and microcomputer systems. These system support packages monitor the performance of computer systems and their use by end users. Performance monitors, like the one shown on page 89, can produce reports containing detailed statistics about the use of system resources such as processor time, memory space, and input/output and secondary storage devices. These reports help managers plan and control the efficient use of computer systems in a computer center or computer network.

Security Monitors

Many operating systems have security features to protect a computer system's resources. For example, they may require passwords and user identification

Figure 3-11
Utility programs such as PC Tools can accomplish a variety of helpful tasks.

🌳	Displays directories in tree format	👜	Puts fragmented files together
	Shows files without opening program		Displays system information
🔍	Searches for misplaced files	☎	Communicates with other PCs
	Recovers data on reformatted disks		Stores programs in RAM for fast load
🕐	Changes date, time, and type of file	🩺	Detects and eliminates viruses
	Recovers deleted files and data		Opens applications from within utility
	Adds color and tones to batch files	⌨	Contains built-in calculator and clock
	Relocates data from bad disk sectors		Backs up files and hard drives
	Repairs damaged files	🔒	Secures files with passwords
	Searches files for specific data		Compresses data to save disk space

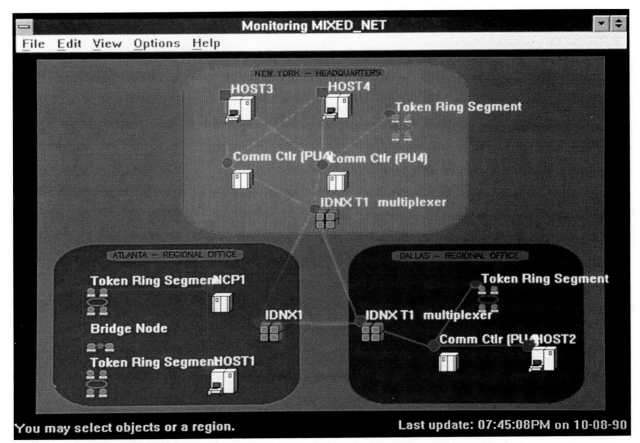

A performance monitor package helps manage the use of a computer system.

Security monitor packages operate with passwords or other gatekeeping features to restrict access to hardware, software, and data.

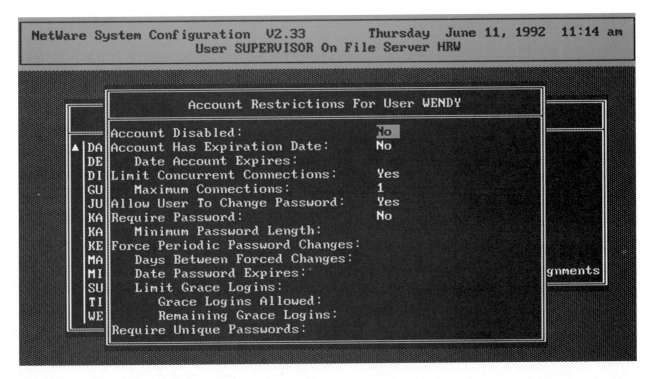

security monitor
A software package that monitors a computer system and protects its resources from unauthorized use, fraud, and vandalism. Security monitor packages operate with passwords or other gatekeeping features to restrict access to hardware, software, and data.

codes *(user IDs)* to sign on to a system or to access restricted files. **Security monitor** packages are available that monitor the use of a computer system to protect its resources from unauthorized use, fraud, and destruction. Such programs provide a high level of security that allows only authorized users to access a system. Security monitors also control use of the hardware, software, and data resources of a computer system. Even authorized users may be restricted to the use of certain devices, programs, and data files. Finally, such packages monitor computer usage and display warning messages and collect statistics on any attempts at improper use. They also produce reports to assist IS managers in maintaining the security of a system. The photograph on page 89 shows a security monitor package that is used to monitor network access.

End Note: End Users and System Software

It's easy to overlook system software. Most end users are more concerned with their application software packages. If you want to do word processing, spreadsheet analysis, or even play a video game, you don't really care about the operating system interface that is displayed when you first turn on your computer. Like most end users, you just want to get on with whatever you have decided to do with your computer. So it's easy to overlook system software in the rush to get your application software running.

But as you can see in this chapter, system software, especially your operating system, is vitally important to end users. You can't use your computer without it. System software manages all of your computer system resources, controls all of your application software, and helps you accomplish all of your computing activities. As you have seen in this chapter, every time you use a keyboard or a mouse, retrieve a file on a disk drive, or switch among tasks, the programs of your operating system are involved. Therefore, understanding the role and capabilities of system software is an important aspect of your computer literacy.

Table 3 1 summarizes some of the capabilities of popular microcomputer operating systems. It highlights some of the features you should consider when you select a microcomputer, its operating system, or any applications software packages you buy. For example, if you want your computer to be easy to use and do several things at the same time, you will want a microcomputer with a powerful main microprocessor and sufficient memory, and an operating system with a graphical-user interface and multitasking and virtual memory capabilities. Then you will need software packages designed to work with the microprocessor and operating system you select.

Features	MS-DOS	OS/2	UNIX	Macintosh System 7
Intel 8088	X			
80286	X			
80386	X	X	X	
80486	X	X	X	
Pentium	X	X	X	
Motorola				
68030			X	X
68040			X	X
Power PC	X	X	X	X
Single-user	X	X		X
Multitasking		X	X	X
Virtual memory		X	X	X
Multiuser			X	

Table 3-1
Typical capabilities of popular operating systems

E T H I C S

Ethical Issues in System Software

System software is often the first line of defense against computer crime. Operating systems may use passwords and user IDs to restrict access to computer resources and databases. System security monitors can also provide tight computer security. They not only protect a system from unauthorized use, but detect, record, and warn of attempts at unauthorized entry.

However, system software is often the first line of attack by computer criminals. They know that breaking into a computer system involves getting past operating system security features. They also know that a **computer virus,** a destructive program that replicates itself, can do its greatest damage if it attaches itself to the operating system—the program that controls the entire computer system. So, good operating security features and the use of other security software such as virus detection and removal programs are important weapons in the fight against computer crime.

You and other end users can also play a direct role in the ethical use of system software. First, you should cooperate with the security features built into the system software you use. Some end users purposely disable such features for their convenience, thus leaving their computer systems vulnerable to computer crime. More importantly, you should refrain from unauthorized copying of software or cooperating with those end users who do.

The COPY utility of most operating systems is the key piece of system software used in such **software piracy.** Copying files is such a useful and necessary part of end user computing that the COPY command is one of the most frequently used utilities in an operating system. But unauthorized copying of software is a different matter. It damages a software developer's financial incentives to develop new and improved software. And it leaves end users with unauthorized copies that they typically do not know well enough to use properly without the documentation and support that only registered owners receive. Software piracy is one ethical issue end users can all do something about.

What Do You Think?

How prevalent are computer viruses and software piracy at your college or university? What steps are being taken to combat the spread of computer viruses? What is being done to discourage software piracy? What more could be done? What do you think?

computer virus
A program that copies its annoying or destructive routines into the computer system of anyone who accesses a computer system that has used the program, or anyone who uses copies of data or programs taken from such computers.

software piracy
Unauthorized copying of software.

Summary

What Is an Operating System?   The most important system software package for any computer is its operating system. An operating system is an integrated system of programs that supervises the operations of the CPU, controls the input/output and storage functions of a computer system, and provides support services. An operating system performs five basic functions by providing user interface, resource management, file management, task management, and utilities.

The User Interface   The part of the operating system that allows you to communicate with it is called the user interface. The three main types are command-driven, menu-driven, and graphical-user interfaces. The trend is away from the use of brief commands, or even menus of options, toward easy-to-use, graphical-user interfaces that employ icons and other images and pointing devices.

Managing Computer Resources   An operating system uses a variety of programs to manage the resources of a computer system, including its CPU, memory, secondary storage devices, and input/output peripherals. Memory management programs keep track of where data and programs are stored. They may also divide memory into a number of sections and swap parts of programs and data between memory and magnetic disks or other secondary storage devices. This may provide a computer system with a virtual memory capability significantly larger than its real memory capacity.

Managing Files   An operating system contains file management programs that control the creation, deletion, and access of files of data and programs. This also involves keeping track of the physical location of files on secondary storage devices by maintaining directories of information about the location and characteristics of files.

Task Management   The task management programs of an operating system manage the computing tasks of end users. They give each task a slice of a CPU's time and interrupt CPU operations to substitute other tasks. Task management may involve a multitasking capability where several computing tasks can occur at the same time. Multitasking may take the form of multiprogramming, where the CPU can process the tasks of several programs at the same time, or time sharing, where the computing tasks of several users can be processed at the same time. The efficiency of multitasking operations depends on CPU processing power and the virtual memory and multitasking capabilities of the operating system.

Popular Operating Systems   MS-DOS is the most widely used microcomputer system. Although a single-user, single-tasking operating system, a graphical-user interface and multitasking capabilities can be achieved by adding an operating environment package like Microsoft Windows. OS/2 is a multitasking operating system for advanced IBM and compatible microcomputers that provides a graphical-user interface and virtual memory. UNIX is a multitasking, multiuser operating system that can run on mainframes, minicomputers, and microcomputers. The Macintosh System 7 is an operating system for Apple Macintosh microcomputers that has a popular graphical-user interface, as well as multitasking and virtual memory capabilities.

Other System Software Operating environment programs add a graphical-user interface to an operating system and may provide multitasking. Programming language translators translate programs into binary codes a computer can execute. Utilities are programs that perform routine computing functions, such as sorting data or copying files, as part of an operating system or as a separate package. Performance monitors are programs that monitor the performance and usage of computer systems to help their efficient use. Security monitors are packages that monitor and control the use of computer systems and provide warning messages and record evidence of unauthorized use of computer resources.

Key Terms and Concepts

command-driven interface	OS/2
cursor	performance monitor
directory	programming language translator
file management	prompt
graphical-user interface	resource management
icon	security monitor
Macintosh System	software piracy
menu-driven interface	system software
mouse	task management
MS-DOS	time sharing
MS-Windows	UNIX
multitasking	utilities
natural language interface	user interface
operating environment	virtual memory
operating system	window

Review Quiz

True/False

_____ 1. System software manages and supports the operations of computers.

_____ 2. An operating system is an integrated system of programs that manages a computer system.

_____ 3. Virtual memory helps you communicate with an operating system.

_____ 4. Resource management programs manage information processing tasks by a computer system.

_____ 5. Task management programs manage the use of CPU time, primary and secondary storage, and input/output devices.

_____ 6. File management programs manage the input/output, storage, and retrieval of data files and programs.

_____ 7. The user interface expands a computer's apparent memory capacity by swapping parts of programs and data between memory and secondary storage devices.

_____ 8. Utility programs perform miscellaneous computing chores for end users.

_____ 9. An operating environment is a graphical-user interface package that coordinates the use of a microcomputer's operating system and application programs.

_____ 10. Multitasking is performing two or more computing tasks at the same time.

Multiple Choice

_____ 1. A movable point of light or other shape that indicates where you should enter data or commands on the screen is called
   a. a menu.
   b. an icon.
   c. a cursor.
   d. a prompt.

_____ 2. A request from the computer for you to enter data or a command is known as
   a. a menu.
   b. an icon.
   c. a cursor.
   d. a prompt.

_____ 3. A small figure that represents a computing activity is called
   a. a menu.
   b. an icon.
   c. a cursor.
   d. a window.

_____ 4. A feature that divides your video screen into separate displays is called
   a. a menu.
   b. an icon.
   c. a cursor.
   d. a window.

_____ 5. A pointing device that moves a cursor on the screen when you move it on a desktop is called
   a. a pointer.
   b. an indicator.
   c. a mouse.
   d. a bug.

_____ 6. A listing of file names and their locations is called
   a. a menu.
   b. an index.
   c. a directory.
   d. a dictionary.

_____ 7. The most widely used microcomputer operating system is
   a. UNIX.
   b. MS-DOS.
   c. OS/2.
   d. the Macintosh System.

d 8. The first widely used graphical-user interface operating system was
a. UNIX.
b. MS-DOS.
c. OS/2.
d. the Macintosh System.

c 9. An operating system developed as a multitasking successor to MS-DOS is
a. UNIX.
b. MS-DOS.
c. OS/2.
d. the Macintosh System.

a 10. A portable, multiuser, multitasking operating system is
a. UNIX.
b. MS-DOS.
c. OS/2.
d. the Macintosh System.

Fill-in

1. You can't do anything with your computer until its *operating system* is loaded and activated.
2. An *operating environment* package enhances the user interface between an end user and its operating system and application programs.
3. More powerful microprocessors and operating systems support a *multitasking* capability where microcomputers can process several tasks at the same time.
4. Most operating systems provide *utilities* that perform miscellaneous computing jobs.
5. Programs that support your use of application software packages are called *system software*.
6. A software package is *command driven* if you must use brief commands to get things done.
7. A software package is *menu driven* if you must choose from a series of menus to get things done.
8. A software package has a *graphical user interface* if you can use pointing devices to select graphics images to get things done.
9. A small pictorial figure displayed on your video screen is an *icon*.
10. A list of choices or options displayed on your video screen is a *menu*.

Questions for Thought and Discussion

1. What is the difference between system software and application software? How does this difference affect end users?
2. Refer to the Real-World Example of the *Chicago Tribune* in the chapter. What other software would newspaper reporters need besides an operating system like OS/2?

3. Macintosh computer users do not spend much time learning about System 7, their built-in operating system. They just turn on their computers and start to point and click at icons and other selections with an electronic mouse. Many users of IBM PC and compatible computers spend a lot of time learning the basics of MS-DOS. What are some reasons for this difference between the two operating systems?

4. What capabilities does an operating environment package add to an operating system?

5. Refer to the Real-World Example of Häagen-Dazs in the chapter. What capabilities does the Windows operating environment give its end users?

6. Graphical-user interfaces are supposed to be the easiest-to-use software interfaces. Yet many users prefer command-driven interfaces. Why?

7. What advantages does OS/2 have over MS-DOS? Disadvantages?

8. What is the difference between multitasking, multiprogramming, and multiprocessing?

9. Refer to the Real-World Example of Garber Travel Services in the chapter. Why would an IS director say that "DOS is dead"?

10. What penalties do organizations pay if they are caught condoning the unauthorized copying of software by their end users? Look up recent articles on this topic in your library. Make a brief report to the class.

Review Quiz Answers

True/False **1.** T **2.** T **3.** F **4.** F **5.** F **6.** T **7.** F **8.** T **9.** T **10.** T

Multiple Choice **1.** c **2.** d **3.** b **4.** d **5.** c **6.** c **7.** b **8.** d **9.** c **10.** a

Fill-in **1.** operating system **2.** operating environment **3.** multitasking **4.** utilities **5.** system software **6.** command driven **7.** menu driven **8.** graphical-user interface **9.** icon **10.** menu

CHAPTER

4

OFFICE AUTOMATION SOFTWARE: USING COMPUTERS FOR COMMUNICATIONS AND PRODUCTIVITY

OUTLINE

LEARNING OBJECTIVES

After reading and studying this chapter, you should be able to

Identify the basic and optional functions of word processing packages.

Identify the resources and activities needed to do desktop publishing.

Describe several benefits of using word processing and desktop publishing to electronically create and publish documents.

Identify four categories of computer graphics and describe how graphics packages help end users analyze data and present information.

Describe how electronic mail, voice mail, facsimile, teleconferencing, and telecommuting systems benefit communications among end users.

You and Office Automation

Office automation is changing the equipment and work habits of end users. You will probably join most end users in our information society who are employed as knowledge workers in offices scattered throughout the world. None of us would like to work in offices where all information processing activities are done manually. We would all agree that office machines such as electric typewriters, copying machines, and dictation machines have made office work easier and more productive. But these mechanized office devices have given way to **office automation (OA),** in which computers, computerized office equipment, and a variety of software packages are automating office work and methods of communications.

Office automation changes traditional manual office methods and paper communications media. For example, a traditional office uses typewriters to produce paper documents that are mailed to customers and business associates. Automated offices, on the other hand, use word processing and electronic mail systems to collect, process, store, and transmit data and information in the form of a variety of electronic messages and computer-produced documents. Thus, office automation applications can improve the efficiency and effectiveness of communications among end users in office work groups and throughout an organization.

Examples of typical office automation applications include word processing, electronic mail, desktop publishing, and teleconferencing. Using computers for office automation can significantly increase the efficiency and effectiveness of office activities. For example, applications like word processing and electronic mail help office workers reduce the time and effort needed to produce and access business messages and documents. Table 4-1 outlines major categories and examples of office automation systems. We will discuss the use of software for most of these applications in this chapter. Let's start with the most widely used office automation application—word processing.

office automation
Using computers, computerized office equipment, and a variety of software to automate office work practices and communications methods.

This airport telephone provides electronic office capabilities to the public with a fax machine and keyboard to communicate with other computers almost anywhere in the world via satellite.

Office Automation Systems	Examples
Electronic Publishing Systems	Word processing and desktop publishing
Electronic Communication Systems	Electronic mail, voice mail, and facsimile
Electronic Meeting Systems	Decision room conferencing, desktop video conferencing, teleconferencing, and telecommuting
Image Processing Systems	Processing and management of document images
Office Management Systems	Electronic office accessories, calendars, directories, and task management

Table 4-1
An Overview of Office Automation Systems

Word Processing

Word processing is the use of computers to create, edit, revise, store, and print text material. You can think of word processing as the processing of *text data* to produce *documents*. First, word processing involves the processing of **text data.** Text data includes the words, phrases, sentences, and paragraphs we use in written communications. Second, word processing results in the creation, editing, and printing of **documents.** In word processing, documents are organized forms of text data such as letters, memos, business forms, and reports.

Word processing packages have become one of the most popular types of application software packages available for use with personal computers. Word processing programs like WordPerfect or Microsoft Word make writing and printing documents dramatically easier than handwriting or using a typewriter. Also, word processing can increase the quality of your writing. First of all, editing, correcting, and revising text material becomes much easier to do. More importantly, word processing encourages your creativity in writing by making it easier to record your thoughts than writing by hand. Thus, word processing encourages "stream of consciousness" writing, so you can easily record what is on your mind, while allowing you to easily revise and improve the communication of your ideas. Figure 4-1 provides a summary of the basic activities of word processing.

Planning for Word Processing

The first step in word processing is planning the kind of document you want to create; for example, a memo, business letter, informal letter, or formal report. Planning is an important activity that gives you an opportunity to clarify in your own mind the purpose of your writing. Planning also enables you to use your imagination to brainstorm the most effective way to communicate your ideas to their intended audience.

Planning may involve making a rough outline or rough draft of the structure and content of your document. The structure of your document should

word processing
The use of computers to create, edit, revise, and print text material.

text data
Words, phrases, sentences, and paragraphs used in documents and other forms of communication.

documents
Organized forms of text data such as letters, memos, business forms, and reports.

Figure 4-1
These are the basic activities in word processing.

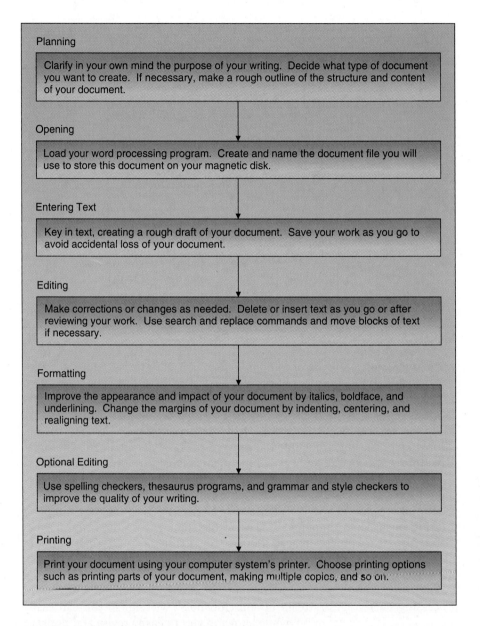

Planning

Clarify in your own mind the purpose of your writing. Decide what type of document you want to create. If necessary, make a rough outline of the structure and content of your document.

Opening

Load your word processing program. Create and name the document file you will use to store this document on your magnetic disk.

Entering Text

Key in text, creating a rough draft of your document. Save your work as you go to avoid accidental loss of your document.

Editing

Make corrections or changes as needed. Delete or insert text as you go or after reviewing your work. Use search and replace commands and move blocks of text if necessary.

Formatting

Improve the appearance and impact of your document by italics, boldface, and underlining. Change the margins of your document by indenting, centering, and realigning text.

Optional Editing

Use spelling checkers, thesaurus programs, and grammar and style checkers to improve the quality of your writing.

Printing

Print your document using your computer system's printer. Choose printing options such as printing parts of your document, making multiple copies, and so on.

follow generally accepted or required standards for quality, readability, and format. For example, the opening and closing text of a business letter differs significantly from those for a memo or informal letter. Thus, planning is an important first step in word processing that results in an acceptable and effective design for the document you wish to create.

Doing Word Processing

Suppose you want to write something using word processing. It can be as simple as a short memo or a long, complex report. In word processing, this is called creating a document. First you load a word processing program from the magnetic disk on which it is stored into the computer's main memory. This should result in an opening screen display on your video monitor. The photograph on page 103 shows you a typical example.

This screen from WordPerfect is a typical opening word processing screen.

Now you can open a **document file** using the appropriate command indicated on the opening display. This involves giving the document you are creating a *file name*. Then you will be able to store the document you created as a file on a magnetic disk in your computer. You can then retrieve it at any time using its unique file name.

Once you enter your document file name, an *editing* screen will be displayed such as shown on page 104. Typically, this includes a **status line** display that helps you keep track of what you are doing. Then you can begin to enter text by using the keyboard and watching what you type as it is displayed on your video screen.

As you type in your words, the word processing program constantly reformats and modifies the appearance of the screen. You do not have to press Enter at the end of every line; you just keep typing, since the program does the "carriage returns" for you. Due to this **word wrap** feature, text material that would extend past the right margin is automatically "wrapped around" to the left margin of the next line. Of course, whenever you want to force the starting of a new line or paragraph (called a *hard return*), you can do so by pressing the Enter key.

document file
Text data in the form of a document that is saved as a file on a magnetic disk or hard drive.

status line
A display that helps you keep track of where you are in a document and what you are editing.

word wrap
A feature that enables you to keep typing without pressing Enter at the end of every line. Text material that would extend past the right margin is automatically "wrapped around" to the left margin of the next line.

Editing Activities

Editing a simple document requires several fundamental editing operations. For example you need to move the cursor around the screen and delete or insert text material. The editing screen might display a menu bar or icons that help you do a variety of editing functions. Or you can use a Help command to bring up a display that tells you how to perform a specific editing activity.

Don't worry about any mistakes you make while trying to record your thoughts. The beauty of a word processing package is that it makes correcting and revising text material easy to do. Once you begin to type a document,

Most word processing programs display a status line at the top or bottom of the screen like the one seen here at the top of this Word-Perfect document.

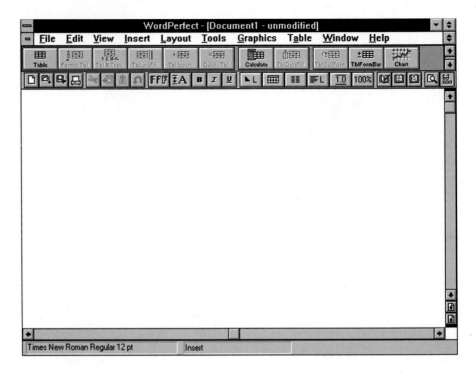

you can use various keys to move your document around on the screen and just type over any mistakes that you make. You will also be able to use specified keys or icons for deleting and inserting characters, words, and lines. This simplifies corrections and changes because it minimizes having to retype incorrect material.

Making Changes

A variety of word processing functions are available to help you make additional changes to a document. For example, you can do search and replace activities, change the format of paragraphs for your entire document, and manipulate sections of your document. You can also use commands that invoke special print effects to take place during the printing process such as printing text in **boldface** or *italics*. In some word processing packages, you can preview such effects before printing using a WYSIWYG (pronounced *wizzywig*) feature, which means "what you see is what you get." So you can see boldface, italics, and other special effects on your screen, exactly as they will look on paper.

Suppose you wish to change certain words or phrases after you have typed a letter, report, or other document. Word processing packages allow you to replace any words and phrases you identify with alternative text. This is called a **search and replace** operation. You could try to visually examine the entire document, but this would be time consuming and difficult. Instead, you can speed up your search by using commands that help you move around your document more quickly, as well as automatically finding, highlighting, and replacing text material.

Formatting

Word processing packages make it easy to control how a document will look when printed. Several common *page-formatting* options are provided that al-

boldface
A special print effect that takes place during the printing process and causes the bolded text to be printed **darker** than surrounding text.

search and replace
Allows you to find and replace any words and phrases you identify with alternative text.

formatting
Commands that allow you to change the layout of what appears on the screen and will eventually be printed.

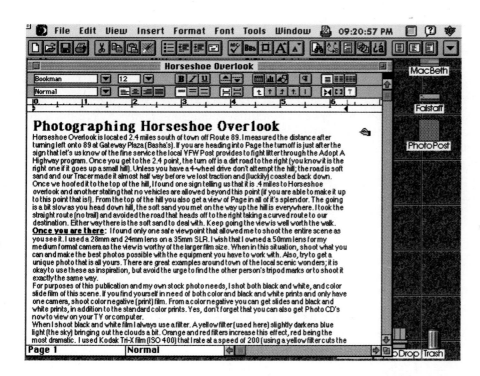

Here you first see a paragraph that runs the full width of the screen before formatting.

low you to have a choice of several formats and styles for whatever type of document you are working on. **Formatting** commands allow you to change the layout of what appears on the screen and will eventually be printed. For example, it is easy to center a title or heading in a document after you have typed it. Formatting also involves automatically **justifying** text. That is, text will usually be left justified, or lined up evenly on the left margin; you can also choose to have text justified on the right margin only, or on both margins.

A word processing program justifies text by automatically adjusting the spaces within each line of a document. However, sometimes you may have to use special commands to format (or reformat) paragraphs in your document. For example, if you change margins or change the words in a paragraph, the spacing will normally need to be changed, too.

justify
A feature found in word processing programs in which text is automatically lined up evenly on the left margin, the right margin, or on both margins.

Block Moves

One of the major capabilities of word processing packages is that they allow you to do "cut and paste" operations to your document. This means that you can move sentences, paragraphs, or pages around within the document, rather than having to retype them. The section of your document that is to be manipulated is called a **block.** A block is a section of your document that has been marked with special commands. Once a block has been marked, you can move it, delete it, copy it, or write it out to its own file. Then you can retrieve it later and insert it in some other document you are working on.

block
A section of the document that has been marked with special commands in order to be moved, deleted, or copied.

Saving and Printing

You should make a habit of continually storing parts of a long document that you are creating on your magnetic disk. Using specified Save command keys or icons will store your document as a text file on your file disk. Saving your work every few minutes will allow you to "save as you go" without leaving the

R E A L - W O R L D   E X A M P L E

Dell Computers: Work Group Publishing

Debby Rosenquist and Alicia Thompson work for Dell Computer, Inc., in Austin, Texas. But they don't help build Dell's microcomputers, which rank as some of the best-selling mail-order PCs produced in the United States. Instead, they help run a 25-member work group that uses networked microcomputer workstations to produce the manuals, brochures, and other documentation needed for Dell's PCs.

Rosenquist manages the company's information development efforts, while Thompson coordinates Dell's documentation for international customers. They rely on software such as WordPerfect for word processing and Aldus PageMaker for desktop publishing. They rely heavily on Novell NetWare, the network operating system, to control the workgroup's sharing of document files and the network's hardware and software resources. Because the group works on several documents at a time, Thompson organizes word processing and desktop publishing activities into four major categories: writing, editing, illustrating, and production. Editing and other changes made by anyone in one of these areas are electronically recorded and communicated to the other three areas. This creates an "edit trail" that helps Dell produce manuals and brochures that are not only attractive but correct as well.

1. How can word processing and desktop publishing become "work group publishing"?

2. Suppose you worked for Dell's documentation group. Which of their four categories—writing, editing, illustrating, or production—would you like to work in? Explain why.

document you are creating. The display of your document remains on the screen. Saving your work minimizes the amount of your document that you would lose due to power failures or other accidental erasures of the contents of main memory. Some programs even allow you to set a timer that will automatically save material after a specified amount of time has passed.

You can always retrieve a copy of a document you saved previously. Just use an appropriate command to load or open a document file. Then enter the name of the document file you wish to retrieve in response to a file name prompt. An electronic copy of your document is then retrieved from the disk and displayed on the screen. You can then begin to work with that document as you did previously, making additional corrections and revisions as needed.

You can print your document at any time by using appropriate Print commands. Usually this is an option provided on the opening menu. A Print command will provide you with a menu of print options, such as previewing your document, printing only parts of your document, making multiple copies, and so on. Then just turn on the printer, select the appropriate options, and print a copy of your document.

Word Processing Options

Many word processing packages provide you with additional features or can be upgraded with supplementary packages. For example, you could buy a *spell checker* that uses a built-in dictionary to identify and correct spelling errors in a document. A *thesaurus* program helps you find a better choice of words to express ideas. *Grammar checkers* and *style checkers* programs can iden-

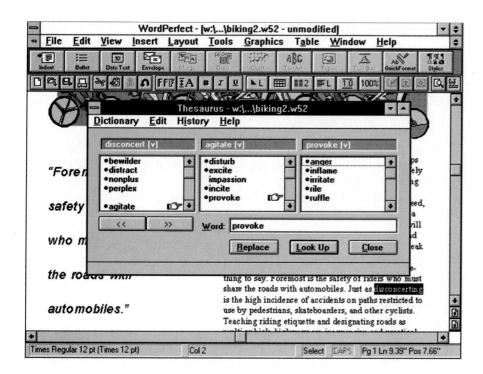

This screen displays WordPerfect's thesaurus function.

tify and correct grammar and punctuation errors, as well as suggest possible improvements in your writing style.

Another text productivity tool is an *idea processor* or *outliner* program. It helps organize and outline your thoughts before you prepare a document or develop a presentation. Also popular is a *mail-merge* program, which can automatically merge the names and addresses in a mailing list file with letters and other documents. Finally, many word processing programs are able to support a limited amount of *desktop publishing* activity. This allows end users to merge text, graphics, and illustrations on each page to produce documents that look professionally published. Let's take a brief look at a few of these options.

Spell Checkers and Thesaurus Programs

Many word processing packages now provide a spell checker capability using a built-in dictionary of thousands of words. The spell checker function automatically "proofreads" your document. It finds and highlights each word that does not agree with the spelling of a similar word in the program's dictionary. Most spell checkers will then suggest alternative words for you to choose from. However, it is up to you to make any change to the word in question. And remember, a spell checker won't discover the incorrect use of a word that is spelled correctly, such as using the word *sea* instead of *see.* So you should still proofread your work to find such errors.

A thesaurus program works much like a spell checker. However, you ask the program to suggest words with similar meanings (synonyms) to or opposite meanings (antonyms) from the one that you highlight or enter. This helps you find a better choice of words to express your ideas.

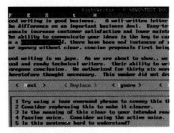

Grammar checking software is available to run with many word processing programs.

Grammar and Style Checkers

Grammar and style checker programs are usually sold as add-on packages for improved word processing. They identify various possible problems in punctuation, sentence structure, word usage, and writing style. For example, GRAMMATIK IV, a best-selling grammar and style checker program, provides sentence analysis, a style and word usage guide, a thesaurus, spell checking, and readability analysis.

Grammar and style checkers contain a dictionary of words, phrases, and punctuation rules that are compared to your writing. The program highlights questionable punctuation, words, phrases, or sentences and offers suggestions for improvement. For example, it may identify usage it considers to be erroneous, sexist, awkward, or inappropriate. Checkers may also count how many times you have used a word, along with other statistics such as the average length of words and sentences. These and other features can help improve your writing style. But remember that writing style is an individual matter. Grammar and style checkers should help, not dictate, your writing style.

Mail-Merge

mail-merge
Allows you to automatically combine names and addresses in a mailing list file with any letters or other documents you want to distribute by mail.

Many word processing programs provide a **mail-merge** feature. It allows you to automatically combine names and addresses in a mailing list file with any letters or other documents you want to distribute by mail. This feature makes possible "personalized" form letters and mass mailings of printed material.

In this application, the mail-merge program inserts names and addresses from a name and address file stored on disk with a file of form letters or standard paragraphs (sometimes called *boilerplate*). This produces a personalized form letter that can be sent to as many people as necessary. The program then uses the name and address file to print envelopes or mailing labels so that the form letter can be mailed. See Figure 4-2.

Quick Quiz

1. Using computers to create, edit, revise, and print text material is _____.

2. The _____ feature automatically adjusts text from the right margin of one line to the left margin of the next line.

3. Activities that change the appearance and layout of your document are called _____.

4. A _____ is a section of your document that you have marked with special commands so you can move and manipulate it.

5. Using a built-in dictionary to identify and correct spelling errors is known as _____.

Answers: 1. word processing   2. word wrap   3. formatting
4. block   5. spell checking

Desktop Publishing

desktop publishing
The use of microcomputers, laser printers, and page composition software to produce a variety of printed materials formerly done only by professional printers.

Desktop publishing turns your microcomputer system into a printing press. That is, desktop publishing allows end users, business firms, and other organizations to produce their own printed materials at significant cost savings

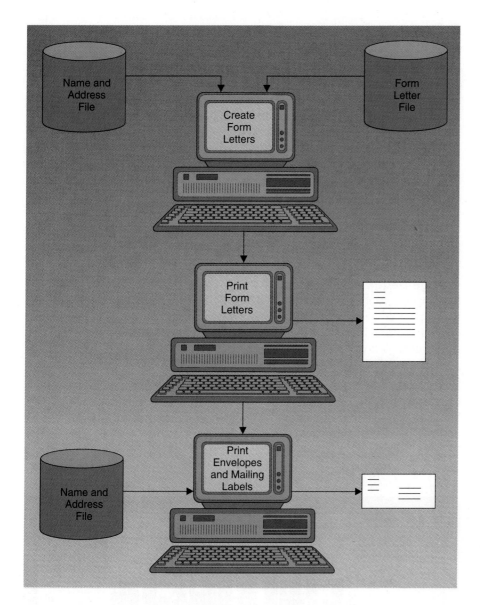

Figure 4-2
A mail-merge capability automatically merges names and addresses with documents you want to distribute by mail.

over commercial publishing. They can design and print their own newsletters, brochures, reports, and manuals with several type styles, graphics, and colors on each page. So desktop publishing has made computer-aided electronic publishing an affordable and attractive application for end users.

Many desktop publishing packages are available. Many word processing packages also provide desktop publishing features. But the desktop publishing process is not easy for the casual end user. Projects involving complex layouts still require experience, skill, and a knowledge of graphics design. However, advances in software are making the job easier in terms of both ease of use and helping you do a better job of graphics design for documents. For example, most desktop publishing packages provide predesigned forms called *templates* or *style sheets* to relieve you of designing many common forms of printed material.

Desktop publishing systems may include a powerful microcomputer with a large-screen, high-resolution monitor that can display an entire 8½ × 11-inch page.

page composition package
A program that enables a desktop publishing system to develop the column and graphics layout of a page using an electronic page makeup process

A Desktop Publishing System

What constitutes a desktop publishing system? Typically, you need a personal computer with a hard disk, a laser printer or other printer capable of high-quality graphics, and software that can do word processing, graphics, and page makeup. Word processing packages and **page composition packages** are available that can do a variety of word processing, graphics, and page makeup functions. For higher-quality printing, end users need to invest in a more powerful computer with advanced graphics capabilities, a high-resolution large-screen color video monitor, graphics, and page composition packages with more extensive features, an optical scanner, and a laser printer with a greater variety of printing capabilities.

Doing Desktop Publishing

How do you do desktop publishing? Very simply, here are the major steps in the process.

- **Page Design and Makeup**
Use a page composition package to develop the format of each page. This page makeup process is where desktop publishing departs from standard word processing and graphics. Your video screen becomes an electronic pasteup board with rulers, column guides, and other page design aids.

- **Text and Graphics Preparation**
Prepare your text with a word processing program or built-in word processor. Create graphics illustrations with a graphics package or built-in drawing tools. You can also use files of clip art—predrawn graphic illustrations—or use an optical scanner to input text and graphics from other sources. Then enter

Almost any type of clip art is available. Clip art can be imported from clip art files into numerous types of page layout and word processing packages.

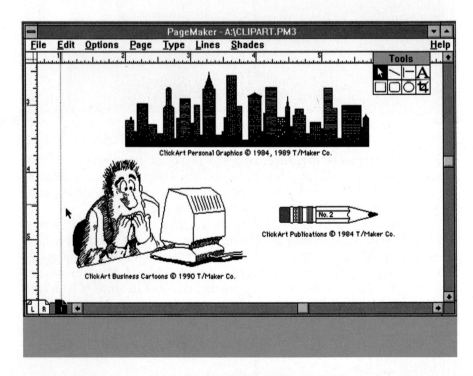

these directly into the document or save them on disk as text and graphics files.

- **Merge Text and Graphics**

Now merge the files of text and graphics into the page format you designed. The page composition software will automatically move excess text from one column to another or from one page to another. It will also help you size and place illustrations and headings.

- **Revise, Store, and Print**

Make sure the pages look the way you want them to on your video screen using the WYSIWYG ("what you see is what you get") features of your page composition software. Then you can store them on your hard disk and print them on a laser printer to produce professional-looking printed material.

Computer Graphics

Computer graphics is the use of computers to produce graphics images. These images can be as simple as a chart or graph of business results, as complex as an engineering drawing of a spacecraft, as beautiful as a simulated seascape at sunset, or as funny as an animated cartoon video. All of these images can be created using computers of all sizes and a variety of graphics software packages.

Computer graphics can be subdivided into four main application areas:

- *Analytical graphics,* which help you better understand data, or discover patterns in collected data.

- *Presentation graphics,* which help you present data or ideas to others in reports, meetings, or other presentations.

- *Computer-aided design (CAD),* in which computer graphics is used by designers in engineering, architecture, and other fields to design products, structures or spaces.

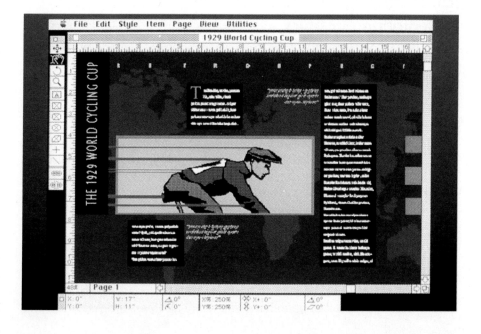

A high-end desktop publishing system can produce newsletters with color graphics and type.

Computer graphics hardware can include a high-resolution graphics adapter board and video monitor and a video camera and recorder.

- *Computer art,* in which computer graphics is used to create visual art, such as pictures, illustrations, and other images.

End User Graphics

It sometimes takes the computing power of a supercomputer or an engineering workstation for expert designers to create the graphics of complex structures or realistic animation. But you can still do a lot of computer graphics on a PC. Attractive and useful analytical and presentation graphics, and even good quality computer art and computer-aided design can be done on most microcomputers using graphics software or other packages that provide graphics features.

Of course, your graphics capabilities and quality increase dramatically if your PC has a more powerful main microcoprocessor, a large memory capacity, a very high-resolution *graphics adapter* circuit board and video monitor, and a software package with more extensive graphics features. You can add even more graphics capabilities with input devices like optical scanners or video cameras to capture photographs and other images, storage media like optical disk drives, and output devices such as laser printers and video and film recorders. (Note: (See the "Computer Graphics" photo essay beginning on page 199 for more information and dramatic examples of computer graphics and art.)

Analytical Graphics

analytical graphics
Graphics that assist end users in analyzing and interpreting data, thus allowing end users to make better decisions.

The use of computer graphics to help end users such as managers monitor business operations and make better decisions is an example of **analytical graphics.** Instead of overwhelming users with large amount of computer-produced data, graphics displays can assist their understanding of data. Not only are graphics displays easier to comprehend and communicate than numeric data, but multiple-color displays can more readily highlight strategic differences and trends in the information your computer is reporting. That's how graphics helps you analyze and interpret data.

Presentation Graphics

presentation graphics
Graphics, such as charts and graphs, used to present information in reports and business meetings.

Which type of output would you rather see, columns of text and numbers or a graphics display of the same information? Most people find it difficult to quickly and accurately comprehend numerical or statistical data that is presented in text and numerical form. A typical example is a report consisting of rows and columns of names and numbers. That is why **presentation graphics** methods, such as charts and graphs, are typically used in technical reports and business meetings. Presentation graphics has proved to be much more effective than tabular presentations of numeric data for reporting and communicating in management reports or in presentations to groups of people. So that's an important reason why office automation stresses the use of graphics software to produce computer-generated graphics displays for effective business communications.

Doing Presentation Graphics

Graphics packages for analytical and presentations graphics convert numeric data into graphics displays such as line charts, bar charts, and pie charts. Many other types of presentation graphics displays are also possible. Analytical and

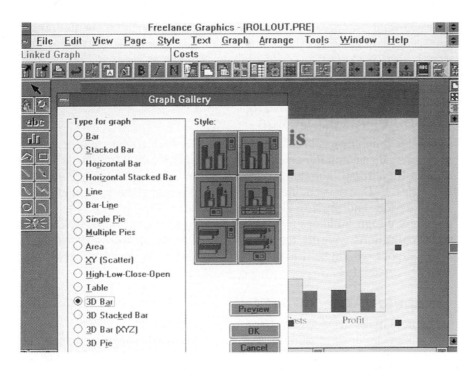

Colorful and informative graphics displays can be created with presentation graphics software like this Freelance Graphics for Windows package.

presentation graphics can be produced by specialized graphics packages such as Harvard Graphics and Lotus Freelance for microcomputers and SAS Graph and Tell-A-Graph for minicomputers and mainframes. The built-in graphics capabilities of electronic spreadsheets or integrated packages are another popular way that many end users do graphics.

To use presentation graphics packages, you typically select the type of graph you want and enter the categories of data you want plotted. This is done in response to prompts displayed on your screen. Or you can highlight the

Color graphics are printed here with a color plotter.

Computer-aided design is accomplished here at a workstation with a drawing pad and mouse-like tracer peripherals.

computer-aided design (CAD)
Using computer graphics in engineering, architecture, and other fields for the interactive design of products and structures.

data you want graphed. The graphics program then analyzes the file of data you specify and generates the requested graphics. Computer printers and devices known as *plotters* can print or draw graphics on paper and other materials, such as overhead transparencies. Other devices known as *film recorders* can produce 35mm color slides of computer-generated graphics.

Computer-Aided Design

Computer graphics has been used for many years in engineering design applications called **computer-aided design (CAD).** This form of graphics is widely used in the aircraft, automobile, machine tool, electronics, and many other industries. CAD assists engineers in designing complex mechanical and electronic devices and physical structures. CAD also helps architects and other designers design buildings, work spaces, and other environments. Complex CAD applications typically require the use of *technical workstations*. These are high-powered, single-user computers with extensive computing power and graphics capabilities.

Computer Art

Computers make the video screen an "electronic canvas" on which artists and illustrators can draw or paint fine art, commercial art, and other visual illustrations. Unlike paper and other traditional media, the art can be changed and revised quickly and easily until the artist is satisfied with his or her work. Then the art can be stored on magnetic or optical disks and reproduced on paper or other media by color laser printers or other devices.

Two basic types of graphics packages are typically used for computer art. One is a *draw program* that allows you to create line drawings and other illustrations. By using a mouse, light pen, graphics tablet, or pen-based computer, you can enter your freehand drawing movements into the computer.

The icons on the left of the window in this draw program represent the drawing options available to the user.

Draw programs usually include a library of predrawn shapes and patterns you can use instead of drawing them from scratch. MacDraw and Windows Draw are popular draw programs.

A *paint program* is the other major type of graphics package for computer art. It allows you to create art as if you were using a paintbrush to paint on canvas. To continue the analogy, a paint program lets you pick "brush" sizes and choose colors from a "palette." Then you can use devices such as a mouse, light pen, or graphics table to paint images whose shapes, colors, and textures best express your artistic ideas. MacPaint and Windows Paintbrush are popular paint programs.

Quick Quiz

1. Using a microcomputer system to produce newsletters, brochures, manuals and other printed materials is _____.
2. A _____ software package is a key component of a desktop publishing system.
3. Files of pre-drawn graphic illustrations are known as _____.
4. Doing _____ helps you graphically present data or ideas to others in reports, meetings, or other presentations.
5. Architects, engineers, and designers use _____ to design products, structures, and spaces.

Answers: 1. desktop publishing 2. page composition 3. clip art 4. presentation graphics 5. computer-aided design

Electronic Office Communications

Office automation has made possible a variety of electronic communications systems such as *electronic mail, voice mail,* and *facsimile.* They allow you to send message in text, video, or voice form or transmit copies of documents and do it in seconds, not hours or days. Office automation hardware and software allow you to transmit and distribute text and images in electronic form over telecommunications networks. This can drastically reduce the flow of paper messages, letters, memos, documents, and reports that flood our present interoffice and postal systems.

Electronic office communications can help achieve two basic benefits. They can make office communications more *cost effective* and *time effective* than traditional written and telephone communications methods. They are designed to minimize *information float* and *telephone tag.* **Information float** is the time (at least several days) when a written letter or other document is in transit between the sender and receiver and thus unavailable for any action or response. **Telephone tag** is the process of (1) repeatedly calling people, (2) finding them unavailable, (3) leaving messages, and (4) finding out later you were unavailable when they finally returned your calls.

Electronic office communications can also eliminate the effects of mail that is lost in transit or phone lines that are frequently busy. The costs of labor, materials, and postage for office communications can be reduced (from more than $5 for a written message to less than 50 cents for an electronic

information float
The time when a document is in transit between the sender and receiver, and thus unavailable for any action or response.

telephone tag
The process that occurs when two people who wish to contact each other by telephone repeatedly miss each other's phone calls.

The graphical user interface of this E-mail program makes it simple to use.

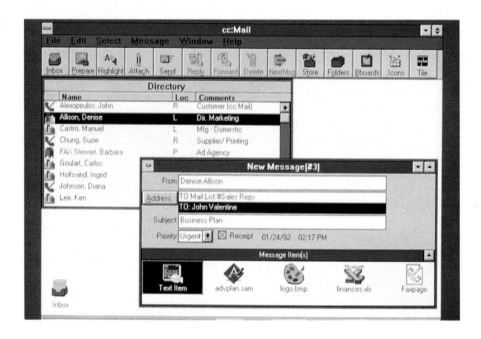

message is one estimate). Also, the amount of time wasted in regular phone calls can be reduced (by one-third according to another estimate).

Easy-to-use, low-cost, and versatile systems are now available for all types of electronic messaging. Computer manufacturers and software suppliers have developed more powerful microcomputer workstations and easy to use office communications packages. These advances in office automation technology are allowing end users to electronically merge voice, data, and images in office communications systems.

Electronic Mail

electronic mail
The transmission, storage, and distribution of electronic text messages over telecommunications networks.

What's the first thing millions of knowledge workers throughout the world do at work each morning? Besides getting a cup of coffee (or tea), they turn on their computers to check their **electronic mail.** Electronic mail (E-mail) has changed the way people work and communicate. E mail lets you send electronic messages instantly to anyone your network can reach. Typically, your message will be stored in *electronic mailboxes* on magnetic disk devices. Whenever they are ready, people can read their electronic mail by displaying it on the video screens of their computers. So, with only a few minutes of effort (and a few microseconds of transmission), a message to one or many individuals can be composed, sent, and received.

E-mail eliminates telephone tag and information float, breaks time-of-day and distance limits, and reduces paper flow and handling. End users and organizations love how it speeds their communications. So, sending and receiving electronic mail messages has become a major activity on the wide area and local area networks of many organizations and work groups. You can also pay a fee to use the networks of telecommunications companies for electronic mail. Companies such as GTE, TELENET, and MCI offer E-mail services, as do personal computer networks such as Compuserve and Prodigy. The photograph at the top of this page shows the video displays provided by an electronic mail package.

Voice Mail

Another variation of electronic mail is **voice mail,** where *digitized voice messages,* rather than electronic text, are used. In this method, you first dial the number of the voice mail service. Once you are accepted, you dial the voice mail number of the person you wish to contact and speak your message. Your voice message is digitized and stored on the magnetic disk devices of the voice mail computer system. Whenever you want to hear your voice mail, you simply dial your mailbox number and listen to stored messages, which the computer converts back into voice form for you to hear.

voice mail
A variation of electronic mail in which digitized voice messages rather than electronic text are accepted, stored, and transmitted to end users.

Facsimile

Facsimile (fax) is not a new telecommunications service. However, advances in this technology have caused a sharp drop in prices and a significant increase in capabilities. As a consequence, sales of fax machines have skyrocketed in the past few years, and *faxing* has become a commonplace office term. Facsimile allows you to transmit images of important documents over telephone or other telecommunication links. In short, the phrase "long-distance copying" might be an appropriate nickname for this telecommunications process.

Usually, a fax machine at one office location transmits to a fax machine at another location, using built-in high-speed modems. Transmission speeds for digital office fax machines range from one to four pages per minute, with quality equivalent to an office copier. A more recent development is the availability of facsimile circuit boards for microcomputers. Installing a *fax board* or *fax modem* and using a fax software package allows a personal computer to transmit digital copies of documents over telecommunications lines to fax machines anywhere. Thus, fax machines can now act as printers for microcomputer users who may be thousands of miles away.

facsimile (fax)
The transmission of text and graphics images and their reconstruction and duplication at a receiving station.

REAL-WORLD EXAMPLE

Comsat World Systems: Down-to-Earth E-Mail

Communications satellite services may be the bread and butter business of Comsat World Systems, but electronic mail for its employees on the ground has made a big impact. Comsat is based in Washington, D.C., but has business all over the world. Its use of E-mail has replaced miscellaneous memos, handwritten notes, phone messages, meeting invitations, and the routing of paper reports. Thus, E-mail has dramatically improved communications among Comsat's 1,300 networked employees.

But Comsat is not going to stop there. According to Bill Voss, director of mobile informa-

tion systems, Comsat is now in the process of integrating facsimile (fax) transmissions and electronic document interchange (EDI) of business documents with the E-mail system. This will make it possible for Comsat employees to easily send and receive fax, E-mail, and electronic documents from their workstations. Voss says these plans "reflect trends in electronic messaging which will revolutionize the way we do business."

1. What are the benefits of E-mail to Comsat?

2. Why would integrating fax, E-mail, and EDI revolutionize the way Comsat does business?

Teleconferencing adds visual contact to what would otherwise be a simple conference call between a group of people in various locations.

teleconferencing
The use of video communications to allow conferences to be held with participants who are geographically dispersed across a region, a country, or anywhere in the world.

Teleconferencing

Why spend travel time and money to attend meetings? *Electronic meeting systems (EMS)* offer a popular alternative. **Teleconferencing** is the most widely publicized form of EMS. Typically, major participants are televised while end users at remote sites take part with voice input of questions and responses. Teleconferencing can also consist of using closed-circuit television to reach several small groups, instead of broadcasting to large groups at multiple sites.

In another type of EMS, participants at remote sites key in their presentations and responses whenever convenient. They use online terminals or workstations connected to a central *conference* computer. Since all participants don't have to do this at the same time, this form of EMS is called *computer conferencing* and is like a variation of electronic mail. Another popular form of EMS is *decision room conferencing,* in which small groups use a local area network of microcomputers and large screen projection in a *decision room* to help them make decisions. *Desktop video conferencing* between the networked computers is a promising form of *EMS.* It enhances collaboration among people by providing face-to-face communications.

Many communications carriers now offer teleconferencing services for events such as sales meetings, new product announcements, and employee education and training. However, you should realize that some organizations have found that electronic meeting systems are sometimes not as effective as face-to-face meetings. This is especially true when important participants are not trained in how to communicate using these systems. Also, the cost of providing electronic meeting services and facilities can be substantial and make EMS not as cost effective as traditional meetings in some situations.

Telecommuting

Why not "commute" to work electronically? **Telecommuting** allows workers to use telecommunications networks to replace commuting to work from their homes. It also describes using telecommunications networks to carry on work activities from temporary locations other than the office and home. In telecommuting, you use a terminal or microcomputer with telecommunications capability to access your company's computer network and databases. Telecommuters and their colleagues use E-mail and voice mail to communicate with each other about job assignments.

Telecommuting is used to some extent by many major corporations and is widely used by independent professionals. It seems to be most popular with people whose jobs involve a lot of individual work, such as programmers, systems analysts, writers, consultants, and so on. It is especially helpful for handicapped persons and working parents of young children. However, studies have shown that telecommuting is not appropriate for some jobs and people. For example, for some workers, productivity and job satisfaction seem to suffer unless they spend a day or two each week at the office or other work sites with their colleagues. So telecommuting is considered only a temporary or partial work alternative for these knowledge workers.

Telecommuting makes it possible for people to work at home or in satellite offices while still connected to the home office's information system.

telecommuting
The use of computers and telecommunications to replace commuting to work from one's home, thus allowing people to work at their homes or other remote sites.

Office Management Software

A popular category of office automation software integrates electronic versions of office calendars, telephone and E-mail directories, appointment schedulers,

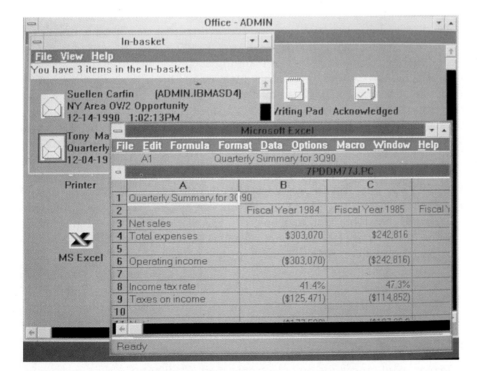

IBM's OfficeVision office management software is an example of a package that provides electronic mail and other services to both small and large office networks.

REAL-WORLD EXAMPLE

Pacific Bell and the Quake: Telecommuting to LA

Urban planners said the earthquake that tore through the Los Angeles area in January 1994 created an unprecedented opportunity for companies to experiment with telecommuting—an option that has long been touted as a solution to the region's air pollution and traffic congestion but that has never gained widespread acceptance. With vital links of the freeway sustem broken and surface streets filled with snaking traffic jams, more workers may decide to use telephone lines and computer linkups to reach the office in minutes instead of battling highway gridlock for hours. "Not everyone has to report into an office. People are using remote computing and cellular phones to try and work," said Michael Dutton of IBM's West Coast marketing and services division.

Large companies are rallying to push the alternative work style. Pacific Bell, for example, has set up a comprehensive package that includes free installation of major telecom services, a $1 million fund to provide modems and terminal adapters, and an assistance hotline. And recently it set up an 800 number for businesses to get information on how to create telecommuting centers. But the alternative work arrangement is not without its doubters. "The biggest anxiety is from managers who want to keep workers in their line of sight," said Kathleen Christensen, a professor at City University of New York who heads up the school's Work Environments Resource Group. Telecommuters may also miss the important exchange of ideas in the office, she said.

1. What are the benefits of telecommuting for urban areas like Los Angeles?
2. What are some of the limitations of telecommuting?

office management software
Software packages that provide computer-based support services to office professionals to help them plan, organize, and accomplish their work activities.

and other office task management tools. **Office management software** packages provide computer-based support service to managers and other office professionals to help them organize their work activities. These electronic services computerize manual methods of planning such as paper calendars, appointment books, directories, file folders, memos, and notes. Individual end users can also get some of the benefits of mainframe office management software by using software known as *desktop accessory* packages.

Office management software packages provide many helpful services to make office work more efficient and productive. For example, you could enter the date and time of a meeting into an electronic calendar program. An *electronic tickler file* program would automatically remind you of important events. Electronic schedulers analyze the electronic calendars of people to help you schedule meetings and other activities for a work group. Electronic mail directories help you contact people easily. And electronic task management packages help you plan a series of related activities so that scheduled results are accomplished on time.

groupware
Software packages that support work activities by members of a work group whose workstations are interconnected by a local area network, allowing them to communicate and work together on joint projects.

Groupware

Groupware is another major category of office management software. Groupware packages support *work group computing*. That is, they allow members of work groups whose microcomputers are interconnected by local area networks to share office management services and office automation applications such as word processing and electronic mail. Groupware packages also sup-

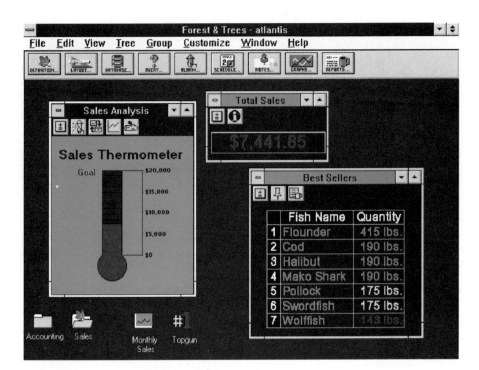

Forest & Trees from Channel Computing is a software package used as groupware, which allows people on a network to access and manipulate the same document.

port group decision making and other work group activities. For example, they allow joint analysis of an electronic spreadsheet, joint word processing of a document, and sharing of electronic mail among members of a work group. Thus, using groupware in office management systems helps end users and work groups organize routine office tasks and work together effectively.

Desktop Accessories

You can get some of the benefits of office automation through the use of **desktop accessory** packages. Desktop accessories are low cost packages that integrate a variety of small programs to help end users organize routine office tasks. A typical desktop accessory package might include programs that provide a calculator, calendar, appointment book, note pad, address book, phone list, alarm clock, and other features. Thus they provide an electronic replacement for many common office devices.

Desktop accessory packages are typically "memory resident" programs that stay in the background until you issue a command. Then they pop up in one or more display windows on your computer's video screen at the touch of a key. For example, you can enter an appointment in an electronic appointment book, jot some notes on an electronic note pad, do some quick calculations on a computer-supplied calculator, and have your computer look up and call the telephone number of a business associate. Then, touch a key to get back to the job you were doing on your computer.

desktop accessories
A software package that provides features such as an electronic calculator, note pad, alarm clock, phone directory, and appointment book that are available as pop-up windows on your display screen at the touch of a key.

Quick Quiz

1. You can send electronic text messages instantly to other computers on a network in a _____ system.

This desktop accessory package displays pop-up windows for its electronic accessories.

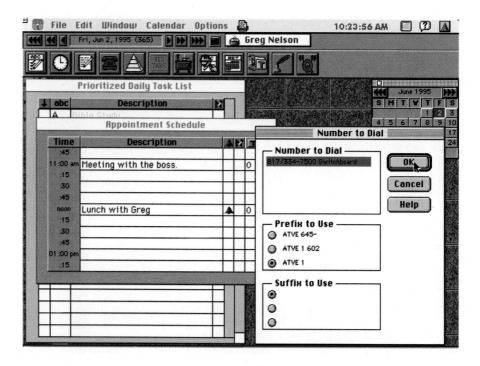

2. Digitized voice messages are stored by a computer system and converted back into voice form in a _____ system.

3. Images of documents are transmitted by a _____ process over a telecommunications network.

4. Groups of people at different sites can participate in a meeting or conference through _____.

5. Work groups can use _____ packages to communicate and work together on group projects.

Answers: 1. electronic mail   2. voice mail   3. facsimile
4. teleconferencing   5. groupware

End Note: End Users and Office Automation

Office automation is a fact of life for most end users today. And it will be even more pervasive in the future. Whatever your future career will be, you will be touched by automated office systems. For example, you will work with professional-looking documents produced by electronic publishing systems. These will be prepared by you or other end users using word processing and desktop publishing systems.

You will also use electronic communications systems for even quicker and more convenient office communications. Electronic mail, voice mail, and facsimile systems will help you keep in touch with co-workers and others so that you can be more productive on the job. Electronic meeting systems will

E T H I C S

Ethical Issues in Office Automation

Office automation applications can raise several ethical issues. This is not surprising, since office automation software provides us with such powerful tools for communications and productivity. However, two leading ethical issues in office automation center on word processing, desktop publishing, and electronic mail.

The first ethical issue concerns **plagiarism**—unauthorized use of another person's written work. Using other people's original writings without their permission or without giving them credit is stealing—pure and simple. It's been a problem as long as we have had published works, especially books and magazines, that are widely reproduced and distributed. The development of the office copier machine made copying printed material easy to do. It thus made plagiarism a bigger problem for authors and publishers.

However, the advent of optical scanning, word processing, and desktop publishing has made plagiarism more tempting and even easier to accomplish. Someone else's text and graphics can be copied by optical scanning, retrieved from a disk, or entered through a keyboard into a computer system. Then the power of word processing can easily be used to modify the original text so that the plagiarism is not readily apparent. Then desktop publishing can be used to make the plagiarized document even more visually attractive and different. But it's still plagiarism. It's an unethical practice all end users should avoid.

The second ethical issue concerns the **right to privacy** and the confidentiality of electronic mail. Reading other people's mail or listening in on their conversations has always been taboo in our society. Unless it's authorized by the people involved or a court order, we call it *mail tampering* and *wiretapping,* both federal crimes when involving the public mail and telephone systems.

But electronic mail has escaped ethical controversy until recently. Some people feel that any organization has a right to monitor the proper use of its computer systems. So some organizations monitor E-mail traffic periodically, supposedly to assure compliance with proper use of company time and computing resources.

Other people aren't so sure that this is an ethical practice. Several corporations are being sued over their monitoring of electronic mail. So the issue is now being debated in the courts, the press, and the halls of Congress.

What Do You Think?

One consumer group says monitoring E-mail is always wrong. Another group of corporations thinks it's okay, as long as employees are warned that their E-mail may be monitored. What do you think?

plagiarism
Unauthorized use of another person's written work.

right to privacy
The right of an individual to freedom from unauthorized monitoring of his or her personal activities and unauthorized disclosure of personal information.

assist your organization or work group in working together as a team. Electronic meetings, teleconferencing, and telecommuting will help you work together on group projects, no matter how far apart you are located from each other.

Finally, your work and the work of your colleagues will be made more productive by office management systems. Software packages for office management will supply you with electronic office accessories like an electronic appointment book, telephone directory, and calendar. Other software will help you, a secretary, or an office manager to schedule appointments and meetings, and to plan work activities for the end users in your office or work group.

So, office automation should increase the efficiency and effectiveness of the communications and work activities of you and other end users. This can only help increase your productivity and the quality of your work and those of others in your office or other work group. Your challenge is to achieve the computer literacy needed to take advantage of the capabilities provided by such automated office systems.

Summary

Word Processing   Software packages for word processing allow you to use your computer to create and edit documents as well as store, retrieve, print, and revise them electronically. Word processing also allows you to easily change the appearance of documents and to use a variety of optional features to correct and improve the spelling, grammar, and style of your writing.

Desktop Publishing   Software packages for desktop publishing allow end users to produce brochures, newsletters, and other documents at significant cost savings over commercial publishing. Page composition packages allow you to perform a page makeup process using your video screen as an electronic pasteup board to design the layout, content, and graphics of each page.

Computer Graphics   Software packages for computer graphics allow you to do analytical graphics to help interpret data and presentation graphics to help you make presentations to others. Graphics packages also allow engineers and architects to do computer-aided design and enable artists and illustrators to draw or paint the images known as computer art.

Electronic Office Communications   Office automation includes a variety of electronic communications services. They help you send electronic text messages (E-mail), voice messages (voice mail), and electronic copies of documents (facsimile). These systems dramatically cut down the flow of paper documents, providing more cost-effective and time-effective communications. Electronic meeting systems save travel time and money through the use of applications like teleconferencing, which provides video and voice transmissions to remote sites within an organization. Telecommuting allows end users to work at home through the use of telecommunications links to their organizations.

Office Management Software   Software packages for office management supply electronic versions of office accessories and tools. Examples include electronic calendar and tickler file programs, electronic task management packages, desktop accessory packages, and groupware packages that support work activities on joint projects by members of a work group.

Key Terms and Concepts

analytical graphics
computer-aided design
computer art
computer graphics
desktop accessories
desktop publishing
document files
documents
draw program

editing activities
electronic mail
facsimile
formatting
grammar and style checker
groupware
information float
justify
mail-merge

office management software
page composition program
paint program
presentation graphics
search and replace
spell checker
status line
telecommuting

teleconferencing
telephone tag
text data
thesaurus program
voice mail
word processing
word wrap
WYSIWYG

Review Quiz

True/False

_____ 1. Word processing is using computers to create, edit, revise, and print text material.

_____ 2. Text data consists of words, phrases, sentences, and paragraphs.

_____ 3. Letters, memos, forms, and reports are examples of documents.

_____ 4. The format feature indicates the file name of a document and whether certain editing features are in operation.

_____ 5. The status line feature automatically sets margins on your document.

_____ 6. WYSIWYG means "what you see is what you get."

_____ 7. End users can produce their own brochures and manuals with electronic mail.

_____ 8. You can use your computer to send and receive electronic mail messages with desktop publishing.

_____ 9. Groupware helps your group work together on group projects.

_____ 10. A search and destroy feature helps you find a word or phrase and change it automatically.

Multiple Choice

_____ 1. The word processing feature that helps correct spelling errors is a

    a. search and replace.
    b. formatting.
    c. thesaurus.
    d. spell checker.

_____ 2. Transmitting electronic images of paper documents is a capability known as

    a. formatting.
    b. facsimile.
    c. transmitter.
    d. copying.

_____ 3. Using graphics to interpret data is

    a. computer art.
    b. computer-aided design.
    c. analytical graphics.
    d. presentation graphics.

_____ 4. Using graphics to present information to others is

    a. computer art.
    b. computer-aided design.
    c. analytical graphics.
    d. presentation graphics.

_____ 5. Using graphics to design products and structures is

    a. computer art.
    b. computer-aided design.
    c. analytical graphics.
    d. presentation graphics

_____ 6. Using graphics to create realistic or abstract images of ideas is

    a. computer art.
    b. computer-aided design.
    c. analytical graphics.
    d. presentation graphics.

_____ 7. When you and the person you want to contact repeatedly miss each other's phone calls, you are playing

    a. round-robin.
    b. roll call.
    c. information float.
    d. telephone tag.

_____ 8. The time a document is in transit between a sender and a receiver is known as

    a. round-robin.
    b. roll call.
    c. information float.
    d. telephone tag.

_____ 9. A word processing feature that helps you find alternatives for words is a

    a. dictionary.
    b. spell checker.
    c. grammar checker.
    d. thesaurus.

_____ 10. A graphics program that lets you pick brush sizes and choose colors from a palette is a

    a. computer-aided design package.
    b. chart package.
    c. paint package.
    d. draw package.

Fill-in

1. Letters or memos you write are stored as _____ files.
2. The _____ features of word processing packages automatically transfers text past the right margin to the left margin of the next line.
3. In word processing, _____ is making changes and corrections to the text content of a document.
4. In word processing, _____ is making changes to the appearance of a document.
5. A _____ is a specially marked part of a document that is typically moved or copied within the document.
6. Using _____ involves televised electronic meetings at remote sites.
7. If you use telecommunications to work at home, you are _____.
8. You can leave _____ messages by using your telephone as an electronic message terminal.
9. A variety of electronic versions of familiar office tools are provided by _____ packages.
10. Doing _____ involves analytical graphics, presentation graphics, computer-aided design, or computer art.

Questions for Thought and Discussion

1. Is word processing just a technical name for computerized typing? Or is there more to word processing than typing? Explain.
2. Refer to the Real-World Example of Dell Computers in the chapter. Is this an example of work group computing? Explain.
3. Should there be a difference in the functions and capabilities of word processing packages for ordinary end users and those meant for professional typists? Why or why not?
4. What is the difference between word processing and desktop publishing? What are the benefits and limitations of each?
5. What are four types of computer graphics? Which type will you most likely use in your future career?
6. What are several benefits and limitations of electronic mail? Voice mail? Facsimile?
7. Refer to the Real-World Example of Comsat World Systems in the chapter. Why didn't the company use its communications satellite network to communicate electronically?
8. What are several benefits and limitations of teleconferencing? Telecommuting?
9. Refer to the Real-World Example of Pacific Bell and the Quake in the chapter. Would you like to be a telecommuter? Explain.
10. Explain some of the ways you could use the office automation software discussed in this chapter in a career you are considering. Make a brief report to the class.

Review Quiz Answers

True/False   **1.** T **2.** T **3.** T **4.** F **5.** F **6.** T **7.** F **8.** F **9.** T **10.** F

Multiple Choice   **1.** d **2.** b **3.** c **4.** d **5.** b **6.** a **7.** d **8.** c **9.** d **10.** c

Fill-in   **1.** document **2.** word wrap **3.** editing **4.** formatting **5.** block
6. teleconferencing **7.** telecommuting **8.** voice mail **9.** desktop accessories
10. computer graphics

5

DECISION SUPPORT SOFTWARE: USING SPREADSHEETS AND OTHER DECISION AIDS

OUTLINE

LEARNING OBJECTIVES

After reading and studying this chapter, you should be able to

Identify the purpose of decision support systems and the major types of decision support software.

Describe how decision support software can help end users do analytical modeling to support decision making.

Identify the functions and benefits of electronic spreadsheet packages.

Describe how you could use a spreadsheet package to provide you with information and decision support.

Identify the components of expert systems and describe how they can be used in decision-making situations.

You and Decision Support

decision support systems (DSS)
Information systems that give end users direct computer support during the decision-making process.

Computers can do more than just help you communicate or be more efficient and productive. Computers can help you make better decisions. Thus, computers and decision support software have revolutionized business decision making. That's because they provide managers and other end users with **decision support systems (DSS),** information systems that give them direct computer support during the decision-making process.

Other types of information systems may use computers to give you information that only indirectly supports your decision making. For example, we saw in the last chapter that office automation systems can provide you with reports produced by word processing and desktop publishing, graphics produced by presentation graphics packages, or messages transmitted by electronic mail systems.

But decision support systems are different. They let you use a computer to explore decision alternatives in an interactive, realtime process. That is, you interact with the displays of a DSS software package by entering data, posing questions, and providing responses as you evaluate alternative solutions to a problem. This process can continue until you feel that you have generated the information you need. Then you can make your decision.

So you see, decision support is more than a computerized process of information reporting. But neither is it a way to have computers make decisions for you. Instead, decision support systems let you use computers and software packages as tools to assist you in the decision-making process.

Decision support software enables end users to analyze and manipulate information, which helps in decision making.

Examples of Decision Support

Let's look at several examples of decision support systems in action. First, let's suppose you are an advertising manager who is trying to decide how much money to spend on TV advertising for a new product. If you knew how to use an electronic spreadsheet package, you could develop and use a *model,* or a hypothetical set of assumptions, on how advertising and sales of similar products are related. Then you could enter different amounts for TV advertising into your computer and see instantly on your video screen how each alternative would affect the sales of your product. After you had repeated this "what-if" process several times, you would probably feel more comfortable about making your TV advertising decision.

Decision support systems are also used for many applications in industry and government. For example, AAIMS (An Analytical Information Management System) is a decision support system used in the airline industry. It was developed by American Airlines but is used by other airlines, aircraft manufacturers, and airline consultants. It supports a variety of airline decisions by studying factors such as aircraft use, utilization of seating capacity, air traffic statistics, market share, and airline revenue and profitability.

Geographic information systems organize data by geographic regions.

Another popular example is GADS (Geodata Analysis and Display System), which was developed by IBM. It constructs and displays maps and other graphics displays that support decisions affecting the geographic distribution of people and physical resources. For example, it can analyze and display the geographic distribution of crimes and thus help decide how to assign police to areas of a city. It has also been used for urban growth studies, defining school district boundaries, and deploying fire department equipment.

Software	Examples
Electronic Spreadsheets	Programs that let you enter and manipulate data and formulas in an electronic worksheet of rows and columns.
DSS Generators	Software packages designed for specific decision support applications on mainframe, minicomputer, and microcomputer systems.
Statistical Analysis Packages	Software used for decision support applications that require extensive statistical analysis.
Group Decision Support Software	Programs that enhance the joint decision making of work groups and other organizational units.
Expert Systems	Software that includes a knowledge base so it can provide expert advice on a specific application area.

Table 5-1
Types of Decision Support Software

Decision Support Fundamentals

A decision support system consists of people, hardware, software, data, and model components. Naturally, managers or other end users make up the people component, while personal computers are the most popular hardware resource. DSS software includes a variety of types of programs. Electronic spreadsheets are the most popular decision support packages for end users. Other types of DSS software include mainframe DSS *generator* packages like IFPS/Plus or statistical analysis packages like the SAS System.

Another type of DSS software are programs used for *group decision support systems (GDSS)*. These software packages help enhance the joint decision making of end user work groups and other organizational units. Even *expert system* packages, which provide expert advice to end users in a specific application area, can also be considered a type of DSS software. Finally, a DSS includes databases and model bases. These store the data and models needed for the decision-making process. See Figure 5-1 and Table 5-1.

Figure 5-1
A decision support system uses hardware, software, data, and model resources to support a manager's decision making.

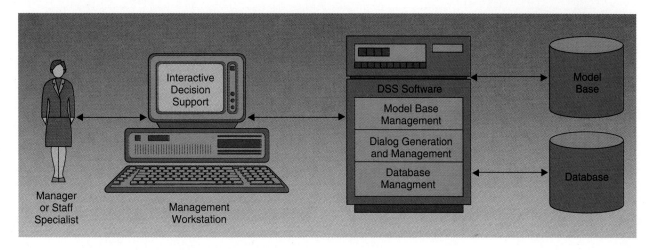

Models

Models are an important component of decision support system. A *model* can be defined as a simplified abstraction of reality that illustrates the fundamental components and relationships of systems in the real world. Models can be *physical models* such as a model airplane, *verbal models* such as a written description of a system, *graphics models* such as an architectural drawing, and *mathematical models,* which can represent the relationships among the components of a system by means of mathematical expressions. See Figure 5-2. For example, many business models express simple accounting relationships mathematically. Thus, whether you are a kid selling lemonade or a tycoon making million-dollar deals, you know that

PROFIT equals SALES minus EXPENSES

Combining several of these relationships together results in the development of a business model that can be used by DSS software for decision support.

Figure 5-2
Models illustrate the components and relationships of real-world systems.

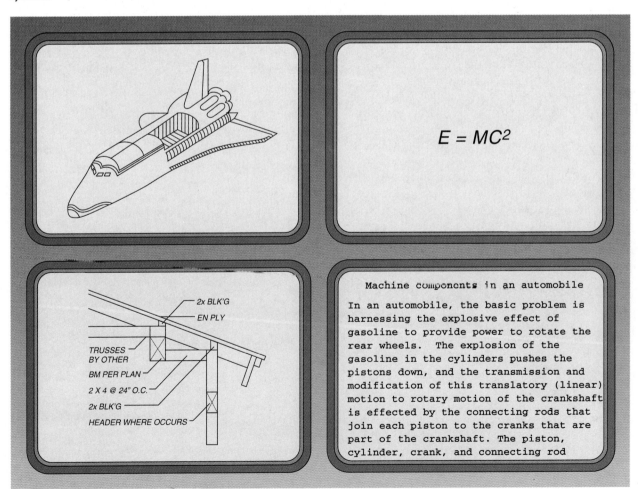

Analytical Modeling

Using an electronic spreadsheet or other software package for decision support involves electronically manipulating models in a process we can call **analytical modeling.** Typically, this involves three basic types of activities:

- What-if analysis
- Goal-seeking analysis
- Optimization analysis

Table 5-2 summarizes the three types of analytical modeling. As you can see, **what-if analysis** involves repeatedly making changes to some of the values in a model to see what effect this has on other values in the model. For example, "If we cut TV advertising expenses, what will happen to sales?"

Goal-seeking analysis sets a target value (a goal) and makes changes to selected values until that goal is reached. For example, "How can we change TV advertising expenses to achieve $3 million in car sales?" Thus, goal-seeking analysis is sometimes called *how-can analysis.* The goal-seeking capability of DSS software packages is sometimes called a *solver* capability, since it "solves" the problem of how to achieve a target value.

Finally, **optimization analysis** attempts to find the optimum or best value for a component of the model, given certain specified *constraints* or limitations. For example, "What's the best amount of TV advertising for us, given the limitations of our budget and the choice of TV stations we have?" Many mainframe DSS generators and statistical analysis packages feature powerful optimization analysis capabilities.

Quick Quiz

1. Computers provide _____ when they help you explore decision alternatives in an interactive, realtime process.
2. A _____ lets you use computers and software packages as tools to assist you in the decision-making process.

analytical modeling
Using computer-based mathematical models to explore decision alternatives using methods such as what-if analysis, goal-seeking analysis, and optimization analysis.

what-if analysis
Observing how changes to selected values affect other values in a mathematical model.

goal-seeking analysis
Making repeated changes to selected values until a chosen value reaches a target value or goal.

optimization analysis
Finding an optimum value for selected variables in a mathematical model, given certain constraints or limitations.

Analytical Modeling	Examples
What-If Analysis	Observing how changes to certain values affect other values. For example, "What if we cut TV advertising expenses—what will happen to sales?"
Goal-Seeking Analysis	Sets a target value (a goal) and makes changes to selected values until that goal is reached. For example, "How can we adjust spending on TV advertising to achieve $3 million in car sales?"
Optimization Analysis	Finds the optimum or best value for a model component, given certain constraints or limitations. For example, "What is the best amount of TV advertising for us, given our budget limitations and choice of TV stations?"

**Table 5-2
Three Basic Types of Analytical
Modeling for Decision Support**

3. A decision support system includes people, hardware, software, data, and _____ components.

4. Three types of _____ modeling include what-if analysis, goal-seeking analysis, and optimization analysis.

5. Repeatedly making changes to some of the values in a model to see the effect on other values in the model is called _____ analysis.

Answers: 1. decision support 2. decision support system 3. model 4. analytical 5. what if

Electronic Spreadsheets

Electronic spreadsheet programs are the most popular software packages for end users' decision support. Spreadsheet packages enable you to use your computer to support your decision making by helping you do analysis, planning, and modeling. They provide an electronic replacement for manual business tools such as accounting worksheets and calculators that were formerly used in planning and budgeting.

A spreadsheet package generates an **electronic spreadsheet,** which is a worksheet of rows and columns stored in your computer's memory and displayed on its video screen. You use the computer keyboard to enter data and mathematical relationships (formulas) into the worksheet. This results in an electronic model of a particular business activity or problem situation you want to analyze. In response to your commands, the computer performs calculations based on the mathematical relationships you defined in the spreadsheet. Then it instantly displays results for you to see and evaluate. Once the

electronic spreadsheet
A program that allows users to do analysis and modeling by entering and manipulating data and formulas into an electronic worksheet of rows and columns.

Electronic spreadsheets like Lotus 1-2-3 for Macintosh or Windows allow users to display multiple related spreadsheets and graphics.

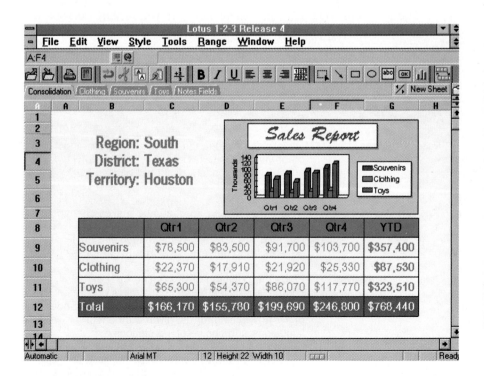

electronic spreadsheet has been developed, it can be stored on disk for later use or printed out as a report.

Many popular electronic spreadsheet packages exist for microcomputers. Most popular is Lotus 1-2-3, followed by Excel and Quattro Pro. Spreadsheet packages are also available for mainframe and minicomputer users. Examples of such electronic spreadsheet products include Lotus 1-2-3M, IFPS, and Focus.

The Layout of a Spreadsheet

An electronic spreadsheet package allows you to build a worksheet with many rows and columns. For example, small spreadsheets might have 63 columns and 254 rows, while medium-size spreadsheets have about 256 columns and 2,048 rows, and some large spreadsheets have 16,000 rows and columns! Since an electronic spreadsheet is so large, only a section is displayed on your video screen at any one time. (See Figure 5-3.)This display screen is a *window* that lets you see a portion of the larger worksheet in memory. Typically, the spreadsheet you see displayed may be 8 columns wide and 20 rows long. However,

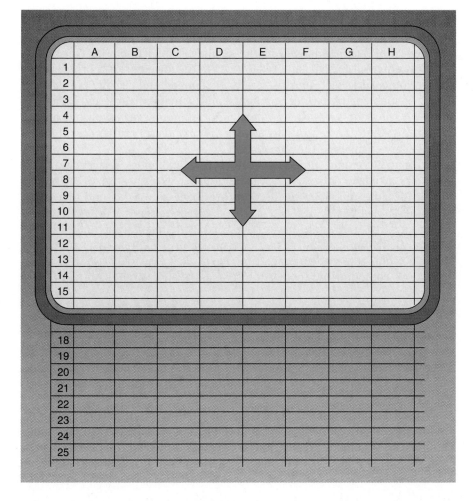

Figure 5-3
Your video screen is a window that lets you see part of the spreadsheet stored in memory.

cells
The spaces formed by the intersection of rows and columns in a spreadsheet.

cell pointer
A cursor located at all times in one of the cells of the worksheet.

you can change the width of the columns or split the screen into two or more windows. Thus, you can move a window around to see and work on any part of the spreadsheet that you wish.

The spaces formed by the intersection of rows and columns are called **cells.** Cells are typically identified by their column and row coordinate (that is, the number or letter of the column and row in which the cell is located). In most spreadsheets, rows are numbered and columns are specified by letters, with the column of a cell mentioned first, then its row. For example, cell C12 identifies a cell at the intersection of the third column and the twelfth row of the spreadsheet. Some spreadsheets allow you to name your cells, so cell C12 could be called SALES if it contained sales data or formulas.

A *cursor,* called a **cell pointer,** is located at all times in one of the cells of the worksheet. Typically, this cursor is a *highlighted* rectangle or a *color bar.* It indicates the *active* cell that will accept data you enter from your keyboard. You use *cursor control keys* or an electronic mouse to move the cursor from cell to cell. To view other parts of the spreadsheet, you move the cell pointer across the worksheet until it reaches the edge of the current window. Then the window begins to shift or *scroll* across the spreadsheet in the direction the cell pointer is moving.

Spreadsheet Modeling

Electronic spreadsheet packages have made it dramatically easier to create and use models of business operations for analytical modeling. You can build a model by entering the data and relationships (the formulas) of a problem into an electronic worksheet, make a variety of changes, and visually evaluate the results of such changes. Once you define all the mathematical and logical relationships in your spreadsheet model, your computer accomplishes all calculations instantly and accurately at your command every time you enter data or make any changes to the spreadsheet.

With an electronic spreadsheet, much time and effort is saved and many errors are avoided compared with using a paper worksheet, pencil, and calculator. Because repetitive calculations are made so quickly and accurately, electronic spreadsheets allow end users to make comparisons, projections, and evaluations that they might never have tried using manual methods. This instant **recalculation** capability is a powerful feature of spreadsheet programs. Thus electronic spreadsheet programs have made it easy to do "what-if" analysis and use computerized models for business analysis and planning.

recalculation
The ability of an electronic spreadsheet package to automatically calculate new values for all spreadsheet entries affected by changes made to other spreadsheet values.

Designing Spreadsheet Applications

Electronic spreadsheet programs are widely used for business applications. However, they can be used for the solution of any problem that requires comparisons, projections, or the evaluation of alternatives. Therefore, electronic spreadsheets are used for many applications in government, education, and science.

Typical business uses include sales forecasting, profit and loss analysis, product pricing, investment analysis, development of budgets, cash flow analysis, financial statement preparation, construction bidding, real estate investment, bank loan analysis, and many other applications. Some examples of nonbusiness applications include budgeting for government agencies, hospital administration, scientific and engineering data analysis, sports management, and so on.

Spreadsheet Application Design

How do you design a spreadsheet application? That is, how do you decide how to use an electronic spreadsheet package to solve a variety of problems or help you do your job better? Figure 5-4 outlines a simple four-step spreadsheet application design process.

Define Spreadsheet Objectives

The first step in spreadsheet design is to define the objectives of the application. That is, how will you use the spreadsheet? What information will you want to receive from spreadsheet displays? What types of analytical modeling will you want the spreadsheet to provide to support your decision making? These are questions you must answer to properly define and evaluate the successful design of your spreadsheet application.

Develop the Spreadsheet Layout

The next step in spreadsheet design is to develop the layout of the worksheet. In this step you must think of the information and decision support you want the spreadsheet to provide in terms of a worksheet format. That is, what should be the headings and content of the rows and columns of your spreadsheet? In this step, you must decide which columns of the spreadsheet should contain descriptive information (such as employee or customer names), data that must be entered (such as salary rates or purchases made), or data that will be calculated (such as salary totals or amounts owed). You should also decide on the placement of other items that should appear in your spreadsheet, such as

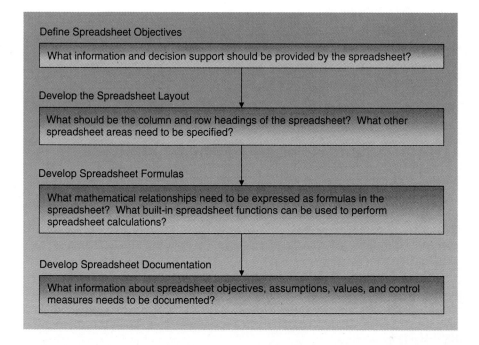

Figure 5-4
These are the basic activities of the spreadsheet application design process.

the title of the spreadsheet and areas for documenting the key values, assumptions, and objectives of the spreadsheet.

Develop Spreadsheet Formulas

In this step, you begin to express the relationships between selected spreadsheet variables as mathematical formulas. For example, as we mentioned earlier, this can be as simple as the relationship among sales, expenses, and profit: (Sales minus Expenses equals Profit). In many cases, the spreadsheet may contain built-in functions (such as Sum or Average) that can be used to perform spreadsheet calculations without having to develop more complex spreadsheet formulas. Therefore, you should identify those functions you can use in your spreadsheet to simplify your work in this step.

Develop Spreadsheet Documentation

In this final step of spreadsheet application design, you should create areas in your spreadsheet that will contain descriptive information about your spreadsheet. This might include brief descriptions of the objectives and assumptions on which the spreadsheet is based. It may also contain a section summarizing the key constants and variables used in spreadsheet formulas. Finally, spreadsheets may contain descriptive notes that document control measures that should be implemented such as testing procedures, protection of spreadsheet contents, and backup copies.

 ## Quick Quiz

1. The most popular software packages for end user decision support are _____.

2. A _____ is a worksheet of rows and columns stored in your computer's memory and displayed on its video screen.

3. The spaces caused by the intersection of rows and columns in a spreadsheet are called _____.

4. You can build a _____ by entering the data and mathematical relationships of a problem into the spreadsheet.

5. Before using a spreadsheet package to solve a problem, you should go through the process of _____.

Answers: 1. electronic spreadsheet programs   2. spreadsheet
3. cells   4. model   5. designing your spreadsheet application

Using a Spreadsheet Program

Figure 5-5 is an example of a simple financial spreadsheet hand-prepared using a calculator and an accounting worksheet. The owner of the XYZ Company developed this simple spreadsheet to analyze the company's recent financial performance. If you were the owner, you could build and use this spreadsheet to help you make better decisions by using an electronic spreadsheet package.

First you would load the spreadsheet program into the computer from a floppy or hard disk. Immediately, the spreadsheet format of rows and columns would appear on the computer's video screen. Then you would begin constructing the XYZ financial performance spreadsheet shown in the photograph on page 142.

REAL-WORLD EXAMPLE

High's Ice Cream: Graphing Decision Support

Using an electronic spreadsheet for decision support is old hat for Oscar Smith, president of High's Ice Cream Corporation of Norfolk, Virginia. He uses the PlanPerfect spreadsheet package to do historical and what-if analysis of sales performance for his chain of 33 ice cream shops. PlanPerfect's ability to generate graphics displays of spreadsheet numbers provides additional decision support. Smith says he produces spreadsheet graphics "so people can quickly conceptualize results."

For example, Smith uses line and bar graphs to compare this year's weekly sales results with last year's and pie charts to compare sales of ten ice cream flavors. Key bits of information to help his decision-making seem to "jump out of the graphics" compared with viewing its standard worksheet format. For example, if cold weather causes a drop in ice cream sales that averages 10 percent for all the stores, but one store registers a 37 percent decrease, it shows up dramatically in a graphics display. Then Smith can get to work doing historical and what-if analysis to discover reasons for the sales drop and formulate ways to get the store back on track.

1. How does Oscar Smith's spreadsheet package give him decision support?

2. How important is spreadsheet graphics to his decision making?

Using Spreadsheet Commands

Electronic spreadsheet programs use a variety of commands to manipulate the worksheet and its contents. For example, you can use a Blank command to erase the contents of a cell. You could use a Copy command to copy the contents of cells throughout the spreadsheet instead of keying in repetitive spreadsheet entries. Or you can insert or delete a column or row by using Insert or Delete commands. You choose commands by making selections from a series of menus or by "pointing and clicking" at icons that represent various command options.

XYZ Company: Financial Performance

	Year 1	Year 2	Year 3	Total
Revenue	100,000—	110,000—	120,000—	330,000—
Expenses	70,000—	77,000—	84,000—	231,000—
Profit	30,000—	33,000—	36,000—	99,000—
Taxes	12,000—	13,200—	14,400—	39,600—
Profit after taxes	18,000—	14,800—	21,600—	59,400—

Figure 5-5
An accounting worksheet is a hand-prepared spreadsheet.

Icons and menus make spreadsheet packages easy to use.

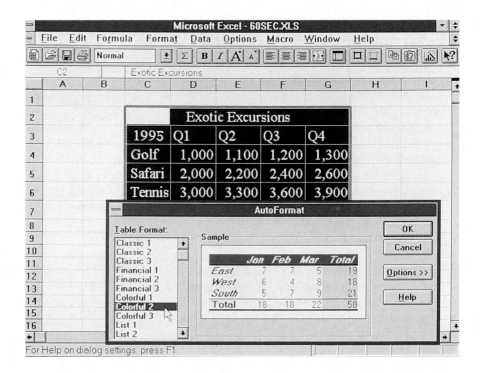

In many spreadsheets, commands are activated by pressing the slash (/) key. This displays a *main menu* of commands above or below the spreadsheet. Selecting any of these main menu commands will provide you with a *command menu* or prompt that specifies various options available to accomplish that command. Selecting one of these options may provide you with a *submenu* of additional options. Thus, several levels of menus may be provided to accomplish major spreadsheet functions.

Entering Data and Formulas

Data is entered in a spreadsheet at the cell location where the cursor is placed. You simply key in the data and press either the Enter key or one of the cursor control keys. You can usually enter many characters of data into a cell. For example, many spreadsheets allow up to 125 characters (or more) in each cell. However, unless you change the standard column width of your spreadsheet, only eight or nine characters may be displayed in the cells on your screen.

Each cell in an electronic spreadsheet can be filled with one of three possible types of information: numbers, words, and formulas. More specifically, you can enter the following:

- Text data, such as titles and other text material, called *labels*.
- Numeric data or numbers, called *values*.
- Mathematical formulas, which you develop to perform standard arithmetic operations (such as add, subtract, multiply, and so on). Formulas can also include special **functions** (to compute a total, average, square root, and so on) that are provided by the spreadsheet program. See Table 5-3. Notice that functions start with an "@" sign.

functions
Specialized preprogrammed formulas provided by a spreadsheet package.

Table 5-3
Examples of Spreadsheet
Functions

Function	Result
AVG(list)	Arithmetic mean of the values in a list
COUNT(list)	Number of nonblank entries in a list
MAX(list)	Largest value in a list
MIN(list)	Smallest value in a list
SUM(list)	Sum of each value in a list

Thus, to construct the XYZ financial performance spreadsheet, you could begin to enter the titles and headings of this spreadsheet shown in Figure 5-6. Then enter dollar amounts into cells where you already know the values that should be included. For example, assuming you knew that sales for 1991 were $100,000, you would enter that amount into the cell established for 1991 sales in your worksheet.

Then you begin entering formulas into the remaining cells that express the relationships you want between each category of values on the spreadsheet. For example, the spreadsheet depicted on page 144 shows that if you want expenses to be 70 percent of the sales, you would enter the formula +B6*.7 into cell B10. That's because 1991 sales are in cell B6, and 1991 expenses are in cell B7. The computer immediately calculates $70,000 as the value for 1991 expenses ($100,000 × .7) and displays it in cell B10.

You would continue this process until all cells contain appropriate formulas and functions and display values calculated by your computer. Notice in Figure 5-6 that even though you entered a formula like +B6*.7 into cell B10, the spreadsheet only displays the calculated value of $70,000. Thus a spreadsheet program must keep track of the formulas "behind" each cell, even though it usually displays only the results of formula calculations in the cells of the spreadsheet.

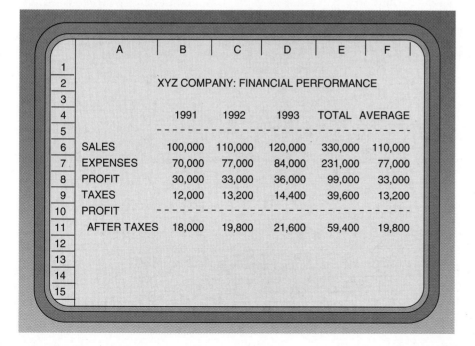

Figure 5-6
This spreadsheet makes it easy to analyze the financial performance of the XYZ Company.

Saving and Printing

Spreadsheets can be stored on a magnetic disk and retrieved later for additional use. A Save command is used to store a spreadsheet on the disk. The Save command will display a prompt that asks you for the name of the file in which the spreadsheet will be saved. Therefore, you must think up a file name, usually of about eight characters. For example, we could use the name PERFORM1 for the spreadsheet file for the XYZ Company's financial performance spreadsheet.

A spreadsheet stored on a magnetic disk can be easily retrieved. You use a Retrieve command that loads a spreadsheet from the disk into the computer's memory. During the execution of this command, the spreadsheet prompt will ask you for the name of the spreadsheet file you wish to load. Once you enter its name, the spreadsheet is retrieved from the disk, stored in memory, and displayed on the screen.

Once you have completed a spreadsheet and used it to analyze a particular problem or opportunity, you will probably want to print a paper copy of the spreadsheet on the printer of your computer system. Use a Print command to output a rectangular area of the worksheet. You can specify the part of the spreadsheet you want printed by entering its cell coordinates in response to a spreadsheet prompt or by highlighting it on the screen. Some programs even allow you to print a spreadsheet sideways on a sheet of paper to help reduce the amount of paper needed to print out large spreadsheets.

Auditing a Spreadsheet

Auditors and managers are often very concerned about the uses to which spreadsheets are put and whether the spreadsheets are valid. Invalid formu-

The formula attached to a particular cell is displayed when the cell is activated.

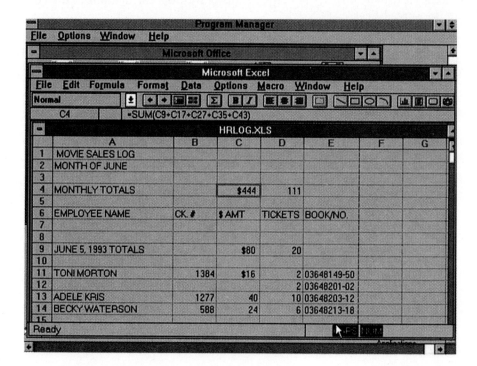

las in a spreadsheet can result in erroneous calculations, costing a company millions of dollars. Therefore, one way to validate a spreadsheet is to examine the formulas and functions used in it. Thus, most spreadsheet programs provide commands that allow you to display and print out the formula and function contents of the cells in a spreadsheet. Such displays and printouts are a vital part of spreadsheet documentation. They help auditors and other specialists examine the formulas used in a spreadsheet to help detect errors in logic or data entry.

What-If Analysis

As we said earlier, an electronic spreadsheet's what-if capability makes a spreadsheet program a simple but important type of decision support system package. An electronic spreadsheet allows you to interact with a computerized model by comparing the effects of alternative proposed decisions. This analytical modeling process significantly assists your decision-making process. After setting up a spreadsheet model, managers and other end users can make what-if changes to quickly and easily discover the effect any change will have on their "bottom line," that is, the key components of their model.

For example, what if we give employees an increase in salary? What if shipping costs increase? What if interest rates go up? What if we purchase, rather than lease, a new truck? What if we cut the recruiting budget? What if we add additional seating capacity? Try it and see the results instantly. Such questions should give you an idea of the variety of uses and the decision support capabilities provided by electronic spreadsheet packages.

Doing What-If Analysis

As an example, suppose you wanted to know *what* would happen to sales of a product *if* advertising expense increased by 10, 20, or 25 percent? To find out, you would simply change the advertising expense formula on a sales forecast worksheet you had developed. First, you would try 10 percent, then 20 percent, then 25 percent. Each time, the affected figures would be recalculated automatically, and a new expected sales figure would be displayed. You would then have a better insight into whether advertising expense should be increased.

Let's look at another example. Suppose you were the owner of the XYZ Company. You would probably want to test the effects of making changes to various spreadsheet values and formulas. You would want to see how this affected the results shown on the financial performance spreadsheet first shown in Figure 5-6. You could make what-if assumptions and change some of the values in the spreadsheet. The spreadsheet program would then automatically perform recalculations based on these assumptions and display the results.

For example, you could change 1991 sales to $200,000 and the computer would instantly calculate and display $36,000 as the profit after taxes for 1991 based on the formulas built into the spreadsheet. You could even develop tables of alternative values *(data tables)* for sales or other items that would automatically make changes to those values in the spreadsheet. This would give you an easy way to generate a variety of what-if results. In this way you could analyze the effect of changes in the past, present, and future financial performance of the XYZ Company.

Quick Quiz

1. Electronic spreadsheets use menus or icons to execute a variety of _____ that manipulate the spreadsheet and its contents.
2. You can enter text data, numeric data, or _____ into the cells of a spreadsheet.
3. Spreadsheet formulas can include special _____ to perform standard arithmetic operations.
4. An electronic spreadsheet package enables you to create and make changes to a spreadsheet _____ to compare the effects of alternative proposed decisions.
5. An electronic spreadsheet's _____ capability makes it a widely used decision support system software package.

Answers: 1. commands 2. formulas 3. functions 4. model 5. what-if analysis

Other Spreadsheet Features

Today's spreadsheet packages don't just do spreadsheets. Most spreadsheet packages allow you to create presentation graphics for displaying information from a spreadsheet. Others contain a variety of predesigned spreadsheets called *templates* or allow you to create three-dimensional spreadsheet models. Still others have grown into multipurpose *integrated packages* that combine spreadsheet capabilities with word processing, database management, graphics, and telecommunications features.

Electronic spreadsheets with graphics capabilities provide decision support to managerial end users.

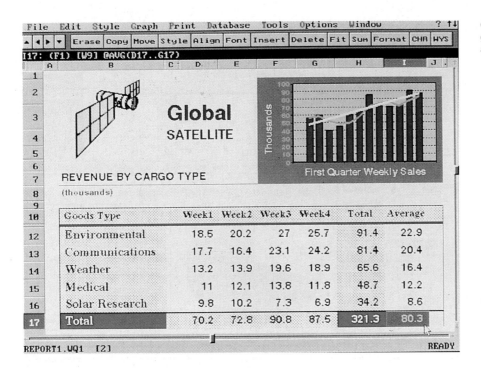

Graphic displays such as this bar graph represent the data in the active spreadsheet.

Using Graphics Displays

One of the outstanding features of most spreadsheet packages is their ability to graph parts of your spreadsheets easily and immediately. Once you enter a simple sequence of graphics commands, your results are displayed instantly. Thus, graphics displays are an attractive way to visualize the information in your spreadsheets, including the results of your what-if analyses. In addition, graphics are a superior way for you to communicate the high points of a spreadsheet and present the results of your what-if analysis to others. Thus, you could issue a series of graphics commands to graph parts of the XYZ financial performance spreadsheet. An example of how you might do spreadsheet graphics is shown in the photograph above.

Templates

Special-purpose spreadsheet models called **templates** make it easy for you to use a spreadsheet package to solve specific problems. Templates are predesigned electronic spreadsheet models that have been developed for specific occupations or classes of problems. Column and row headings are already set up, and formulas and special functions defining relationships between the elements in the spreadsheet are already included. Templates are available as separate programs or are included in advanced spreadsheet packages.

Typically, these worksheet models are developed for specific applications such as accounting, real estate, and engineering. For example, you can buy spreadsheet templates for doing your income taxes, calculating mortgage payments, analyzing athletic team statistics, and so on. You can also develop and store your own templates. Any spreadsheet model you develop and save without entering variable data is a template you can use when you need it.

templates
Predesigned electronic spreadsheet models that have been developed for specific occupations or classes of problems.

Tax preparation software provides templates for entering income and expense information.

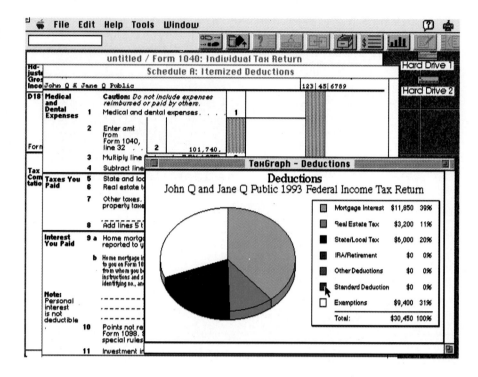

Spreadsheet templates designed for tax accounting, financial analysis, or real estate investment applications are very popular. The appeal of templates is that you only need to enter data to produce results. For example, you can produce a completed tax return by entering your income, expenses, and other data into a spreadsheet tax return template.

Macros

macros
Allows you to use one or a few keystrokes to represent a series of keystrokes to perform a spread-sheet or other software operation.

Most spreadsheet packages let you create and save **macros** to help you auto-mate some of the ways you use a spreadsheet program. The simplest form of macro allows you to use one keystroke to represent a series of keystrokes you would use to perform a spreadsheet operation. For example, saving an updated spreadsheet file to your disk requires at least five keystrokes (/FS Enter R) in many spreadsheets, while erasing the spreadsheet in memory typically takes another four keystrokes (/WEY). Instead, you could create and use a two-key-stroke macro (Alt S). Then all you would have to do is hold down the Alt key and press the S key whenever you wanted to save an updated spreadsheet and erase it in memory.

A more advanced form of macros involves programming in the *command language* provided by some spreadsheet packages. Custom programs of spread-sheet commands can then be developed to make using a spreadsheet a lot eas-ier for inexperienced end users.

Three-Dimensional Spreadsheets

Several popular spreadsheet programs now let you develop three-dimensional worksheets called *workpads* or *cubes* of up to 16,000 rows, 16,000 columns, and 16,000 pages, for a total of 4 trillion cells!

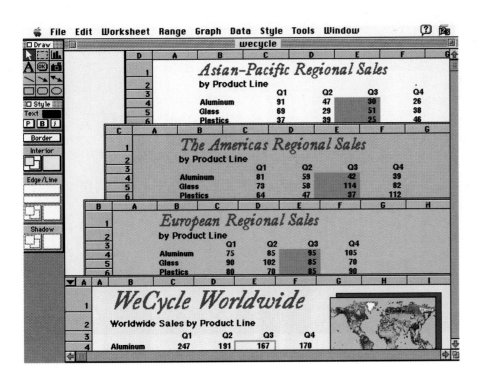

Three-dimensional spreadsheets provide more cells than most end users would ever need.

Of course, most end users would never use such spreadsheet capacities. But the concept of worksheet *pages* as a third spreadsheet dimension can be a useful feature. For example, you could develop this month's family budget on the first worksheet page of a workpad or cube, next month's budget on the second worksheet page, and so on. Thus, it would take 12 worksheet pages to hold a year's worth of monthly budgets. If you then made an adjustment to this month's budget that affected future months, the spreadsheet package would recalculate all 12 budgets to reflect the change.

Integrated Packages

Integrated packages combine the abilities of several general-purpose application programs into one software package. These packages were developed to give end users the convenience of having the features of several types of packages combined into one. Integrated packages also make it easier to transfer data files among applications you are working on. Examples of popular integrated packages are Microsoft Works, Symphony, Framework IV, PFS: First Choice, and Enable. These packages typically combine the popular functions of electronic spreadsheets, word processing, and database management with graphics and telecommunications.

Thus, integrated packages allow you to process the same file of data with one package, moving from one function (such as a spreadsheet) to another (such as graphics) by pressing a few keys on your keyboard. You can view displays from each function separately or together in multiple windows on your video screen. Some integrated packages may compromise on the speed, power, and flexibility of their functions in order to achieve integration. Therefore, ex-

The Microsoft Works integrated package provides word processing, spreadsheet, database, telecommunications, and graphic capabilities all in one package.

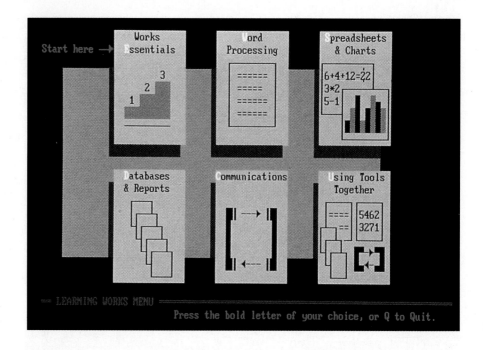

perienced end users may prefer single-function packages for applications they use heavily.

However, many end users prefer integrated packages. They love the convenience of using just one package with a common user interface and a common set of commands. This reduces the time it takes to learn how to use many software features. Also, buying an integrated package is less costly than buying several separate programs. Several popular integrated packages are priced significantly below leading individual-function packages.

Expert Systems

artificial intelligence (AI)
A science and technology whose goal is to develop computers that can think, as well as see, hear, walk, talk, and feel. Examples include intelligent robots and *expert systems* that can give end users expert advice in a specific area.

expert system
A computer-based information system that uses its knowledge about a specific subject area to act as an expert consultant to users. It consists of a *knowledge base* and software that performs inferences on the knowledge and communicates answers to a user's questions.

The newest developments in decision support software are being affected by exciting developments in the field of **artificial intelligence (AI).** Artificial intelligence is an area of computer science that is attempting to develop computers that can think as well as see, hear, walk, talk, and feel! For example, current AI projects include the development of natural languages for programming computers, advanced industrial robots, and more *intelligent* computers. Thus, one major AI effort is in developing computer capabilities normally associated with human intelligence, that is, reasoning, learning, and problem solving. One of the most practical applications of this particular area of AI is the development of *expert systems*.

An **expert system** is a *knowledge-based* information system that uses its knowledge about a specific subject area to act as an expert consultant to end users. The components of an expert system consist of a *knowledge base* and software that performs inferences on the knowledge and communicates answers to a user's questions. Figure 5-7 illustrates the interrelated components of an expert system.

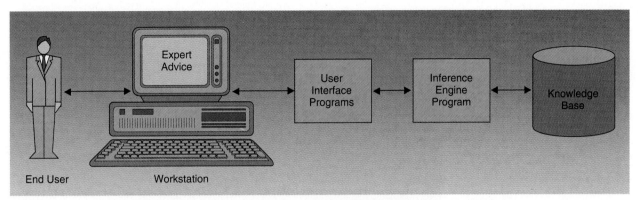

Figure 5-7
An expert system uses software and a knowledge base to provide expert advice to an end user.

An expert system's **knowledge base** typically consists of a *rule base* of IF-THEN rules and a *database* of facts and other information about a subject. Its software component usually consists of an *inference engine* program and other programs for refining knowledge or communicating with users. The inference engine program processes the rules and data related to a specific problem. It then makes inferences resulting in recommended courses of action.

For instance, if a knowledge base contained rules and data about systems analysts, an expert system might make the following simple inferences:

knowledge base
A collection of knowledge about a subject in a variety of forms, such as facts and rules of inference.

- IF Joan is a systems analyst,
  and
- IF systems analysts need high-powered computers,
- THEN Joan needs a high-powered computer.

REAL-WORLD EXAMPLE

Consumer Health Services, Inc.: Changing Spreadsheets

Electronic spreadsheets have undergone quite a transformation since the first spreadsheet software, VisiCalc, was unveiled at the West Coast Computer Faire in 1979. Users were thrilled that an electronic spreadsheet made extinct the painstaking manual calculation of ledger sheets; today, much more is expected of spreadsheets. The current leader of the Windows spreadsheet market is Microsoft Excel for Windows. But Lotus 1-2-3 still commands a major share of the DOS spreadsheet market and is selling a lot of a much improved version of 1-2-3 for Windows and an analytical spreadsheet called Improv for Windows.

To Frank Gregg, senior data analyst at Consumer Health Services, Inc., a physicians' information and referral service in Boulder, Colorado,

the ability to make changes on the fly and immediately see the results displayed is the most important feature of a spreadsheet. "In Lotus 1-2-3, that's enhanced even further by being able to see changes on a graph roght on the spot," Gregg said. "We bought Lotus 1-2-3 as a spreadsheet, though we've taken it beyond the capabilities of a simple spreadsheet via macros," he said. "The physician-tracking system I developed on 1-2-3 runs from menu selections, which access files of macro instructions that automate everything."

1. What changes have occurred in how electronic spreadsheets are used?
2. What do you think is the most important feature of a spreadsheet?

This expert system allows pilots to determine a course of action in any given situation.

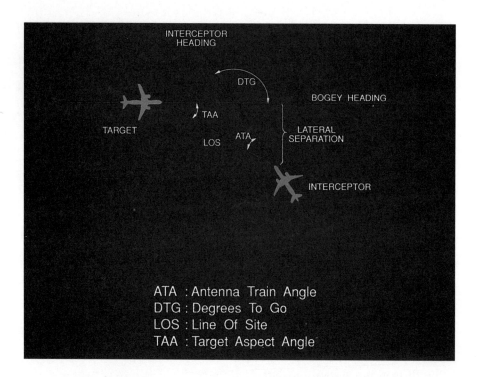

Applications of Expert Systems

Expert systems are being used in many different fields, including medicine, engineering, the physical sciences, and business. Expert systems now help diagnose illnesses, search for minerals, analyze compounds, recommend repairs, and do financial planning. The applications of expert systems are limited by the willingness and ability of human experts to transform and transfer their knowledge into a computerized knowledge base. Of course, no one can be an expert on everything. So expert systems must be limited to relatively narrow, well-defined problem areas. But that still leaves a lot of room for expert systems applications. See Table 5-4.

One classic example of expert systems is Mycin, which was developed at Stanford University in the mid-1970s. Mycin diagnoses and prescribes treatment for meningitis and other bacterial infections during the first 48 hours of an infection. This is a time when symptoms are unclear and human diagnosis is difficult. Mycin was designed by painstakingly interviewing many doctors about their diagnosis and treatment practices, and it took more than 20 person-years to complete. It contains more than 500 rules and uses its knowledge of infectious organisms, results of lab tests, and patient history and symptoms to make its diagnosis and prescribe treatment. Mycin has proven more accurate than human diagnosis in its area of expertise.

Another good example is an expert system called *Authorizer's Assistant*. It's used by American Express to help credit authorizers decide on requests for credit. With more than 20 million U.S. cardholders, American Express developed this expert system to cut down on losses from incorrect credit authorizations. American Express has no preset credit limit, which makes credit authorization more difficult. It also has a policy of reaching approval/denial

Table 5-4
Some Applications of Expert Systems

Application	Examples
Decision Support	Loan portfolio analysis Employee performance evaluation Insurance underwriting
Diagnostics	Equipment calibration Help desk operations Medical diagnosis
Scheduling	Maintenance scheduling Production scheduling Education scheduling
Configuration Design	Manufacturability analysis Communications network design Optimum assembly plans
Classification and Selection	Material selection Delinquent account identification Suspect identification
Process Control	Machine control Production monitoring Chemical testing

Doctors now use expert systems to help diagnose certain medical conditions.

An expert system asks the user questions and explains its reasoning once it has drawn a conclusion.

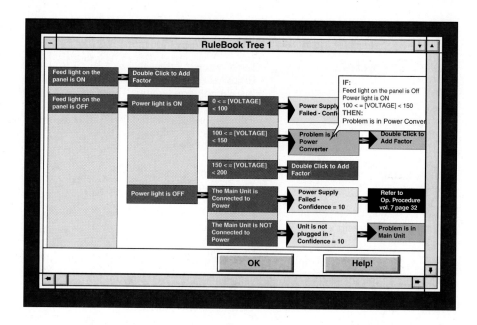

decisions within 90 seconds or less. Thus, the risks of a bad decision are great. The knowledge base of Authorizer's Assistant contains the expertise of several experienced credit authorizers. Thus, it helps credit authorizers recognize charge requests that are outside typical credit patterns. Therefore, any unusual requests that do not fit its profile are declined.

Using an Expert System

Using an expert system involves an interactive computer-based session in which the solution to a problem is explored, with the expert system acting as your consultant. The expert system asks you questions, searches its knowledge base for facts and rules, explains its reasoning process when asked, and gives you expert advice in the subject area being explored. The photograph above illustrates part of the dialogue between an end user and an expert system.

Developing an Expert System

Relatively low-cost software packages are available that help expert system developers, known as *knowledge engineers,* and end users develop their own expert systems on microcomputers. These expert system development packages or **shells** allow knowledge engineers or end users to capture the knowledge of experts and develop the knowledge base and software modules for an application without starting from scratch. For example, one shell uses a spreadsheet format to help you develop IF-THEN rules, while another automatically generates rules based on examples you furnish.

shells
Expert system development packages that allow knowledge engineers or end users to capture the knowledge of experts and develop the knowledge base and software for an expert system.

Quick Quiz

1. Most spreadsheet packages allow you to create _____ displays of parts of your spreadsheet.

REAL-WORLD EXAMPLE

Broadway Department Stores:
Experts in Retailing

What's the most fiercely competitive retail and fashion market in America? A lot of retailers think it's Southern California. And that's where the Broadway, a Los Angeles-based chain of 43 department stores, must compete. They ring up more than 57 million customer transactions a year, so they must be doing something right. Their strategy is simple: superior customer service and highly qualified retail managers. And one other ingredient, too: expert systems to help store managers.

Everyday management of each store is handled by 645 area sales managers (ASMs), many of whom are recent college graduates with only a few years of retail experience. So the Broadway's executives and IS staff built an expert system based on the knowledge of eight of their top producing sales managers, which they called Area Sales Man-

ager Expert System Consultant or the ASM-ESC. It has six modules covering sales technique, staffing, product knowledge, product procurement, floor layout, and motivation. When a store manager uses ASM-ESC, it asks for specific store data and then identifies potential problems and suggests solutions. Many of the Broadway's ASMs say that the expert system helps them make decisions much more quickly—and makes the Broadway more competitive and successful.

1. Why is retail store management a good application of expert systems?
2. What other occupational areas could be helped by expert systems? Explain.

2. Special-purpose, predesigned spreadsheet models are called _____.
3. A _____ allows you to use one or two keystrokes to repeat a series of keystroke commands.
4. A(n) _____ combines the capabilities of an electronic spreadsheet program with the capabilities of word processing, graphics, database, and other programs.
5. An _____ uses an inference engine program and a knowledge base to serve as an expert consultant to end users.

Answers: 1. graphics   2. templates   3. macro   4. integrated package   5. expert system

End Note: End Users and Decision Support

In this chapter, you've learned that computers can do more than electronically process data to give you information quickly and attractively. Computers can help you make decisions. Decision support software like electronic spreadsheet packages and DSS generators won't make decisions for you. But they will allow you to quickly explore your decision options.

E T H I C S

Ethical Issues in Decision Making

What factors influence your decision making when you are faced with ethical choices? That's an issue researchers in ethical behavior have been studying for many years. A simplistic answer would involve using *situational ethics*, that is, "It depends on the situation." A more complex but more realistic answer would be, "A lot of factors are involved in making ethical choices."

Figure 5-8 outlines many of the key factors that affect our decision-making process when we must choose between ethical and unethical behavior. Notice how much our ethical choices are affected by our environment—our personal, professional, work, government, legal, and social environments. Then notice how our own individual attributes affect our ethical behavior. For example, your moral code, personal goals, motivation, and position or status in society and your personal self-concept, life experience, personality, and demographics (age, sex, religion, location, and so on) are important factors that affect your ethical choices.

Finally, notice that our ethical decision-making process is affected by how we acquire and process information and by our *cognitive style* (that is, how we think). The potential for losses or rewards we perceive in any given situation also plays a big part. So you see, there are many factors involved any time you must make a decision that has ethical consequences. You should also realize that decision support software does not and cannot make such decisions for you. You bear the ultimate responsibility for how the factors in your environment and your own individual attributes affect your ethical decision-making process. That is the cornerstone of your personal freedom and responsibility in our society.

What Do You Think?

Could decision support software influence your ethical decision making? Would there be ethical dangers in your use of expert systems? Or are other environmental and individual factors more important? What do you think?

Once you have generated enough information about your alternatives, you will have gained insight into the decision situations you face. Then you can make your decisions with more confidence in their outcome. That's the essence of the decision support concept.

Electronic spreadsheets are the most popular type of software package that gives end users this kind of decision support. That's because they allow you to build electronic worksheet models of business or other situations. Then you can analyze past and present performance or forecast future results by

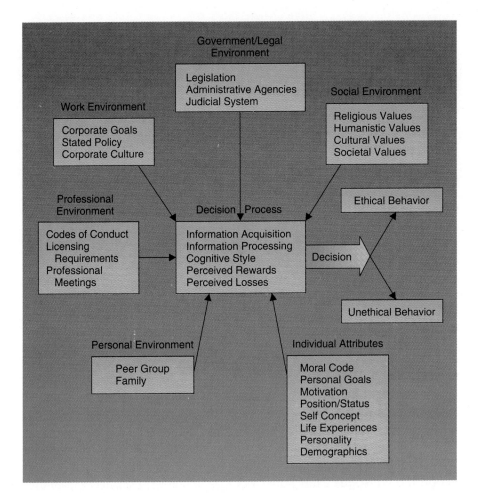

Figure 5-8
Our ethical behavior is affected by a variety of environmental and individual factors.

doing analytical modeling. That is, you can use your spreadsheet package to do what-if, goal-seeking, or optimization analysis to find out what the effects of alternative decisions might be. You can even graph the results of your modeling so you can create graphics displays of your decision alternatives. So an electronic spreadsheet program or the spreadsheet component of an integrated package is a valuable decision support tool for end users.

Of course, you can also use an exciting development in artificial intelligence that gives you the decision support of experts. That's what expert systems do. These software packages will give you expert advice on very specific and limited subjects to help you make better decisions. Expert systems can't tell you everything you need to know. But since they do contain the knowledge of experts on specific subjects in their knowledge bases, they can be a big help in certain problem situations. That's why expert systems are being used to help end users make decisions in medicine, education, and government, as well as in industry and many other fields. So changes are that expert systems will be supporting decisions you make in the future, whatever your career will be.

Summary

You and Decision Support   Computers and decision support software make decision support systems (DSS) possible. A DSS package allows you to explore and evaluate decision alternatives in an interactive process that helps you make better decisions.

Decision Support Fundamentals   In a decision support system, managers and other end users use computers, databases, model bases, and DSS software to provide interactive support for decision making. DSS software includes electronic spreadsheets, DSS generators, statistical analysis packages, group decision support software, and expert systems. End users utilize a DSS package to develop and manipulate mathematical models to do three basic types of analytical modeling: what-if analysis, goal-seeking analysis, and optimization analysis.

Electronic Spreadsheets   Spreadsheet programs are the most popular software packages for end user decision support. They generate an electronic worksheet of rows and columns in which you enter data and formulas to construct a model of a business or other situation. Then you can do analytical modeling, such as what-if analysis, to support your decision-making efforts.

What-If Analysis   An electronic worksheet allows you to interact with a computerized model to compare the effects of proposed decisions. In what-if analysis, a spreadsheet's ability to perform instant recalculations lets you observe how changes you make to some spreadsheet values affect other values. This gives you insight into what the effect of proposed decisions might be.

Other Spreadsheet Features   Most spreadsheet packages let you create presentation graphics of data from a spreadsheet. Other spreadsheet options include predesigned spreadsheet templates, macros, and three-dimensional spreadsheets.

Integrated Packages   Integrated packages combine spreadsheet capabilities with word processing, database management, graphics, and telecommunications features. They give you the convenience of having the features of several programs combined into one lower-cost package.

Expert Systems   An expert system is a knowledge-based information system that uses its knowledge about a specific subject area so it can act as an expert consultant to end users. The components of an expert system consist of a knowledge base and software that performs inferences on the knowledge and communicates advice to support end user decision making.

Key Terms and Concepts

analytical modeling	functions
artificial intelligence	goal-seeking analysis
cell	integrated package
cell pointer	knowledge base
decision support software	labels
decision support system	macros
electronic spreadsheet	models
expert system	optimization analysis
expert system shell	recalculation

scroll
spreadsheet graphics
templates
three-dimensional spreadsheet

values
what-if analysis
window

Review Quiz

True/False

_____ 1. An electronic spreadsheet is a worksheet of rows and columns stored in your computer's memory and displayed on its video screen.

_____ 2. A decision support system lets you explore decision alternatives in an interactive process.

_____ 3. A spreadsheet package lets you do analytical modeling.

_____ 4. A value is a simplified abstraction of a real-world system.

_____ 5. A cell pointer is a cursor that you can move around the spreadsheet.

_____ 6. Text data such as titles are the primary components of spreadsheet models.

_____ 7. A label is a number or a formula in a spreadsheet.

_____ 8. Scrolling is moving the display screen window across the spreadsheet in memory.

_____ 9. Spreadsheets allow instant calculation of changes you make to a cell.

_____ 10. When you use a macro, one keystroke can represent a series of keystrokes.

Multiple Choice

_____ 1. A spreadsheet model that has interrelated worksheet pages is called a

  a. framework.
  b. macro.
  c. template.
  d. three-dimensional spreadsheet.

_____ 2. A predeveloped spreadsheet model available for specific applications is a

  a. framework.
  b. macro.
  c. template.
  d. three-dimensional spreadsheet.

_____ 3. Computer science is trying to develop computers with the capability of

  a. agility.
  b. movement.
  c. artificial intelligence.
  d. all of the above.

_____ 4. An expert system shell is a software package for

   a. developing expert systems.
   b. an expert system user interface.
   c. expert system spreadsheets.
   d. auditing expert systems.

_____ 5. A spreadsheet display is a

   a. physical model.
   b. visual model.
   c. verbal model.
   d. mathematical model.

_____ 6. A spreadsheet model of business or scientific relationships is usually a

   a. physical model.
   b. graphics model.
   c. verbal model.
   d. mathematical model.

_____ 7. Programs that let you manipulate data and formulas in a worksheet are

   a. expert systems.
   b. electronic spreadsheets.
   c. DSS generators.
   d. group decision support packages.

_____ 8. Programs that provide expert advice to end users are

   a. expert systems.
   b. electronic spreadsheets.
   c. DSS generators
   d. group decision support packages.

_____ 9. Programs that are designed for specific decision support applications are

   a. expert systems.
   b. electronic spreadsheets.
   c. DSS generators.
   d. group decision support packages.

_____ 10. Programs that enhance joint decision making by work groups are

   a. expert systems.
   b. electronic spreadsheets.
   c. DSS generators.
   d. group decision support packages.

Fill-in

1. Three basic forms of _____ modeling are what-if analysis, goal-seeking analysis, and optimization analysis.

2. Observing how changes to certain values affect other values is known as _____ analysis.

3. Setting a target value and making changes to selected values until a goal is reached is called _____ analysis.

4. Finding the best value for a model component, given certain limitations, is called _____ analysis.

5. The space formed by the intersection of a row and column is called a _____.

6. The display screen is like a _____ that lets you see part of the spreadsheet stored in memory.

7. Mathematical formulas and computational routines are provided as _____ by the spreadsheet program.

8. A _____ package combines the functions of several packages into one.

9. A _____ is a knowledge-based information system that offers expert advice to end users.

10. A collection of facts and rules gathered from experts is called a _____.

Questions for Thought and Discussion

1. How does computer-based decision support differ from the reporting and presentation of information by computers?
2. Why do you think that what-if analysis is the most popular form of analytical modeling?
3. Refer to the Real-World Example of High's Ice Cream Corporation in the chapter. What kinds of models do you think Oscar Smith develops?
4. Why do you think electronic spreadsheet programs have become such a popular software package for end user computing?
5. Why is a spreadsheet package a form of decision support system (DSS) software?
6. Many spreadsheet packages provide the capability to graph parts of a spreadsheet. Is the use of such graphics displays an example of decision support? Explain.
7. Refer to the Real-World Example of Consumer Health Services, Inc. in the chapter. What capabilities do spreadsheet packages offer that are most important to end users?
8. Do you think computers will ever be able to think? Explain your answer in light of the capabilities of expert systems.
9. Refer to the Real-World Example of Broadway Department Stores in the chapter. What kind of decision support do expert systems provide?
10. Investigate how you could use the capabilities of the latest spreadsheet packages to support your decision making in a career you are considering. Make a brief report to the class.

Review Quiz Answers

True/False   **1.** T **2.** T **3.** T **4.** F **5.** T **6.** F **7.** F **8.** T **9.** T **10.** T

Multiple Choice   **1.** d **2.** c **3.** d **4.** a **5.** b **6.** d **7.** b **8.** a **9.** c **10.** d

Fill-in   **1.** analytical **2.** what-if **3.** goal-seeking **4.** optimization **5.** cell **6.** window **7.** functions **8.** integrated **9.** expert system **10.** knowledge base

C H A P T E R

6

DATABASE MANAGEMENT SOFTWARE: MANAGING YOUR DATA RESOURCES

OUTLINE

LEARNING OBJECTIVES

After reading and studying this chapter, you should be able to

Explain how the database management approach benefits organizations and end users more than a file processing approach.

Identify fundamental data elements and data structures used to organize data for easy access by end users.

Identify the basic tasks you can accomplish with database management packages.

Identify several benefits provided by personal information managers and software packages for managing text databases, image databases, hypertext, and hypermedia.

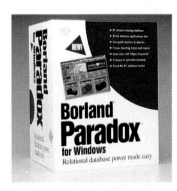

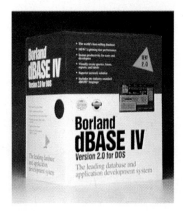

Database management packages have become a popular category of end user software.

file processing
Information processing in which data are stored in independent files, and each file is processed by different application programs.

database management
An approach to the storage and processing of data in which independent files are consolidated into a common database of records available to different application programs and end users for processing and reporting.

database
A collection of logically related records that consolidates records previously stored in separate files so that a common pool of data records serves many applications.

You and Database Management

In Chapter 4, we discussed how word processing programs help you organize and manipulate text data to provide you with attractive computer-produced documents. In Chapter 5, we saw that spreadsheet programs help you organize and manipulate data and formulas in electronic worksheets to provide you with easy-to-use modeling tools for decision support. In this chapter, we will see how database management programs can help you organize and access data in your files and databases. Database management packages have thus become an important part of *information resource management (IRM)*. This concept emphasizes that data and information are vital resources that must be managed effectively for the benefit of all end users in an organization.

Database management packages have many uses for both end users and organizations. For example, you could use database packages to keep track of assets, to store bibliographic research information, or to maintain family budget data. Both large and small businesses may use them to maintain important business data such as the records of their customers, employees, and products. Database packages may also be used by medical offices to maintain medical histories and billing data. Or they can be used by libraries to keep track of checkout information, determine when books are overdue, or track the current location of their inventory of books. So database management software has proven its usefulness in many types of organizations and end user computing situations.

The Database Management Approach

How would you feel if you, as the owner of a computer-using company, were told that since your business uses a **file processing** approach, some information you want about your employees is too difficult and too costly to obtain? Suppose you were given the following reasons:

- The information you want is in several different files, each organized in a different way, thus making access difficult.

- Each file has been organized to be used by a different application program, none of which produces the information you want in the form you need.

You would probably be frustrated and disenchanted if your computer systems could not provide you with employee information simply and easily. That's how end users can be frustrated when an organization relies on file processing systems. In this approach, data are organized, stored, and processed in independent files of data records as we described.

In the **database management** approach, on the other hand, files are consolidated into a common pool, or **database,** of records that are available to many different application programs. Thus, a database integrates data that had formerly been scattered in many different independent files. In addition, database management software packages provide a helpful software interface between end users and their databases. Thus, a database management approach helps end users easily access and use the records stored in databases. See Figure 6-1 for example.

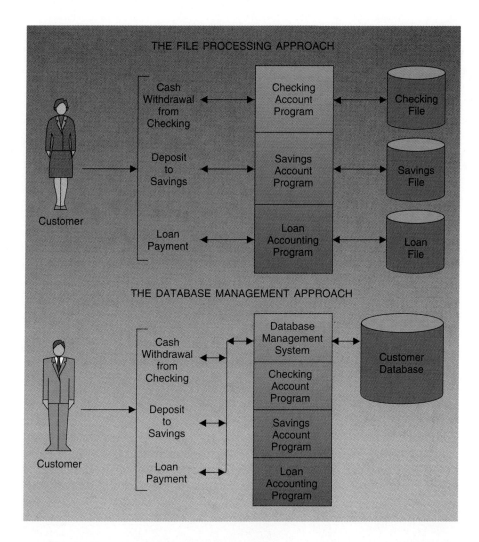

Figure 6-1
A database management approach consolidates files of customer records into a common database with the help of database management software.

The database management approach has other advantages over the file processing approach, especially if several files of data are used by several different applications. For instance, you don't need to duplicate employee names and addresses in multiple files, such as a payroll file, employee benefits file, employee performance file, and so on. This not only saves disk space, it reduces the chance for errors caused by entering the same data several times into multiple files.

Database Management Software

Early attempts to develop database management programs resulted in the development of **file management packages.** These programs use a "filing card" or "flat file" structure to organize stored data. They store a group of related data as individual records in a single independent file. A file management program works with one file at a time, helping you access your stored records to find information you need, just as you would if you had a file of index cards on a certain subject. File managers allow you to electronically extract infor-

file management package
A program that organizes stored data as individual records in a single independent file.

This database management package allows end users to use the SQL and QBE query languages to specify the information they need.

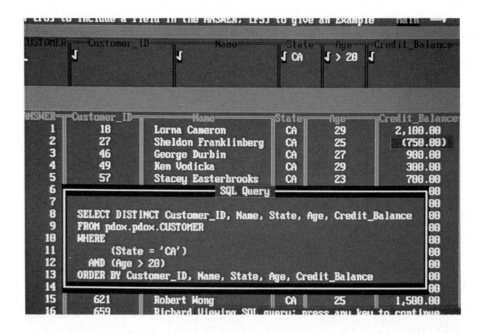

mation in the form of displays, listings, and reports from the various files stored in your computer system.

Database Management Systems

database management system (DBMS)
A generalized set of computer programs that controls the creation, maintenance, and use of databases.

Technically, a database management package is known as a **database management system (DBMS).** A database management system is a group of programs that manages the creation, maintenance, and use of the databases of end users and organizations. It allows you and other end users to easily ac-

This dBASE IV database package is displaying a "help" dialogue box.

cess and share the use of the same database for different applications. A DBMS also simplifies the process of retrieving information from a database in the form of displays and reports. Instead of having to write programs to extract information, end users can pose simple questions in a *query language* or design their own report forms to receive immediate displays of the information they need.

Examples of mainframe DBMS packages that are quite popular are DB2 by IBM and Oracle by the Oracle Corporation. Oracle is also widely used on minicomputer systems. Popular microcomputer database management packages are dBASE IV and Paradox by Borland International and Foxbase by Microsoft.

Microcomputer database management programs allow you to set up a database of interrelated records on your personal computer system. With such computerized records, you can store and retrieve information much faster and more efficiently than with a manual filing system using paper files. Most DBMS packages allow you to perform four primary jobs. See Figure 6-2.

- *Database development* helps you define and organize the content, relationships, and structure of the data needed to build your databases.
- *Database maintenance* helps you add, delete, update, correct, and protect the data in your databases.
- *Database reporting* helps you access the data in your databases. This typically involves information retrieval and report generation. Thus, you can selectively retrieve and display information and produce printed reports and documents.

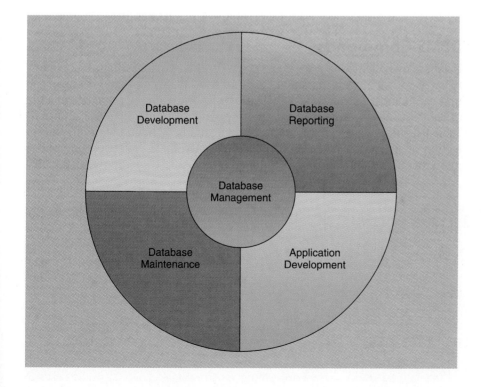

Figure 6-2
A database management package helps you accomplish these four database tasks.

Table 6-1
Some Typical Database
Management Commands

Command	Action
Browse	Provides full-screen window viewing and editing.
Copy	Makes a copy of an existing database file.
Create	Creates new database files.
Display	Displays records, fields, and expressions.
Edit	Alters specific data fields in a database.
Insert	Inserts data into a file.
Join	Creates a new file from two other files.
List	Lists the records in a file.
Locate	Finds a record that fits a condition.
Report	Formats and displays a report of data.
Sort	Sorts the records in a file on one or more data fields.
Use	Specifies the database file to be used.

- *Application development* helps you design data entry screens, forms, reports, programs, and other aspects of a proposed end user application. We will discuss application development in Chapter 10.

DBMS Commands

Database management packages use a variety of commands, menus, and icons to carry out their operations. For example, the Create command is one of the first commands you may use. You would use it to create the structure of a file or database. A sample of typical database management commands is shown in Table 6-1. In a menu-driven approach, the opening or main menu offers a selection of alternative database management operations. Selecting one of the main menu choices leads you to submenus of database operations, data entry

Figure 6-3
Pull-down menus offer you a variety of options when using some database management packages.

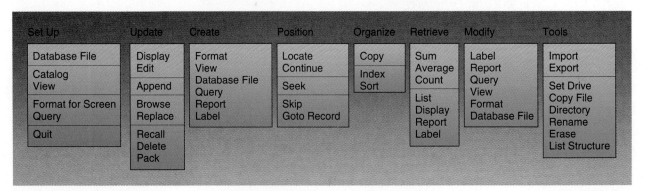

REAL-WORLD EXAMPLE

Fairfield University:
Community Database Services

What do college students, community service, and practicing database management have in common? Helping the hungry and the homeless, that's what. At Fairfield University in Connecticut, students of business professor Alfred Katz developed a database management application for the Food Bank of Fairfield County using the DataEase database management program. The food bank had been having trouble keeping track of food contributed by federal, state, and private sources that was then distributed to local soup kitchens and needy families. The database management application solved that problem and gave students a practical project to work on.

A similar application using a database management program was developed by students for other community service agencies. This application keeps track of students who help out at shelters for the homeless and other community service programs. For example, it matches students' skills, interests, and class schedules with the needs of various community service agencies.

1. How typical are the information needs of community service agencies?

2. How can database management packages help meet those needs?

screens, instructions, prompts, and so on. Figure 6-3 shows the variety of menu options provided by a widely used database management package.

Database Management Fundamentals

Before we can explain the use of database management packages, we need to review the meaning of several important data concepts. These fundamental concepts will help you understand how the data resources of computer-using organizations are organized so they can be easily accessed and managed by end users.

Data Elements

In Chapter 2, we mentioned that data are organized into *characters, fields, records, files,* and *databases,* just as writing can be organized in letters, words, sentences, paragraphs, and documents. Examples of these **logical data elements** are shown in Figure 6-4.

logical data elements
Data elements (such as records and files) that are used to logically organize data.

Characters

The most basic logical data element is the **character,** which consists of a single alphabetic, numeric, or other symbol. We might argue that the *bit* or *byte* is a more elementary data element, but remember that those terms refer to the *physical* storage elements provided by the computer hardware as we discussed in Chapter 1. From a user's point of view (that is, from a *logical* as opposed to a *physical* or hardware view of data), a character is the most basic element of data that can be observed and manipulated.

character
A single alphabetic, numeric, or other symbol.

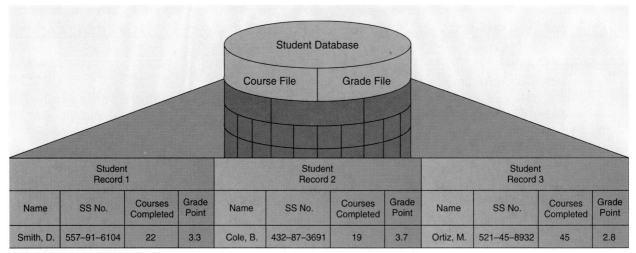

Student Record 1				Student Record 2				Student Record 3			
Name	SS No.	Courses Completed	Grade Point	Name	SS No.	Courses Completed	Grade Point	Name	SS No.	Courses Completed	Grade Point
Smith, D.	557–91–6104	22	3.3	Cole, B.	432–87–3691	19	3.7	Ortiz, M.	521–45–8932	45	2.8

Figure 6-4
Data can be logically organized into fields, records, files, and databases.

field
A grouping of characters that describes a particular characteristic of a person, place, thing, or event.

attribute
A characteristic or quality of an entity.

entity
A person, place, thing, or event.

record
A grouping of related data fields treated as a unit. A record represents a collection of attributes that describes an entity.

file
A collection of related data records treated as a unit.

transaction file
A data file containing relatively transient data describing current transactions.

master file
A data file containing relatively permanent information, which is utilized as an authoritative reference and is usually updated periodically.

Fields

The next higher level of data is the **field,** or *data item*. A field consists of a grouping of characters. For example, the grouping of alphabetic characters in a person's name forms a *name field,* and the grouping of numeric characters in a sales amount forms a *sales amount field*. Specifically, a data field represents an **attribute** (a characteristic or quality) of some **entity** (person, place, thing, or event). For instance, a person's age could be a data field that represents one of the many attributes of an individual. You or an IS analyst must analyze your data needs to decide how many characters should be specified as the maximum *field length* for each field. Depending on your uses for the data, you might specify a name field of up to 20 characters, and address field length of up to 30 characters, and so on.

Records

Related fields of data are grouped to form a **record.** So, a record represents a collection of attributes that describes an entity. An example is a student's course record, which consists of data fields such as the student's name, social security number, and course grades.

Files

A group of related records is known as a data **file.** Thus, a *student file* would contain the records of the students in a university. Files are frequently classified by the application for which they are primarily used, such as a *course file* or a *registration file*. Files are also classified by their permanence, for example, a sales *master file* versus a sales *weekly transaction file*. A sales **transaction file,** then, would contain records of all sales transactions occurring during a period and would be used periodically to update the permanent records contained in a sales **master file.** A *history file* is an obsolete file retained for backup purposes or for long-term, historical storage, called *archival storage.*

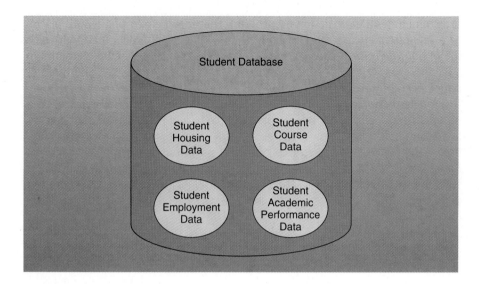

Figure 6-5
Student data formerly kept in separate files can be consolidated into a student database.

Databases

A *database* is an integrated collection of logically related records and files. A database consolidates records previously stored in separate files into a common pool of data records that can be accessed by many different application programs. For instance, the *student database* for a university consolidates data formerly segregated in separate files for student course, academic performance, employment, and housing records. Thus, a student database would allow easy access to different types of student data that might be needed by university administrators. See Figure 6-5.

Data Dictionaries

Data dictionaries play an important role in the database management approach. A **data dictionary** consists of a directory or catalog of information that describes the field, record, and file contents and relationships of a database.

data dictionary
A directory of information that defines the field, record, and file contents and relationships of a database.

```
F1-Help    F2-Files    F3-Features    F4-Print    F5-Edit    F6-Style
Database   TEST.FOL                                1% Full    Line    1
  [          1          2          3          4          5          6          7        ]

  First Name: 2w10      Last Name: 1w15

  Company: 3w20
  Address: 4w15
  Suite: 5w15
  City, State, Zip: 6w25

  Phone: 7w15        FAX: 8w15

  Client Type: 9w15
```

The data dictionary of a common database package shows the width for each field in the database in number of characters.

It also includes a data dictionary program that may be part of a DBMS or can be a separate software package. Thus, you can think of a data dictionary as a file of *data definitions* that define the characteristics of the data elements in a database, as well as a program that manages the creation, use, and maintenance of the information in the data dictionary.

A data dictionary contains the names and descriptions of all types of data records in a database as well as their interrelationships. It also contains information specifying the procedures required for end users' access of databases, the use of databases by application programs, and database security. Some *active data dictionaries* may even enforce standard data definitions whenever a DBMS is used to access a database. As an example, an active data dictionary would not let you enter the name of a student into a student database if it exceeded the size of the name field specified in the dictionary.

Database Structures

Database management packages organize data in several basic ways. That is, these packages establish relationships among the records in a database using one of several different database *models* or *structures*. Then the DBMS package can use this structure to provide you with quick and easy access to information stored in databases. At the present time, most database management packages use *hierarchical, network,* or *relational* structures to organize data. See Figure 6-6.

The Hierarchical Structure

hierarchical structure
A logical data structure in which the relationships between records form a hierarchy or tree structure. Typically, the relationships among records are one-to-many, since each data element is related only to one element above it.

Early mainframe database management system packages used a **hierarchical structure.** In the hierarchical structure, the relationship among records forms a *hierarchy,* or tree structure. In the traditional hierarchical model, all records are dependent and arranged in multilevel structures, consisting of one *root* record and one or more *subordinate* levels. Thus, all of the relationships among records are *one-to-many,* since each data element is related only to one element above it. The data element or record at the highest level of the hierarchy (the "department" data element in Figure 6-6) is called the *root.* Notice that a data element can be located by moving downward from a root and along the *branches* of this structure until a desired record (such as the student data element) is located.

The Network Structure

network structure
A logical data structure that allows many-to-many relationships among data records. It allows access of a data element by following several paths because any data element or record can be related to any number of other data elements.

Many mainframe DBMS packages still use a **network structure.** The network structure was designed to represent more complex logical relationships by allowing *many-to-many* relationships among records. That is, the network model can access a data element by following one of several paths, because any data element or record can be related to any number of other data elements. For example, in Figure 6-6, departmental records can be related to more than one student record, and student records can be related to more than one course record. Thus, you could locate all student records for a particular department or all course records related to a particular student.

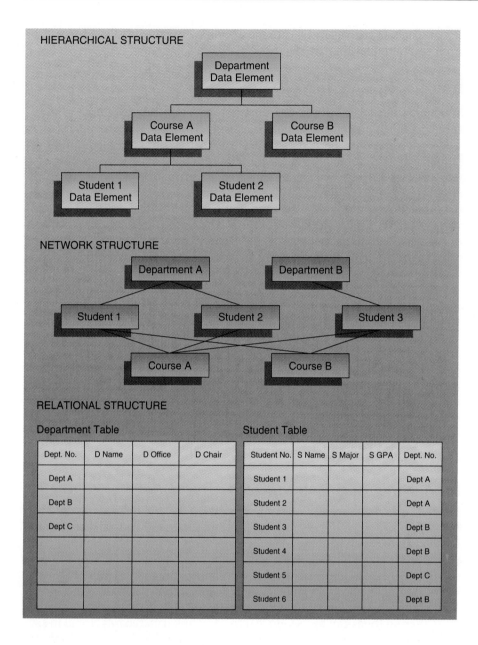

HIERARCHICAL STRUCTURE

NETWORK STRUCTURE

RELATIONAL STRUCTURE

Department Table

Dept. No.	D Name	D Office	D Chair
Dept A			
Dept B			
Dept C			

Student Table

Student No.	S Name	S Major	S GPA	Dept. No.
Student 1				Dept A
Student 2				Dept A
Student 3				Dept B
Student 4				Dept B
Student 5				Dept C
Student 6				Dept B

Figure 6-6
Data can be organized using hierarchical, network, or relational structures.

The Relational Structure

Microcomputer database management system (DBMS) packages typically use a more flexible kind of database structure—the **relational structure.** Many mainframe and minicomputer DBMS also use this relational structure, so it has become the most popular of the three database models. Relational database management systems are easy to understand and use. As shown in Figure 6-6, a relational DBMS allows a user to think of data as arranged in *tables,* with the records as rows and the fields as columns. This simple tabular file structure is a major benefit of the relational database model. A rela-

relational structure
A logical data structure that uses a tabular structure in which data elements are arranged in tables, with records as rows and fields as columns.

tional database management package also allows you to easily retrieve data from several tables that are logically related in some way.

Which Structure Is Best?

The hierarchical data structure is a natural model for databases used in structured, routine types of transaction processing. However, there are many cases where information is needed about records that do not have hierarchical relationships. For example, as we saw in Figure 6-6, students can enroll in several courses offered by several different departments. While hierarchical structures can be modified to allow such multiple relationships, a network data structure could more easily handle the many-to-many relationships involved. It is thus more flexible than the hierarchical structure for many types of business operations. However, like the hierarchical model, its relationships must be specified in advance. So, the network model cannot easily handle nonroutine, *ad hoc* (as needed) requests for information by end users.

Relational databases, on the other hand, can easily provide information in response to your *ad hoc* requests. That's because all of the relationships among the data elements in a relationally organized database do not need to be specified when the database is created. Database management software can create new tables of data relationships using parts of the data from several tables. Thus, relational databases are easier for programmers to work with and easier to maintain than the hierarchical and network models. The major limitation of the relational model is that a relational DBMS cannot process large numbers of business transactions as quickly and efficiently as those based on the other models. However, this performance gap is narrowing with the development of advanced relational DBMS software.

Identifying and Linking Data

The data structures we have just mentioned use several different methods to help you locate and retrieve data from files and databases. Thus, all data records usually contain one or more identification fields or **keys,** which identify the record so it can be located. For example, the social security number of a person is often used as a **primary key** field because it uniquely identifies the data records of individuals in a student, employee, customer and other personnel files and databases.

Other methods can be used to identify and link data records stored in several different database files. For instance, hierarchical and network databases may use **pointer fields.** These are fields within a record that indicate (point to) the location of another record that is related to it in the same file or in another file. Hierarchical and network database management systems use this method to link records so they can retrieve information from several different files. See Figure 6-7.

Relational database management packages use *primary keys* to link records. Each file or table in a relational database must contain a primary key. This field (or fields) uniquely identifies each record in a file and must also be found in other related files. In Figure 6-8, "department number" is the primary key in the department records table and is also a field in the student records table. So a relational database management package could easily pro-

keys
One or more fields within a data record that are used to identify it or control its use.

primary key
A field within a data record that uniquely identifies that record so it can be located. A social security number is an example of a typical primary key field.

pointer fields
Fields within a record that point to the location of another record that is related to it in the same or different file.

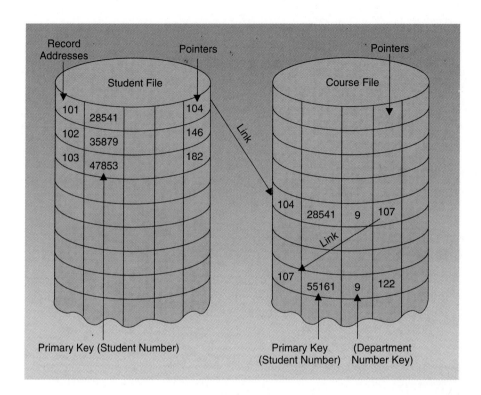

Figure 6-7
Keys and pointers can be used to locate records.

vide you with information from both tables. Suppose you asked, Who is the department chair for student 5's major? Within seconds the DBMS would *join* the two tables, locate the appropriate records, retrieve the appropriate fields, and display the answer "D. Thomas" on your video screen.

Quick Quiz

1. A _____ approach consolidates data into a database of records available to many application programs.

Figure 6-8
Common keys help you retrieve data from several tables.

Department Table

Dept. No.	D Name	D Office	D Chair
Dept A			J. Wilson
Dept B			S. Alvarez
Dept C			D. Thomas

Student Table

Student No.	S Name	S Major	S GPA	Dept. No.
Student 1				Dept A
Student 2				Dept A
Student 3				Dept B
Student 4				Dept B
Student 5				Dept C
Student 6				Dept B

2. A _____ package helps you do database development, maintenance, reporting, and application development.

3. Data can be organized into data fields, records, _____ , and databases.

4. A _____ describes the field, record, and file contents and relationships of a database.

5. A _____ database structure organizes data into interrelated tabular formats.

Answers: 1. database management   2. database management system   3. files   4. data dictionary   5. relational

Using Database Management Packages

Let's take a look at how you could use a database management package to help manage your data. For example, you could use a DBMS package to help you manage the data about the employees of a business or other type of or-

Figure 6-9
These are the basic activities of the database management process.

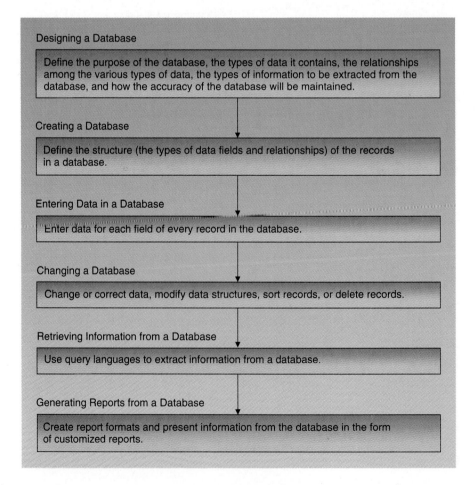

ganization. Figure 6-9 outlines the six steps of the database management process you could use.

Designing a Database

The first step of the database management process is to design the database you will create and use. You should decide on the purpose of the database, the form and content of information you will want to extract from the database, the types of data it will have to contain, the relationships between the various types of data, and how you will maintain the accuracy of the database. For example, you may decide that you want to:

- Develop a database of employee records
- Retrieve selected information about employees
- Produce a variety of reports about employees
- Periodically update the records in the database to reflect changes in employee job status and wage payments

Before you create a database, you should carefully think about the *design* or *structure* of the records in each file or table that might be created. You should also consider how these files or tables can be related to other files and tables. For example, suppose you decide that you want to create an *employee database* that includes a *payroll file* for the employees of your company. This payroll file will contain important payment information about your company's employees. Each payroll record will contain data fields about individual employees required to properly pay them what they are owed each week.

Creating a File

The next thing you do when using a database management program is to *create* the structure of the files or tables you want in your database. What this means is that you are going to specify the characteristics of the fields that make up each record in a file you are creating for a particular application. This procedure is also known as *defining* the structure of the records in your database. That procedure is supported by the *data dictionary* function of a database management package.

For demonstration purposes, let's assume an application where we can limit each record to seven fields with the following field definitions in each record:

1. Employee name (NAME), 15 character positions
2. Social security number (SSNO), 9 character positions
3. Gender (GENDER), 1 character position
4. Department (DEPT), 14 character positions
5. Hourly rate of pay (RATE), 5 numeric positions, 2 decimal places
6. Number of hours worked (HOURS), 4 numeric positions, 1 decimal place
7. Amount of pay (PAY), 6 numeric positions, 2 decimal places

Figure 6-10 illustrates the entries you might make in creating the record format for a simple payroll file. This is a typical *record definition* screen displayed by a database management package.

Figure 6-10
Creating a database file involves
specifying the characteristics of
the fields in your data records.

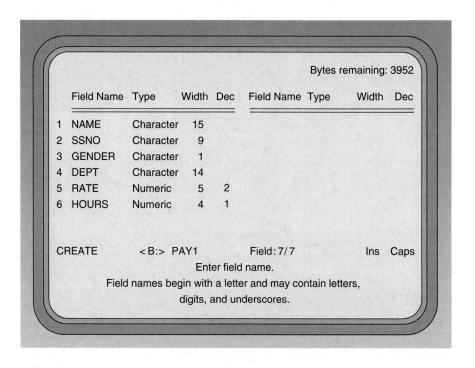

	Field Name	Type	Width	Dec
1	NAME	Character	15	
2	SSNO	Character	9	
3	GENDER	Character	1	
4	DEPT	Character	14	
5	RATE	Numeric	5	2
6	HOURS	Numeric	4	1

Bytes remaining: 3952

CREATE   < B:> PAY1   Field: 7/7   Ins   Caps
Enter field name.
Field names begin with a letter and may contain letters,
digits, and underscores.

Entering Data into a Database

Once you have created the structure of a file, you really have created an
"empty" file. Your next step is to begin to enter data into that file. Most database management packages provide a *data entry screen* to help you with entry of data into files and databases. You can then begin to type in data into
each field of a record. Figure 6-11 shows what a data entry screen looks like
while you are entering data into the fields of a record in the payroll file. Most
database management packages automatically save each data record or groups
of data records you enter onto a magnetic disk of your computer system. They
also allow you to retrieve a copy of a file or database from disk and load it into
the memory of your computer.

Changing a Database

After you have used your database for a while, you may decide that some
changes are needed. Most database management packages help you change a
database in one of the four following ways:

- You can change or correct data in specific fields for selected records in
  a file. For example, an employer might give selected employees a pay
  raise. This would be shown by increasing their hourly rate as recorded
  in a payroll file.

- You can change the structure (the characteristics of selected fields) of
  the records in a file. For example, you can increase the size (the number
  of characters allowed) in the name field of employees.

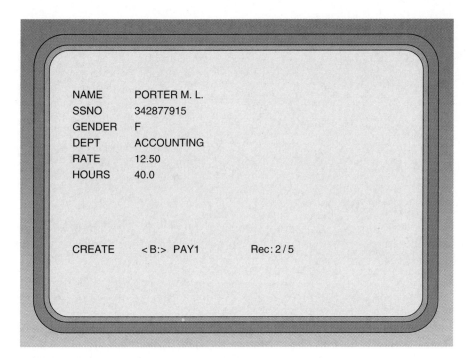

Figure 6-11
You can key in data to create a
data record in a database file.

- You can also change the order of records in a file by sorting activities. For example, you can sort a payroll file into alphabetical order by employees' names.
- Finally, you can generate new files that are variations of the files already in the database and delete unwanted records and files. For example, you can remove the records of terminated employees from a payroll file.

Retrieving Information from a Database

You can now see that a database management package allows you to create, enter, and change data in a database file. It's time to see how to retrieve information from a database. Database management programs provide several methods to assist in the retrieval of information. This allows you to be selective in both the format and contents of information you wish to see displayed or printed.

You can use a database management package to ask for information from a database and receive an immediate response in the form of video displays or printed reports. No difficult programming is required. A **query language** feature lets you easily obtain immediate responses to *ad hoc* inquiries: You merely key in a few short inquiries. A **report generator** feature allows you to quickly specify a report format for information you want presented as a report.

Query Languages

Query languages allow you to display or print out information in several basic ways. Easiest of all is to merely list all the data fields of all data records in

query language
A high-level, English-like language provided by a database management package that enables users to easily extract data and information from a database.

report generator
A feature of database management system packages that allows an end user to quickly specify a report format for the display of information retrieved from a database.

a file or database. However, this detailed *file listing* is not very easy to use since too much information is provided for most end users to absorb quickly.

It would be more productive for you to display only the data fields you want from selected records in a file or database. For instance, you could query a payroll file to display the names and departments of all female employees who worked more than 40 hours in a specific week. Finally, a query language can do mathematical calculations and provide you with statistics about the data records in a file or database. You could count the number of male and female employees who worked overtime, or compute the total amounts of overtime paid to groups of employees as recorded in a payroll file.

SQL and QBE

Figure 6-12 illustrates the use of a query language for a simple request for employee information. A query language that is becoming a standard for many database management system packages is called SQL, or *structured query language*. The basic form of an SQL query is:

SELECT . . . FROM . . . WHERE

SELECT lists the characteristics or *attributes* you want reported, FROM indicates which files or *tables* contain the information you are looking for, and WHERE specifies the *conditions* the reported information must meet.

For example, if a hospital personnel manager wanted to display information about hospital employees who are female physicians, he or she might use the SQL query shown in Figure 6-12a. That SQL query retrieves the names, specialties, and departments of female physicians from the Employee table and department managers' names from the Department table in the hospital's Personnel database, and displays them as shown in Figure 6-12b. This database operation is called a *join* because it combines data from the two tables based on a primary key field (Department) found in both tables.

Another popular query language is QBE or *query by example*. This method is simpler than using SQL queries. All you have to do is fill in or check boxes displayed on your video screen to ask for information you want. For example, Figure 6-13 shows how you could request information using the query-by-example method with a popular database management package like Paradox or dBase IV.

report generator
A feature of database management system packages that allows an end user to quickly specify a report format for the display of information retrieved from a database.

report form
Specifies the title and column headings of the report you want to produce, lists which data fields from your database will be included, and specifies any subtotals and totals that may be required.

Generating Reports

As we have just seen, most database management packages let you make quick database inquiries. Responses can be quickly displayed on your video screen or printed on your system printer. However, what if you want output printed or displayed in a report format that you can use repeatedly, with features such as titles, columns, headings, and totals? Then you should use the report generation capabilities provided by the **report generator** feature that is part of most database management packages.

The first thing you must do is create a **report form** or *report format*. This report form specifies the title and column headings of the report you want to produce. It should also specify what data fields from your database will be in-

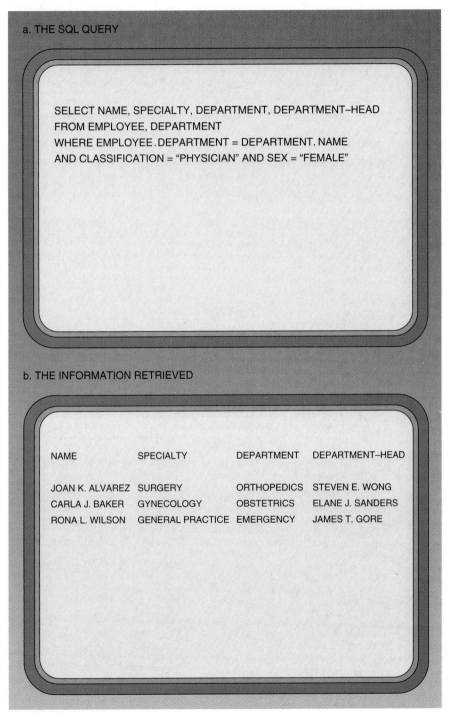

a. THE SQL QUERY

SELECT NAME, SPECIALTY, DEPARTMENT, DEPARTMENT–HEAD
FROM EMPLOYEE, DEPARTMENT
WHERE EMPLOYEE.DEPARTMENT = DEPARTMENT.NAME
AND CLASSIFICATION = "PHYSICIAN" AND SEX = "FEMALE"

b. THE INFORMATION RETRIEVED

NAME	SPECIALTY	DEPARTMENT	DEPARTMENT–HEAD
JOAN K. ALVAREZ	SURGERY	ORTHOPEDICS	STEVEN E. WONG
CARLA J. BAKER	GYNECOLOGY	OBSTETRICS	ELANE J. SANDERS
RONA L. WILSON	GENERAL PRACTICE	EMERGENCY	JAMES T. GORE

Figure 6-12a
This SQL query selectively retrieves information about employees.

Figure 6-12b
This is how SQL might display requested employee information.

cluded and whether subtotals and totals are required. Once this blank report form is created, it can be stored on your magnetic disk for later use. Whenever you wish, you can use the form to extract and present data from your

Figure 6-13
QBE makes it easy to retrieve information. In this example, 125 is an "example operator" that is placed in the Cust ID field to join the ORDERS and CUSTOMER tables in order to display selected name and address information for all customers who have ordered stock number 519.

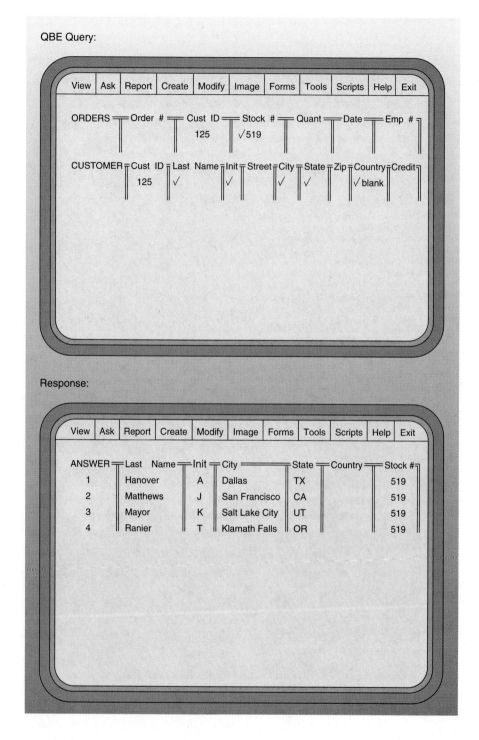

database. The photograph on page 183 shows the use of a *report format screen* provided by a database management package to create the format of a report.

Thus, database management packages enable you to generate reports based on report forms you create. You can use these forms to display or print

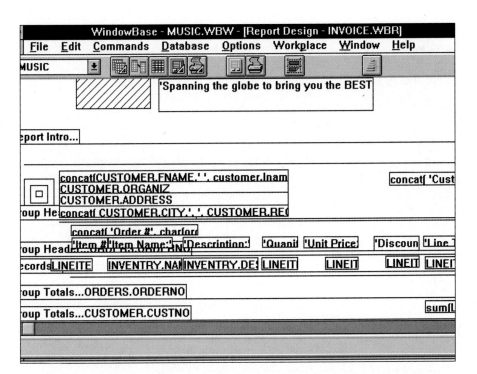

This is a report format screen in a database management package for specifying the columns in a report you wish to create.

This report produced by a database management package presents selected data extracted from a customer order file.

reports using data extracted from any file or database you have. This not only includes data already stored in the database, but information resulting from calculations (totals, averages, and other simple arithmetic functions) performed for you by the DBMS. This gives you a powerful reporting capability.

REAL-WORLD EXAMPLE

The Seattle Symphony: SQL for the Arts

SQL and a database management package have been a big help to the Seattle Symphony. Its IS director, Deborah Braun, says a database management approach using the SQL query language has enabled the symphony to really personalize its ticketing and fundraising applications. The symphony uses Artsoft/SQL as an add-on package to its SQL-based Sybase database management system. This combination provides marketing, ticketing, accounting, fundraising, and box office management applications to the symphony.

Braun particularly likes the ability of the ticketing system to display a three-dimensional seating chart that allows box office telephone operators to check seating availability for several concerts at a time. With this system, operators can find the best available seat "with the touch of a button, instead of having to hunt around the charts," she says. The marketing capabilities of the system are also a big hit. For example, subscribers can easily be identified based on many different factors. This ability is really important to the symphony's marketing and fundraising efforts. That's because when it comes to promotional mailings, says Braun, the symphony is "always looking for a new base of people to hit."

1. How does an SQL capability help the Seattle Symphony?

2. Why do you think the Sybase DBMS package needed an add-on package like Artsoft/SQL for this application?

For instance, you could print payroll reports for all employees or only for employees who worked overtime, including totals, subtotals, and average wages paid. The photograph on page 183 shows a report produced by a database management package. The Orders for Customer Report presents selected data from a customer order file.

Quick Quiz

1. In _____ a database, you define the purpose, types of data and relationships, and types of information to be extracted from a database.

2. In _____ a database, you use a DBMS to define the structure of the records in a database.

3. Once you have defined the structure of the records in a database you can _____ into the database.

4. A _____ lets you easily obtain immediate responses to inquiries from a database.

5. A _____ lets you quickly specify a format for information you want presented as a report.

Answers: 1. designing 2. creating 3. enter data 4. query language 5. report generator

Other Data Management Software

Developments in information technology have created many useful and novel ways to manage a variety of forms of data. For example, software is now available to manage everything from miscellaneous bits of data for end users to large text databases, image databases, and even multimedia databases. Let's take a brief look at how these data management developments help end users and organizations manage diverse forms of data resources.

Personal Information Managers

A popular software package you can use for information management and retrieval is the **personal information manager (PIM).** These packages help end users store, organize, and retrieve text and numerical data in the form of notes, lists, clippings, tables, memos, letters, reports, and so on. As an example, you can enter information randomly about people, companies, deadlines, appointments, meetings, projects, and financial results. The PIM package will automatically organize such data with minimal instructions from you.

Relationships are automatically established among pieces of data by the software based on specifications you provide. The PIM might establish relationships between items based on key words you specify that are common to several topics in the PIM's *information base*. Then the PIM will help you by retrieving pieces of related information in any order and in a variety of forms. Information can be retrieved as a list of appointments, meetings, or other things to do; the timetable for a project; or a display of key facts and financial data about a competitor.

Text Database Management

Text databases are a natural outgrowth of the use of computers to create and store documents electronically. Commercial bibliographic data banks of business, economic, and other information are stored in large text databases. Some

personal information manager (PIM)
A software package that helps end users store, organize, and retrieve text and numerical data in the form of notes, lists, memos, and a variety of other forms.

text databases
Any database of text documents containing information in the form of abstracts or complete articles from newspapers, magazines, and other published sources.

```
File  Edit  Schedule  Clear  Write  Lookup  Phone  View  Report

    Name: Joswick International Data     Addrs: 6721 Brookside
 Contact: Alec Turner                         : Suite 273
   Phone: 214-555-3423  X:        CC:         :
   Title: Owner                         City: Dallas
     Sec: Chris                        State: TX
    Dear: Mr. Turner                     ZIP: 76062

    Call:▼ 1/10/92    9:30 am   Re: Follow up on information sent
 Meeting: 1/17/92   11:00 am   Re: Final demo
   To-Do: 1/09/92    3:35 pm   Re: Make travel arrangements

 Last Results: Had public relations send company info
    ID/Status: Prospect              Referred by: Jason Newman

Next Objective: Close Sale        Industry Type: High tech
   Probability: 30,000                 Birthdate: 6/25/52
   YTD Revenue: 350,000             Company Size: Small

      Reminder: Currently seeking other proposals
        User 8:
        User 9:
 C:\ACT2\DATABASE\ACT                        A Name 116 of 327
F1=Help  Thu 09-Jan-92  9:58 am
```

Personal information management packages allow for information to be organized in a variety of ways.

Figure 6-14
Public information services provide a wealth of information from online data banks.

Dow Jones Information Service
Provides statistical data banks on stock market and other financial market activity, and on all corporations listed on the New York and American stock exchanges, plus 800 selected other companies. Its Dow Jones News/Retrieval system provides bibliographic data banks on business, financial, and general news from *The Wall Street Journal, Barron's,* the Dow Jones News Service, The Associated Press, *Wall Street Week,* and the 21–volume American Academic Encyclopedia.

Mead Data Central
Lexis bibliographic data bank provides legal research information, such as case law, court decisions, federal regulations, and legal articles. *Nexis* provides a full text bibliographic database of over 100 newspapers, magazines, newsletters, news services, government documents, and so on. It includes full text and abstracts from *the New York Times* and the complete 29–volume Encyclopedia Britannica.

Lockheed Information Systems
DIALOG system offers over 75 different data banks in agriculture, business, economics, education, energy, engineering, environment, foundations, general news publications, government, international business, patents, pharmaceuticals, science, and social sciences.

text databases are marketed on CD-ROM (compact disk read-only memory). These compact optical disks are designed for use with microcomputer systems. Major corporations and government agencies have developed large text databases containing documents of all kinds. They use *text database management systems* software to help create, store, search, retrieve, modify, and assemble documents and other information stored as text data in such databases. Microcomputer versions of such software are available to help you manage and use text databases on compact disks.

Access to large, privately owned databases, or **data banks,** is available for a fee to end users and organizations from commercial information services networks, such as Interactive Data Corporation, Dow Jones Information Services, Lockheed Information Systems, and Mead Data Central. Data is available in the form of statistics on economic and demographic activity from *statistical* data banks. Or you can receive abstracts from hundreds of newspapers, magazines, and other periodicals from *bibliographic* data banks. See Figure 6-14.

data banks
A comprehensive collection of libraries of data, especially large statistical and text databases owned by government agencies or private organizations.

Image Database Management

Image management is a fast-growing form of data management. It allows you to electronically capture, store, process, and retrieve images of all kinds, especially business and government documents. These documents may include numeric data, text, handwriting, graphics, photographs, and video segments. One of the fastest growing image management applications is *transaction document image processing.* Documents such as customers correspondence, sales orders, invoices, application forms, and service requests are captured electronically and routed to end users throughout the organization for processing.

image management
A form of data management that allows you to electronically capture, store, process, and retrieve images of all kinds, especially business and government documents.

For example, a customer application form for a bank loan might be captured by an optical scanner and indexed by an image database management system. It would then be electronically routed to various end user workstations for editing and financial and credit analysis. Finally, it could be retrieved electronically and displayed at a loan officer's workstation where a decision on the loan application is made. Such image management systems have resulted in significant productivity improvements and cost savings.

Hypertext

Hypertext is a technology that allows you to use text databases interactively. A *hypertext document* is text in electronic form that is indexed so that it can be quickly searched by the reader. If you are using a hypertext software package, you can highlight a term on a hypertext document displayed on your computer video screen, press a key, and the computer will instantly display a passage of text related to that term. Once you finish reading that *pop-up* display, you can return to what you were reading originally or jump to another part of the document instantly. Thus, using hypertext software provides an environment for *interactive reading* of text material.

hypertext
A methodology for the construction and interactive use of text material in which a body of text in electronic form is indexed in a variety of ways so that it can be quickly searched by a reader.

Several software packages are available for the development of hypertext documents. One of the most widely used is the HyperCard package for the Apple Macintosh microcomputer. In HyperCard, the basic unit of text is called a *card.* A hypertext document consists of *stacks,* or collections, of interrelated

Hypertext and hypermedia allow the user to point to an element on the screen to access further information related to the subject in text or other forms of media.

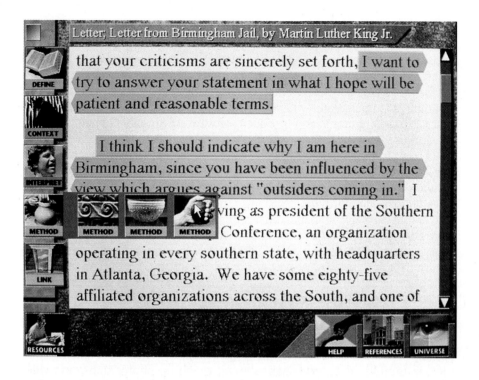

and indexed cards. Thus, hypertext document packages are sometimes called *stackware*. Hypertext documents can be programmed to let a reader *navigate* through a document by following one or more *scripts*. This kind of hypertext document can lead the reader through its contents in several different ways. For example, a reader could choose several different plots or story lines in a hypertext novel.

Hypermedia And Interactive Video

hypermedia
Documents that contain multiple forms of media, including text, graphics, video and sound, that can be interactively searched like hypertext.

By definition, hypertext contains only text and a limited amount of graphics. **Hypermedia** technology provides you with multiple forms of media, including text, graphics, video, sound, and so on. To experience hypermedia, you need to add a multimedia circuit board and a CD-ROM drive to your PC. Proponents of hypermedia expect electronic multimedia documents to become as popular as more traditional paper documents such as books, encyclopedias, magazines, and newspapers. Figure 6-15 shows a diagram of the components of the Perseus Hypermedia Project. Perseus will contain up to 100 megabytes of hypertext and 10,000 hypermedia images of the ancient Greek civilizations.

interactive video
The integration of image processing with text, audio, and video processing technologies that makes possible interactive multimedia presentations.

When hypermedia contains animated video images, it uses a technology called interactive video. Interactive video systems integrate image processing with text, audio, and video processing technologies. To use software for developing **interactive video** applications, you need a microcomputer with significant processing power and memory, add-on circuit boards, and both hard and optical disk storage. This allows you to digitally capture, edit, and combine text, pictures, and sound into multimedia business and educational presentations.

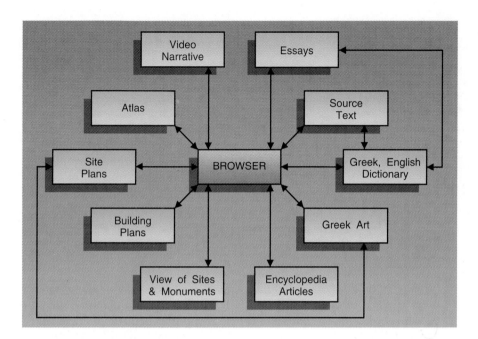

Figure 6-15
The Perseus hypermedia project
provides an electronic multimedia
resource on ancient Greece.

Education and training are prime prospects for interactive video applications. For instance, an interactive video session for training auto mechanics has been produced on optical disks. It combines animated graphics displays of engine parts, electronic diagnostic charts, lists of major topics and facts, video clips of mechanics working on vehicles, and engine sounds helpful in engine diagnostics. Interactive video can use hypermedia technology so you can see and hear material *interactively*. That is, you do not have to view a pro-

This interactive video display
system includes a laser disk
player, touchscreen, and projection
screen.

REAL-WORLD EXAMPLE

Volkswagen Corporation:
Object-Oriented Database Management

Volkswagen is constructing a new on-line system that monitors every task involved in building, distributing, selling, and servicing automobiles built by the German firm, such as all Volkswagen and Audi models. Dubbed Euro Elan, the application—expected to reach some 110,000 end users by 1997—is an effort to link car dealerships and factories across several continents to better track inventory, building processes, and other aspects of the car business. Volkswagen chose an object-oriented database management system from Versant Object Technology Corp. to underpin the system. "The idea is to build a system that all our distributors can use to track cars, from the building of them through selling and maintenance, all the way to recycling them later on," said Joseph Bayrhammer, manager of the technical team at Euro Marketing Systems, a Volkswagen subsidiary made up of representitives from 12 Volkswagen and Audi importers across Europe.

Although the Volkswagen is the most popular car in Europe, after taxes and other fees are deducted, the company makes a profit of only about $26 on each car sold, according to *AutoWeek* magazine. Volkswagen sold 3.5 million cars worldwide in 1992. Finding a way to streamline costs is imperative for Volkswagen, which *AutoWeek* said is the highest-cost high-volume carmaker in the world. Volkswagen expects to see gains from this application in the form of reduced parts inventory and faster customer service. For example, if a customer walks through a showroom looking for a black Volkswagen Jetta with sunroof, antilock brakes, and no air conditioning, a sales representative could use Euro Elan to search for such a vehicle at any of 10,000 dealerships. Currently, such a search is time consuming because it involves many phone calls and manual "eyeballing" of production records, Bayrhammer said.

1. What is one possible reason why Volkswagen chose object-oriented database management as the foundation of its Euro Elan application?

2. How will Euro Elan help Volkswagen lower its costs?

---

gram sequentially. You can move among various segments randomly or according to pre-established paths indicated by menus and prompts. Though expensive to produce, interactive video is being used for training purposes by large business firms, government agencies, and other organizations.

 ## Quick Quiz

1. A _____ package helps you store, organize, and retrieve miscellaneous data and information.

2. A _____ database is used by commercial data bank services for business, economic, political, and other information.

3. An _____ database can store images of business and government documents.

4. A _____ capability enables you to read a document interactively.

5. A _____ capability can provide you with text, graphics, video, and sound.

Answers   1. personal information manager   2. text   3. image
4. hypertext   5. hypermedia

E T H I C S

Ethical Issues in Database Management

Any use of computers to manage data can quickly raise several ethical questions. Whose data is it? Who should manage the data? How and why should access to the data be controlled and protected? If databases contain data about individuals, the questions can get even more intense. Do you have a right to privacy concerning data about you? What about the public's right to know? Do organizations have any property rights to data they collect about you? As you can see, these questions are real, not just topics for academic discussion.

Many ethical issues about data today concern the use of data about individuals captured by transaction processing systems and stored in organizational databases. We're not talking about sensitive personal data about people in confidential personnel files. Personal transaction data is retrieved from every check you write, every credit card purchase you make, every magazine you subscribe to, and every insurance form you fill out.

The power of computers, the intelligence of analytical software, and the efficiency of computerized databases are combined to extract data about your demographics, your finances, your health history and accident record, and your buying habits and preferences. This information is then used by organizations for everything from targeting you for telemarketing campaigns and mass mailings to deciding whether or not to extend you credit or car insurance. What makes this issue even more serious is that, many times, information about you is sold to other organizations so they can target you for their own purposes. Companies known as *information brokers* now do business by arranging such deals.

One way to confront this issue has been formulated by Richard Mason of Southern Methodist University.[1] It is based on the concept that information forms the *intellectual capital* of individuals, and information systems should not rob people of their intellectual capital. For example, people should not lose information without compensation and without their permission or be denied access to information or be exposed to erroneous information.

Mason proposes a new *social contract,* where information systems will help ensure everyone's right to fulfill his or her human potential. In this social contract, information systems would be designed to ensure accuracy and not invade a person's privacy. Channels of information would be protected and information made accessible to avoid information illiteracy. Finally, information systems would be designed to protect an individual's intellectual capital from unauthorized exposure, loss, or damage.

(continued on following page)

(continued from previous page)

What Do You Think?

Mason summarizes the ethical questions involved with the acronym PAPA—Privacy, Accuracy, Property, and Accessibility:

- *Privacy.* What information about you or your associations must you reveal to others, under what conditions, and with what safeguards?

- *Accuracy.* Who is responsible for the authenticity, fidelity, and accuracy of information?

- *Property.* Who owns information? What are the just and fair prices for its exchange?

- *Accessibility.* What information does any person or organization have a right or privilege to obtain, under what conditions, and with what safeguards?

What do you think?

---

[1] Richard Mason, "Four Ethical Issues of the Information Age," *MIS Quarterly*, March 1986, pp. 5-12.

End Note: Data Management versus Decision Support

Which should you use—a database management package or an electronic spreadsheet? That's a question that concerns many end users and end user consultants. The familiarity of a spreadsheet's worksheet format and the computational power and ease of use of spreadsheet programs made them a runaway choice of millions of end users. Microcomputer database management packages came on the scene later, and did not have the same power, familiarity, or easy-to-use features that spreadsheets provided. So spreadsheet programs are still much more widely used than database management packages.

But some end user consultants question this state of affairs. They feel that too many end users are using spreadsheets for jobs that could be better done by database managers. That is, electronic spreadsheets, whose forte is analysis and decision support, are being used to store, manage, and report data, which, as you have seen in this chapter, are the key functions of database management packages.

Much of the reason for this reluctance to use a DBMS package is the inertia of millions of end users who have become accustomed to using spreadsheets as a versatile productivity tool. So they continue to use spreadsheets to help them do jobs that could be done better by other packages. Another major reason is that most database management packages do not have the computational, easy-to-use, and presentation features of many spreadsheet packages.

All this is changing, thanks to significant improvements in the features offered by newer versions of database management packages. Many now provide menu-driven and graphical-user interfaces to make them a lot easier for you to use. Their computational power has been increased with the addition of built-in mathematical functions. And some even do graphics!

So now the question for end users is a basic one—do you want to do data management or decision support? That is, do you want to do a lot of *ad hoc* analytical modeling and mathematical computations to help you analyze business situations and make decisions? If so, a spreadsheet is the package for you. On the other hand, do you want to build files and databases to organize, protect, and store data and to routinely update that data due to transactions that occur? Do you want to quickly and easily retrieve data and present information in the form of queries and a variety of reports? Then you should use a database management package.

It's that simple. Use electronic spreadsheets to give you analytical power and decision support. And use database management packages to manage and retrieve information from your data resources.

Summary

You and Database Management   Database management has become a popular end user application. For many years, organizations depended on a file processing approach in which separate computer programs were used to update independent data files and produce documents and reports. In the database management approach, the data needed by different applications is consolidated into several common databases instead of being stored in several independent data files.

Database Management Software   The database management approach involves using a database management package to manage updating and maintaining common databases and sharing of the data in a database by different application programs. Database management packages allow you to create a file or database structure, enter data, and update and make other changes to maintain the database. You can also receive quick responses and create reports by using the query language and report generator features of the DBMS. Finally, a database management package helps you design and develop end user applications.

Database Management Fundamentals   Data must be organized in some logical manner so it can be efficiently accessed and processed. Thus, data is commonly organized into logical data elements: characters, fields, records, files, and databases. Most database management packages use hierarchical, network, or relational structures to organize data. Key fields are used to identify records so that they can be located. Definitions of data elements and their interrelationships are typically stored in a data dictionary for use by a DBMS.

Other Data Management Software   Software is now available to manage a variety of forms of data. This includes personal information managers to organize miscellaneous pieces of end user information, software to manage text and image databases, and software packages for interactive use of hypertext and hypermedia systems.

Key Terms and Concepts

character
creating a database
data banks
data dictionary
data management versus decision
  support
database
database maintenance
database management approach
database management system
field
file
file management package
file processing approach
hierarchical structure
hypermedia
hypertext

image databases
image management
interactive video
key
network structure
personal information manager
pointer
primary key
query by example
query language
record
relational structure
report form
report generator
structured query language
text database

Review Quiz

True/False

_____ 1. A database management approach relies on independent data files.

_____ 2. A file processing approach consolidates records into a single common file.

_____ 3. A database is a collection of interrelated records and files.

_____ 4. A character is a single alphabetic, numeric, or other symbol.

_____ 5. A database management package allows you to easily display information and produce reports.

_____ 6. A file management package controls the creation, interrogation, and maintenance of a database.

_____ 7. Most microcomputer database management packages use a relational database structure.

_____ 8. When you create a database, you specify the characteristics of each field in the records of a database.

_____ 9. A key is an identification field in a record.

_____ 10. A primary key is an identification field that uniquely identifies a record.

Multiple Choice

_A_ 1. A predesigned report format from a database management package is a

    a. report form.
    b. template.
    c. menu.
    d. macro.

_D_ 2. A field in a data record that identifies the location of a related record is a

    a. key.
    b. primary key.
    c. index.
    d. pointer.

_D_ 3. When you can interactively use a text database, you are using

    a. data management.
    b. text management.
    c. hypermedia.
    d. hypertext.

_C_ 4. When you can interactively use text, graphics, images, sound, and video, you are using

    a. data management.
    b. text management.
    c. hypermedia.
    d. hypertext.

_____ 5. Your name is an example of a

    a. field.
    b. record.
    c. file.
    d. database.

_____ 6. Your name, employee number, department, and salary might form a

    a. field.
    b. record.
    c. file.
    d. database.

_____ 7. A collection of student registration records might form what is called a

    a. field.
    b. record.
    c. file.
    d. database.

_____ 8. An integrated collection of various types of student records would be a

    a. field.
    b. record.

  c. file.
  d. database.

_____ 9. A package that helps an end user store and retrieve miscellaneous pieces of information is a

  a. file manager.
  b. data manager.
  c. personal information manager.
  d. data dictionary.

_____ 10. A program that defines and catalogs the data definitions in a database is a

  a. file manager.
  b. data manager.
  c. personal information manager.
  d. data dictionary.

Fill-in

1. The _____ approach uses independent files of data and specialized programs for each major information processing job of end users.

2. The _____ approach uses integrated collections of data records accessible by end users through a database management system.

3. In the _____ structure, the relationships among records in a database form a tree-like structure.

4. The _____ structure can represent relationships between records in a database where any data element can be related to any number of other data elements.

5. In the _____ structure, the relationships between records in a database can be represented as a series of interrelated tables.

6. When you change, update, or correct the data in a database, you are doing database _____.

7. With a _____ , you can easily interrogate a database to get information you need.

8. Most database management software provides a _____ , which allows you to specify and produce reports from a database.

9. An _____ system electronically captures, stores, processes, and retrieves images of documents and other visual media.

10. Two popular query languages are _____ and _____ .

Questions for Thought and Discussion

1. Why is a database management approach better than a file processing approach?

2. Refer to the Real-World Example of Fairfield University in the chapter. What are several ways the food bank could use its database management package?

3. Why do you think most microcomputer database management packages use a relational database structure instead of the hierarchical or network structures?

4. Refer to the Real-World Example of the Seattle Symphony in the chapter. Could other types of organizations also benefit from this approach? Explain.

5. Do you think that hypertext and hypermedia will replace traditional publications like newspapers, magazines, and books? Explain.

6. What types of end users could benefit most from using personal information managers? Explain.

7. Who owns the information about you captured by the transaction processing systems of banks, retail stores, and insurance companies? What limitations should be established for its use?

8. Which software package would you rather use, an electronic spreadsheet program or a database management system? Explain why, discussing their use for decision support and data management.

9. Refer to the Real-World Example of the Volkswagen Corporation in the chapter. Could other types of organizations benefit from a similar system? Explain how.

10. Identify several types of data management software that you might be able to use in a career you are considering. Briefly explain what they do as well as their benefits and limitations. Make a brief report to the class.

Review Quiz Answers

True/False   1. F 2.. F 3. T 4. T 5. T 6. F 7. T 8. T 9. T 10. T

Multiple Choice   1. a 2. d 3. d 4. c 5. a 6. b 7. c 8. d 9. c 10. d

Fill-in   1. file processing 2. database management 3. hierarchical 4. network 5. relational 6. maintenance 7. query language 8. report generator 9. image processing 10. SQL and QBE

VIEWPOINT

THE WORLD OF COMPUTER GRAPHICS

Computers can help you draw, paint, design, analyze, and present your ideas graphically. That's what **computer graphics** is all about. As we said in Chapter 4, computer graphics can take a variety of forms. All you need is your personal computer and a graphics software package to turn your ideas into graphical reality. Thus, you can

- Create unique forms of visual art with draw and paint programs.

- Design products and structures with computer-aided design and software.

- Analyze data and present results with analytical and presentation graphics packages.

The following pages should give you a good idea of the potential for graphics applications available at your fingertips, whatever your future career choices and opportunities will be.

COMPUTER ART

Computers help artists create stunning visual images of many kinds. Here are a few examples.

Computers help artists create fine art—everything from contemporary art to replicas of the old masters.

Computers can do *fractals* (that is, the geometry of fractured shapes) to create stunningly intricate images.

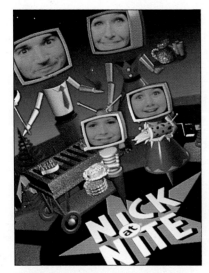

Computers can add motion that brings visual art alive in everything from animated cartoons to TV commercials to flight simulation.

Computer art can now appear surprisingly realistic.

Computers help commercial artists in advertising and publishing create dramatic graphics for advertisements, posters, and product packaging.

COMPUTER-AIDED DESIGN

Computer-aided design (CAD) helps designers in engineering, architecture, interior design, fashion design, and other fields create intricate designs for products, structures, and environments.

Architects use CAD to design buildings and other structures.

Engineers can design complex products and devices with CAD packages and engineering workstations.

Clothing designers use graphics packages to create fashion concepts and detailed patterns.

ANALYTICAL AND PRESENTATION GRAPHICS

In many situations, graphics can help people analyze and communicate better than words or numbers. That's why computer graphics are used to analyze data and present results. For example, **analytical graphics** can help you analyze and interpret data for better decision making by finding patterns in the data that numbers or words may not reveal.

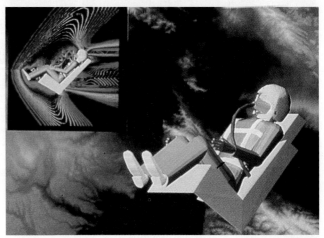

Analytical graphics help scientists analyze everything from the structure of molecules and crystals to weather patterns and the aftereffects of earthquakes and supersonic aerodynamics.

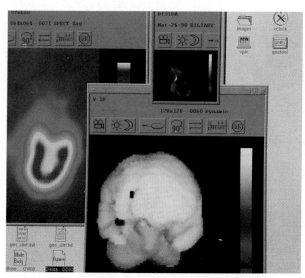

Analytical graphics in health care create three-dimensional images of the human body by using computer-aided tomography (CAT), magnetic resonance imaging (MRI), and ultrasound scanners. Thus, computer graphics dramatically improve diagnostic methods in medicine.

Presentation graphics can help you improve communication of information or ideas in reports, meetings, and other types of presentations. Presentation graphics can be as simple as a bar or pie chart in a report or as elaborate as a computer-controlled "slide show" presentation of video images. Thus, computer graphics can produce visual aids that dramatically increase the effectiveness of your presentations.

Line charts, bar charts, pie charts, and their variations are the most popular types of presentation graphics.

PART III

HARDWARE

In the following chapters, we explore hardware from an
end user's perspective by examining the basic types, capabilities, and applications of computer systems, peripheral devices, and telecommunications networks.
Coverage of computer systems and peripherals stresses
end user and organizational computing uses. You will
also learn how telecommunications networks enable end
users to communicate electronically and share computing resources.

C H A P T E R

7

COMPUTER SYSTEMS: MACHINES FOR END USER AND ORGANIZATIONAL COMPUTING

OUTLINE

You and Computer Systems

The Central Processor

Computer Memory

Types of Computer Systems

Microcomputer Systems

Minicomputer Systems

Mainframe Computer Systems

Networked Computer Systems

Technical Note: How Computers
 Work

Ethics: Ethical Issues in Computer
 Systems

End Note: End Users and Computer
 Systems

LEARNING OBJECTIVES

After reading and studying this
chapter, you should be able to

Describe how computers represent
data and execute instructions.

Outline the major differences in the
capabilities and uses of
microcomputers, minicomputers,
mainframes, and networked
computer systems.

Identify benefits, limitations, and
trends in the major types of
computer systems.

You and Computer Systems

In Chapter 1, you learned that computers are systems of interconnected information processing devices. You also learned that there are several different categories of computer systems. In this chapter, we will expand on those topics and also discuss basic concepts of how computers work.

How computers process data and execute instructions is an important topic. Of course, as a computer-literate end user, you do not need a detailed technical knowledge of computer operations. However, you do need to understand some basic facts and concepts about how computers work. Therefore, in the first part of this chapter, we will explore basic concepts about the functions of computer CPUs and memory, how computers execute instructions, and how computers represent data.

As a computer-literate end user, you also need a basic understanding of how different types of computer systems are designed to meet the information processing needs of end users and their organizations. So later in this chapter, we will discuss the capabilities and uses of the major types of computer systems in use today. This should help you become an informed user of microcomputers and other computer systems.

The Central Processor

central processing unit (CPU)
The unit of a computer system that includes the circuits that control the interpretation and execution of instructions. In many computer systems, the CPU includes an arithmetic-logic unit, a control unit, and other processing and control circuitry.

The **central processing unit (CPU)** is the most vital hardware component of a computer system. It is also known as the central processor, the instruction processor, and the main microprocessor in a microcomputer. As noted in Chapter 1, the two major subunits of the CPU are the arithmetic-logic unit and the **control unit.** The CPU includes specialized circuitry such as **registers** for high-speed, temporary storage of instruction and data elements, and subsidiary processors such as those for arithmetic operations, input/output, and telecommunications support.

The Control Unit

control unit
A unit of the CPU that interprets and directs the execution of instructions.

The control unit directs and controls every other component of a computer system. A control unit obtains instructions from the primary storage unit and, after interpreting the instructions, it transmits directions to the appropriate components of the computer system, ordering them to perform their tasks. For example, the control unit tells the input and secondary storage devices what data and instructions to read into memory. It tells the arithmetic-logic unit where the data to be processed is located in memory, what operations to perform, and where in memory the results are to be stored. Finally, it directs secondary storage and output devices to store processed data and communicate information to end users.

The Arithmetic-Logic Unit

arithmetic-logic unit (ALU)
A unit of the CPU that performs arithmetic and logical operations.

The **arithmetic-logic unit (ALU)** is where arithmetic and comparison operations occur. Data may be transferred from primary storage to the arithmetic-logic unit and then returned to storage several times before processing is complete. The arithmetic-logic unit allows a computer to perform the arithmetic operations of addition, subtraction, multiplication, and division.

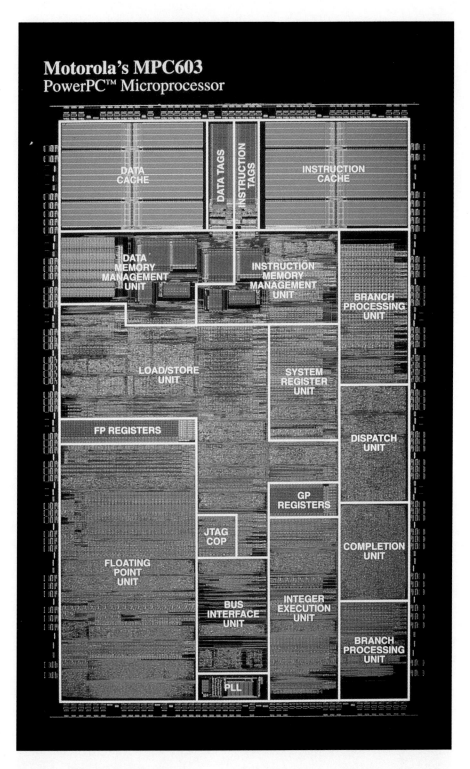

Motorola's MPC603
PowerPC™ Microprocessor

DATA CACHE

DATA TAGS

INSTRUCTION TAGS

INSTRUCTION CACHE

DATA MEMORY MANAGEMENT UNIT

INSTRUCTION MEMORY MANAGEMENT UNIT

BRANCH PROCESSING UNIT

LOAD/STORE UNIT

SYSTEM REGISTER UNIT

DISPATCH UNIT

FP REGISTERS

GP REGISTERS

JTAG COP

COMPLETION UNIT

FLOATING POINT UNIT

BUS INTERFACE UNIT

INTEGER EXECUTION UNIT

BRANCH PROCESSING UNIT

PLL

This Motorola PowerPC microprocessor packs more than 3 million transistors onto a chip.

Through its ability to make comparisons, the ALU can test for various conditions during processing and then perform appropriate operations. Basically, the ALU can compare two numbers to determine which is higher than, equal to, or lower than the other. This ability of the ALU to make comparisons gives computers a *logic* capability. Therefore, computers can make logical changes from one set of program instructions to another based on the results of comparisons made during processing.

Computing overtime pay is a typical example. In a payroll program, the ALU allows a computer to test whether the hours worked by hourly employees exceed 40 hours per week. If the hours are over 40, those employees may have earned overtime pay. If so, a computer would compute overtime pay using a different sequence of instructions than that used for employees who did not work overtime.

CPU Alternatives

The CPUs of many current computer systems use a variety of designs for their processing functions. For example, instead of having one CPU with a single control unit, arithmetic-logic unit, and primary storage unit (called a *uniprocessor* design), CPUs may use a **multiprocessor** design that contains several types of processing units.

multiprocessor
A computer that contains several CPUs or other types of processing units.

Most computers use specialized microprocessors to help the main CPU perform a variety of functions. These microprocessors may be used for input/output control, primary storage management, arithmetic computations, or telecommunications, thus freeing the main central processor (sometimes called the *instruction processor*) to do its main job of executing program instructions. For instance, a microcomputer typically uses specialized support microprocessors such as *arithmetic coprocessors, video display controllers,* or *magnetic disk controllers*. A large computer may also use support microprocessors called *channels* to control the movement of data between the CPU and input/output devices.

Many mainframes and supercomputers use a *multiprocessor* design that consists of multiple CPUs. These systems can then do *multiprocessing*. That

CPU alternatives include math coprocessor chips like the one shown here.

is, they can execute instructions from several different programs at the same time in each of their CPUs. However, some of these computers are designed to provide organizations with a *fault tolerant* capability. This means that computers with multiple CPUs provide a built-in backup to each other if one of them fails. Such computers are widely used in bank ATM systems, airline reservation systems, national credit card systems, and other networks where a fault tolerant capability is essential.

Parallel Processors

One of the newest multiprocessor designs uses hundreds or even thousands of instruction processors organized in clusters or networks. These *parallel processing* systems can therefore execute many instructions at a time in *parallel*. This is a radical departure from the design of most current computers, (called the *von Neumann design*), which execute instructions serially (one at a time). Some parallel processor designs are based on simple models of the human brain, which has more than 10 billion processors called *neurons*. These *neural network* designs are considered to be a key technology in providing advanced artificial intelligence capabilities to future generations of computers.

RISC Processors

Many engineering workstations and other powerful computers rely on a reduced instruction set computer (RISC) processor design. This contrasts with most current computers that use CISC (complex instruction set computer) processors. RISC processors produce a faster CPU by using a smaller *instruction set*. That is, they use a smaller number of the basic *machine instructions* that a processor must execute. By keeping the instruction set simpler than CISC processors, a RISC processor can reduce the time needed to execute program instructions. Though they need more complex software, computers that use RISC processors have become popular for computational-intensive applications, such as those in engineering and the physical sciences. However, RISC technology is the basis for advanced microprocessors like the IBM/Apple/Motorola designed Power PC for a new generation of high-performance personal computers.

This PowerPC microprocessor was designed based on RISC technology.

Computer Memory

A computer's storage activities take place in the memory circuits of its *primary storage unit* and in secondary storage devices such as magnetic disks and tape. All data and program instructions must be moved into the primary storage unit (also called *main memory* or *main storage*) before they can be processed. Thus, a computer stores both data and instructions internally in its memory. This enables a computer to "remember" the details of its assignments and to proceed from one assignment to another automatically, since it can retain data and instructions until needed. Because computers can store their operating instructions internally, they can process data *automatically,* that is, without continual intervention by end users.

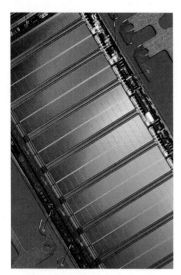

This is an enlargement of a powerful memory chip.

A computer's primary storage unit is organized into many small groups of storage circuits called *storage positions* or *storage locations*. It's frequently compared to a group of mailboxes, where each mailbox has an address and is capable of storing one item of data. Each position of storage has a specific location number called an *address*, so that data stored in it can be readily located. In most modern computers, each position of storage can hold at least one character, that is, a number, a letter, or other symbol.

Direct-Access or Random-Access Memory

Another important memory concept concerns *random-access* and *direct-access* memory. Both terms mean that elements of data or instructions can be directly stored and retrieved by selecting and using any storage location. They also mean that each storage position (1) has a unique address and (2) can be individually accessed in approximately the same length of time as any other without having to search through other storage positions. For example, each memory cell on a computer memory chip can be individually sensed or changed just as quickly as any other.

Memory Chips

A computer's primary storage consists of *memory* chips. Millions of storage circuits can be packed on silicon chips using *very large-scale integration (VLSI)* technology. Thus, memory chips with capacities of 256K bits, 1 million bits (1 megabit), 4 megabits, and 16 megabits are currently used in computer systems.

Memory chips are small, fast, shock and temperature resistant, and relatively inexpensive compared to earlier computer memories. One major disadvantage of most memory chips is their *volatility*. That is, an uninterrupted electrical charge must be supplied to these circuits or their contents will be

This high-speed memory board contains numerous memory chips.

lost. Therefore, they require standby electrical power (battery packs or emergency generators) to save their contents in case of power failure. That's why it's advisable to save your work frequently when using microcomputers.

As seen in Chapter 1, today's computers use two basic types of memory chips: *random-access memory (RAM)* and *read-only memory (ROM)*. Most primary storage consists of volatile RAM circuits. Each memory position of RAM chips can be both sensed (read) or changed (written). So RAM is sometimes called direct-access or read/write memory.

Typically, ROM contains parts of a computer's operating system and other selected programs. ROM is a *nonvolatile* memory used for permanent primary storage. It can only be read, not "written" (that is, changed). Its contents are permanently burned into the storage circuits during manufacture.

Quick Quiz

1. The _____ is the central processing unit for a microcomputer.
2. The _____ interprets and executes instructions.
3. The _____ performs computations and comparisons.
4. The _____ stores instructions and data during processing.
5. Most computer memories consist of volatile _____ chips, while _____ chips are used for more permanent primary storage.

Answers: 1. main microprocessor   2. control unit
3. arithmetic-logic unit   4. primary storage unit   5. RAM, ROM

Types of Computer Systems

Look at Figure 7-1. Notice how many variations of the three basic categories—microcomputers, minicomputers, and mainframe computers—there are. Why are there so many varieties of computer systems? Many computer categories are attempts to describe the variations of *computing power* that computer systems provide for you to use. This means that computers may differ in their processing speed and memory capacity, as well as in the amount and capabilities of peripheral devices for input, output, and storage that they can support. In addition, computers are frequently placed in *application* categories such as *network servers* or *technical workstations*. These categories classify computers by the primary jobs for which you can use them.

Moreover, Figure 7-1 illustrates that computer classifications do overlap each other. For example, you will find microcomputers that are more powerful than some minicomputers, and minicomputers more powerful than some mainframe computers. Also, you can find both microcomputers and minicomputers used as network servers or engineering workstations. In addition, some experts predict that several computer categories will soon merge or disappear. For example, they argue that minicomputers and many mainframe computers are being made obsolete by growth in the power and versatility of networks of microcomputer systems.

Because computer manufacturers also typically produce *families,* or *product lines,* from which you can choose, computers can come in a variety of models with different processing speeds, memory capacities, and other

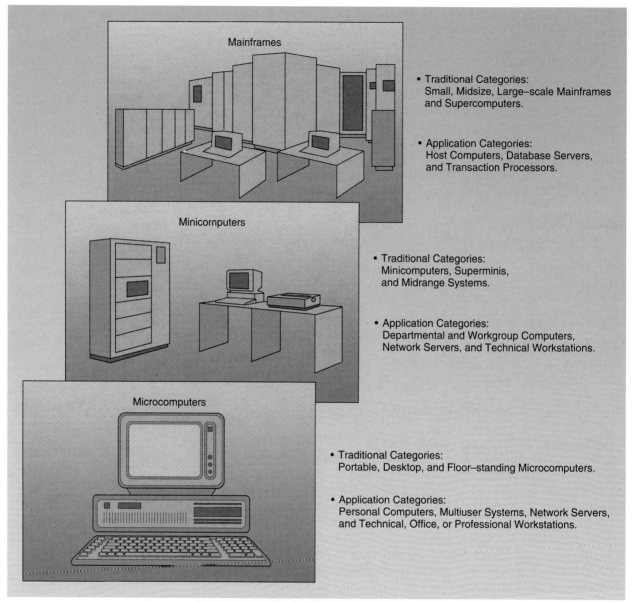

Figure 7-1
Computers come in a variety of categories for a variety of uses.

capabilities. This lets manufacturers provide a range of choices, depending on your information processing needs. Most models in a family are *compatible*. That is, programs written for one model can usually be run on other models of the same family, with little or no change, so you can move up to larger models of the same computer product line as your computing needs grow.

Microcomputer Systems

microcomputer
A small computer typically used by an end user as a computing workstation.

Microcomputers are the most important category of computer systems for end users. A microcomputer is typically called a *personal computer*, or PC. However, microcomputers have become much more than small computers used by individual persons. With a microcomputer, your computing power exceeds that of the mainframes of previous computer generations at a fraction of the cost. You can think of them as powerful computing *workstations* for use by end users in business firms and other organizations.

Microcomputers come in a variety of models for a variety of purposes, as the photographs below illustrate. For example, microcomputer size categories include *handheld, notebook, laptop, portable, desktop,* and *floor-standing* models. Most microcomputers are *desktop* units designed to fit on top of an office desk. Or they are *portables* designed to be conveniently carried by end users, such as salespersons or consultants, who do a lot of traveling as part of their job assignments.

Most microcomputers are really single-user *professional workstations* designed to support the work activities of a particular end user. Very powerful microcomputers may be used by engineers and scientists as *technical workstations* to perform advanced simulation and computational tasks. In addition, powerful *multiuser* machines are available that support computing by several end users at multiple terminals. And *network servers* coordinate processing in *local area networks (LANs)* of microcomputers and other devices.

A Microcomputer System

The typical hardware components of a microcomputer are shown in Figures 7-2 and the photograph on page 213. A microcomputer system may resemble a small portable TV with a keyboard. Or it may be too large to fit on a desktop and include a variety of peripheral devices. However, no matter what it

Microcomputer systems vary considerably in size and style. Shown here, clockwise from top left, are Macintosh LC 575, Dell 486P/20, Compaq Systempro, and Texas Instruments TravelMate 3000.

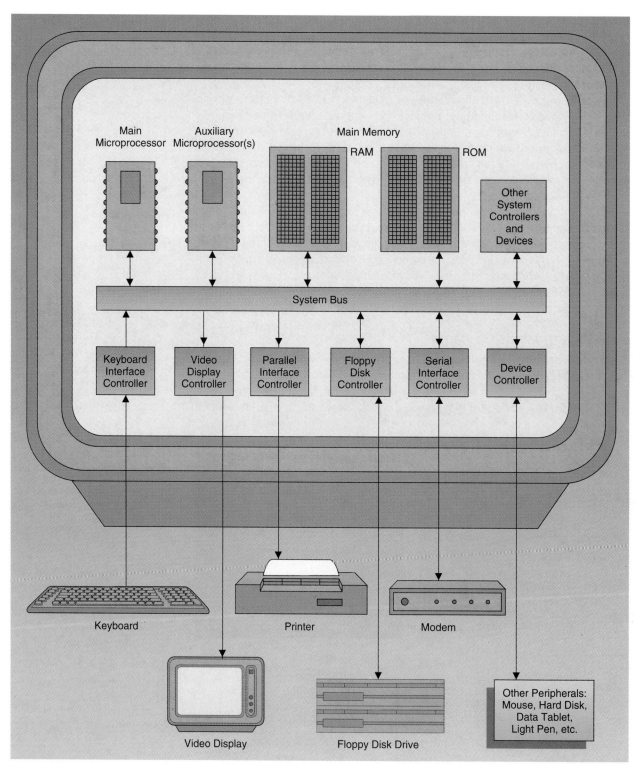

Figure 7-2
These are typical components of a
microcomputer system.

This IBM PS/2 microcomputer supports a double disk drive, high-resolution monitor, mouse, and extended keyboard.

looks like, remember that a microcomputer is a *computer system*. Its components must perform the system functions of input, processing, output, storage, and control that we explained in Chapters 1 and 2.

Input and Output

Keyboards and the *electronic mouse* are the most widely used input devices for microcomputers. Other devices such as touchscreens, pen-based LCD screens, optical scanners, and voice input devices are also used. Video monitors and printers are typically used for output, and other devices are available, such as audio speakers and graphics plotters.

Processing and Control

Microcomputers are powered by a main microprocessor and several support microprocessors. These and other chips control memory access and input/output devices that are installed on one or more circuit boards. Typically, they are housed in a *main system unit* to which peripheral devices can be connected. The main microprocessor and other electronic components serve as the central processing unit and as specialized processing and control devices. The most popular main microprocessors for IBM and other similar microcomputers are the Intel 80386, 80486, and Pentium microprocessors. Some versions of the Apple Macintosh use Motorola 68030 and 68040 microprocessors, while Apple's Power Macintoshes use the Power PC microprocessor.

The Intel Pentium microprocessor contains more than 3 million transistors and features dual execution units and high-speed memory caches that give it a top processing speed exceeding 100 million instructions per second.

Speed

Many microprocessors can operate at nanosecond speeds. Some of them can thus process over 50 million instructions per second (MIPS). Another impor-

REAL-WORLD EXAMPLE

Snow, Christensen & Martineau and Others: Laptops for All

Let's say you're an attorney in Salt Lake City defending a client who's being sued by someone represented by the law firm of Snow, Christensen & Martineau. One of its 55 lawyers brings a laptop computer into the courtroom. "That sometimes surprises the attorney on the other side," says Paul J. Graf, a partner in the firm. It sure does. But not for long. Other attorneys are realizing that with a laptop PC in court, they can access a database of legal precedents at will, or display the sworn statements of witnesses to check for discrepancies when they are testifying.

Or let's say you're a student at the prestigious Harvard Business School. No more exam blue books for you. Now, along with your 1,500 other classmates, you take exams on your laptop PC, and hand in a floppy disk when you are finished. Or let's say you're any kind of business person. "In the 1970s and 1980s, you could say, 'Let me have your card and I'll get back to you,'" says J. Bowman Rodgers, executive VP of Poquet Computer Corporation. In the 1990s, he says, your customers will expect you to use a laptop PC to give them price quotes or estimates right on the spot.

1. Are laptop computers toys or tools, fads or necessities? Explain.

2. How could you use a laptop now or in your future career?

tant measure of processing speed for a microprocessor is its *megahertz* (MHz) rating (millions of clock cycles per second). That's why microcomputers are typically described by the MIPS and MHz ratings of their microprocessors. However, megahertz ratings can be misleading. That's because a computer's processing speed in MIPS depends on a variety of factors. For example, speed is dependent on the size of the *bus* or circuitry paths that interconnect microprocessor components. Also, specialized microprocessors such as a *math coprocessor* can be added to do arithmetic calculations faster.

Storage

Memory chips on circuit boards in the main system unit provide primary storage. Memory capacities typically range from 2 to 16 megabytes of semiconductor storage, though larger capacities are becoming more common. *Secondary storage* is provided by floppy disk drives, hard disk drives, optical disks, and other devices. These can be part of the main system unit or can be externally connected. They provide from several hundred kilobytes to several hundred megabytes of online storage.

Use of Microcomputers

Microcomputers have many uses. How you use them depends on the many types of software packages available for them that are discussed in the four chapters of Part II. For example, of the most popular uses of microcomputers include word processing, spreadsheet modeling, database management, presentation graphics, electronic mail, and, of course, video games! Thousands of software packages are available for microcomputers, so they are being used for thousands of applications by end users in every field.

Minicomputer Systems

Minicomputers are *midrange* systems that are typically larger and more powerful than most microcomputers but smaller and less powerful than large *mainframe* computer systems. However, this is not a precise distinction. High-end models of microcomputer systems (*supermicros*) are more powerful than some minicomputers. High-end models of minicomputers (*superminis*) are more powerful than some mainframe computers. In addition, local area networks (LANs) of interconnected microcomputers have more processing power than many minicomputer and mainframe models. Thus, a controversy exists on the prospects of minicomputers remaining a separate computer category. But for now, minicomputers have a wide range of processing capabilities and hardware features.

Minicomputers are designed to handle many different types of jobs and peripheral devices. They are typically less costly to buy and operate than mainframe computers. Most minicomputers can also function in ordinary operating environments and do not need special air conditioning or electrical wiring. Therefore, they can be placed in most offices and work areas. In addition, since they are comparatively easy to operate, the smaller models of minicomputers can be operated by properly trained end users.

Uses of Minicomputers

Minicomputers are used for a large number of business and scientific applications. They first became popular for use in scientific research, instrumentation systems, engineering analysis, and industrial process monitoring and control. Minicomputers can easily handle such uses because these applications are narrow in scope and do not demand the processing versatility of mainframe systems. They are thus popular as industrial process-control and manufacturing-plant computers, where they play a major role in computer-aided manufacturing (CAM). Minicomputers can take the form of powerful *engineering workstations* for computer-assisted design (CAD) applications. They are also widely used as *front-end* computers, meaning that they help mainframe computers control telecommunications networks with large numbers of data-entry terminals.

Minicomputers have become popular as *departmental* computers where they serve the computing needs of individual departments. They can even act as *network servers* to help control *local area networks (LANs)*. In this capacity, they help manage networks of microcomputer workstations, data-entry terminals, and shared disk drives, laser printers, and other devices. In addition, some organizations have demonstrated that minicomputers can provide more processing power and online storage, while supporting more end users, than local area networks of microcomputers.

Mainframe Computer Systems

Mainframe computers are large, powerful computers that are still the "big iron" for computing at many large corporations as well as other organizations. Mainframes are physically larger than micros and minis and usually have one or more central processors, faster processing speeds, and larger primary storage capacities. For example, they may be able to process from 10 to 200 mil-

minicomputer
A midsize or midrange computer, typically with more computing power than most microcomputers, but not as powerful as most mainframe computers.

The DEC VAX 3400 minicomputer system is driven by this midsize processing unit.

mainframe computer
A larger computer system, typically with one or more central processing units, faster processing speeds, larger memory capacities, and able to handle more peripheral devices than a microcomputer or minicomputer.

lion instructions per second (MIPS). Their main memory capacity can range from 32 megabytes to several gigabytes of storage positions. The computing power of a mainframe is impressive. Large mainframes can process hundreds of different programs and handle hundreds of different peripheral devices (terminals, disk and tape drives, printers, and so on) for thousands of different users at the same time.

Uses of Mainframes

Many organizations are "downsizing" their computing resources to save money by replacing their mainframes with minicomputers or networks of microcomputers. However, mainframe computer systems are still popular for a variety of uses. Mainframes are particularly popular for high-volume transaction processing and maintenance of large corporate databases. Large organizations such as major banks, credit card companies, retailers, and stock exchanges must process millions of transactions each day. Many of them still rely on mainframes to handle the processing of customer inquiries, sales trans-

IBM's 3090 is an example of a large mainframe computer system.

actions, passenger reservations, money transfers, customer and corporate accounting entries, and inventory changes, to name a few.

Large organizations and commercial *time-sharing* companies use mainframes to manage access by many end users at the same time to large centralized databases and libraries of application programs. Large mainframes may also be used to handle the great volume of complex calculations involved in scientific and engineering analysis and simulation of complex design projects, such as spacecraft design. Mainframes have also found an important role as *host computers* or *super servers* for networks of many computer terminals, microcomputer workstations, and minicomputers.

Supercomputer Systems

Supercomputers are a category of extremely powerful systems designed for high-speed numeric computation. They work on mathematical problems or simulations that would take years to accomplish with other computers. Primary users of supercomputers are large government research agencies, military defense contractors, national weather forecasting agencies, large

supercomputers
The most powerful computer systems available, designed for high-speed numeric computation so they can solve massive computational problems.

This trademark from Columbia Pictures was made possible by computer animation created on a Silicon Graphics supercomputer system.

The black box in the foreground is a Silicon Graphics mini-supercomputer.

networked computer systems
Computer systems interconnected by telecommunications links so they can work together and share hardware, software, and data resources.

The networked computer system of the *Home Shopping Club* processes thousands of consumer product orders every day.

time-sharing networks, and large corporations and universities. However, supercomputers have also been put to work doing incredibly realistic computer animation for movies and TV.

Cray Research, along with NEC, Fujitsu, and a few others are the leading makers of supercomputers. These computers can process hundreds of millions of instructions per second (MIPS). They perform arithmetic calculations at a speed of billions of *floating-point operations per second* (gigaflops). This means supercomputers can do in a second or two what it would take hours for most microcomputers to do. Purchase prices for many supercomputers are in the $5 million to $50 million range. However, the use of *parallel processing* designs of interconnected microprocessors has spawned a new breed of *mini-supercomputers* with prices below $1 million. These and other supercomputers continue to advance the state of the art for the entire computer industry.

Networked Computer Systems

Computer systems rarely "stand alone" anymore. That is, they are increasingly *networked* or interconnected by telecommunications links with other computer systems. These **networked computer systems** allow end users to share computer hardware, software, and data resources. Interconnected networks of smaller computers have also become a major alternative to larger computer systems. For example, networks of several minicomputers can replace a large mainframe computer system. More commonly, networks of microcomputers are replacing both minicomputers and mainframes in many organizations.

Networked computer systems may rely on microwave and satellite telecommunications links throughout a large geographic area to form wide area networks (WANs). Or they may consist of computers interconnected by wire, cable, or other methods in local area networks (LANs) at offices or other

REAL-WORLD EXAMPLE

Georgia Pacific and Canadian Pacific: Micros, Minis, and Mainframes

Georgia Pacific is a major manufacturer of forest products. Georgia Pacific has eliminated its IBM 3081 mainframe in Atlanta and replaced it with a network of 20 IBM AS/400 minicomputers and 150 microcomputers distributed throughout the company. It is "downsizing" to micros and minis to save money. "Our costs in this new environment are significantly lower," says IS director Paul Pavloff. "Most of the savings have been in computer operations and technical support areas."

Canadian Pacific, a nationwide railroad company, has other ideas. "We need information flowing through the business, not concentrated in certain areas," says George Sekely, vice president of computers and communications. So Canadian Pacific continues to develop a huge nationwide network of personal computers and terminals that are connected to mainframes, with no minicomputers involved. "The PCs now add so much intelligence and provide user friendliness and speed for transactions," Sekely says. "This is not old-fashioned personal computing, like spreadsheets. I'm talking about enhancing mainframe transactions, working in a closer way with the mainframe."

1. Why do you think Georgia Pacific and Canadian Pacific disagree on the use of minicomputers and mainframes?

2. Which one do you think is right? Explain.

work sites. The distribution of computing power throughout an organization in this way is known as *distributed processing*. This approach is replacing large *centralized* mainframe computer facilities and the *decentralized* operations of independent computers with networks of end user microcomputers (*clients*) and network servers in what frequently is called *client/server* computing.

Uses of Networked Computers

Networked computer systems are being assigned many jobs formerly given to large minicomputer and mainframe computer systems. As an end user, you will probably use a microcomputer as a *professional workstation* in both local area and wide area networks to accomplish your work activities. For example, you might use a spreadsheet package provided by your local area network server to analyze data transmitted (downloaded) to your workstation from a mainframe computer system.

Networks of microcomputer workstations enable you to share hardware, software, and data resources and communicate with other end users in your work group as you work on joint projects. This is called *work group computing*. You might, for example, send *electronic mail* messages and transfer data files to colleagues who are working with you to prepare a major project proposal or report.

Besides providing end user computing support, networks of microcomputers can produce enough computing power to replace minicomputers and mainframe computer systems in many *transaction processing* applications. For instance, some organizations are using networked microcomputers instead of mainframes to process thousands of daily credit reports, money transfers, credit card purchases, customer account inquiries, and other business transactions.

Technical Note: How Computers Work

Read the next few pages of this section if you want to know in more detail how computers execute instructions and represent data in the components and circuitry of their CPUs. This will give you a brief look at how computers work.

How Computers Execute Instructions

Computers do their work by executing instructions, that is, following and completing the instructions in a program. The execution of an instruction can be divided into two segments, the *instruction cycle* and the *execution cycle*. Simply stated, the **instruction cycle** consists of activities in which an instruction is fetched from primary storage and interpreted by the control unit. The **execution cycle** consists of performing the operations specified by the instruction that was interpreted.

Figure 7-3 is a simplified illustration and explanation of what happens in a CPU during its instruction and execution cycles. Notice the basic operations that occur in this simple example:

During the instruction cycle:

1. First, an instruction is *fetched* from its location in primary storage and temporarily stored in the registers of the control unit.
2. Next, the instruction is *interpreted* by the circuitry of the control unit.
3. Finally, the control unit prepares electronic circuitry "paths" within the CPU to carry out the required operations.

During the execution cycle:

1. First, the data to be processed are fetched from their locations in primary storage and temporarily stored in storage registers of the arithmetic-logic unit.
2. Next, the operation specified by the instruction are performed (addition, subtraction, comparisons, and so on).
3. Finally, the result arising from the manipulation of the data is moved from an accumulator register and stored in primary storage.

Figure 7-3 illustrates the execution of an instruction from a payroll program, where a computer is told to add the amount of hours worked today by an employee to his or her total hours worked this week. The CPU adds today's hours (8), which had been stored in memory at address 006, to the amount (32) contained in an *accumulator register*, and moves the result (40) to memory location 008.

Machine Cycles

A CPU's timing circuitry, or *internal clock*, generates a fixed number of electrical pulses. It determines the timing of such basic CPU operations as fetch-

instruction cycle
Activities in which an instruction is fetched from primary storage and interpreted by the control unit.

execution cycle
Performing the operations specified by an instruction that has been interpreted by the control unit.

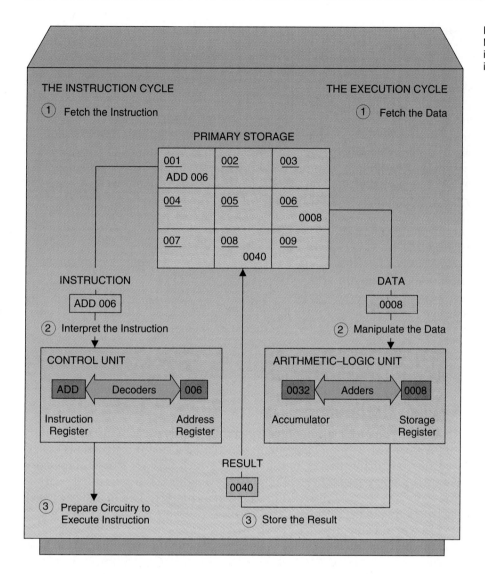

Figure 7-3
Notice some of the steps involved
in executing a simple computer
instruction.

ing and interpreting instructions. The time period to accomplish each basic
operation is called a **machine cycle.** The number of machine cycles required
to execute an instruction varies with the complexity of the CPU's design and
the instruction being executed.

machine cycle
The time period to accomplish a
basic CPU operation as determined by a fixed number of electrical pulses emitted by the CPU's
timing circuitry.

Registers

During each machine cycle, electrical pulses generated by the internal clock
energize circuitry that senses and interprets instructions and data. These are
moved in the form of electrical pulses among various components of the CPU.
One of the most important of these are **registers**—small high-speed storage
circuits used for the temporary storage of parts of an instruction or an element of data during the operation of a CPU.

registers
Small high-speed storage circuits
used for temporary storage of
parts of an instruction or data element during CPU operation.

REAL-WORLD EXAMPLE

Royal Caribbean Cruise Lines: PCs and Minis

Computers on cruise ships? Yes. In fact, Miami-based Royal Caribbean Cruise Lines uses Tandem Integrity minicomputers and a variety of PCs on six cruise ships. Royal Caribbean carefully considered several computers with multiple central processing units from AT&T to IBM before choosing the Integrity dual processor mini. John Pomeroy, manager of information technology for the line's OnBoard Systems Group, says the minicomputers must be able to keep operating under all sea conditions, so a fault-tolerant capability was a must.

Operated by one technician per ship, the minicomputers track passengers' on-board purchases of meals, drinks, and gifts after collecting point-of-sale data from about 20 personal computers on each ship. The results are downloaded to Royal Caribbean's IBM AS/400 minicomputers when the ships return to Miami. The cruise line's two-year experience with Integrity has been positive. So Royal Caribbean is installing more of the minicomputers on its other ships. "Knock on wood," Pomeroy said, "but it's been working out flawlessly."

1. Why do you think Royal Caribbean selected fault-tolerant minicomputers and PCs for its cruise ships?

2. What other computer uses would have similar requirements?

Logical Computing

Unless you intervene, a computer will automatically execute instructions until the final instruction of a program is executed. Usually, instructions are executed sequentially, that is, in the order in which they are stored in memory. An *instruction counter,* which automatically advances in sequential order to the address of the next instruction stored in memory, is used to indicate which instruction is to be executed next.

However, computers frequently make *logical* changes in the order that they execute instructions. For example, sometimes the next instruction to be executed is a *branch instruction.* This might require the arithmetic-logic unit to perform a *test* or *comparison* to see if a certain condition is present. If it is, the control unit may have to execute an instruction in another part of the program.

Let's look at the payroll example we mentioned earlier. Most payroll programs use a different sequence of instructions for hourly employees who work more than 40 hours per week. That's because these employees may have earned *overtime pay.* In this case, the computer would test each eligible employee's total weekly hours to see if it was greater than 40 hours. Therefore, to compute overtime pay, the CPU would branch to another part of the program and begin executing instructions for computing overtime pay, rather than regular pay.

How Computers Represent Data

The letters of the alphabet in this text are symbols that, when properly organized or "coded" into the English language, will represent data you can process into information. Thus, words, numbers, and punctuation are the *human-sen-*

sible code by which data are represented in this book. Similarly, data must be represented in a *machine-sensible* code before they can be processed by a computer system.

In Chapter 1, we said that data are represented in computers by either the presence or absence of electronic or other signals in the computer's circuitry or in the media it uses. This is called a **binary,** or two-state, representation of data, since only two possible states or conditions are possible. For instance, electronic circuits can be either in a conducting (ON) or nonconducting (OFF) state. Media such as magnetic disks and tapes can also indicate these two states. They represent data with magnetized spots whose magnetic fields can have two different directions or *polarities*.

That's why the **binary number system** (which has only two symbols, 0 and 1) is the basis for representing data in computers. For example, in a computer's electronic circuits, the conducting (ON) state represents a 1 and the nonconducting (OFF) state represents a 0. Thus a computer performs all of its operations by manipulating groups of 0s and 1s that represent data through the use of various binary-based computer codes.

binary
Data represented by the presence or absence of electronic or other signals in a computer's circuitry or the media it uses.

binary number system
A number system that uses only two symbols, 0 and 1.

Computer Codes

In computerese, a 0 or 1 is called a **bit** or *binary digit*. In the binary number system, any number can be expressed as a group of binary digits or *bits*. Computers employ binary-based codes that use groups of bits to represent each character of data. These codes make the job of communicating with a computer easier and more efficient than using long "strings" of binary digits. You can consider them as shorthand methods of expressing binary numbers within a computer.

Table 7-1 shows examples of the most widely used computer code—the American Standard Code for Information Interchange (ASCII) (pronounced *as-key*). Its standard form is a seven-bit code, but it is now widely used in its "extended" form (Extended ASCII), an eight-bit code that can represent 256 different characters. ASCII is used by most microcomputers and minicomputers, as well as by many larger computers. It has been adopted as a standard code by national and international standards organizations. Another computer code is the Extended Binary Coded Decimal Interchange Code (EBCDIC) (pronounced *eb-si-dick*). It is an eight-bit code used by IBM and other mini and mainframe computers. See Appendix A for more information about the binary number system and the ASCII and EBCDIC codes.

bit
A contraction of "binary digit." It can have the value of 0 or 1.

Bytes and Words

Computers store *bytes*. A **byte** is a basic grouping of *bits* (binary digits) that the computer stores as a single unit. A byte typically consists of eight bits and is used to represent a character of data in the ASCII and EBCDIC coding systems. For example, each tiny storage location on an electronic chip or a magnetic or optical disk can represent at least eight binary digits. Thus, each storage location can hold one character. That's why the capacity of a computer's memory, magnetic disks, and other secondary storage devices is typically expressed in terms of bytes.

Computers work with *words*. A **word** is a group of binary digits (usually larger than a byte) that is operated on as a unit by the CPU. Thus, a computer with a 32-bit *word length* might have registers with a capacity of 32 bits and

byte
A grouping of, typically, eight bits that represents a character of data in the ASCII and EBCDIC coding systems.

word
A group of bits operated on as a unit by the CPU.

Table 7-1
Examples of the Extended ASCII Computer Code

Character	ASCII Code	Character	ASCII Code
0	00110000	I	01001001
1	00110001	J	01001010
2	00110010	K	01001011
3	00110011	L	01001100
4	00110100	M	01001101
5	00110101	N	01001110
6	00110110	O	01001111
7	00110111	P	01010000
8	00111000	Q	01010001
9	00111001	R	01010010
		S	01010011
A	01000001	T	01010100
B	01000010	U	01010101
C	01000011	V	01010110
D	01000100	W	01010111
E	01000101	X	01011000
F	01000110	Y	01011001
G	01000111	Z	01011010
H	01001000		

should process data faster than computers with a 16-bit or 8-bit word length. However, remember that processing speed also depends on the size of a CPU's *buses,* the circuits that interconnect various CPU components. For example, some microprocessors have 24- and 32-bit registers but only a 16-bit data bus. They thus move data and instructions only 16 bits at a time. Therefore, they are slower than microprocessors that have 32-bit registers and data paths.

Representing Data

Figure 7-4 illustrates how data can be represented in computers using the eight-bit ASCII code. Figure 7-4 shows how each character in the term *"end-user"* can be represented by an eight-bit code. The circles represent semiconductor circuit elements or other forms of storage media. The darker blue

Figure 7-4
This is how a computer's memory circuits represent the term *end user* using the ASCII code.

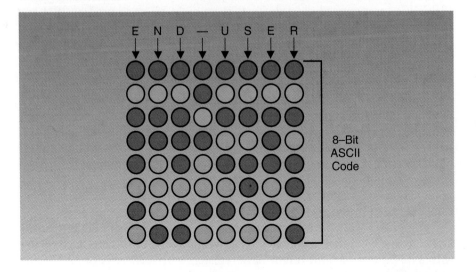

E T H I C S

Ethical Issues in Computer Systems

The topic of computer systems raises many ethical issues. One of the major issues is the ethical use of computers. In Chapter 1, we briefly introduced the topic of computer crime and ethics, that is, criminal and irresponsible behavior with computers. We will discuss this topic in much more detail in Chapter 12. However, other uses of computers are not so obviously criminal or irresponsible as the theft of money or data, or the unauthorized use of someone else's hardware and software. Let's look at two examples. First, should computers be used in military weapons systems? Second, should computers be used to create robots with artificial intelligence? Each situation creates an ethical controversy. For instance, the following are four applications proposed recently by the U.S. Department of Defense for research and development using artificial intelligence techniques:

- Nuclear missile target detection from satellite sensing systems
- Detection of quiet submarines by advanced sonar systems
- Battlefield radar and infrared surveillance systems
- Detection of "stealth" aircraft using infrared systems

Do any of these military uses of computers seem unethical to you? To peace activists, most offensive and defensive military applications of computers are unethical. They see many military applications as provocative acts that can only lead to military escalation and war.

Our other example is the ethical issues raised in building computerized robots with artificial intelligence. First, you should realize that the term *robot* is used to describe any programmable machine that displays simple human-like capabilities like grasping and moving objects, using tools, or moving from place to place. Thus robots have become a fact of life in industry and society. Second, in Chapter 1, we mentioned that one of the goals of the science of artificial intelligence (AI), is to develop software for computers (and robots) so they can display some of the characteristics of human intelligence. However, remember that since this software is developed by human programmers, it also embodies the ethical values, assumptions, and goals of its human creators.

What ethical values should be installed in robots? That's a question that has been debated for many years. One answer came from Isaac Asimov, the brilliant writer of science fiction stories. Asimov's robots have artificial brains whose circuits are designed with three built-in safeguards that Asimov called the three Laws of Robotics.

1. A robot may not injure a human being or, through inaction, allow a human being to come to harm.
2. A robot must obey the orders given it by human beings except where such orders conflict with the first law.

(continued on next page)

(continued from previous page)
3. A robot must protect its own existence as long as such protection does not conflict with the first or second law.

One of the problems with Asimov's laws is the interpretation that our ethical values give to words like "injure" and "harm." Other science fiction writers have written horror stories of despotic robots that refuse to let humans do anything (work or play) that might injure or harm them. The world then becomes a giant prison, with robots as our electronic guards.

What Do You Think?
Are most military applications of computers provocative acts of war? What kind of ethical values should be built into robots? What do you think?

circles represent an electronic or magnetic ON state, while the lighter blue circles represent an OFF state.

Quick Quiz

1. During its instruction cycle, a computer fetches and interprets _____ in the control unit.
2. During its execution cycle, a computer may fetch and manipulate _____ in the arithmetic-logic unit.
3. A computer executes the instructions in a computer program _____ unless a branch instruction directs it to the instructions in another part of the program.
4. A _____ typically consists of eight bits.
5. The most widely used computer code is _____ .

Answers: 1. instructions 2. data 3. sequentially 4. byte
5. ASCII (American Standard Code for Information Interchange)

End Note: End Users and Computer Systems

In this chapter you have seen how the different components of a computer system work to execute instructions and represent data. You have also seen that the term *computer system* covers many different types of computers. From microcomputers to minis to mainframes, from single-user systems to multiuser networks, they are all designed to serve the computing needs of end users and organizations. Of course, the microcomputer is the favorite of end users. It's become the knowledge worker's *professional workstation,* designed to support your work activities with desktop computing power. Then, when it is part of a telecommunications network, it can bring the computing power of other micros, minis, and mainframes to your work site.

Minicomputers and mainframes still have important roles to play in end user and organizational computing. Minis act as process control and manufacturing control computers, engineering workstations, telecommunications control computers, departmental computers, and network servers. Mainframes are still the choice of many large organizations for high-volume transaction processing, time-sharing services, and as network hosts or super servers. Supercomputers are still indispensable in solving problems involving complex calculations in seconds or minutes that would take years for other computers to do.

Of course, computer systems rarely stand alone anymore. Thanks to telecommunications networks, computers are now tied together to share hardware, software, and data resources. For example, networked microcomputers in a local area network have become so popular they are replacing both minis and mainframes in some applications. Networked microcomputers also support the development of *work group computing,* where end users use their computer workstations to work on joint projects together.

So, whatever your computing needs, computers are available to meet them. To be a computer-literate end user, you need to learn how to use computer systems to effectively support your work activities. This chapter should have helped you learn about how computers work and about the many types of computer systems in use today. But as we said in Chapter 1, you also need hands-on practice in using computers to get things done. Hopefully, you are gaining such experience at school or work right now. Only then will you be able to realize the full potential of computer systems.

Summary

The Central Processor In most computers, a CPU includes a control unit, arithmetic-logic unit (ALU), and primary storage unit, as well as support microprocessors for specialized functions. The control unit interprets instructions and directs their execution by a computer system. The ALU performs arithmetic operations and makes logical comparisons. The primary storage unit (memory) stores instructions and data during processing. Most computer memories consist of random-access memory (RAM) chips, as well as read-only memory (ROM) for permanent storage of selected programs. Some computers may use a multiprocessor design with more than one CPU, while others may use a network of parallel processors to execute many instructions at the same time.

Types of Computer Systems Many computer categories describe the relative computing power or different uses of computer systems. Traditional categories such as microcomputers, minicomputers, and mainframes differ in their processing speeds, memory capacities, and ability to handle peripheral devices. However, these categories do overlap. Also, the growing power of networked microcomputers makes obsolete some minicomputer and mainframe models.

Microcomputer Systems Microcomputers are used as personal computers, workstations, and multiuser systems. A microcomputer system typically uses a keyboard for input, a system unit containing the main microprocessor for processing and control, semiconductor RAM and ROM circuits for primary storage, floppy or hard disk drives for secondary storage, and a video display and printer for output. Popular applications for microcomputers include word processing, decision analysis and support, database management, graphics, communications, application development, business and engineering applications, and personal and home applications.

Other Computer Systems   Minicomputers are larger and more powerful than most microcomputers. These midrange systems are used by small groups of end users for many business and scientific applications. Mainframe computers are larger and more powerful than most minicomputers. Mainframes are usually faster, have more memory capacity, and can support more peripheral devices. They are designed to handle the information processing needs of large organizations. Mainframes and minicomputers are being replaced in many organizations by networks of microcomputer systems. Supercomputers are a special category of extremely powerful computer systems designed for massive computational assignments.

Executing Instructions   The execution of a computer instruction can be subdivided into an instruction cycle and an execution cycle. In the instruction cycle, an instruction is fetched from primary storage and interpreted by the control unit. In the execution cycle, a computer performs the operations specified in the instruction that was interpreted.

Representing Data   Data are represented in a computer in a binary form because of the two-state nature of the electronic, magnetic, and optical components of computers. Most computers use special codes based on the binary number system, including the ASCII and EBCDIC codes. Within the computer, data are usually organized into bits, bytes, and words. Each storage position can store one byte and has a specific address, so the data stored in its contents can be readily located.

Key Terms and Concepts

arithmetic-logic unit
ASCII
binary number system
binary representation
central processing unit
computer codes
computer systems
control unit
EBCDIC
how computers execute instructions
mainframe computer
memory chips
microcomputer

microprocessor
minicomputer
multiprocessor designs
networked computer systems
primary storage unit
RAM
ROM
registers
secondary storage
supercomputer
volatility
word

Review Quiz

True/False

_____ 1. A CPU can be subdivided into an arithmetic-logic unit and control unit.

_____ 2. The control unit performs computations and comparisons.

_____ 3. The ALU interprets instructions and directs processing.

_____ 4. Instructions and data are stored in primary storage during processing.

_____ 5. A main microprocessor is the central processing unit for a microcomputer.

_____ 6. A minicomputer is typically used as an individual computing workstation.

_____ 7. A microcomputer is a midrange computer that may be used as a departmental or work group computer.

_____ 8. Mainframes may be used as host computers, transaction processors, and organization-wide systems.

_____ 9. A supercomputer is the most powerful type of computer.

_____ 10. Computer systems can have multiple CPUs.

Multiple Choice

_____ 1. Computer systems are frequently connected in

    a. telecommunications networks.
    b. random networks.
    c. serial networks.
    d. parallel networks.

_____ 2. Microelectronic storage circuits on silicon chips include

    a. RAM.
    b. ROM.
    c. memory chips.
    d. all of the above.

_____ 3. You can store and erase data in these memory chips:

    a. RAM
    b. ROM
    c. magnetic chips
    d. CD-ROM

_____ 4. Data are permanently stored in these memory chips:

    a. RAM
    b. ROM
    c. magnetic chips
    d. CD-ROM

_____ 5. Parts of an instruction or an element of data are stored by the CPU in

    a. controllers.
    b. registers.
    c. recorders.
    d. instructors.

_____ 6. Computers execute instructions by

    a. fetching and interpreting an instruction.
    b. fetching and manipulating data.
    c. moving data and instructions into registers in the ALU and the control unit.
    d. all of the above.

_____ 7. Representing data by the presence, absence, or change in direction of electric current, magnetic fields, or light rays in computer circuits and media is known as

    a. cell representation.
    b. text representation.
    c. binary representation.
    d. decimal representation.

_____ 8. The binary number system has a base of

    a. one.
    b. two.
    c. three.
    d. zero.

_____ 9. This element equals 16 bits or 32 bits for most current microcomputers.

    a. bit
    b. byte
    c. word
    d. page

_____ 10. An eight-bit code that represents data in many computers is

    a. Extended decimal.
    b. Extended ASCII.
    c. Extended binary.
    d. Extended EBCII.

Fill-in

1. The CPU of a microcomputer is called a _____.
2. Various models of _____ can be used as professional and technical workstations, network servers, and multiuser systems.
3. Some experts think _____ will be made obsolete by the rapid growth of networked microcomputers.
4. Some _____ act as super servers for telecommunications networks containing minicomputers and microcomputers.
5. Most of a microcomputer's memory is called _____.
6. Parts of the operating system and some application programs may be permanently stored in memory chips called _____.
7. It typically takes _____ bits to represent a byte in widely used computer codes.
8. The speed of microprocessors is typically expressed in terms of _____ and _____.
9. A(n) _____ computer consists of a network of microprocessors executing many instructions at the same time.
10. The most widely used computer code is called _____.

Questions for Thought and Discussion

1. Are minicomputers and mainframe computers being made obsolete by networked computers? Why or why not?

2. Why are some models of microcomputers or minicomputers called workstations?

3. Refer to the Real-World Example of Snow, Christensen & Martineau in the chapter. What other professions could be affected significantly by using laptop computers? Explain.

4. What is the capacity of the memory (RAM and ROM) and magnetic disk devices of a microcomputer you use? What is the name, word size, and speed rating of its main microprocessor? What other types of microprocessors does it use?

5. Refer to the Real-World Example of Georgia-Pacific and Canadian Pacific in the chapter. Why do you think one company eliminated mainframe computers, while the other sees no need for minicomputer systems?

6. What are the advantages and disadvantages of networked computer systems?

7. What are the potential benefits of RISC processors? Parallel processors? What are their limitations?

8. Why do computers use the binary number system? Why do they use codes like ASCII?

9. What are the ASCII codes for each letter of your first name? Your last name?

10. What types of computer systems do you use now? What activities do you accomplish with each of these computers? Make a brief report to the class.

Review Quiz Answers

True/False: 1. T 2. F 3. F 4. T 5. T 6. F 7. F 8. T 9. T 10. T

Multiple Choice: 1. a 2. d 3. a 4. b 5. b 6. d 7. c 8. b 9. c 10. b

Fill-in: 1. microprocessor 2. microcomputers 3. minicomputers 4. mainframes 5. RAM 6. ROM 7. eight 8. MHz, MIPS 9. parallel processor 10. ASCII.

8

COMPUTER PERIPHERALS: INPUT, OUTPUT, AND STORAGE DEVICES

OUTLINE

LEARNING OBJECTIVES

After reading and studying this chapter, you should be able to

Describe trends in computer peripherals that improve user interface and data entry methods.

Identify the major types and uses of computer peripherals for input, output, and storage.

Identify the benefits and limitations of several popular peripherals that provide methods of input and output for end users.

Describe trends and trade-offs in computer peripherals and media used for storage of data resources.

You and Computer Peripherals

A computer is just a "box" without peripherals. Its microprocessor may be able to process several million instructions per second (MIPS). Its memory may be able to hold several million bytes (megabytes) of data and programs. Still, the box would just sit there idle, if there was no way you could get data and instructions into it, no way you could get information out of it, and no way to store anything for your later use. That's why computers need peripherals. Without peripherals, a computer is a processing box, not a computing *system*.

So this chapter covers many of the computer peripherals you can use for input, output, and secondary storage. Why are so many types of peripherals available? Because the perfect device you need for input, output, or storage does not exist. As you will see in this chapter, every peripheral device you can use has its advantages and disadvantages. For example, a keyboard is great for entering text, but not very good at selecting images displayed on your video screen. A mouse doesn't "do" text, but it's great for selecting icons and other displayed images.

As you can see, the advantages and disadvantages you face with any peripheral device arise from the things you need to do when using computers. This problem is compounded if you consider the many different types of end users, work environments, and applications that we have for computers. So the computer industry has responded by developing many different devices for input, output, and secondary storage. As a computer-literate end user, you need to know something about the capabilities and limitations of many of these peripherals. That is the purpose of this chapter.

Input/Output Trends

How do you communicate with a computer? Typically, you use various input devices to issue commands, make selections, and enter data. Your computer responds using a variety of output devices to display or print information.

Figure 8-1
Trends in computer input and output methods help provide a more direct and natural user interface.

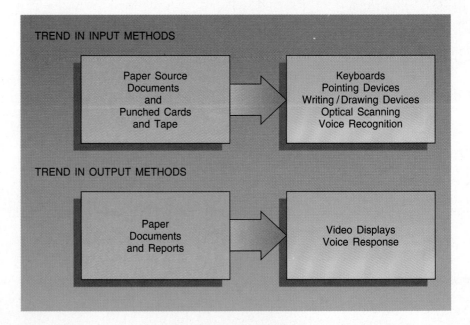

TREND IN INPUT METHODS

| Paper Source Documents and Punched Cards and Tape | → | Keyboards Pointing Devices Writing/Drawing Devices Optical Scanning Voice Recognition |

TREND IN OUTPUT METHODS

| Paper Documents and Reports | → | Video Displays Voice Response |

Thus, we can say that computer input and output devices provide you with **user interface hardware** for communicating with computers. Figure 8-1 shows you major trends in the use of input and output peripherals. Along with software developments covered in Chapter 3, these hardware developments help provide you with a more direct and natural user interface.

user interface hardware
Input and output peripheral devices for communication with computers.

Interface Hardware Trends

Figure 8-1 emphasizes that most end users now enter data and instructions directly into a computer system through a keyboard, *pointing devices* such as the electronic mouse, or writing/drawing devices such as *light pens*. Other methods such as optical scanning and voice input reduce the need to key in text material or an end user's responses. Another hardware interface trend is the direct output of information through video displays and voice response devices instead of through output of paper documents and reports.

Data-Entry Trends

The input activity in many organizations involves a process of **data entry**. In this process, data is captured, edited, and entered into a computer system. Data-entry activities have always been a bottleneck in processing the many transactions that take place in an organization. It's always been a problem getting data into computers accurately and quickly enough to match their awesome processing speeds. Older methods of data entry rely on end users to capture data on **source documents** such as purchase orders, payroll time sheets, and sales-order forms. In many cases, these documents are accumulated and transferred to data entry specialists who use the keyboards of video terminals to key the data into a computer system.

data entry
The process of capturing, editing, and entering data into a computer system.

source document
A document that is the original record of a transaction, such as a purchase order or a sales-order form.

Most organizations have found that such manual methods are slow, costly, and error prone. As you will see in this chapter, manual data entry is rapidly being replaced by direct, automated methods. As Figure 8-1 illustrates, older methods of data entry that relied on paper source documents or punched cards have been replaced in many cases by direct entry activities that use keyboards, writing/drawing devices, and optical scanning methods. For example, many retail stores use optical scanning devices to automatically capture data from **bar codes** printed on products you buy. This speeds up and reduces the errors and costs of the data entry process for the stores and their customers.

End User Terminal Trends

Until microcomputers were developed, most end users relied on a variety of **terminals** for access to minicomputer and mainframe computer systems. Any input/output device connected by telecommunications links to a computer can be called a *terminal*, so even a touch-tone phone can be a computer terminal. However, most terminals today use a keyboard for input and a video screen for output. They are called **visual** (or video) **display terminals (VDTs)** or CRT (cathode ray tube) terminals. Terminals allow you to access the computers in a network to make inquiries, enter data about transactions, and perform other computing tasks.

terminal
Any input/output device connected by telecommunications links to a computer.

visual display terminals
Terminals that use a keyboard for data entry and a video screen for output.

Many terminals are *dumb terminals*, that is, they have no processing capability by themselves. However, the trend is toward *smart terminals*, which

The video display terminals in this office are connected to the mini-computer in the background.

intelligent terminals
Terminals with the capabilities of a microcomputer that can thus perform many functions without accessing a larger computer.

transaction terminals
Terminals used in banks, retail stores, factories, and other sites that are used to capture transaction data at its point of origin.

add some microprocessors and memory circuits. **Intelligent terminals** are really microcomputers that are used as telecommunications terminals to larger computers. Therefore, they can perform data entry and other information processing tasks by themselves.

Another big trend is the widespread use of **transaction terminals**. You have probably seen and used transaction terminals in banks, retail stores, offices, and other sites. Typical examples are automated teller machines (ATMs), factory work-process terminals, portable inventory recorders, and retail point-of-sale (POS) terminals. These terminals use a variety of input/output devices, such as keypads, touchscreens, optical scanning wands, and video display screens. They all capture transaction data from end users and transmit it over telecommunications networks to computer systems for processing.

Keyboards and Pointing Devices

Keyboards are the most widely used input devices for computers. The typewriter-like keyboard allows you to interact with and enter data and text material directly into a computer system. When you strike its keys, you send electronic binary codes (like ASCII) representing characters or other functions to the computer's CPU. Most keyboards use a traditional layout of alphanumeric keys, along with a numeric key pad, *cursor control keys,* and a variety of special-purpose *function keys.*

pointing devices
Devices that allow an end user to move the cursor to an appropriate spot on the video screen and press one or more buttons to issue commands, select alternatives, and respond to prompts.

electronic mouse
A small device electronically connected to a computer and moved by hand on a flat surface in order to position the cursor. Buttons on the mouse allow users to issue commands and make selections.

Pointing devices are better alternatives than keyboards for issuing commands, selecting alternatives, or responding to prompts, especially if your computer is displaying a graphical-user interface. Several pointing devices allow you to use an easy *point-and-click* method to move the cursor and choose from menu selections or icons on your video screen.

The **electronic mouse** is the most popular pointing device to move the cursor and make icon and menu selections or perform other actions. Most mice use a roller ball, which moves the cursor in the direction the ball is rolled. Others use an optical sensing technology that recognizes points on a

Computer keyboards come in a variety of styles and layouts such as the ergonomic keyboard shown here.

special pad. By moving the mouse on your desktop or pad, you can move the cursor over to an icon or menu selection displayed on the screen. You then press a button on the mouse to begin the task you selected.

The **trackball** and the **joystick** are other popular pointing devices. A trackball is a stationary pointing device; you turn a rollerball with just its top exposed outside its case to move the cursor on the screen. Trackballs are thus easier to use than mice for many end users. They are becoming more popular and are built into several laptop computer keyboards. A joystick resembles a small gearshift lever set in a box. Joysticks are used for computer-assisted design and are also popular control devices for microcomputer video games.

Why not use your finger as a pointing device? **Touch-sensitive screens** enable you to use a computer by touching the surface of its video display screen. Such screens emit a grid of infrared beams, sound waves, or slight electric current that is broken when the screen is touched. The computer senses the point in the grid where the break occurs and responds with an appropriate action. You can indicate your selection on a menu display by touching the screen next to that menu item.

trackball
A rollerball device used to move the cursor; an "upside down" mouse.

joystick
A small lever set in a box that moves the cursor.

touch-sensitive screens
An input device that allows users to issue commands and make selections by placing a finger on or close to the video screen.

Pointing devices include the electronic mouse and trackball of various designs.

Drawing devices include digitizers like these pens, puck, and pressure-sensitive drawing board.

Pen-based Computing

Several pen-like devices are available that allow your handwriting and drawing to be directly entered into a computer system. They are especially popular with artists, architects, engineers, and designers. One example is the **light pen**. It's a pen-shaped device that uses photoelectric circuitry so you can enter data into a computer through its video screen. You can *write* or draw on the video display because the light-sensitive pen enables the computer to calculate the coordinates of the points on the screen being touched by the light pen.

A **graphics pad** is another writing/drawing device. Generically, it's called a *digitizer*, since what you draw or write on its pressure-sensitive surface is digitized into binary codes by the computer and accepted as input. You can use a *stylus* or other penlike device to write or draw on a graphics pad. Or you may use another hand-held device (a *puck*) that contains a small glass window with crosshairs to trace over forms, maps, or drawings laid on the graphics pad. Other devices even allow you to capture a three-dimensional image of an object by tracing over its outline with a digitizing pen.

Graphics pad and light pen technologies are being used to develop a new generation of **pen-based computers** that recognize handwriting. These *notebook* PCs are tablet-style portable microcomputers that contain software able to recognize your handwriting. They have a pressure-sensitive layer like a graphics pad under their slatelike liquid crystal display (LCD) screen. So instead of writing or drawing on a paper form fastened to a clipboard, inspectors, field engineers, and other mobile workers can use a pen to enter handwritten data directly into a computer.

light pen
A photoelectric device that allows data to be entered or altered by writing or drawing on the face of a video display screen.

graphics pad
A pressure-sensitive surface that digitizes what is drawn or written on it and enters it into a computer system.

pen-based computers
Tablet-style portable microcomputers that recognize handwriting or hand drawing done by a pen-shaped device on their display screens.

REAL-WORLD EXAMPLE

State Farm and Kaiser Permanente Hospital: Pen-based Computing

What do insurance claims adjusters and hospital nurses have in common? Well, you might say that they both have to fill out a lot of forms in performing their jobs. Of course claims adjusters are concerned with estimating the repairs needed by your car, while nurses are more concerned with tracking repairs to your health. In any case, hospitals and insurance companies have been looking for ways to cut down on the paperwork required in these two occupations.

Now comes the pen-based computer. These tablet-sized computers recognize printed handwriting on their LCD screens and transform it into digitized data that can be stored and used for any computing task. So it's a natural for filling out electronic forms stored in the computer and displayed on the screen. For example, some State Farm claims adjusters are using pen-based computers to fill out insurance forms electronically while inspecting damaged cars at auto repair shops. Then the computer automatically calculates repair estimates based on allowable parts and labor charges. Some of the nurses at Kaiser Permanente Hospital in Hayward, California, are using pen-based PCs to update patient medical charts electronically. Nurse Carol Graham says that since nurses spend as much as 60 percent of their day on paperwork, automating such tasks should give them more time for patients.

1. What features of pen-based computers make them a good input device? A good output device?

2. What other jobs could benefit from pen-based computers?

This notebook PC recognizes handwriting on its slate-like screen.

Video Input and Output

Computers use TV technology for input as well as output. Input from a VCR, camcorder, or TV receiver can be digitized, compressed, and stored by a computer on magnetic or optical disks in *snapshot* or *full-motion* images. Capture of snapshot video images is not too costly, but full-motion video technologies like *digital video interactive (DVI)* are quite expensive. For example, you might have to spend thousands of dollars to upgrade a high-powered PC with additional software, circuit boards, memory, and magnetic or optical disk capacity to achieve a DVI capability. Another expensive option you could add is a *multimedia development* capability. This would allow you to merge TV images with text, graphics, and sound to develop your own computer-generated video presentations.

Video Output

cathode ray tube (CRT)
An electronic vacuum tube (television picture tube) that displays the output of a computer system.

Video displays are the most common type of computer output. Most video monitors and terminals use a **cathode ray tube (CRT)** similar to the picture tube in home TV sets. The clarity (*resolution*) and colors of the display depend on the type of video monitor used and the graphics circuit board or *video adapter* installed in your microcomputer or terminal. These components offer several levels of resolution. Examples are EGA (enhanced graphics adapter), VGA (video graphics array), or *super* VGA. Having a high-resolution graphics capability is important if your software provides extensive graphics displays and a graphical-user interface.

Low-resolution video monitors have a *character addressable* display. That is, the screen is typically divided into 25 rows and 80 columns, which provides 2,000 character locations. Each character on the screen is composed of dots called *pixels*. For example, displaying a letter of the alphabet might take 128 (8 × 16) pixels. Higher-resolution video monitors may use a *bit-mapped* display, where each pixel can be assigned a location on the screen. For example, a medium-resolution (VGA) color monitor contains more than 300,000 pixels (640 × 480) and can display 64 colors. High-resolution (Super VGA) displays can provide almost 800,000 pixels (1024 × 768) and 256 colors. Some high-powered microcomputer workstations can generate displays of near-photographic quality that contain more than 4 million pixels and 4,000 colors.

Video images, left, may be captured on a PC for multimedia presentations. This realistic display, right, was generated by an IBM RISC 6000 Powerstation.

Video display alternatives include the gas plasma display as seen in the IBM Portable 70, left, and the LCD display of the Macintosh Powerbook, right.

liquid crystal display (LCD)
Video displays formed by applying an electrical charge to silicon crystals.

plasma display
A video display technology that generates displays with electrically charged particles of gas trapped between glass plates.

Liquid crystal displays (LCDs) are no longer relegated to electronic calculators and watches. LCDs are primarily used as an alternative to CRT displays in portable microcomputers and terminals. That's because LCD displays need a lot less electric current and provide a thin, flat display. Technology advances have improved the size and clarity of LCD screens, which formerly were hard to see in bright sunlight or artificial light. In addition, LCDs that provide full-color displays are now available.

Plasma display devices provide an alternative to CRT displays and LCDs in a limited number of applications. Plasma displays are generated by the glow of electrically charged particles of gas (plasma) trapped between glass plates. Plasma display units provide a flat, thin display technology but are significantly more expensive than LCD units. However, they use less power, provide more clarity and faster display speeds, and are easier to see from any angle and in any light. Thus, plasma displays continue to be used in some portable microcomputers.

Quick Quiz

1. Peripheral devices for input and output are being designed to provide a direct and natural _____.
2. An automated teller machine (ATM) is an example of a _____.
3. The electronic mouse, trackball, and joystick are examples of _____.
4. Tablet-style microcomputers that can recognize your handwriting are an example of _____.
5. Most video monitors use _____ technology, while most portable computers use a _____ technology.

Answers: 1. user interface 2. transaction terminal 3. pointing devices 4. pen-based computers 5. cathode ray tube (CRT), liquid crystal display (LCD)

Printers and plotters produce hard copy display. This is an example of an office-type laser printer.

Printed Output

Many times, video displays of information are not permanent enough. That's why most computer systems use **printers** to produce permanent output or *hard copy*. You need such printed material if you want to take copies of output with you and share them with others. You may also need hard copy output for legal documentation. Printers can produce reports for management and documents such as payroll checks and bank statements, as well as printed copies of graphics displays. **Plotters** are peripherals that use ink pens or other methods to draw graphics displays on paper in many scientific and engineering design applications. The photograph above illustrates one type of computer printer.

Printers are available in a variety of sizes, prices, technologies, and performance levels. Printers can print a single character, line, or page using an *impact* or *nonimpact* process. A *dot matrix* printer for a microcomputer or a

printer
A hard-copy output device used to print computer output on paper.

plotter
A hard-copy output device used to produce drawings and graphical displays on paper or other materials.

Figure 8-2
How a variety of printers work.

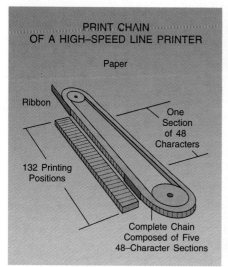

PRINT CHAIN OF A HIGH–SPEED LINE PRINTER

Paper

Ribbon

One Section of 48 Characters

132 Printing Positions

Complete Chain Composed of Five 48–Character Sections

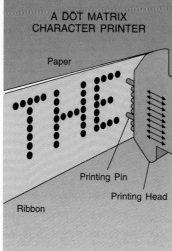

A DOT MATRIX CHARACTER PRINTER

Paper

Printing Pin

Printing Head

Ribbon

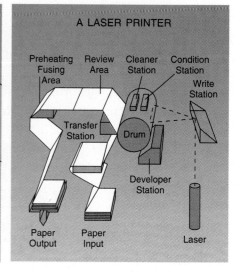

A LASER PRINTER

Preheating Fusing Area

Review Area

Cleaner Station

Condition Station

Write Station

Transfer Station

Drum

Developer Station

Paper Output

Paper Input

Laser

mainframe *line* printer both print by the impact of printing elements against paper. Laser printers used by both microcomputers and mainframes are a popular example of nonimpact printers. Figure 8-2 shows how several types of printers work.

Dot Matrix Printers

Dot matrix printers are the most widely used impact printers for personal computer systems. Their comparatively low cost, acceptable speed, and ability to do both text and graphics make them a popular choice. They use a print head containing electromagnets that fire short wires or pins to form a character as an array (a *matrix*) of dots. Dot matrix printers with 9-pin print heads produce fast *draft quality* printing, while 24-pin printers can produce slower, *near letter-quality* output. Thus the speed of dot matrix printers can range from 50 to more than 400 characters per second (CPS), with prices from a few hundred to under a thousand dollars.

Like other impact printers, the dot matrix printing process is noisy but can produce multiple copy forms. An important dot matrix advantage is that you can make some adjustments to type size and type *font* at the direction of the software that you use. For instance, you don't have to change print heads to print boldface or italics, use a more compact type size, or print foreign language characters.

dot matrix printers
Printers that use a print head containing pins that form a character as an array or matrix of dots.

Line Printers

High-speed **line printers** are still used in mainframe and minicomputer systems. These impact printers generate an entire line at a time (up to 132 characters) at speeds up to 3,000 lines per minute. They use a moving metal chain or drum of characters as their printing element. Line printers are expensive. Depending on their speed and print quality, their cost can exceed $100,000, so they are being replaced by high-speed laser printers in many mainframe systems.

line printer
A device that prints all the characters of a line as a unit.

Laser Printers

Laser printers formerly were available only as high-priced *page printers* for mainframes. Now they are a popular and affordable choice for many microcomputer systems. Laser printers are fast, quiet, versatile, and do high-quality printing of both text and graphics. Like other nonimpact printers, they don't print multiple copy forms.

Most laser printers use a laser beam to create electrostatic images of computer output on a rotating drum. The images on the drum attract a *toner* similar to that used in *xerographic* copiers and are then transferred to paper. A typical laser printer for your microcomputer system might print from 4 to 20 pages per minute. Prices range from about $500 to $5,000. Mainframe models are fast, but expensive. Though they can exceed 350 pages or 21,000 lines per minute, they can cost several hundred thousand dollars. The operating cost of laser printers must also be considered. It might cost a hundred dollars to replace a toner cartridge after each 4,000 pages of output from a microcomputer's laser printer.

laser printers
Printers that use a laser to create electrostatic images on a rotating drum and transfer them to paper.

Figure 8-3
Printers use a variety of methods to provide output.

ABCDEFGHIJKLMNOPQRSTUVWXYZ
abcdefghijklmnopqrstuvwxyz1234567890

ABCDEFGHIJKLMNOPQRSTUVWXYZ
abcdefghijklmnopqrstuvwxyz1234567890

ABCDEFGHIJKLMNOPQRSTUVWXYZ
abcdefghijklmnopqrstuvwxyz1234567890

The big attraction of laser printers is the quality and versatility of their printing of text and graphics. They are a must for most *desktop publishing* and other graphics applications. For example, if you have a microcomputer and desktop publishing software, you can combine text and graphics to produce attractive newsletters, forms, brochures, and manuals on your laser printer, as illustrated in Figure 8-3. As the costs of new technologies (like color laser printing) continue to decline, desktop publishing should become even more popular.

Ink-jet Printers

ink-jet printers
Printers that spray tiny particles of ink from fast-moving nozzles against paper.

Ink-jet printers are a lower-cost alternative to laser printers for versatile printing of text and graphics—even in color. They are also a quiet, higher-quality, nonimpact alternative to dot matrix printers. Ink-jet printers spray tiny ink particles from fast-moving nozzles against paper. Electrostatic charges placed on the paper attract the ink, which forms characters of high print quality. One disadvantage is that sometimes the ink may smear. Ink-jet printers cost $200 to $1,500 and can print more than 300 characters per second.

Thermal Printers

thermal printers
Printers that use heated wires and heat-sensitive paper, or a heat-sensitive waxed ribbon and regular paper, to print output.

Thermal printers use heated wires to produce characters on heat-sensitive paper. Some small, slow, but inexpensive and quiet thermal printers are used as printers for portable computers. However, their print quality is poor and fades with time. Newer, more expensive and faster *thermal wax* printers use a heat-sensitive waxed ribbon and regular paper and can print quality color output. Prices for thermal printers can range from a few hundred dollars to more than $10,000, with speeds from 10 to 300 characters per second.

Voice Recognition and Response

voice recognition
Direct conversion of spoken data into electronic binary codes for entry into a computer system.

voice response
Computer output consisting of spoken words generated by mainframe audio response units, micro- and minicomputer voice messaging systems, and speech synthesizer microprocessors.

Voice recognition and **voice response** systems provide the easiest user interface for data entry and conversational computing. That's because speech is an easy, natural, and efficient means of human communication. Voice recognition and voice response technologies have become cost-effective for a variety of specialized applications.

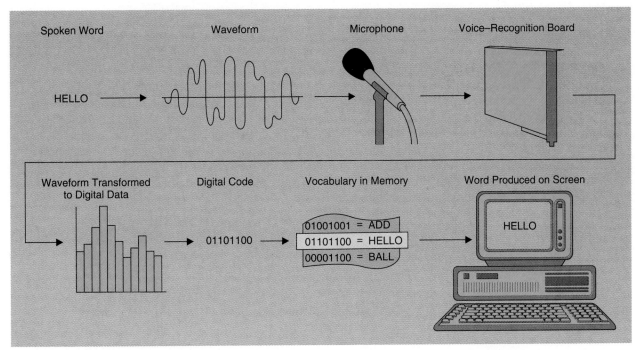

Spoken Word   Waveform   Microphone   Voice–Recognition Board

HELLO

Waveform Transformed   Digital Code   Vocabulary in Memory   Word Produced on Screen
to Digital Data

01101100

01001001 = ADD
01101100 = HELLO
00001100 = BALL

HELLO

Figure 8-4
A spoken word can be digitized
and accepted as input in voice
recognition systems.

Voice Recognition

Voice recognition systems analyze speech or vocal tract patterns and transform them into binary codes. Most systems require "training" the computer to recognize a limited vocabulary of standard words for each user. For example, you could train the system to recognize your voice by repeating each word in its vocabulary (about 10 times) until it got it right. Some systems use a voice recognition circuit board and software, a microphone, and a video terminal to display their spoken input. See Figure 8-4.

Voice data entry is a typical application of voice recognition. It is used in situations where workers need to perform data entry while their hands are busy with a task. Thus, voice recognition is being used for inspection, inventory, and quality control in manufacturing; by doctors and medical technicians for recording patient evaluations and diagnoses; and by airlines and parcel delivery companies for voice-directed sorting of baggage and parcels.

Speaker recognition is another application of voice recognition technology. It identifies individuals by their unique "voice print" before allowing them entry into restricted areas or computer systems. Voice recognition can also be used with many microcomputer software packages for voice input of data and commands. However, voice recognition for word processing is expected to become a very popular application in the next few years. Personal dictation software for word processing is now available for microcomputers for under $1,000 for a 34,000-word vocabulary system.

Voice Response

Examples of voice response devices range from mainframe *audio-response* units, to voice messaging micro- and minicomputer systems, to *speech synthesizer microprocessors* found in toys, appliances, and other products. Com-

REAL-WORLD EXAMPLE

Circuitest, Inc.: No Hands Computing

Circuitest, Inc. in Nashua, New Hampshire, is using voice recognition systems to free the hands of printed circuit board testers, who typically use both of their hands to inspect board with a pair of electronic probes. The Verbex system, priced at $695, consists of Listen for Windows software and a digital signal processing (DSP) circuit board that converts continuous human speech into keystrokes that a Microsoft Windows application software package can understand. "Voice recognition applications require lots of calculations that are provided by fast RAM in DSP boards. The price of fast RAM has come down to the point where we can now offer a Windows product on PCs," says Verbex President Larry Dooling.

Verbex can recognize up to 300 words out of a total vocabulary of 420 words supplied by the system. Circuit board testers can also display and manipulate a drawing of a board while they test it. "It makes an incredible difference. The testers are about 30 percent more productive." says Mike Gowing, a software engineer at Circuitest.

1. Why would circuit board testing be a good application for voice recognition?

2. What other applications do you think would be good candidates for voice recognition technology?

puters with audio-response or voice messaging units use voice response software to verbally guide you through the steps of a task. They also can allow computers to respond to your touch-tone input over the telephone. You have probably already experienced voice response in computerized telephone switching systems, *telemarketing* surveys, or when registering for classes in a computerized telephone registration system. Many banks also offer voice re-

This man is using a personal dictation system, one form of voice recognition technology.

sponse systems where you can use a touch-tone phone to pay your bills or check your credit and account balances.

Optical and Magnetic Recognition

Computers can read. You can use **optical scanning** devices to convert text or graphics into digital input a computer can recognize. For example, **optical character recognition (OCR)** and optical mark recognition (OMR) equipment are designed to read a variety of marks, characters and codes on many kinds of documents. You can also use *optical scanners* to read pages of text and graphic images. Therefore, capturing text and graphics with scanners is popular in *desktop publishing* applications.

Optical scanning and OCR eliminate having to key in data from source documents into a computer system. Instead, scanners employ lasers and photoelectric devices to scan the characters or graphics on documents. Reflected light patterns from the documents are converted into electronic impulses that are accepted as digitized data by computer systems.

Hand-held optical scanning **wands** are used by many retail stores to read the vertical bars of **bar coding** or other characters that you see on most merchandise tags, products and many other items. For example, supermarkets use checkout scanners to read the Universal Product Code (UPC) bar coding on packages of food and other items. These scanners emit laser beams, which read the Universal Product Code on products you are buying. The digitized product data is sent to an in-store minicomputer, which transmits the price and other information back to the scanner to be displayed and printed on your receipt. The photograph on page 000 shows a hand-held optical image scanner.

Magnetic Data Entry

How do computers read checks? **Magnetic ink character recognition (MICR)** lets bank computer systems read checks and deposit slips so they can be posted to customer checking accounts. The identification numbers of the bank and the customer's account number are preprinted on the bottom of checks with an iron oxide-based ink. The first bank receiving a deposited check encodes the amount in magnetic ink in the check's lower right-hand corner. Then the bank's MICR *reader-sorters* magnetically read and sort checks at speeds of up to 2,400 checks per minute. Several large banks have begun replacing MICR technology with optical scanning systems.

A **magnetic stripe** technology helps computers read credit and debit cards. That's why there's a dark magnetic stripe on the back of your credit cards. It's the same iron oxide coating used on magnetic tape for computer and audio or video recordings. Your customer account number is recorded on the strip so it can be read by bank ATMs, credit card authorization terminals, and other "mag stripe" readers.

Quick Quiz

1. Computer systems use various kinds of _____ and _____ to produce permanent output on paper.

2. The most widely used printers for personal computer systems are _____ , while _____ are most popular for desktop publishing applications.

optical scanning
Using lasers and photoelectric devices to scan text and graphics and convert them into digital input.

optical character recognition (OCR)
Optical scanning of special-purpose characters such as bar codes.

wand
A hand-held OCR device used for data entry.

bar coding
Vertical marks or bars placed on merchandise tags or packaging that can be sensed and read by optical character-reading devices.

magnetic ink character recognition (MICR)
Computer recognition of characters printed with magnetic ink; primarily used for check processing by the banking industry.

magnetic stripe
A stripe of iron oxide coating on the back of credit cards or other cards that enables computers to magnetically read information stored on the stripe.

The ScanMan is a hand-held optical image scanner.

3. The easiest user interface for data entry and conversational computing is provided by _____ and _____.

4. An _____ wand can read bar coding or merchandise packaging.

5. Computers typically use _____ technology to read checks in banking.

Answers: 1. printers, plotters 2. dot matrix, laser printers 3. voice recognition, voice response 4. optical scanning 5. magnetic ink character recognition

Storage Trends and Trade-offs

Individuals and organizations store their data resources on a variety of storage devices until they are needed. For example, you may store data on pieces of paper in a notebook or on paper documents in file folders locked in a filing cabinet. Many organizations still store a lot of data that way. With computer-based information systems, however, data resources are stored temporarily in a computer's memory circuits, and more permanently on a variety of secondary storage media and devices. Then data is available when needed for processing into information products for end users.

Figure 8-5 illustrates the major categories of primary and secondary storage media. Notice some of the trade-offs as you move from one type of computer storage to another. If you use larger-capacity storage media like optical disks, you sacrifice some access speed but pay less per bit of storage. On the other hand, if you use large amounts of volatile semiconductor memory circuits (RAM), you gain fast access speeds, but sacrifice some security and storage capacity and pay more per bit of storage.

Of course, these trade-offs are continually changing as developments in storage technology continue. For example, the capacity of semiconductor memory chips continues to increase, while their cost per bit of storage is dropping steadily. The same holds true for the speed, capacity, and cost of

Figure 8-5
Each type of storage media requires trade-offs in speed, capacity, and cost.

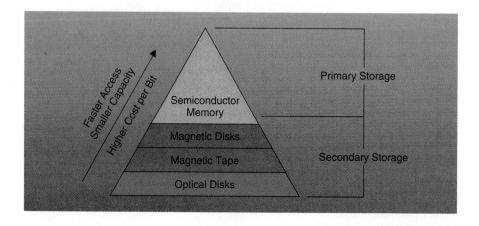

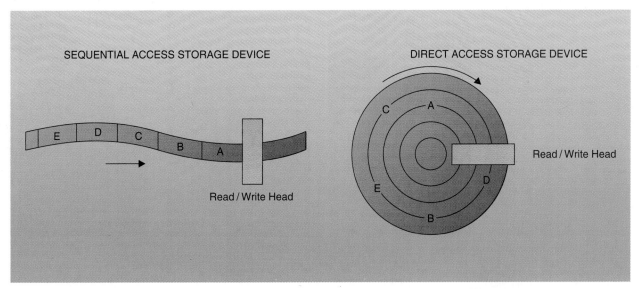

Figure 8-6
Direct access devices let you access data directly instead of sequentially.

magnetic disk and tape media as they compete with the fast-growing use of larger-capacity but slower-speed optical disks. For now, semiconductor memory chips are the media that computers use for primary storage and a limited amount of high-speed secondary storage. Magnetic disks lead the pack as the most widely used form of secondary storage media, followed by magnetic tape and optical disks.

Direct versus Sequential Access

Another trade-off among storage devices is their capability for *direct* versus *sequential* access to stored data. As we saw in Chapter 7, semiconductor memory chips are a **direct access** storage media we call random-access memory (RAM) or read-only memory (ROM). Magnetic and optical disk devices are other *direct access storage devices* (DASDs). This means that any data element stored on a magnetic or optical disk can be accessed directly in approximately the same time as any other. This is similar to directly selecting a specific song on a compact disk (CD) that is spinning in a CD player. The laser reading head can move directly to the track where the song you want to hear begins. That's direct access. See Figure 8-6.

Magnetic tape is a **sequential access** medium. The storage locations on magnetic tape do not have unique addresses and therefore cannot be directly addressed. Instead, data elements must be recorded or retrieved one after another in a predetermined sequence on the tape. For instance, all the records of students could be stored on a magnetic tape in a numerical order based on their student ID numbers. Therefore, if you wanted to locate the record of a particular student, your computer might have to search most of the recorded data on a tape until it found the correct student ID. This is like using *fast forward* or *rewind* on a stereo cassette tape deck to find a specific song you want to hear. That's sequential access.

direct access
A method of storage in which each storage position has a unique address and can be individually accessed in approximately the same period of time without having to search through storage positions.

sequential access
A method of storing and retrieving data in which elements are recorded in a predetermined sequence.

Magnetic storage media include, from far left, floppy disks, mainframe magnetic tapes, hard magnetic disk drives, and removable disk packs.

Magnetic Disk Storage

Magnetic disk media provide fast access and large secondary storage capacities at a reasonable cost. Therefore, they are used as direct access storage devices (DASDs) in most types of computer systems. Magnetic disks are of two types: conventional (hard) metal disks and flexible (floppy) plastic diskettes. They come in a variety of disk arrangements, including multiple disk units, removable disk packs and cartridges, and fixed disk units. Removable disk devices are popular because they can be used interchangeably in magnetic disk drives and stored offline when not in use.

Magnetic disks are thin metal or plastic disks that are coated on both sides with an iron oxide recording material. One or more disks may be mounted on a vertical shaft, which may rotate at 300–3,600 revolutions per minute (rpm). Electromagnetic read/write heads are positioned by access arms slightly above both surfaces of each disk to magnetically read or write data on concentric circular **tracks.** Data is recorded on tracks in the form of tiny magnetized spots that form the binary codes representing characters as bytes of data. Thousands of bytes can be recorded on each track with several hundred data tracks on each disk surface. Each track is subdivided into a number of portions called **sectors.** A sector can hold from a few hundred to several thousand bytes, depending on the disk drive's recording density. See Figure 8-7.

Sealed disk drives have grown in popularity. Their control of the disk environment results in faster, more reliable operation and more compact, high-density storage capacity. The read/write heads in magnetic disk devices "float" or "fly" on an air cushion above the disk surface; clearance is usually less than 50 microinches (millionths of an inch). Thus, many magnetic disk units have air filtration systems to remove airborne particles, such as smoke or dust. Such particles can cause the read/write head to come in contact with the disk (called a *head crash*), which usually results in the loss of data on that portion of the disk. That's why it's so important for you to keep your floppy disks clean

magnetic disks
Thin metal or plastic disks coated with iron oxide that allows data to be recorded in the form of tiny magnetized spots.

tracks
Concentric circular positions on a magnetic disk surface on which data is stored as tiny magnetized spots that form binary codes.

sectors
A division of a track on a magnetic disk surface.

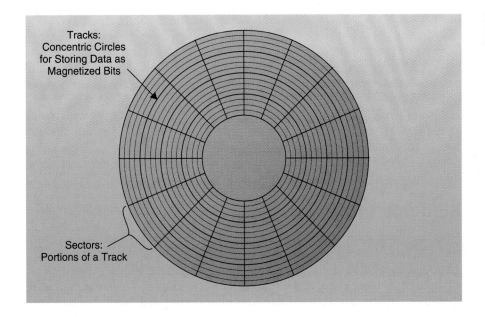

Figure 8-7
Magnetic disks are organized into sectors and tracks.

Tracks:
Concentric Circles
for Storing Data as
Magnetized Bits

Sectors:
Portions of a Track

and protected. It's also why hard disks are sealed and filtered to eliminate particles greater than 17 microinches. The read/write head can then fly less than 20 microinches above the disk surface. See Figure 8-8.

Floppy Disks

Floppy disks, or *magnetic diskettes*, consist of polyester film covered with an iron oxide compound. A single disk rotates freely inside a protective plastic jacket, which has an opening to accommodate the read/write head of a disk drive unit. Most floppy disks come in $5^1/_4$-inch and $3^1/_2$-inch sizes. The $5^1/_4$-inch disk has a flexible plastic jacket and was the most widely used in microcomputers. However, the $3^1/_2$-inch disk has rapidly become a new standard. Its hard plastic jacket and metal cover for its read/write opening provide a more protective, stable environment. Currently, $5^1/_4$-inch disks hold from 360 kilobytes to 1.2 megabytes, while $3^1/_2$-inch disks have capacities from 720 kilobytes to 1.44 and 2.8 megabytes. Higher-capacity floppys, such as $3^1/_2$-inch

floppy disk
A small magnetic disk consisting of plastic coated with iron oxide and enclosed in a protective case.

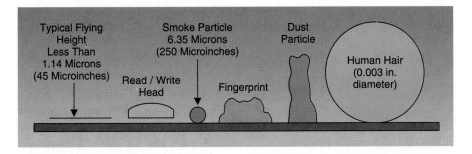

Figure 8-8
These magnetic disk pollutants cause *head crashes*.

Typical Flying
Height
Less Than
1.14 Microns
(45 Microinches)

Read / Write
Head

Smoke Particle
6.35 Microns
(250 Microinches)

Fingerprint

Dust
Particle

Human Hair
(0.003 in.
diameter)

disks holding up to 25 megabytes, are available for special, very high-density disk drives.

Floppy disks provide an economical and convenient form of direct access storage for microcomputers. They are also removable and interchangeable and can be stored conveniently offline when not needed. They are thus a popular way to provide backup storage for data or programs stored on your microcomputer's hard disk unit. The floppy's main limitations are its slow speed and small capacity compared to hard disk drives. For example, one double-spaced page of text contains about 2K bytes of data. While a 1.44 megabyte floppy can hold about 720 pages of text, a 40 megabyte hard drive can store up to 20,000 pages of text.

Hard Disk Drives

hard disk drive
A magnetic disk device consisting of several metal disks, access arms, and read/write heads in a sealed module.

Most magnetic **hard disk drives** consist of several metal disks, access arms, and read/write heads in a sealed module. This technology allows higher speeds, greater data-recording densities, and closer tolerances within a more stable environment. Most hard disk drives are nonremovable, but removable *disk cartridge* versions are also popular. Removable, open *disk packs* are still used by some mainframe systems, but since they are not sealed devices, their use is declining.

Hard disk drives for microcomputers contain one to four disks with diameters of $2^1/_2$, $3^1/_2$, and $5^1/_4$ inches. Capacities range from 10 to more than 500 megabytes. Mainframe hard disk units typically contain from six to 11 disks with either 8-inch or 14-inch diameters. Capacities of these drives range from 500 megabytes to several gigabytes (billions of bytes). However, some companies are replacing their mainframe hard disk drives with *disk arrays* of several interconnected microcomputer hard disk drives for billions of bytes of direct access storage.

The major advantage of hard magnetic disks is that they give you fast, high-capacity, direct access storage. A major limitation is the possible loss of your data and programs due to head crashes. Therefore, you need to "back up" hard disks with floppy disks or magnetic tape devices that provide backup storage. Lack of removability is another limitation, though removable hard disk cartridges are now available to provide you with convenience, backup, and security. Hard disk units are more expensive than floppy disk drives, but their cost is steadily declining with advancements in storage technology.

Magnetic Tape Storage

magnetic tape
A plastic tape with an iron oxide surface on which data can be stored by selective magnetization of portions of the surface.

Magnetic tape is an important sequential-access medium. Though its access time is slower than magnetic disks, it is a compact, stable, large-capacity form of secondary storage. It is popular for storing large amounts of infrequently used data and for backing up magnetic disk drives.

Data on magnetic tape are recorded as magnetized spots on the iron oxide coating of 1/4-inch or 1/2-inch plastic tape by the read/write heads of magnetic tape drives. Magnetic tape is usually divided into horizontal *tracks* to accommodate the recording of bits into binary computer codes. Figure 8-9 illustrates the format of data recorded on nine tracks in the EBCDIC computer code on magnetic tape.

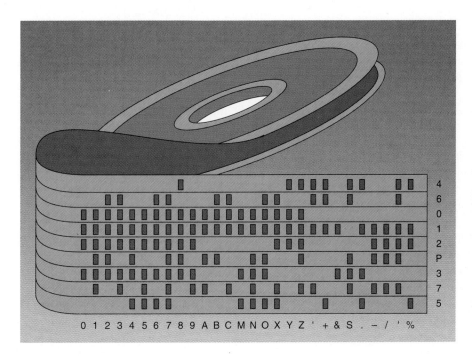

Figure 8-9
Magnetic tape stores data as magnetic spots arranged in binary computer code.

Another magnetic medium is the magnetic tape cartridge.

Magnetic tape comes in several forms including tape reels, cartridges, and cassettes. Mainframe computers are increasingly using magnetic tape cartridges instead of the traditional magnetic tape reel. These cartridges can hold more than 200 megabytes, and are much more compact, and easier to load and unload. In fact, automatic *cartridge library* systems that hold thousands of cartridges are being used by many large organizations to automate tape loading, unloading, and management on their mainframe systems. Magnetic tape cassettes and cartridge units, including 8-millimeter video tape cassette drives, can store hundreds of megabytes of data. They have become popular for making backup copies of data and programs stored on hard disk drives.

Optical Disk Storage

Optical disks are a direct access storage medium used for very large-capacity (*mass*) storage. Mainframe optical disk devices use 8-inch and 12-inch plastic disks with capacities of several gigabytes of information. Another version is called **CD-ROM** (compact disk read-only memory). It uses a 12-centimeter (4.7-inch) compact disk (CD) similar to the ones used in stereo music systems. Each disk can store more than 500 megabytes. Data are recorded by using a laser to burn permanent microscopic pits in a spiral track on a master disk from which compact disks can be mass produced. Then CD-ROM disk drives use a laser device to read the binary codes formed by those pits.

Another optical disk technology is **WORM** (write once, read many) disks. End users with microcomputers and WORM recorder drives can record data once on an optical disk and then read it indefinitely. The major limitation of CD-ROM and WORM systems is that recorded data cannot be erased. However, this makes them a great choice for *archival* storage applications where

optical disk
A mass storage device using laser technology to record and read tiny spots on a plastic disk.

CD-ROM
Compact disk read-only memory; a small optical disk on which data is permanently stored.

WORM disks
Write once, read many; optical disks on which data can be recorded once by end users and then read indefinitely.

REAL-WORLD EXAMPLE

Arthur Andersen and the Attorneys: CD Libraries

No more lugging heavy books and reference manuals to each audit. The international accounting firm of Arthur Andersen and Company used to allocate a 500-pound library of accounting and auditing manuals to each member of its audit staff. All of that material has been replaced with one CD-ROM optical disk, only 4.7 inches in diameter, that weighs less than an ounce. Known as the Audit Reference and Resource Disk (AARD), this optical disk contains 150 library files and software programs to assist auditors when they are auditing the financial records of their clients.

No more searching through musty law libraries. Attorneys are increasingly using CD-ROM libraries because more legal databases are becoming available on CDs each month. For example, National Legal Databases of Tulsa, Oklahoma, publishes LawDisc CD-ROM—California Civil Cases. This is a two-disk set that contains the full text of all California civil cases from the 1930s to the present. National Legal Databases also publishes CDs on civil case law from other states as well as a variety of federal law libraries.

1. What are the benefits and limitations of CD-ROM in accounting and law?

2. What other occupations could benefit from the use of CD-ROM libraries?

---

erasable optical disk
An optical disk that records and erases data by using a laser to heat microscopic points on the disk's surface.

This CD-ROM is an optical disk.

an easily accessible but permanent record of legal and business documents and reference materials is needed.

Erasable optical disk systems are the latest optical disk technology. This is the form that is expected to challenge magnetic disks and tape as storage media. Erasable technology records and erases data by using a laser to heat a microscopic point on the disk's surface. In some versions, a magnetic coil changes the spot's reflective properties from one direction to another, thus recording a binary 1 or 0. A laser device can then read the binary codes on the disk by sensing the direction of reflected light. See Figure 8-10.

One of the major uses of optical disks is in *image processing*, where long-term archival storage of historical files of document images must be maintained. As an example, banks and insurance companies use optical scanners to capture digitized images of customer documents. They store them on WORM optical disks as an alternative to using microfilm. The major benefit of CD-ROM disks is that they provide fast access to reference materials and data banks in a convenient, compact form. This could include encyclopedias, directories, manuals, periodical abstracts, parts listings, and statistical databases of business and economic activity. You will also find that interactive multimedia educational and industrial training courses have been developed on CD-ROM disks.

Optical disks have thus become a popular storage medium for archival storage, image processing, and multimedia applications. They appear to be a promising alternative to magnetic disks and tape for providing end users and organizations with mass storage capabilities. However, the optical erasable technology is still being perfected, while the capabilities of magnetic disks

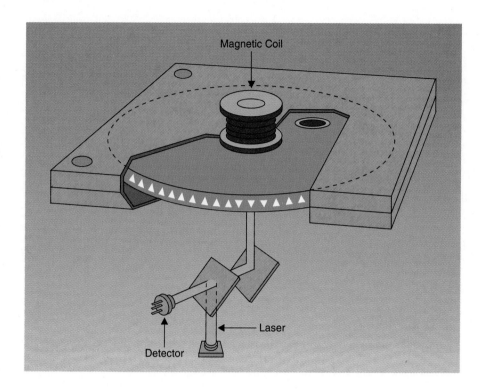

Magnetic Coil

Laser

Detector

Figure 8-10
An erasable optical disk uses a
laser to record and erase data.

continue to increase. Also, optical disk devices are significantly slower and, in
the case of WORM and erasable versions, more expensive than magnetic disk
drives. As a result, optical disk systems are not expected to displace magnetic
disk technology in the near future.

Other Storage Methods

Several other forms of secondary storage are available. For example, you could
command your operating system to treat part of your computer's semiconductor memory (RAM) as if it was another magnetic disk drive. This effectively
makes part of memory a form of high-speed secondary storage called a *RAM
disk*. Its major drawback is its volatility. That is, unlike a magnetic disk, its
contents will be lost if power is interrupted.

Several manufacturers have developed non-volatile memory chip devices
called *flash memory* for use with notebook microcomputers. One version is
called the *Flash RAM card*. These removable credit card-size devices provide
up to 40 megabytes of erasable direct access secondary storage. Industry fore-
casters predict that Flash RAM cards may replace magnetic disks as their storage capacity continues to increase.

Other semiconductor memory devices are being offered as secondary storage media. For instance, the magnetic stripe technology on credit cards has
begun to be replaced in some applications by **smart cards**. These cards con-

smart cards
Cards containing information
stored in ROM semiconductor
memory. Some versions may contain a microprocessor chip.

This pen-based computer uses a Flash RAM card for secondary storage.

tain information about you stored in ROM semiconductor memory chips. Other versions even contain a microprocessor. Some organizations are experimenting with *optical cards* that use optical disk technology. For example, a complete history of all of your medical records or credit transactions could be stored on a single optical card, which would be updated each time you used it.

Quick Quiz

1. Semiconductor memory chips have faster storage _____, while optical disks have greater storage _____.
2. The most widely used storage media are _____ for primary storage and _____ for secondary storage.
3. Magnetic disks are a _____ storage media, while magnetic tape is a_____ storage media.
4. The most widely used forms of magnetic disk technology for microcomputers are removable _____ and large-capacity _____ drives.
5. CD-ROM is a popular form of _____ storage technology.

Answers: 1. access, capacity 2. semiconductor memory chips, magnetic disks 3. direct access, sequential access 4. floppy disks, hard disk 5. optical disk

E T H I C S

Ethical Issues in Computer Peripherals

One of the ethical issues raised in the use of computers concerns their *accessibility* to the handicapped and disadvantaged. Some ethical scholars argue that a case can be made that there should be a "right of access" to computers for all citizens. This argument is based on the premise that because our society has become so dependent on computers, access to computers has become necessary to achieve other rights, that is, our constitutional rights as citizens.

Another example of the computer accessibility issue is the Rehabilitation Act Amendments of 1986, which contains a Section 508 entitled "Electronic Equipment Accessibility." The impetus for this section was the fact that government offices were developing into *electronic offices* where a microcomputer on every desk was becoming commonplace. Section 508 was developed to guarantee that persons with disabilities could gain or keep their jobs with the federal government. So the section was written to make *accessibility* to microcomputers and other electronic equipment a requirement of federal law.

Let's look at a few of the federal regulations that were developed to guide government agencies to see how they affect the *hardware interface* provided by computer peripherals. For example, the regulations state:[1]

Federal agencies shall provide handicapped employees and non-handicapped employees equivalent access to electronic office equipment. Agencies shall consider:

- Utilization of special peripherals to attain equivalent end results by handicapped and nonhandicapped employees.
- Access to and use of equivalent communications capabilities by handicapped employees.

These regulations are then made more specific by "functional specifications" for input and output that must be considered by federal agencies when acquiring computer peripherals. Examples of such specifications include:

- Some programs require a fine motor control device such as a mouse. An alternative method such as voice input or key strokes may be required.
- An alternative input device may be needed to replace or supplement a keyboard or mouse. Alternative input methods may include speech input, eye scan, suck and puff, or headtracking.
- Auditory output capable of speech with adjustable volume control and headset jack or a visual alternative to warning beeps and other auditory output may be required.
- Visual output from video monitors may need to be enlarged, reproduced verbally, or modified in some way.

(continued on following page)

(continued from previous page)

What Do You Think?

Should user interface hardware be designed to provide accessibility to all end users? Should the "right of access" be a civil right? What do you think?

[1]Richard E. Ladner, "Computer Accessibility for Federal Workers with Disabilities: It's the Law," *Communications of the ACM*, August, 1989, pp. 952–956.

End Note: End Users and Computer Peripherals

This chapter emphasizes the important role peripheral devices play in helping you use a computer. Input devices like keyboards and electronic mice help you enter data and give commands. Output devices like video monitors and printers let you see what you and the computer are doing, and let you display or print the information products you produce. And secondary storage devices like magnetic disks or CD-ROM help you store data and programs until you are ready to use them.

You have also seen that the reason there are so many peripheral devices to choose from is that none of them is the perfect device for all applications. For example, keyboards do text, mice don't. Video monitors can't produce hard copy output like printers do. And magnetic disk drives can't store as much data as CD-ROM, but they access data faster.

Finally, we've pointed out several important trends that are driving developments in computer peripherals. One is the trend toward a more direct, easier-to-use, and more natural hardware interface for end users. Developments like touchscreens and voice recognition and voice response all point in this direction. Another trend is moving us toward secondary storage devices that are smaller and faster but yet have massive storage capacities. CD-ROM is an example of a step in that direction.

The development of computers that are easy to use and yet have more computing capabilities is not just a matter of developing more powerful processors and better software packages. It also depends on the continued development of better computer peripherals.

Summary

Input/Output Trends Developments in peripheral devices for input and output are designed to provide a direct and natural user interface. Examples include pointing devices like the electronic mouse and touchscreen and automated data-entry methods like optical scanning, which replace older methods that require manual processing of source documents. End user terminals are becoming more intelligent and are increasingly being used to capture transaction data in many applications.

Keyboards and Pointing Devices   Keyboards are the most widely used input devices for computers. Pointing devices like the electronic mouse, joystick, and trackball use a point and click action to move the cursor and make selections. The touchscreen allows you to use your finger as a pointing device.

Writing/Drawing Devices   Several devices enter your handwriting and drawing into a computer system. The light pen allows you to write or draw directly on the display screen. The graphics pad and the LCD screen of pen-based computers digitize what you draw or write on their pressure-sensitive surfaces.

Video Input and Output   Computers can accept video input from a VCR, camcorder, or TV receiver for later use in video or multimedia presentations. Video output is provided by video monitors using cathode ray tube (CRT), liquid crystal display (LCD), and plasma display technologies. The resolution of these displays depends on the capabilities of the video monitor and the graphics circuit board in your computer system.

Printed Output   Several devices are available to produce permanent printed output for convenience and documentation. Dot matrix and line printers print by impact on paper. Other printers use a nonimpact process. Laser printers use a technology similar to xerographic copy machines, while ink-jet printers spray small jets of ink to form characters. Plotters use ink pens or other methods to draw graphics displays on paper.

Voice Recognition and Response   Voice technologies provide the easiest and most natural user interface. Voice recognition hardware and software analyze speech or vocal patterns and transform them into binary codes. Applications include voice data entry, speaker recognition, and voice operation of some software packages. Voice response systems are available for mainframes, minicomputers, and microcomputer systems. Speech synthesizer microprocessors can also be found in toys, appliances, and other products. Voice response systems allow computers to verbally respond to your use of a touch-tone phone for telemarketing surveys and customer inquiries.

Optical and Magnetic Recognition   Optical scanning technology relies on scanning lasers and photoelectric devices to convert pages of text or graphics into digital computer input. Optical scanning wands and other scanners are also used to read special bar codes on merchandise tags. One form of magnetic data entry involves the use of magnetic ink character recognition technology by banks to read checks and deposit slips for computer processing. Account numbers recorded on a magnetic stripe on the back of many credit and debit cards can be read by bank ATMs and other devices.

Storage Trends and Trade-offs   End users make trade-offs in speed, capacity, and cost whenever they choose storage media. Semiconductor memory has fast access speed but costs more per bit of storage capacity than magnetic or optical disks. Other factors such as the volatility of RAM semiconductor memory and the sequential access nature of magnetic tape must also be considered.

Magnetic Disk Storage   Magnetic disks provide direct access secondary storage for most computer systems. Floppy disks for microcomputers come in two sizes and can provide several megabytes of storage. They are economical, removable, and interchangeable, though relatively slow and limited in capacity. Hard disk drives, both fixed and removable, provide fast, large-capacity storage. Microcomputer hard disk drives offer capacities from ten to several hundred megabytes. Mainframe hard disk drives provide several gigabytes of capacity.

Magnetic Tape Storage   Magnetic tape is a sequential access storage medium. Data is stored in a sequential order on the tape. Magnetic tape is compact, stable, and has a large storage capacity, though it is slower than hard magnetic disks. It is a popular medium for making backup copies of data and programs stored on hard disk drives.

Optical Disk Storage   Optical disks can store vast amounts of data on a compact direct access medium. They have larger capacities but are slower and more costly than magnetic disk and tape media. CD-ROM is an optical disk similar to those used in compact disk music systems. It provides easy access to more than 500 megabytes of reference materials. Write once, read many (WORM) optical disks can be recorded once to create a permanent copy of several billion bytes of document images for long-term storage. Erasable optical disk systems are the latest optical disk technology. They are expected to challenge magnetic disk and tape technologies in the future.

Key Terms and Concepts

bar coding	mouse
CD-ROM	optical character recognition
cathode ray tube	optical disk storage
daisy wheel printer	optical scanning
data entry trends	pen-based computing
direct access storage	plasma display
dot matrix printer	plotters
erasable optical disks	pointing devices
graphics pad	semiconductor memory chips
icons	sequential access
ink-jet printer	storage media trade-offs
input/output trends	terminals
joystick	thermal printer
laser printer	touchscreen
light pen	trackball
line printer	user interface hardware
liquid crystal display	video input
magnetic disk storage	voice recognition
magnetic ink character recognition	voice response
magnetic stripe card	wand
magnetic tape storage	

Review Quiz

True/False

_____ 1. Computer input and output methods for end users are becoming more direct and natural.

_____ 2. Hardware and software should be safe and easy to use.

_____ 3. Manual processing of source documents is replacing direct, automated methods.

_____ 4. A video display terminal uses a keyboard and video display with telecommunications links to a computer.

_____ 5. You just point the keyboard at what you want done.

_____ 6. Moving a mouse along your desktop moves the cursor on the screen.

_____ 7. A joystick is a popular pointing device for video games.

_____ 8. You can communicate with some computers by touching their display screens.

_____ 9. A trackball helps you "write" on the video screen with a light-sensitive device.

_____ 10. A data tablet captures data by writing on a pressure-sensitive surface.

Multiple Choice

_____ 1. This promises to be the easiest, most natural way to communicate with a computer:
  a. a mouse.
  b. a trackball.
  c. a keyboard.
  d. voice recognition.

_____ 2. The most common video display technology is
  a. CRT.
  b. LCD.
  c. plasma.
  d. electroluminescent.

_____ 3. This device produces hard copy output such as paper documents and reports:
  a. CRT.
  b. LCD.
  c. CD-ROM.
  d. printer.

_____ 4. This printer prints a character by the impact of metal pins:
  a. daisy wheel.
  b. dot matrix.
  c. line.
  d. laser.

_____ 5. This printer prints a page at a time of high-quality output:
  a. daisy wheel.

     b. dot matrix.
     c. line.
     d. laser.

_____ 6. Capturing data by processing light reflected from images is known as

     a. light processing.
     b. image capture.
     c. optical scanning.
     d. light scanning.

_____ 7. A flexible magnetic disk in a plastic jacket is called a

     a. floppy disk.
     b. hard disk.
     c. cassette disk.
     d. cartridge disk.

_____ 8. This adds large magnetic disk capacity to a computer:

     a. floppy disk.
     b. hard disk.
     c. soft disk.
     d. cassette disk.

_____ 9. A storage technology that uses a laser to read microscopic points on plastic disks is

     a. a CD-ROM.
     b. a magnetic disk.
     c. an erasable optical.
     d. all of the above.

_____ 10. Permanent storage on small optical disks is called

     a. CD-ROM.
     b. WORM.
     c. erasable optical.
     d. all of the above.

Fill-in

1. In a(n) _____ device, each storage position can be accessed in approximately the same time.

2. A(n) _____ is like a stationary electronic mouse.

3. The same display technology as electronic watches and calculators is used by a(n) _____ video screen.

4. A(n) _____ is a hand-held device that reads bar coding.

5. Bank check processing uses _____ technology.

6. Printing a character by spraying tiny jets of ink is the technology of _____ printers.

7. A(n) _____ printer prints a character by using heated wires.

8. A(n) _____ lets you write on its pressure-sensitive LCD screen.

9. The _____ stores data in the form of magnetic spots on metal or plastic disks.

10. End users can only record data on _____ disks once.

Questions for Thought and Discussion

1. Do you think computers are becoming easier to use? Why or why not?

2. Why are there so many types of input, output, and storage devices?

3. Which input devices would you choose for entering data from (a) printed questionnaires, (b) telephone surveys, (c) bank checks, (d) merchandise tags, and (e) engineering drawings? Explain your choices.

4. Which output devices would you choose for producing (a) visual displays for portable microcomputers, (b) legal documents, (c) engineering drawings, (d) financial results for top executives, and (e) responses for telephone transactions? Explain your choices.

5. Refer to the Real-World Example of State Farm and Kaiser Permanente Hospital in the chapter. What are the benefits and limitations of pen-based computing compared to the computers you are currently using?

6. Refer to the Real-World Example of Circuitest, Inc. in the chapter. Why isn't voice recognition more widely used?

7. Which devices would you choose for (a) primary storage, (b) large-capacity, permanent storage, (c) large-capacity, fast direct access storage, (d) large files for occasional processing, and (e) inexpensive, portable, direct access storage? Explain your choices.

8. Refer to the Real-World Example of Arthur Andersen and the Attorneys in the chapter. What different applications could WORM or erasable optical disks have compared to CD-ROM?

9. What improvements to the transaction terminals you use (bank ATMs or POS terminals in retail stores) can you suggest that would make them easier to use?

10. What improvements to the computer peripheral devices or software packages you have used can you suggest to provide a better user interface? Make a brief report to the class.

Review Quiz Answers

True/False: **1.** T **2.** T **3.** F **4.** T **5.** F **6.** T **7.** T **8.** T **9.** F **10.** T

Multiple Choice: **1.** d **2.** a **3.** d **4.** b **5.** d **6.** c **7.** a **8.** b **9.** d **10.** a

Fill-in: **1.** direct access **2.** trackball **3.** LCD **4.** wand **5.** magnetic ink character recognition **6.** ink-jet **7.** thermal **8.** pen-based computer **9.** magnetic disk **10.** WORM

C H A P T E R

9

TELECOMMUNICATIONS NETWORKS: SHARING INFORMATION AND COMPUTING RESOURCES

OUTLINE

You and Telecommunications

Telecommunications Networks

Network Alternatives

Telecommunications Media

Telecommunications Processors

Telecommunications Software

End User Telecommunications

Technical Note: Communications Alternatives

End Note: End Users and Telecommunications

Ethics: Ethical Issues in Telecommunications

LEARNING OBJECTIVES

After reading and studying this chapter, you should be able to

Describe the basic components and major types of telecommunications networks.

Identify several major types of hardware, software, and media used in telecommunications networks.

Identify several major alternatives in telecommunications network designs and communications capabilities.

Describe several typical uses of telecommunications by end users.

You and Telecommunications

No matter what your career, you will probably need to exchange information and share computer resources with other end users. So to accomplish your work activities, you are going to have to depend on telecommunications networks to support your information processing and communications needs. That's why you need to study how end users and organizations use telecommunications technologies.

What is telecommunications? **Telecommunications** is the sending of information in any form (voice, data, text, and images) from one place to another using electronic, laser, or other technologies. Thus, it can refer to TV and radio broadcasting, as well as communications between computers and end users. *Data communications* more narrowly describes transmitting and receiving data over communication links between one or more computer systems and input/output terminals. Some people use the terms *teleprocessing* and *telematics* to emphasize the integration of telecommunications and computer-based information processing. However, it's a fact that all forms of telecommunications now rely heavily on computers and computerized devices. Since the broader term *telecommunications* includes data communications activities, we will use these terms interchangeably.

It is important that you understand some of the major alternatives in telecommunications networks, resources, and services. This understanding will help you be an informed user of telecommunications. However, a general understanding and appreciation, not a detailed knowledge, is sufficient for most end users. Therefore, in this chapter, we will first discuss the basic components and types of telecommunications networks. Then we will discuss a variety of telecommunications topics to give you a brief introduction to important characteristics found in telecommunications networks today. Finally, we will discuss some of the major uses of telecommunications for end user computing that you may experience in your use of telecommunications.

Telecommunications Networks

Before we can discuss the uses of telecommunications, you should understand some basic concepts of telecommunications networks. Generically, we can define a *communications network* as any arrangement where a *sender* transmits a *message* to a *receiver* over a *channel* consisting of some type of *medium*. Let's look at a **telecommunications network** as an example.

Figure 9-1 illustrates the five basic components of a *telecommunications network,* which we will discuss in this chapter.

- *Terminals* are an obvious component. As we saw in Chapter 8, any input/output device that uses telecommunications networks to transmit or receive data is a terminal. This might include video terminals, microcomputers, telephones, office equipment, and transaction terminals such as automated teller machines (ATMs) and point-of-sale (POS) terminals.

- *Telecommunications processors* are less well-known components. They support data transmission and reception between terminals and computers in a network. Devices such as *modems* and *multiplexers* may

telecommunications
The sending of information in any form from one place to another using electronic, laser, or other technologies.

telecommunications network
A system of computers, terminals, communications processors and software, interconnected by telecommunications channels and media.

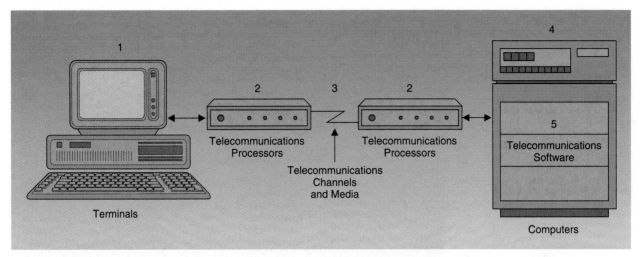

Figure 9-1
Telecommunications networks have five basic categories of components.

convert data from analog to digital signals and back, or control the flow of communications traffic between computers and terminals.

- *Telecommunications channels* are the highways over which data are transmitted and received in a network. Telecommunications *channels* typically use combinations of *media* to get the job done. Media such as copper wires, coaxial cables, fiber optic cables, microwave systems, and communications satellite systems would probably all be used in regional and global telecommunications networks.

- *Computers* of all sizes and types are interconnected to provide information processing power and telecommunications management in a network. A mainframe computer may serve as a *host computer* for a large network, a minicomputer can act as a *front-end processor* in support of a mainframe, and a microcomputer may act as a *network server* for a small network of microcomputer workstations.

- *Telecommunications software* is a vital network component. These programs are used by various computer systems in a network for telecommunications support and management. Examples are *communications packages* for microcomputers, *network operating systems* for network servers, and telecommunications *monitors* for mainframe host computers.

Whether your microcomputer is only connected to a few others in a small office network or is part of a worldwide network of thousands of computers and end users, these five basic components must be at work to support your telecommunications activities. Millions of end users and organizations rely on these telecommunications network components to exchange information and carry out their activities. Therefore, you should use this framework to help you understand the many telecommunications networks in use today.

Wide Area Networks

There are many varieties of telecommunications networks. However, from an end user's point of view, there are two basic types: *wide area* and *local area* networks. Telecommunications networks covering a large geographic area are

Figure 9-2
Wide area networks span cities,
countries, and the world with
telecommunications links.

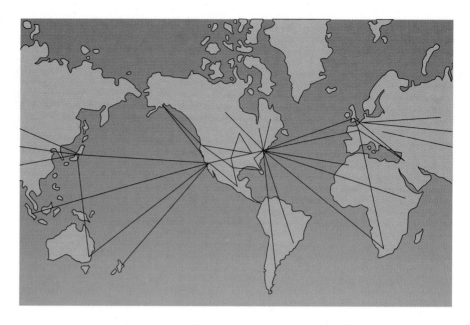

wide area networks (WANs)
A telecommunications network
covering a large geographic area.

popularly called **wide area networks (WANs).** Even networks that cover a large city or metropolitan area *(metropolitan area networks)* can also be included in this category. Wide area networks allow you to transmit and receive information across cities, regions, countries, or the world. For example, Figure 9-2 illustrates a worldwide area network. Such large networks are a necessity for carrying out the day-to-day activities of many organizations and their end users. So they are used by large manufacturers, banks, retail chains, transportation companies, government agencies, school districts, and many other organizations.

Mosaic is a popular "browser" for
the World Wide Web, a part of the
Internet.

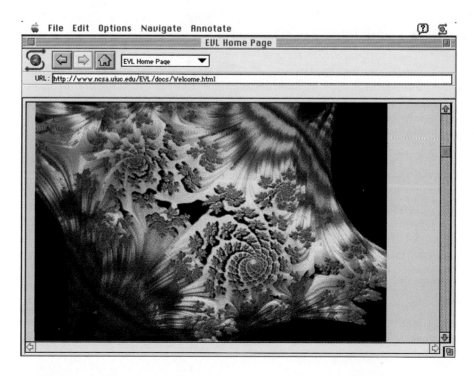

Sprint's global data network is operated from this control center.

The Internet and the Information Superhighway

The **Internet** is the largest "network of networks" today and the closest model we have to the information superhighway of tomorrow. The Internet is more than a wide area network. It is a rapidly growing global web of thousands of business, educational, and research networks connecting millions of computers and their users in over 100 countries to one another. The Internet evolved from a research and development network (ARPANET) established in 1969 by the U.S. Department of Defense to enable corporate, academic, and government researchers to communicate with E-mail and share data and computing resources. The Internet grew to over 25,000 networks and 20 million users in early 1994, with a rate of growth estimated at 7 to 10 percent per month.

The most popular Internet application is E-mail. Internet E-mail is fast, faster than many public networks. Messages usually arrive in seconds or a few minutes, anywhere in the world. And Internet E-mail messages can take the form of data, text, fax, and video files. The Internet also supports bulletin board systems formed by thousands of special interest groups. Anyone can post messages on thousands of topics for interested users to read. Other popular applications include accessing files and databases from libraries and thousands of organizations, logging on to other computers in the network, and holding realtime computer conversations with other Internet users.

Networks like the Internet and other developments in telecommunications technology have made the concept of an **information superhighway** technically possible. In this concept, local, regional, nation-wide, and global networks will be integrated into a vast "network of networks." The information superhighway system would connect individuals, households, businesses,

Internet
A network of thousands of business, educational, and research networks connecting millions of computers and their users in over 100 countries.

information superhighway
A national network of networks that would interconnect individuals, households, and institutions with interactive voice, data, video, and multimedia communications.

government agencies, libraries, universities, and all other institutions and would support interactive voice, data, video, and multimedia communications. Proponents argue that the information superhighway could dramatically increase our nation's competitiveness by improving economic communications and collaboration. For example, the information superhighway could provide electronic mail and videoconferencing services to enable businesses throughout the country to build products faster through an electronic collaboration in the product design process. Or the highway could support an interactive video home shopping and entertainment system that could revolutionize the retailing and entertainment industries.

Communications Carriers

Companies called **common carriers** provide many of the wide area communications networks used by computer-using firms and individuals. They have been authorized by government agencies to provide a selected number of communication services to the public. Examples are US West, Pacific Telesis, Southeastern Bell, General Telephone and Electronics, and many independent telephone companies. Other common carriers specialize in selling long-distance voice and digital data communications services, including AT&T Long Distance, ITT World Communications, U.S. Sprint, and MCI Communications.

Common carriers can provide several wide area telecommunications network options. For example, an organization could use regular, voice-grade, direct distance dialing (DDD), which is more expensive, slower, and less reliable than other options. Or it could sign up for a wide area telephone service (WATS) and pay a monthly fee for unlimited use of a set amount of telephone line capacity. Or it could lease its own communications lines (called *leased* lines) from telephone companies and be guaranteed exclusive use of a low-noise, fast communications channel. However, this last alternative is economically feasible only for large corporations, large universities, and government agencies with massive data communications needs. Another expensive option is the use of commercial communications satellite services, or using a *bypass* system in which an organization installs its own dish antennas and directly leases the use of communications satellites.

Other major communications carriers include companies called **value-added carriers** that operate networks called value-added networks (VANs). They lease communications lines from common carriers and offer communications services to customers. Typically, messages from customers are transmitted in groupings called *packets*. Therefore, their networks are sometimes called *packet-switching networks*. Value-added carriers offer their customers high-quality, relatively low-cost service in return for a membership fee and usage charges based on the amount of communications activity accomplished. Examples of such carriers are GTE Telenet, General Electric's Mark Net, and Compunet by CompuServe.

Local Area Networks

Local area networks (LANs) connect computers and other devices within a limited physical area, such as an office, building, manufacturing plant, or other work site. LANs became a major type of telecommunications network after end users in offices, departments, and other work groups began to use mi-

common carriers
An organization that supplies communications services to other organizations and to the public as authorized by government agencies.

value-added carriers
Companies that lease telecommunications lines from common carriers and offer a variety of telecommunications services to customers.

local area network (LAN)
A telecommunications network that typically connects computers, terminals, and other computerized devices within a limited physical area such as an office, building, or other work site.

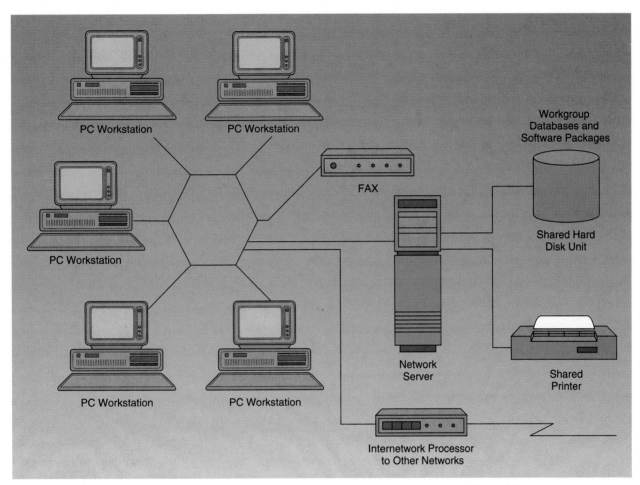

PC Workstation

PC Workstation

Workgroup
Databases and
Software Packages

PC Workstation

FAX

Shared Hard
Disk Unit

PC Workstation

PC Workstation

Network
Server

Shared
Printer

Internetwork Processor
to Other Networks

Figure 9-3
Local area networks allow end
users in a workgroup to share
hardware, software, and data resources.

crocomputers. LANs can interconnect your microcomputer with other end
users' workstations, other computer systems, and various types of computer
peripherals. This helps you and other end users in a work group communicate electronically and share hardware, software, and data resources. For instance, end users whose microcomputers are part of a LAN can share the use
of laser printers and magnetic hard disk units, copies of word processing or
electronic spreadsheet packages, and project databases. See Figure 9-3.

Most LANs include a microcomputer with a powerful main microprocessor and a large hard disk capacity that serves as the network's *file server* or
network server. This server contains a network operating system program that
controls network telecommunications and the use of network resources. For
example, it may distribute copies of common data files and software packages
to you and other end users, and control your access to laser printers and other
network peripherals. Some local area networks can also connect you to the
computing resources and databases of wide area networks. They use communications processors such as *bridges, routers,* and *hubs* to interconnect with
other LANs, or to form a connection to a WAN called a *gateway.* LANs have
thus become a powerful resource for end user and work group computing in
many organizations.

network server
A computer that contains a network operating system program to
control network telecommunications and the use of network
resources.

REAL-WORLD EXAMPLE

Tadpole Technology: Using the Internet

What is made up of more than 25,000 connected networks, has several million connected computers, and has more than 20 million users? Answer: the Internet. The Internet, which is the world's largest computer network, has been doubling in size (number of hosts and networks) every year since 1988. Many companies are being enticed by the Internet's speedy, low-cost global communications, its appropriateness for collaborative work, its online software, and its unique databases. Many organizations see the mega-network as a complement to their existing network. With the low connection cost—often a flat monthly fee for leased line and dial-up access—users can access commercial and noncommercial services to the United States and 100 other countries.

Notebook computer vendor Tadpole Technology, Inc., with headquarters in Cambridge, England, and with offices in Austin, Texas, San Jose, California, Dallas, New York, Washington, D.C., and France, keeps everyone connected through the Internet. "Even when the salespeople are traveling, they carry notebooks and connect to us through the Internet from the customer premises, their hotel room, or even from the airport lounge," says Jim Thompson, a Tadpole scientist.

1. What are the advantages of Internet to end users?

2. How could you benefit from using Internet at your college or university?

Quick Quiz

1. The five basic components of _____ are terminals, telecommunications processors, telecommunications channels, computers, and telecommunications software.

2. A _____ is any input/output device that is part of a telecommunications network.

3. A _____ is a telecommunications network covering a large geographic area.

4. Companies that provide a variety of telecommunications networks and services to the public are called _____.

5. A _____ is a telecommunications network that connects computers and other devices in a room, office building, or other work site.

Answers: 1. telecommunications networks 2. terminal 3. wide area network 4. communications carriers 5. local area network

Network Alternatives

Several basic alternatives are used in the design of telecommunications networks. The two simplest types of network designs are *point-to-point lines* and *multidrop lines*. When point-to-point lines are used, each terminal is connected by its own line to a computer system. When multidrop lines are used, several terminals share each communications link to a computer. Obviously,

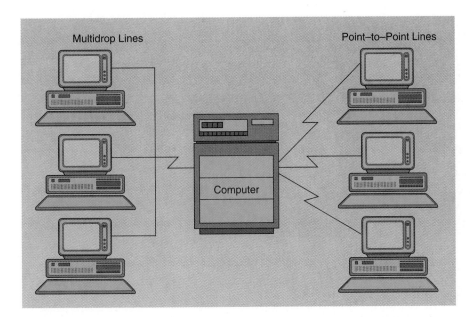

Figure 9-4
Multidrop and point-to-point lines are two basic ways to connect terminals to a computer.

a point-to-point line is more expensive because all of its communications capacity and equipment is being used by a single terminal. Therefore, point-to-point lines are used if there is almost continuous communication between computers and terminals. A multidrop line decreases communications costs because each line is shared by many terminals. Typically, multiplexers or concentrators may be used to help many terminals share the same line. See Figure 9-4.

Star, Ring, and Bus Networks

Figure 9-5 illustrates three basic designs used in wide area and local area networks. A **star network** ties end user computers to a central computer. In a **ring network,** computers are tied together to form a loop on a more equal basis. A **bus network** is a network in which computers share a single *bus,* or

star network
A network that connects end user computers to a central computer.

ring network
A network in which computers are interconnected to form a loop on a more equal basis.

bus network
A network in which computers share a single bus, or communications channel.

Figure 9-5
Star, ring, and bus networks are the three basic forms of network designs.

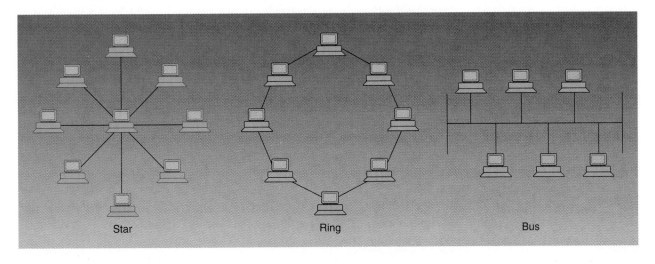

Star   Ring   Bus

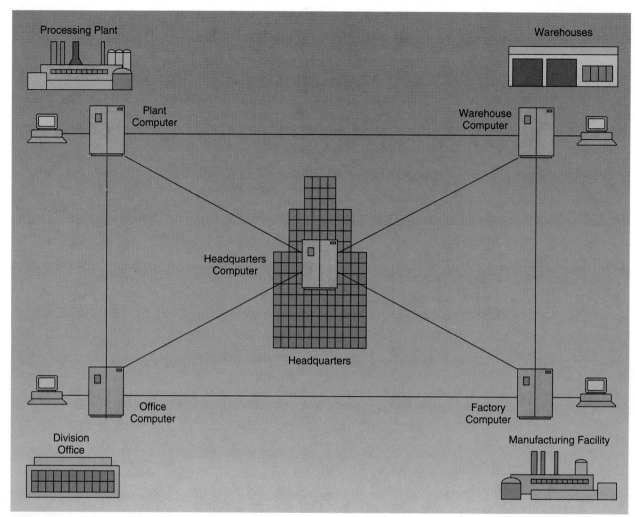

Figure 9-6
This distributed network combines star and ring approaches.

communications channel. In many cases, star networks take the form of *hierarchical networks*. For example, an organization might have a hierarchical network in which a large headquarters computer is connected to medium-size computers at the divisional level, which are connected to small computers at the departmental or work group level.

Star network variations are common because they can support the *chain-of-command* and hierarchical structures of many organizations. Ring and bus networks are most common in local area networks. Ring and bus networks are considered more reliable and less costly for the type of communications that are common in LANs. For example, if one computer in a ring network goes down, the other computers can continue to process their own work as well as communicate with each other. See Figure 9-6.

Protocols

Computer manufacturers and national and international organizations have developed standards called *protocols* to encourage the development of improved telecommunications network designs. That's because it is quite common to find a lack of compatibility between the telecommunications hardware and software of different manufacturers. For instance, it still is difficult to build telecommunications networks that include IBM, DEC, and Apple computer systems. Special multiplexers, called *protocol converters,* may be used to establish communications between incompatible computer systems. This situation has hampered the use of telecommunications, increased its costs, and reduced its effectiveness.

A **protocol** is a standard set of rules, procedures, or specifications for the control of communications resources and activities in a network. Many competing and incompatible protocols are in use today. As an example, some protocols establish standards for the physical design of the cables and connectors you use between terminals, computers, modems, and communications lines. Other protocols establish the rules for *handshaking.* This is the process of exchanging predetermined signals and characters so you can start a telecommunications session between you and other computers. Still other protocols deal with control of transmission reception in a network, packet and other switching techniques, internetwork connections, and so on.

protocol
A set of rules and procedures to control communications in a telecommunications network.

Network Architectures

The goal of **network architectures** is to promote an open, simple, flexible, and efficient telecommunications environment. So network architectures specify standard protocols, standard communications hardware and software interfaces, and a standard interface between end users and computer systems. For example, the International Standards Organization (ISO) has developed a seven-layer Open System Interconnection (OSI) model to serve as a standard for network architectures. Other examples of popular network architectures include IBM's Systems Network Architecture (SNA) and the Digital Network Architecture (DNA) of the Digital Equipment Corporation. Figure 9-7 illustrates the seven levels of the OSI model network architecture.

network architecture
A master plan designed to promote an open, simple, flexible, and efficient telecommunications environment through the use of standard protocols and standard communications hardware and software interfaces.

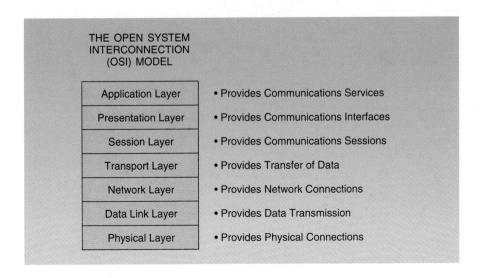

Figure 9-7
The OSI model communications network architecture is recognized as an international standard.

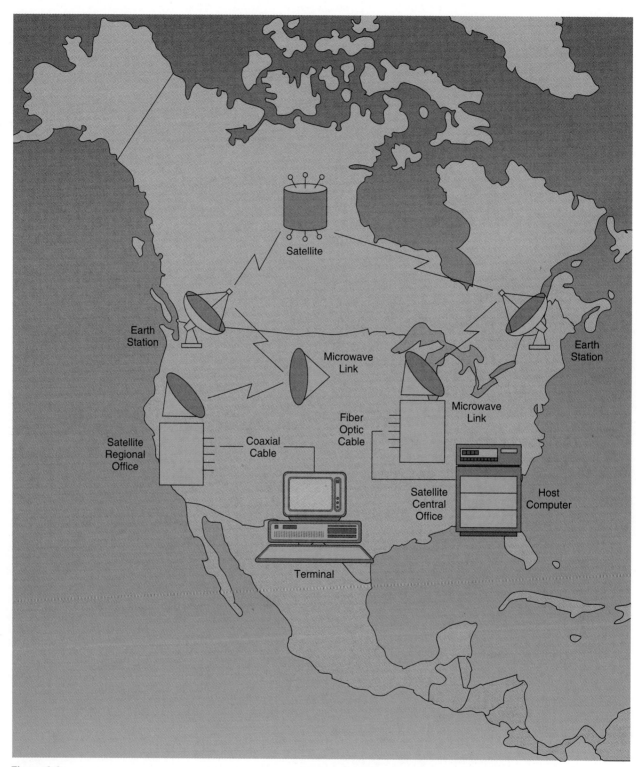

Figure 9-8
This wide area network uses a variety of telecommunications channels and media.

Integrated Services Digital Network

An exciting development in network architectures is ISDN, the Integrated Services Digital Network. This is a set of international standards that establishes digital telecommunications networks capable of handling voice, data, image, and video communications throughout the world. ISDN would replace the many types of networks in use today with a single type of digital network. Many communications carriers and corporations are developing and using the communications technologies needed to implement ISDN networks. ISDN is scheduled to be available in major U.S. cities by the mid-1990s and in most U.S. and major international locations by 2010.

Telecommunications Media

As we indicated earlier, data and other communications move on *telecommunications channels* in a telecommunications network. Every telecommunications channel uses a variety of **telecommunications media.** Examples include twisted-pair wire, coaxial cables, and fiber optic cables. These media physically link the devices in a network. Other alternatives, such as microwave systems, communications satellite systems, and cellular radio, use microwave and other radio waves to transmit and receive data. Figure 9-8 illustrates some of the major types of media used in a wide area telecommunications network.

telecommunications media
Materials and methods such as twisted-pair wire, coaxial and fiber optic cables, and microwave transmissions that link the devices in a network.

Wire and Cable

Ordinary telephone wire consisting of copper wire twisted into pairs, called **twisted-pair wire,** is used in communications networks throughout the world for both voice and data transmission. A **coaxial cable** consists of a sturdy copper or aluminum wire wrapped with spacers to insulate and protect it. This insulation minimizes interference and distortion of the signals the cable carries. Groups of coaxial cables may be bundled together in a big cable for ease of installation. These high-quality lines can be placed underground and laid on the floors of lakes and oceans. They allow high-speed data transmission and are used instead of twisted-pair wire lines in high-service metropolitan areas, for cable TV systems, and for short-distance connection of computers and peripheral devices. See Figure 9-9.

twisted-pair wire
Ordinary telephone wire, consisting of copper wire twisted into pairs, utilized in communications networks throughout the world for both voice and data transmission.

coaxial cable
A sturdy copper or aluminum wire wrapped with spacers to insulate and protect it.

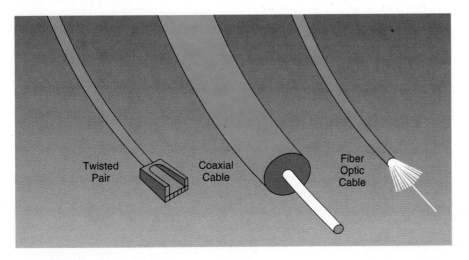

Figure 9-9
Twisted-pair wire, coaxial cable, and fiber optic cable are the most widely used telecommunications media.

Twisted Pair   Coaxial Cable   Fiber Optic Cable

Fiber Optics

fiber optics
The technology that uses cables consisting of very thin filaments of glass fibers that can conduct the light generated by lasers at frequencies that approach the speed of light.

Fiber optic cables consist of bundles of one or more glass fibers.

terrestrial microwaves
High-speed radio signals transmitted in a line-of-sight path between relay stations spaced approximately 30 miles apart.

communications satellites
Earth satellites placed in stationary orbits above the equator that serve as relay stations for microwave signals transmitted from earth stations.

The Intelsat VI communications satellite is seen here with clouds and open ocean as backdrop.

cellular radio
A radio communications technology that divides a metropolitan area into a honeycomb of cells to greatly increase the number of frequencies and thus the users that can take advantage of mobile phone service.

Fiber optics has become a major type of communications media. It uses cables consisting of one or more hair-thin filaments of glass fiber wrapped in a protective jacket. Fiber optics can conduct light pulses generated by lasers at transmission rates as high as 2 billion bits per second. This is about ten times greater than coaxial cable and 200 times better than twisted-pair wire lines. Fiber optic cables give you substantial size and weight reductions as well as increased speed and greater carrying capacity. For example, a half-inch-diameter fiber optic cable can carry up to 50,000 channels, compared to about 5,500 channels for a standard coaxial cable.

Fiber optic cables are not affected by and do not generate electromagnetic radiation. Therefore, multiple fibers can be placed in the same cable. Fiber optic cables don't need a lot of devices known as *repeaters* to retransmit their signals, like electrical wire media do. Fiber optics also has a much lower data error rate than other media and is harder to tap than electrical wire and cable. The biggest disadvantage of fiber optics is the difficulty of splicing the cable to make connections, though this is also a security advantage that limits line tapping.

Microwave and Satellite Systems

Terrestrial (earthbound) **microwave** systems transmit high-speed radio signals in a line-of-sight path between relay stations spaced approximately 30 miles apart. Microwave antennas are usually placed on top of buildings, towers, hills, and mountain peaks, and they are a familiar site in many sections of the country. They are still a popular medium for both long-distance and metropolitan area networks.

Communications satellites also use microwave transmission. Several dozen communications satellites from various nations placed into stationary "parking orbits" approximately 22,000 miles above the equator. Satellites are powered by solar panels and transmit microwave signals at a rate of several hundred million bits per second. They serve as relay stations for communication signals transmitted from *earth stations*. Earth stations beam microwave signals to the satellites, which amplify and retransmit the signals to dish antennas at other earth stations thousands of miles away.

While communications satellites were first used for voice and video transmission, they are now also used for high speed transmission of large volumes of data. Communications satellite systems are operated by several firms, including AT&T, Western Union, American Satellite Company, and Intelsat, an international consortium of more than a hundred nations. Large corporate and other users are also developing networks of small satellite dish antennas and directly leasing communications satellite capacity to connect their distant work areas. These are called *bypass networks* because these companies are bypassing the communications networks provided by communications carriers.

Cellular Radio

Cellular radio is a communications technology that divides a metropolitan area into a honeycomb of *cells*. Each cell has its own low-power transmitter, rather than having one high-powered radio transmitter to serve an entire city.

This significantly increases the capacity of the radio frequencies available for mobile phone service. However, this technology requires the use of computers and other communications equipment to coordinate and control the transmissions of thousands of mobile phone users as they drive from one cell to another. The use of cellular phones has increased dramatically as cellular radio has become an important communications medium for mobile voice and data communications.

Telecommunications Processors

As we mentioned early in the chapter, **telecommunications processors** such as modems and other devices support communications among the terminals and computers in a telecommunications network. Let's take a look at some examples of the devices that are typically found in telecommunications networks.

Modems

Typically, you will have to add a communications processor called a *modem* to your microcomputer. **Modems** are the most common communications processor for end user computing. Their main job is to convert a computer's *digital* signals into *analog* frequencies, so they can be transmitted over ordinary telephone lines. A modem at the other end of the communications line converts the transmitted data back into digital pulses at a receiving computer. This process is known as *modulation* and *demodulation*. The word *modem* is a combined abbreviation of those two words.

Notice in Figure 9-10 that a computer transmits data as *digital* signals, that is, as a series of discrete (noncontinuous) voltage pulses. For instance, for many computers, +5 volts represents a binary 1 and –5 volts represents a binary 0. However, telephone systems were originally designed to carry *analog* signals, that is, continuous signals of varying intensity. Because the human voice generates continuous signals consisting of sound waves that vary in pitch, tone, and volume, a telephone converts this into continuous electromagnetic frequencies (analog signals). These signals are then transmitted over our public telephone systems.

Thus modems are a necessity any time you use a public telephone system for data communications. Modems must convert your computer's digital voltage pulses into analog transmission frequencies, and vice versa. However, many communications companies have developed *digital communications networks* that now transmit digital voltage pulses. So these networks don't

telecommunications processors Devices such as modems, multiplexers, concentrators, and controllers that provide a variety of telecommunications support services and may allow a communications channel to carry simultaneous data transmissions from many terminals.

modems A device that converts a computer's digital signals into analog frequencies so they can be transmitted over ordinary telephone lines.

Portable cellular telephones or radio terminals are growing in popularity.

Figure 9-10
Modems convert a computer's digital signals to analog and back.

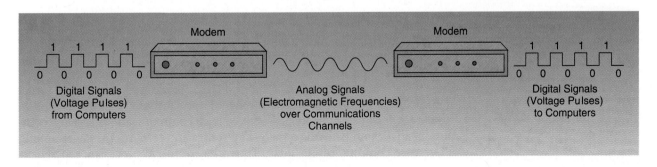

Digital Signals (Voltage Pulses) from Computers | Analog Signals (Electromagnetic Frequencies) over Communications Channels | Digital Signals (Voltage Pulses) to Computers

Modems consist of modem circuit boards, stand-alone modems, modems on a chip, and acoustic coupler modems.

need modems that only perform the traditional digital to analog conversion function.

Many modems support a variety of telecommunications functions. *Intelligent modems* use special-purpose microprocessors to support additional capabilities. Examples include simultaneous data and voice transmission, transmission error detection, automatic dialing and answering of calls, and a faxing capability.

Modems come in several forms, including external units, internal circuit boards, *acoustic couplers,* and microelectronic modem chips. The external modem is a separate unit that is connected by a telephone jack between your microcomputer and the telephone line. The internal modem consists of a circuit board that plugs into one of the expansion slots inside your microcomputer. It has a telephone jack so you can connect it to a telephone outlet. The acoustic coupler modem has a special holder or cradle into which the telephone handset is placed. This connects the modem to the telephone line so the modem can process audible analog tones.

Modems differ in their data transmission speeds, which is typically expressed in *baud* rates. Technically, baud refers to the number of signal changes that can take place in one second. However, it is often popularly used as the equivalent of one bit per second (BPS). Typically, speeds vary from 2,400 BPS for a slow-speed modem, to 9,600 BPS for medium-speed modems, and more than 14,400 BPS (14.4 kilo baud) for high-speed modems. A 2,400 BPS modem (or one that provides several speeds) is a popular choice. Cost typically ranges between $100 and $700 but can go higher. A faster modem may cost more, but saves on time and telephone line charges. For example, a ten-page, double-spaced report would take 10 minutes to transmit with an outmoded 300-baud modem and only 1 ¼ minutes at 2,400 baud.

Multiplexers

multiplexer
An electronic device that allows a single communications channel to carry simultaneous data transmission from many terminals.

A **multiplexer** is a communications processor that allows a single communications channel to carry simultaneous data transmissions from many terminals that are sharing the channel. Typically, a multiplexer merges the transmissions of several terminals at one end of a communications channel, while a similar unit separates the individual transmissions at the receiving end. This is accomplished in two basic ways. In *frequency division multiplexing (FDM),* a multiplexer effectively divides a high-speed channel into multiple slow-speed channels that can be used by many slow-speed terminals. In *time division multiplexing (TDM),* the multiplexer divides the time each terminal can use a high-speed line into very short time slots.

Front-End Processors

front-end processor
Typically, a smaller, general-purpose computer that is dedicated to handling data communications control functions in a communications network, thus relieving a mainframe computer of these functions.

A **front-end processor** is typically a minicomputer dedicated to handling the data communications control functions for large mainframe computer systems. For example, a front-end processor can poll remote terminals to determine if they have a message to send or if they are ready to receive a message. It controls access to a network and allows only authorized users to use the system, assigns priorities to messages, logs all communications activity, computes statistics on network activity, and routes and reroutes messages among alternative communication links. Thus, the front-end processor can relieve the host computer of its communications control functions so it can concentrate on other information processing chores.

Private Branch Exchange

A **private branch exchange (PBX)** is a communications processor that serves as a switching device between the telephone lines within a work area and the local telephone company's main telephone lines, or *trunks*. In recent years, PBXs route telephone calls within an office and also provide other services, such as automatic forwarding of calls, conference calling, and least-cost routing of long-distance calls. Some PBX models can control communications among the terminals, computers, and other information processing devices in local area networks of offices and other work areas. Other PBXs can integrate the switching of voice, data, and video in an *integrated services digital network (ISDN)*.

Telecommunications Software

As we said earlier, software is a vital component of all telecommunications networks. Several types of programs are used to control and support communications activities occurring in telecommunications networks. For instance, telecommunications software packages for mainframe computers in wide area networks are frequently called *telecommunication monitors* or *teleprocessing (TP) monitors*. Local area networks (LANs) rely on software called *network operating systems*. And of course, many communications software packages are available to use with microcomputers.

Microcomputer Communications Packages

Telecommunications software makes telecommunications happen. Therefore, you need to load a communications package into your microcomputer and use it to direct your telecommunications sessions. Communication packages for microcomputers are fairly easy to use. Once you load the program, you are usually provided with a display that asks you to set *communications parameters* for your session. Communications parameters include the baud rate in bits per second and other factors that help your computer communicate with another. The section on "Communication Alternatives" later in this chapter discusses many of the parameters you may have to specify in a communications session.

Most packages let you store telephone numbers and the parameters for computers and networks you communicate with regularly in a dialing directory. Your computer and modem can then automatically dial and select the necessary parameters for you. Most packages then provide you with a series of prompts or menus to guide you in sending or receiving messages, information, or files.

Communications packages can let your microcomputer act as a generic *dumb terminal* that can only send, receive, and display data one line at a time. Typically, however, communications software lets your PC act as a generic *intelligent terminal* and transmit, receive, and store on disk everything from brief messages to entire files of data and programs. Also, many packages allow you to specify that your microcomputer *emulate* (act like) a specific

private branch exchange (PBX)
A switching device that serves as an interface between the many telephone lines within a work area and a telephone company's main telephone lines. Computerized PBXs can handle the switching of both voice and data in the local area networks that are needed in such locations.

This cabinet contains multiple private branch exchanges (PBXs).

This is a display from Terminal Plus, a telecommunications package.

```
┌─ Dialer - [MAIL-NFO.DCD] ─────────────────────── ▼ ▲ ┐
│  File   Edit   Phone   Help                            │
│ ┌─Entries──────────┐  ┌─Service─────────────────────────────────┐ │
│ │ AT&T             │  │ Name:       VAX-Research                 │ │
│ │ BIX              │  │ Number:     713-555-4805   ┌Prefix/Suffix...┐│ │
│ │ CompuServe       │  │ User ID:    smithw                       │ │
│ │ Delphi           │  │ Password:   *******                      │ │
│ │ Dow Jones        │  │ Network ID:                              │ │
│ │ FutureSoft       │  └──────────────────────────────────────────┘ │
│ │ GEnie            │  ┌─Session──────────────────┐┌─Communications─┐│
│ │ MCI              │  │ Terminal Emulation: TTY (Generic) ▼│ Port: COM1: ▼│
│ │ NewGraphics BBS  │  │ Transfer Protocol:  XModem  ▼ │ Baud Rate: 9600 ▼│
│ │ VAX-Accounting   │  │ Settings File:      None    ▼ │ Parity: None ▼│
│ │ VAX-Research     │  │ Login Script:       None    ▼ │ Data Bits: 8 ▼│
│ │                  │  │ Post-Login Script:  None    ▼ │ Stop Bits: 1 ▼│
│ │                  │  └────────────────────────────┘└──────────────┘│
│ │                  │  ┌─Statistics───────────────────────────────┐ │
│ │ ┌New...┐┌Sort...┐│  │ Date of last call: 05/29/92  Total Calls: 1│ │
│ │ ┌─Clear Marks──┐ │  │ Cost per hour ($): 0.00  Total Cost: $0.00 ┌Clear┐│
│ │ ┌────Dial──────┐ │  └────────────────────────────────────────────┘ │
│ │ ┌Exit Dialer Mode┐│                                                │
└───────────────────┘                                                  │
```

type of terminal, especially popular models used with large computer systems.

Files of data and programs can be *downloaded* from another computer to your microcomputer and stored on disk. Or files can be *uploaded* from your microcomputer to another computer. Communications packages allow you to transfer data files quickly, thus saving you the time and cost of keying in the data by hand. Some programs even allow files to be transferred automatically between unattended computer systems. Files may have to be converted to a standard ASCII computer code format before they can be transmitted. Therefore, many software packages let you specify an ASCII format when saving your files. For instance, you can store a spreadsheet or a word processing document as an ASCII file.

Telecommunications Software Functions

access control
Establishes connections between terminals and computers in a network. Communications software works with a communications processor to connect and disconnect communications links and establish parameters such as transmission speed, mode, and direction.

You should realize that telecommunication software packages provide a variety of communications support functions. One example is **access control**, which establishes connections between terminals and computers in a network. The software works with a communications processor (such as a modem) to connect and disconnect communications links and establish parameters such as transmission speed, mode, and direction. It may also involve automatic telephone dialing and redialing, logging on and off with appropriate account numbers and security codes, and automatic answering of phone calls from another computer. Many communications packages also include a *script language,* which allows you to program an automatic sequence of commands to customize access control. For example, you can develop programs to automatically access other computers at night or while you are away. Figure 9-11 illustrates the tasks performed by a network operating system for a local area network.

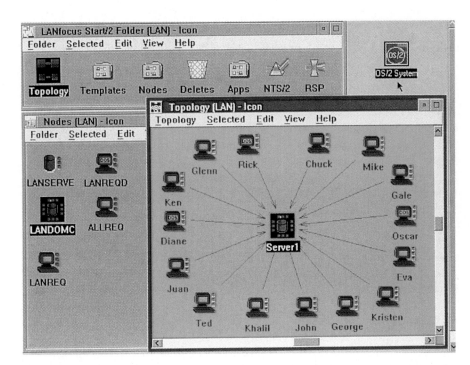

Figure 9-11
This network operating system
display provides a view of all
users connected to the network
file server.

Network management is another important software function. software such as LAN network operating systems and WAN telecommunications monitors determine transmission priorities, routes messages, polls terminals in the network, and forms waiting lines *(queues)* of transmission request. They also may log statistics of network activity and the use of network resources by end users in the network.

network management
Managing telecommunications network activity by determining transmission priorities, routing messages, polling terminals, and so on.

Error control, which involves detection and correction of transmission errors, is another major job of telecommunications software. Many errors are caused by distortions such as line noise and power surges. Communications software controls errors in transmission by several methods. Additional *control codes* are usually added to the message itself. These specify such information as the destination of the data, their priority, and the beginning and end of the message. If errors are detected, a signal is usually sent back to the computer to retransmit the previous message.

error control
Detecting and correcting transmission errors in a telecommunications network.

Security management is another important software function that protects a communications network from unauthorized access. For instance, access software may restrict your access to data and the computing resources in a network. This typically involves procedures that limit your access to part or all of a network depending on your security classification. The software may also use automatic disconnection and callback procedures to allow only authorized users to use a network. With such software, if you try to access a network, the host computer would automatically hang up and calls back using your computer's or terminal's authorized phone number. Finally, coding techniques called **encryption** may be used to scramble data into a coded form before transmission and decode it upon arrival at its destination.

security management
Protecting a telecommunications network from unauthorized access and use of its resources.

encryption
To scramble data or convert it, prior to transmission, to a secret code that masks the meaning of the data to unauthorized recipients.

REAL-WORLD EXAMPLE

RhoMed, Cullen/Burr, and SED Systems: LAN Tales

Local area networks (LANs) are spreading like wildfire among PC users in the world of work. Estimates indicate that over half of all PCs in organizations are networked together by LANs, and that number is increasing every day. So whether you are a scientist or attorney, a secretary or architect, chances are you are connected to other PCs in your organization, no matter how large or how small it may be.

Take RhoMed, a small research and development firm in Albuquerque, New Mexico. Its ten PCs are linked by a LAN so scientists and attorneys can share software like WordPerfect for word processing and Paradox for database management. Then there's Cullen/Burr Associates Architects of Phoenix, Arizona. The company has seven high-powered PCs it uses for CAD (computer-aided de-

sign) applications networked together so architects can share the files of drawings for projects they are working on. Or take SED Systems, a space engineering company in Saskatoon, Saskatchewan. This Canadian firm uses a small LAN to network the PCs of its four secretaries so they can share word processing files of correspondence and project proposals. Like Cullen/Burr, they rely on the LANtastic network operating system package to coordinate the sharing of software and document files among the PCs in the LAN.

1. What telecommunications network components are in a local area network?

2. What capabilities does a LAN provide for people who work in an office or other work group?

Quick Quiz

1. Star, ring, and _____ networks are three basic network designs.
2. Fiber optic cables and microwave radio are examples of _____.
3. The most common telecommunications processor for microcomputers is the _____.
4. Your microcomputer needs a _____ package to access and act like a terminal in a network.
5. A _____ is a standard set of telecommunications rules, procedures, or specifications.

Answers: 1. bus   2. telecommunications media   3. modem
4. communications package   5. protocol

End User Telecommunications

It is useful for you to think of telecommunications as supporting a variety of end user and organization-wide activities. We'll discuss end user telecommunications in this chapter, and applications of organizational telecommunications in Chapter 11. As we said in Chapter 3, you should view your microcomputer as an end user workstation. Typically, your workstation is tied by telecommunications links to other workstations in a local area network, with a more powerful microcomputer operating as a *network server*. Or workstations might be connected to larger networks, using departmental mini-computers or corporate mainframes as *hosts* or *super servers*.

Office Automation

Computers and telecommunications networks are automating office work practices and communications methods. That's what we call *office automation*. This topic was thoroughly covered in Chapter 4, so we won't duplicate it here. But you should realize that most end users in an information society work in offices that are dependent on telecommunications networks. Let's look at several important examples.

Electronic mail, voice mail, and facsimile are the leading applications in the use of telecommunications among office workers. *Electronic mail (E-mail)* lets you use your computer to send electronic text messages to other end users. E-mail messages are stored on the network computer's magnetic disk devices until they are retrieved and displayed on the workstations of the people you send them to. *Voice mail* works the same way, only with digitized voice messages. *Facsimile (fax)* has become a common way to electronically send copies of documents over the phone lines. *Faxing* is popular because you can send a hard copy of a document in a few seconds anywhere there is a phone connection.

Other office automation applications make heavy use of telecommunications technologies. Local area networks can provide an *electronic meeting room* for group decision making. End users at terminals can conduct meetings where issues can be explored anonymously and decisions reached quickly. Or *teleconferencing* can be used to conduct meetings and conferences over wide area networks to participants all over the world. Finally, telecommunications allows you to work in your office at home and still be connected to your fellow workers' computers in what is popularly called *telecommuting*. So you see, telecommunications networks are essential for office automation.

Work Group Computing

Many times, end user computing is a group effort that depends on telecommunications networks. That's because organizations frequently form one or more work groups that work on a variety of projects as a team. This is known as **work group computing.** For instance, you and other members of a work group might use a local area network to share the use of software packages like Lotus Notes for spreadsheet analysis, electronic mail, and report generation in order to accomplish group assignments. So such packages are now being called *groupware*.

Local area networks help make work group computing possible by letting end users share hardware, software, and data resources. LANs tie office workstations together with other office devices, such as laser printers, and frequently link work groups to department and wide area corporate networks. Software packages and common databases are also shared by teams of end users. So, work group computing means you can share data, perform joint analysis, and integrate the results of efforts by other members of your work group who are working with you on joint projects.

work group computing
End user computing in a work group environment in which members of a work group use telecommunications networks to communicate and share hardware, software, and databases to accomplish group assignments.

Public Information Networks

Gaining access to a variety of public data banks and information services is easy if you have a personal computer equipped with a modem and a commu-

Lotus Notes is an example of a groupware package.

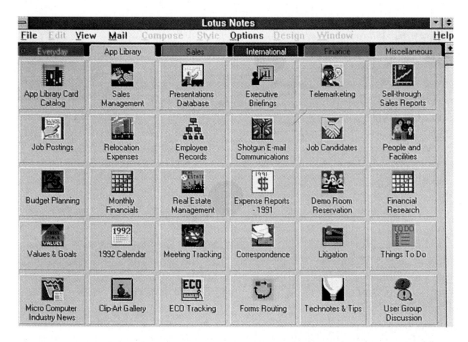

nications software package. In Chapter 6, we discuss some of the *data banks* offered to the public by commercial information services. In addition, companies such as CompuServe and GEnie offer a variety of information services for a fee to anyone with an appropriately equipped personal computer. They offer such services as electronic mail, financial market information, use of software packages for personal computing, electronic games, home banking and shopping, news, sports, weather information, and a variety of specialized data banks. Many other organizations offer information services, sometimes

This menu lists some of the information services available on CompuServe.

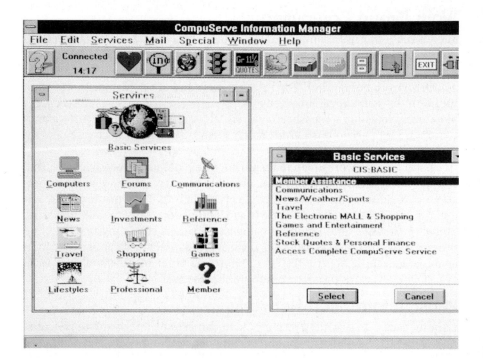

Service	Telephone	Cost
CompuServe CompuServe, Inc.	800-848-8199	$6–12 per hour
DIALOG Dialog Information Services, Inc.	800-334-2564	$30–300 per hour
Dow Jones Information Service Dow Jones & Co.	800-225-3170	$60–174 per hour
GEnie G.E. Information Service	800-638-9636	$6–18 per hour
LEXIS Mead Data Central	800-543-6862	$39 per hour
NEXIS Mead Data Central	800-229-9597	$39 per hour
PRODIGY Prodigy Services Co.	800-PRO-DIGY	$14.95 per month

Table 9-1
Public Information
Services and Data Banks

for free. For example, the Internet offers free use of many of the same services as commercial networks. See Table 9-1

Videotex

Another way you can get information using an information services network is **videotex.** In its simplest form *(teletext),* videotex is a one-way, repetitive broadcast of pages of text and graphics information to your TV set. This method uses cable, telephone lines, or standard TV transmission. A control device allows you to select the page you want to display and examine. Videotex, however, is an *interactive* information service provided over phone lines or cable TV channels. You use either a terminal connected to your TV set or a PC with specialized communications software. Then you select specific video displays of data and information, such as electronic *Yellow Pages* or an electronic bank checkbook to do banking and shopping electronically.

Videotex is widely used in Europe. Many companies in the United States tried pilot programs of videotex services in the 1980s, but most efforts failed to generate sufficient consumer interest. Videotex services are currently available from several sources, including personal computer networks such as Prodigy and the CompuServe Bank-at-Home and Shop-at-Home services.

Prodigy is a joint venture of IBM and Sears. It is an attractive videotex service whose best feature is its low cost. Other services typically charge an hourly fee each time you use them. Prodigy charges a low monthly fee ($14.95 per month), which allows up to six family members to use their communications software to access the system, even from different locations. This gives you access to a variety of services, including electronic mail, bulletin board systems, banking and shopping at home, news, weather, stock quotes, and video games.

videotex
An interactive information service provided over phone lines or cable TV channels to a home computer or terminal connected to a TV set.

One of the videotext services provided by Prodigy is this Personal Control Financial Network.

One of Prodigy's disadvantages is that it is a *closed network,* that is, you cannot access other public networks (such as Internet) to send E-mail or other data. CompuServe, on the other hand, does provide *gateways* so you can communicate with people on other networks from their service. Unlike CompuServe and other services, Prodigy's special communications software also takes control of your PC so you cannot download financial data (such as stock market statistics) into a spreadsheet or database management program, store it on disk, or print it on your printer. So Prodigy's chief appeal is as a low-cost videotex network for home use.

America Online provides an electronic bulletin board for people interested in the environment.

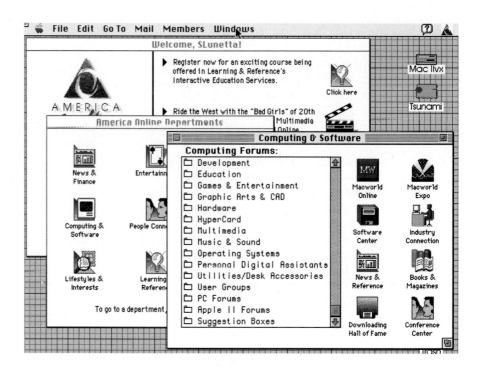

Bulletin Board Systems

Imaging using an electronic **bulletin board system (BBS)** that allows you to "post" public or private messages that other end users can read by accessing the BBS with their computers. That's why bulletin board systems are a popular telecommunications service for end users. You can use a BBS provided by public networks such as the Internet, CompuServe, and Prodigy, or enroll in those offered by thousands of business firms, organizations, and user groups.

Establishing a BBS requires at least a microcomputer with a hard disk drive, a BBS software package, and a modem and telephone line for as many simultaneous users as the BBS computer can handle. A bulletin board system serves as a central location that allows you to post and pick up messages or upload and download data files or programs 24 hours a day. Once you are assigned a user account number, you can call the BBS to ask questions, get advice, locate and share information, place advertisements, and get in touch with other end users. Thus, many bulletin board systems are used by business firms and other organizations as a convenient, low-cost way to enhance the flow of information among their employees and customers.

bulletin board system (BBS)
A computer network in which electronic messages, data files, or programs can be stored for other subscribers to read or copy.

Distributed and Cooperative Processing

Distributed processing and *cooperative processing* are major forms of end user and organizational telecommunications. In **distributed processing**, information processing is accomplished by a network of computers interconnected by telecommunications links. Many organizations are moving to distributed processing instead of relying on one large *centralized* computer facility or on the *decentralized* operation of several independent computers. For example, a distributed processing network may consist of mainframes, minicomputers, and microcomputers dispersed over a geographic area and interconnected by wide area networks, or they may be distributed within end user departments and work groups in local area networks.

Cooperative processing takes this concept one step further. It allows the computers in a distributed processing network to share the processing of parts of an end user's application. As an example, you could use a spreadsheet package provided to your microcomputer workstation by a local area network server to perform financial analysis on data provided by a mainframe computer system. This is sometimes called **client/server computing,** where end user workstations *(clients)* are connected to LAN servers and possibly to mainframe *superservers*. See Figure 9-12.

distributed processing
A form of decentralization of information processing made possible by a network of computers dispersed throughout an organization.

cooperative processing
Allows the various types of computers in a distributed processing network to share the processing of parts of an end user's application.

client/server computing
A computing environment where end user workstations (clients) are connected to micro- or mini-LAN servers and possibly to mainframe superservers.

Quick Quiz

1. Electronic mail, voice mail, and faxing are examples of _____ applications of telecommunications.
2. When end user computing is a group effort supported by telecommunications it is called _____.
3. A variety of information services and data banks are provided by _____ to microcomputer users.
4. You can read and post electronic messages on a _____.

REAL-WORLD EXAMPLE

The National Football League: Wide Area Receivers

If there's one thing National Football League teams demand from the league office, it's absolute equality of treatment among the teams in all matters. If there is any inequality among the teams in football skills, they want it settled on the playing field, not in the back office. "It is important that we make information available to each club at the same time as its competitors receive it," says Mary Oliveti, who is manager of information processing at NFL headquarters in New York City. So the NFL has a wide area network linking VAX minicomputers at each of the 28 team offices across the country.

The network allows instant distribution of data to all the teams, as well as allowing teams to communicate electronically with each other. For example, Bill Consoli, who is a member of the IS staff for the Los Angeles Rams, says: "If we're on

the road, we talk to another club over the network about accommodations, ticket requests, and even what the weather's like." Of course, the league office is busy using the network for more than 2,000 transactions per week to all teams, including roster adjustments, waiver notices, game statistics, and officiating changes. It also uses the network for interoffice memos and exchange of player contracts, as well as for balloting for Pro Bowl teams, processing Super Bowl information, maintaining officials' schedules, and sharing press releases.

1. Is the NFL's wide area network an example of a distributed processing network? Explain.

2. Why does the NFL need this network? Couldn't it accomplish the same thing using telephones, fax machines, and express delivery?

5. In _____, the computers in a distributed processing network may consist of end user microcomputer workstations, network servers, and mainframe superservers.

Answers: 1. office automation 2. workgroup computing 3. public information networks 4. bulletin board system 5. client/server computing

Figure 9-12
Computing power can be distributed throughout an organization by a client/server network.

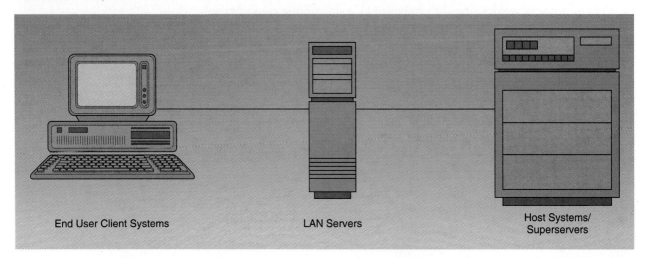

End User Client Systems   LAN Servers   Host Systems/Superservers

Technical Note: Communications Alternatives

Read the next few pages of this section if you want to know in more detail how communications channels provide a variety of capabilities to support your telecommunications needs. For example, the networks you use may have different transmission speeds, offer single or multiple transmission of data, or use different switching and access methods. As we said earlier, every time you begin a telecommunications session, your communications package will ask you to specify some of these *parameters* or will select them for you. So this section gives a brief look at some common alternatives you may experience in your telecommunications activities.

Transmission Speed

The communication capabilities of a telecommunication channel can be classified by *bandwidth,* which determines its maximum transmission rate, typically measured in *baud* or in bits per second (BPS). *Voiceband,* or low-speed channels allow data transmission rates from 300 to 9,600 BPS, though speeds of up to 1 million BPS are possible. These channels use unshielded twisted pair wire for "voice-grade" telephone communications. These are communications lines are the ones you will typically use with microcomputers, video terminals, and fax machines.

Medium-band or medium-speed channels using shielded twisted pair lines can handle data transmission speeds from 9,600 to 10 million BPS. *Broadband,* or high-speed, digital channels provide transmission rates at intervals from 19,200 BPS to several billion BPS. They typically use microwave, fiber optics, or satellite transmission. Examples are 64,000 BPS for digital telephone service and 1.54 million BPS for the T1 communications channels used in many large private communications networks. See Figure 9-13.

Parallel or Serial Transmission

The two basic methods of transmitting bits of data are *parallel* and *serial* transmission. Parallel transmission involves transmitting all the bits needed

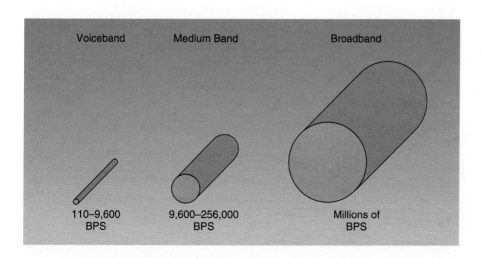

Voiceband	Medium Band	Broadband
110–9,600 BPS	9,600–256,000 BPS	Millions of BPS

Figure 9-13
The bandwidth of a telecommunications channel determines its range of transmission speeds.

Figure 9-14
Serial transmission is typically used in telecommunications networks.

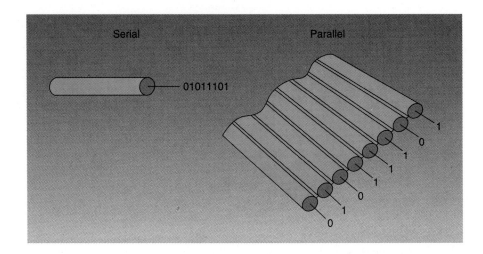

to represent a character simultaneously. Serial transmission, on the other hand, involves sending each of the bits composing a character one at a time. Parallel transmission is obviously faster and more expensive than serial transmission because more telecommunications channels are required. Therefore, parallel transmission is typically used for data transfers over short distances, especially between a computer system and its peripheral devices. For instance, most microcomputers use a *parallel port* or *interface* as a connection to a printer, while serial transmission through a *serial port* is traditionally used between computers and modems for data communications over telephone networks. See Figure 9-14.

Transmission Mode

Two modes of transmitting data are called *asynchronous* and *synchronous* transmission. Asynchronous transmission transmits one character at a time, with each character preceded by a *start bit* and followed by a *stop bit*. Asynchronous transmission is normally used for low-speed transmission at rates below 2,400 BPS. Synchronous transmission transmits groups of characters at a time, with the beginning and end of a character determined by the timing circuitry of a communications processor. Synchronous transmission is normally used for transmission speeds exceeding 2,400 BPS. See Figure 9-15.

Figure 9-15
Asynchronous transmissions transmit one character at a time, while the synchronous approach transmits many characters at a time.

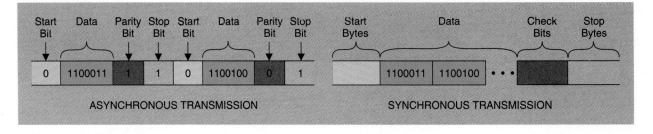

| Simplex Line | Half–Duplex Channel | Duplex Channel |

Figure 9-16
Telecommunications networks may provide simplex, half-duplex, or duplex channels.

Transmission Direction

Communications channels can provide three types of data transmission directions. A *simplex* channel allows data to be transmitted in only one direction. A *half-duplex* channel allows transmission in either direction, but in only one direction at a time. This is usually sufficient for low-speed terminals (such as transaction terminals). That's because alternating the sending and receiving of data is a typical characteristic of their normal communications activities. The *full-duplex* channel allows data to be transmitted in both directions at the same time. It is used for high-speed communications between computer systems. See Figure 9-16.

Switching Alternatives

Regular telephone service relies on *circuit switching,* in which a circuit is opened to establish a link between a sender and receiver and remains open until the communication session is completed. In *message switching,* a message is transmitted a *block* at a time from one switching device to another. *Packet switching* is a widely used method for data communications that involves subdividing communications messages into groups called *packets,* typically 128 characters long. The packet-switching network carrier uses computers and other communications processors to control the packet-switching process and transmit the packets of various users over its leased lines.

Access Methods

How can terminals and other devices access and share a network to transmit and receive data? A variety of *access methods* are used to provide this capacity. In the *polling* approach, a host computer or communications processor polls (contracts) each terminal in sequence to determine which terminals have messages to send. Thus, the transmission of each terminal is based on a "roll call" of each terminal on the line. Polling can be an effective method because the speed of mainframes and communications processors allows them to poll and control transmission by many terminals sharing the same line, especially if communications consist of brief messages and inquiries.

In the *contention* approach, line use is on a first-come, first-served basis, where a terminal can transmit data if the line is not in use, but it must wait if it is busy. So a terminal or other device must monitor the network and send a message only if it senses the network is not in use. If there is a "collision" with another message, a terminal typically stops transmission, waits until the network is clear, and tries again.

Another widely used method in local area networks is *token passing.* A *token* is a special signal code sent around the network. If a terminal or other device wants to transmit a message, it must wait for the token to come by, take it off the network, and transmit its message. After transmission is completed, the token is returned to the network. See Figure 9-17.

Figure 9-17
Three basic access methods may
be used to send and receive data
in a network.

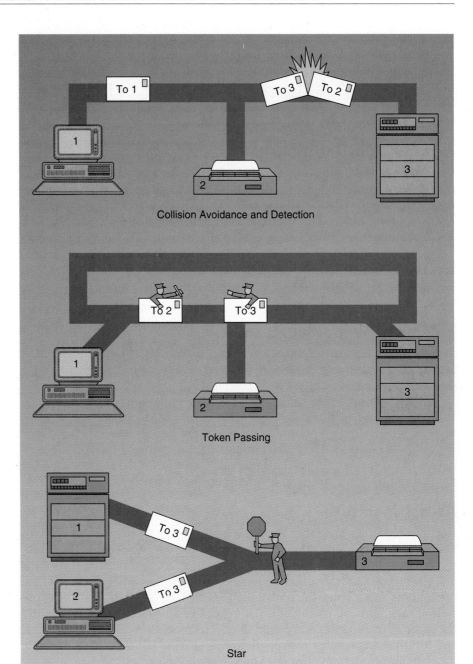

End Note: End Users and Telecommunications

Telecommunications is now an indispensable ingredient in the activities of
end users in our information society. You will depend on telecommunications
networks to get things done, no matter what your future career will be. You
will probably use a local area network to connect you to others in an office
or other work group. Then you will be able to share hardware, software, and
data resources, communicate electronically, and work on joint projects. In ad-

ETHICS

Ethical Issues in Telecommunications

The use of telecommunications networks generates many ethical issues. For example, in other chapters, we mention the issues of *right to privacy* arising from the unauthorized monitoring of electronic mail networks and the computer monitoring of employee productivity in data entry networks. In this chapter let's talk about some of the ethical issues arising from the use of a nationwide videotex network, the Prodigy information service.

We described the use of Prodigy earlier in this chapter. The Prodigy service provides elaborate graphics capability and has further features not provided by other information services. This added capability is provided by Prodigy's special software that must be used to access the system—standard communications packages won't work. In addition, the software running during an online session is downloaded into the PC during that session. The net effect of this method is to put the PC under the control of the Prodigy system. Unlike information services like CompuServe, subscribers then have minimal control of their own machines.

This means that the Prodigy system could accidentally erase a subscriber's hard disk or inadvertently transmit computer viruses into their subscribers' computer systems. Prodigy also disables the normal screen-dump capability of a PC. Thus it has complete control of what information an end user may and may not print or store to disk. In addition, there has been some controversy about Prodigy's ability to examine information on an end user's disk.

Prodigy has also been embroiled in controversy concerning racist comments users placed in its electronic bulletin board system. Then, when Prodigy tried to control usage of its BBS, it was accused of censorship! So you see, even a videotex service that provides an attractive telecommunications network for home computer users can involve activities that have ethical implications.

What Do You Think?

Should Prodigy be in control of your computer during a telecommunications session? What about the potential for accidental erasure of your disk or computer virus infection? Should it control what you may store on your disk or print on your printer? What about its ability to examine the information on your computer's disk? Should Prodigy screen messages before they are posted on its BBS? These are just some of the ethical questions raised by the use of a videotex network. What do you think?

dition, you will probably be connected to a wide area network, so you can communicate with colleagues across the country or around the globe.

Thanks to these networks, you will use office automation services such as electronic mail, voice mail, and facsimile to communicate electronically and avoid the delays and costs of paper-based communications. You will also be able to use a variety of information services to access external data banks or gain entry to even more network services such as videotex and bulletin board systems. Finally, telecommunications makes distributed and cooperative processing happen. This allows you to share in the computing power of the micros, minis, and mainframes that may be part of your organization's networks.

Telecommunications itself is changing from voice-oriented telephone systems to integrated digital networks that carry voice, data, and video anywhere. Fiber optics, satellites, and cellular radio are the media of these communications highways of the future. So you can look forward to telecommunications networks that instantly and effortlessly allow you to share information and computing resources with your co-workers anywhere in the world.

Summary

You and Telecommunications   Telecommunications is the sending of information in many forms from one place to another using electronic and other technologies. No matter what your career will be, you will have to depend on telecommunications networks to help you accomplish your work activities.

Telecommunications Networks   The major components of a telecommunications network are (1) terminals, (2) telecommunications processors, (3) communications channels, (4) computers, and (5) telecommunications software. There are two basic types of telecommunications networks: wide area networks (WANs) and local area networks (LANs). WANs cover a wide geographic area, while LANs interconnect end user workstations and other devices at local work sites.

Network Alternatives   There are several alternatives in telecommunications network design. This includes point-to-point lines, where each terminal has its own line to a computer, and multidrop lines, where several terminals share a communications link. Star networks tie end users to a communications control computer. Ring networks tie computers together in a ring on a more equal basis. In bus networks, computers share the same channel. Protocols, which are standard sets of rules, procedures, or specifications for the control of resources and activities in a network and network architectures, promote open, simple, and flexible network interfaces and designs.

Telecommunications Carriers   A wide variety of telecommunications services, including data communications, are provided by authorized common carriers to organizations and the public. More specialized data communications, such as packet-switching networks, are provided by companies called value-added carriers.

Telecommunications Media   Telecommunications channels are a variety of media, including twisted-pair wire, coaxial cable, and fiber optic cable, which physically link the devices in a network. Other alternatives, such as land-based microwave, communications satellites, and cellular radio use microwave and other radio waves to transmit and receive data.

Telecommunications Processors   Telecommunications networks rely on a variety of telecommunications processors. Modems convert your computer's digital signals to analog frequencies for transmission over ordinary telephone systems. At the receiving end, a modem converts analog frequencies back to digital for entry into a computer system. Multiplexers allow a single communications line to carry simultaneous data transmissions from many terminals. Front-end processors are typically minicomputers that handle data communications chores for mainframe computer systems. A private branch exchange (PBX) controls communications among telephones, terminals, and computers in some office local area networks.

Telecommunications Software   Several types of programs are used in controlling and supporting telecommunications networks. Examples include telecommunications monitors for mainframe computers in wide area networks, network operating systems for local area networks, and microcomputer communications packages. These packages provide a variety of support functions, including access control, network management, error control, and security management. Communications packages are the software resources that allow you to set up a telecommunications session in which your microcomputer acts like an intelligent terminal to send messages and transfer files between computer systems.

End User Telecommunications   Your microcomputer is an end user workstation that is typically part of local area and wide area networks. This allows you to share hardware, software, and data resources while working on group projects, faxing documents, and sending electronic and voice mail messages to other end users. You can also use a variety of business and personal information services, bulletin board systems, and videotex services to exchange information to carry on your work activities. Telecommunications also makes distributed and cooperative processing possible through networks of interconnected computers.

Communications Alternatives   Communications channels offer a variety of capabilities to support different communications needs. Thus, networks may have different transmission speeds or offer single or multiple transmission of data, such as serial or parallel transmission, or simplex or duplex channels. Or they may use different switching or access methods, such as message or packet switching, polling, contention, or token passing, to allow terminals to share use of communications lines.

Key Terms and Concepts

bulletin board system	distributed processing
cellular radio	encryption
client/server computing	fiber optic cable
coaxial cable	front-end processor
common carriers	host computer
communications satellites	information superhighway
cooperative processing	Internet

local area network
microwave systems
modem
multiplexer
network architecture
network server
private branch exchange
protocol
public information network

telecommunications channels and
  media
telecommunications network
telecommunications processors
telecommunications software
value-added carriers
videotex
wide area network
work group computing

Review Quiz

True/False

_____ 1. The basic components of a telecommunications network are terminals, telecommunications processors, channels and media, computers, and control software.

_____ 2. A local area network is a communications network covering a large geographic area.

_____ 3. A wide area network is a communications network in an office, a building, or other work site.

_____ 4. Communications carriers provide a variety of communications networks and services to the public.

_____ 5. Public information services provide telecommunications network resources and computing services to end users.

_____ 6. Videotex is an interactive information service for home computers.

_____ 7. Centralized computing depends on computers at central and local sites interconnected by a network.

_____ 8. In cooperative processing, networked computers share the processing of parts of an end user's application.

_____ 9. In work group computing, members of a work group share computer resources to jointly accomplish work assignments.

_____ 10. ASCII is a coding technique for data communications security.

Multiple Choice

_____ 1. Both satellites and land-based relay stations use this telecommunications technology:
   a. coaxial cable.
   b. microwave.
   c. fiber optics.
   d. cellular radio.

_____ 2. A communications medium that uses pulses of laser light in glass fibers is
   a. coaxial cable.
   b. microwave.
   c. fiber optics
   d. cellular radio.

_____ 3. This supports mobile data communications in urban areas:

   a. coaxial cable.
   b. microwave.
   c. fiber optics.
   d. cellular radio.

_____ 4. Telecommunications software controls communications network

   a. access.
   b. transmission.
   c. security.
   d. all of the above.

_____ 5. A common communications processor for a microcomputer is a

   a. modem.
   b. multiplexer.
   c. simulator.
   d. condenser.

_____ 6. This device helps a communications channel carry simultaneous data transmissions from many terminals:

   a. modem.
   b. multiplexer.
   c. simulator.
   d. condenser.

_____ 7. This device handles the switching of both voice and data in a local area network:

   a. modem.
   b. switcher.
   c. PBX.
   d. condenser.

_____ 8. A master plan for a standard interface for telecommunications networks is a

   a. protocol.
   b. network architecture.
   c. interface architecture.
   d. interface network.

_____ 9. A standard set of rules, procedures, and specifications for control of communications in a network is a

   a. protocol.
   b. network architecture.
   c. interface architecture.
   d. interface network.

_____ 10. This technology promises to merge voice, data, and video communications into a single type of digital network:

   a. OSI.
   b. ISI.
   c. ISDN.
   d. SNA.

Fill-in

1. Companies known as _____ lease lines from common carriers and offer specialized telecommunication services.

2. End users can post public or private messages for other computer users on _____ systems.

3. You can access a variety of information services at home with _____.

4. Telecommunications network support _____ computing, where end users work together on group projects.

5. Many organizations are implementing _____ computing, in which end user workstations are networked to LAN servers and larger super-servers.

6. Computers at central and local sites interconnected by a network allow _____ .

7. A _____ is a microcomputer that controls the software and data resources of a local area network.

8. Telecommunications _____ includes modems, multiplexers, and front-end processors.

9. A _____ computer is the main computer in a wide area network.

10. A _____ process or is typically a minicomputer dedicated to handling communications functions for a mainframe.

Questions for Thought and Discussion

1. Digital networks are expanding and telecommunications capabilities are being built into computers. Will this make modems obsolete? Explain.

2. Refer to the Real-World Example of RhoMed, Cullen/Burr, and SED Systems in the chapter. What similarities and differences do you see in the use of LANs in each of these firms?

3. Are telecommunications packages for microcomputers really necessary? Couldn't their functions be built into other types of software? Explain.

4. Refer to the Real-World Example of the National Football League in the chapter. How else could the NFL use telecommunications? Explain.

5. What is work group computing? Why is it dependent on telecommunications?

6. List several benefits and limitations of videotex and other public information services.

7. Refer to the Real-World Example of Tadpole Technology in the chapter. What are some benefits and limitations of the company's use of the Internet for telecommunications?

8. What are the benefits of distributed processing networks compared to centralized telecommunications networks?

9. Why do you think there is a trend toward cooperative processing and client/server computing?

10. What are some of the ways you use telecommunications at school or work? What telecommunications hardware, software, and network resources do you use? Make a brief report to the class.

Review Quiz Answers

True/False: 1. T 2. F 3. F 4. T 5. T 6. T 7. F 8. T 9. T 10. F

Multiple Choice: 1. b 2. c 3. d 4. d 5. a 6. b 7. c 8. b 9. a 10. c

Fill-in: 1. value-added carriers 2. bulletin board 3. videotex 4. workgroup 5. client/server 6. distributed processing 7. network server 8. processors 9. host 10. front-end

VIEWPOINT

AN END USER'S GUIDE TO COMPUTER SELECTION

HOW TO BUY A COMPUTER

Practically everybody wants a computer. But the process of buying computer hardware or software is usually more involved than just visiting your local computer store and making a purchase. Before making that visit, there are some important questions you need to answer. Do you really need a computer or is there a more cost-effective way to do the job? If you decide that a computer is needed, what are the exact jobs you will need to perform? Are there special peripheral devices that you need to include? What kind of software do you need? How much should you anticipate spending and what will it cost you to use and maintain your computer system? These are just a few examples of the questions that you will be able to answer in a good computer selection process.

The computer spectrum ranges from mainframes to microcomputers.

The process used to define your computing needs is much the same whatever size or type of computers you are considering. Of course, complexity increases at the high end where the diverse needs of many end users must be considered. However, It is important that you define your requirements in an organized manner, even if you are considering buying a personal computer for professional or home use. Figure 1 presents a computer systems specification road map that identifies important steps in defining a system to meet your needs. The purpose of this guide is to help you

- determine your need for a personal computer.

- prepare a statement of your computer requirements.

- develop the specifications for a computer system.

- evaluate and select a source for the purchase of your system.

- make a trip to a computer store as a knowledgable customer.

Do You Really Need a Computer?

Most people start with the assumption that using a computer is the best way to get the job done. However, buying and installing a computer should only be done when you determine that it is the best alternative for your situation. Before you make that decision, there are several questions you need to answer so you can make an informed decision.

- *Need for a change* Do you really need a computer or can you continue with a manual system? Sometimes, the simplest and most cost-effective solution to meet your requirements is to improve and continue to use a noncomputerized system. In exploring the costs involved, you

should first define the cost of doing the task manually and then look at the cost of acquiring and maintaining a computer-based system.

- *Tasks to accomplish* Can the tasks you want to accomplish be done on a personal computer? Next you should determine if the tasks you want to accomplish are within the capabilities of microcomputers. Assuming you want to do applications like word processing, spreadsheets,

Microcomputers are commonly found in small businesses.

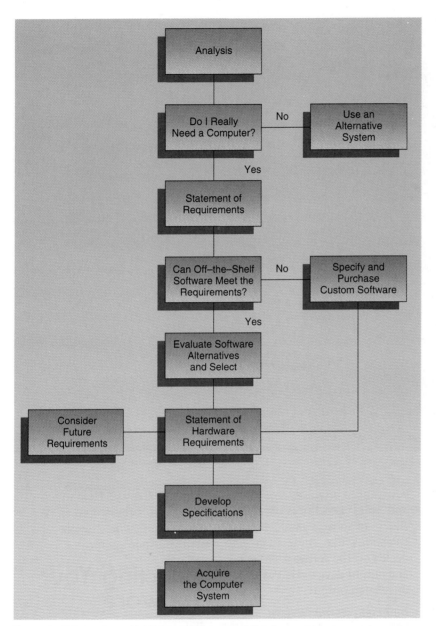

Figure 1 This road map highlights major steps to follow in acquiring a computer system.

the data accumulated in the system, which usually requires special equipment. The maintenance of the operating system and application software is also a consideration. You may have to pay for occasional updates for your software packages, though many times upgrading to revised versions is not necessary. Finally, the cost of documentation such as manuals and operating supplies must be estimated.

Defining Your Computer Requirements

You have now looked at the alternatives and determined that a personal computer will meet your computing needs. Now it's time to define your requirements. The first step is to develop a clear idea of what you want to accomplish. To do this, you will need to answer questions like the following:

- *Tasks to perform* What are the actual tasks you want to perform? In asking this question, you need to list exactly what you intend to do with the information system. It is not enough to say, "I'm going to do word processing" or "I'm going to use spreadsheets." For instance, you need to determine whether you will use word processing for correspondence and reports, spreadsheets for budgeting and sales analysis, graphics for presentations at meetings, and so on.

- *Information products* What displays, reports, or documents do you need and how will they be used? The information prod-

database management, and graphics, a microcomputer would be quite capable of fulfilling your needs.

- *Costs involved* How much will you have to spend and what are the operating costs? Many advertisements for personal computers make their cost seem

quite reasonable. However, the initial cost is not the only cost associated with the operation of a computer system and you should be aware of all costs before you make the final decision to buy. For example, the cost of maintaining system hardware in top operating condition must be considered as well as protecting

Computers are now found in all types of businesses.

ucts you produce will affect your computer system requirements. For example, will you need to print out a lot of correspondence, reports, and forms? Or do

A point-of-sale terminal's optical scanning wand captures data on bar code labels.

you want to produce newsletters and sales brochures or color slides of charts and graphs? Questions like these help you decide on the software packages and output devices that can produce such output.

• *Input and storage of data* How will you enter data into the system? How much input data will there be? How much data will need to be stored? Data can come from many different sources, and its volume and the way in which it is captured will affect your system requirements. For example, will you need just a keyboard and a mouse or trackball? Or will you need to optically scan a lot of bar codes or documents? What about pen-based

computer entry? How much data will need to be stored as files by the system? What storage capacity will you then require?

Selecting Your Software

Before you can develop a detailed set of your computer requirements you must make several software decisions. For instance, the operating system and the applications software you select will have a significant impact on system requirements. Each operating system and application software package alternative may also require different computer system resources. Computer system memory size, processor speeds, input devices, and other features are affected by such software decisions. Therefore, you must determine what software you will be using before you can determine the hardware requirements for your computer system. Several questions must be answered when selecting software. Does your application consist of one task, a number of individual tasks, or several related tasks? Which of the available operating systems (such as MS-DOS, OS/2, or UNIX) will best satisfy your needs? Do you need to consider an operating environment package (such as Microsoft Windows or DesqView) in addition to the operating system? Is there a commercially available applications software package, or will you need custom software?

A Software Evaluation Matrix

Once you understand your software requirements, you can compare the features of available applications software packages with them. One way to do this is to create an evaluation form similar to that shown in Table 1. This lists some important software requirements along one side of the matrix and the software products to be evaluated along the top. Comparing each requirement to the capabilities of each available product should result in a "picture" that will make your selection decision easier.

Hardware Requirements of Software

Notice that the comparison matrix provides a place for recording the hardware system requirements for each application program. Memory requirements and any special hardware requirements should be recorded for later consideration when you develop hardware specifications. As part of the software selection process, you must identify the hardware requirements of each software package. For example, how much memory is required for the application? What, if any, special hardware devices are required by the application? Is a particular main microprocessor recommended for this software package?

Evaluating End User Software

Comparing software specifications is often not as easy as it may sound. There may be technical terms involved that you do not understand, the differences between products may be subtle, and the specifications may be misleading in some cases. However, there are publications available in many retail magazine racks that specialize in comparing computer hardware

Table 1
Application Software Evaluation Matrix

Criteria	Package #1	Package #2	Package #3
Operating system/ environment required			
Reliability			
Ease of use			
Quality of documentation			
Customer support			
Provisions for customizing			
Hardware requirements			
Total points assigned			

Rating scale (relative performance to the specifications):

Software Performance Factor	Points
• Fully conforms to your requirements	10
• Meets all critical requirements, but lacks some desired features	8
• Functional, but would require acceptable changes in your methods	6
• Lacks critical features that would require additional software to meet your needs	2
• Includes exceptional features that are useful but not specified as a requirement	+2 (added to 10)

Software package comparisons are printed in many computer magazines.

and software. They will present you with easy-to-understand comparisons of software products.

Published software comparisons often include valuable comments by users of the products. If possible, you should contact any users you know for the type of packages you are considering and ask them for their evaluations and experiences. If you can gain access to electronic information services like CompuServ, GEnie, and Prodigy, you can also scan their bulletin board messages for helpful comments from users on the merits of various hardware devices and software packages.

Defining Your Hardware Requirements

Now it's time to define your hardware requirements. Some of the factors you should consider are as follows:

- *System availability* Can your application tolerate periods of downtime in case of power or system failure? If not, you will need to consider backup electric power and computer systems.

- *Growth plans* Do you plan on adding applications in the next two years? Will you require larger data storage capabilities in the near future? If you answer yes to these questions, you should consider purchasing larger disk storage and a more powerful main microprocessor.

- *Communications with other systems* Will you want to communicate with other systems within the company or outside the company? If the answer is yes, networking options or telecommunications devices may be a factor in your hardware specifications.

- *Operating systems* Which operating system will best meet your needs? Will an operating environment package be included? Each operating system and operating environment requires particular hardware considerations that must be factored into your hardware specifications.

Table 2
Hardware Specification Checklist Example

Criteria	Decision	System Requirements	Memory Required	Storage Required
Operating system	MS-DOS Version 5	MS-DOS compatibility	100K	1.2 MB
Operating environment	Microsoft Windows	MS-DOS compatible	500K	10 MB
Applications program	Works for Windows	Windows compatible	350K	1.5 MB
Future applications programs	Various	Windows compatible	2 MB	100 MB
File storage space	20 MB/year	N/A	N/A	20 MB
Hard disk requirement	200 MB	1/2-height bay	N/A	200 MB
Floppy disk requirement	3.5" HD	System slot & 1/2-height bay	N/A	1.44 MB
Main microprocessor requirement	Intel 80486SX	Intel microprocessor	N/A	N/A
Monitor requirement	14" SVGA color	Super VGA card	On board	On board
Keyboard requirement	101 key	Serial port	N/A	N/A
Other input required	Electronic mouse	Serial port	N/A	N/A
Printer	Ink jet	Parallel port	N/A	N/A
Communications requirement	Fax modem	2400/9600 BPS modem card	N/A	N/A

The Hardware Checklist

The hardware requirements for a system must include a number of elements relating to input, output, storage, and processing speed. A hardware specification checklist provides a convenient way for you to consolidate your requirements and to assure yourself that all elements have been taken into account. Table 2 is an example of a hardware specification checklist.

System Specifications

Once you have completed the software and hardware checklists you are ready to prepare a final list of specifications. These specifications should describe the hardware and software requirements of your system. They should be stated in sufficient detail to assure consistency in the price quotations of different suppliers who may bid on the system. The specifications should also contain any requirements you might have for warranty, service, installation, and supplies. Table 3 is an example of the specifications for a basic end user computer system.

Selecting a Source

There are several alternatives for acquiring a computer system for a small business or for a personal purchase. Most often computer dealers, mail order firms, or discount stores are your alternative sources. In these situations, the system specifications is an important tool in communicating your needs and for comparing the proposals from various sources. Let's discuss two options for the purchase of your system—mail order and a computer store. But first, there are several important points you should consider when determining where you will buy your system.

- Does the dealer run a reputable business that demonstrates the stability necessary to assure you that your purchase will be supported during the warranty period?

- Does the dealer have references that you can contact to verify customer satisfaction?

- Are the dealer's representatives easy to talk to, technically competent, and knowledgeable about computers and the products they represent?

- Does the dealer offer after-the-sale support and training?

- Has the dealer made provisions for prompt service and/or system replacement in case your system fails?

- Does the dealer have a warranty or customer satisfaction policy that will let you return the system without penalty if it does not perform to your specifications?

Mail Order Sources

At first glance the advertisements from mail order sources offer the most favorable pricing for systems. You should approach this carefully—conditions described in the small print can result in a final price well above the one that attracted your attention. Mail order sources often offer custom brands of personal computers in addition to name brand systems. Peripheral devices (printers, tape devices, and so on) are usually brand name products offered at heavily discounted prices.

Your contact with a mail order source is usually limited to the phone or mail and may be somewhat impersonal. You cannot view the actual equipment or operate the equipment in the manner you will use it, and you cannot see the source's operations or service facilities.

Table 3
System Specification Example

Software
Operating system: MS-DOS version 6.0—installed
Operating environment: Microsoft Windows 3.1—installed
Application software: Microsoft Works for Windows—installed

Hardware
Main microprocessor: Intel 80486SX
Main memory: 4 MB RAM
Hard disk drive: 200 MB
Floppy disk drive: 3.5 inch/1.44 MB
Video monitor: 14-inch Super VGA color
Enhanced 101-key keyboard
Electronic mouse—3 button
Ink jet printer
Fax modem—2400/9600 BPS internal card
Super VGA accelerator card
Desktop or mini-tower case with 6 expansion slots
Power supply—200 watts/surge protector/all cables

Computer systems can be ordered through mail order catalogs.

The offerings from mail order firms are often very attractive from a price standpoint and can be a "good deal" if you are a knowledgeable and cautious buyer. However, if you are a first-time buyer, you should carefully consider the disadvantages associated with having to select from a distance. While you ultimately may be able to correct any mistakes you or the dealer make, it takes a long time to accomplish this through the mail. See Table 4.

A Trip to the Computer Store

Now that you have developed a good working knowledge of your needs in both software and hardware and have made some of the hard decisions regarding features, it is time to visit your local computer dealer. When you select the dealer you intend to visit, don't forget the questions asked earlier in "Selecting a Source."

The computer store is usually arranged to display several personal computer configurations and their peripheral devices (printers, monitors, and so on). Some stores advertise the qualifications of their salespeople, so it is possible to receive assistance from very qualified people. It is important that you deal with someone who is not there just to sell you a computer system. He or she should be able to interpret your needs and suggest alternatives to meet your computing requirements.

Full-service computer stores usually offer name brand computers, custom branded (*clone*) computers, and name brand peripheral devices. Unlike the mail order process, you will usually have an opportunity to operate the equipment. You may also be able to use your own software to test a computer system. In addition to these conveniences, you will have the opportunity to inspect the store's service facilities. Finally, you can easily return to the computer store in case of problems with your purchases.

Talking to a Salesperson

You should start by showing the salesperson your specifications and discussing your needs. Most salespeople will probably have specific questions about the items you have described in your specification. This helps them understand your needs and recommend the kinds of hardware you need.

Often a salesperson will suggest possible upgrades or features that are available at an additional cost that might enhance the ability of the system to meet your needs. You should be cautious at this point. Sometimes these features are not really required in your application but will add significant cost to your system. Remember, one reason you spent the time developing your specifications is to avoid getting more than you need or want.

Cover your requirements step by step until you are fully satisfied that you and the salesperson are in agreement. Ask for demonstrations of all features on a computer system identical to the one in which you are interested. Next ask for a price quotation. The sales-

Table 4
What to Consider When Buying Direct-Mail PCs

Price
The lowest PC list price is not always the best buy. Consider costs of upgrades, repairs, and service calls when purchasing.

Brand
Look for an established name, or get recommendations by asking the company for two or three customer reference sites. If they won't give you references, don't bother.

Customer Service
Call a direct-mail supplier's service department before buying. Users warn of increasing difficulty in getting quality customer service by telephone.

On-Site Support
New buyers should have strong technical support staffs in-house. Without a dealer channel to go through, customers need more than telephone support, and outside service programs are becoming more expensive than ever.

User Reaction
Turn to on-line public computer forums such as CompuServe to gauge existing customers' satisfaction levels. Many direct-mail buyers have set up special mailboxes on these services to communicate with each other.

Large computer stores carry computers from many major manufacturers.

person should understand that you are going to compare performance and value at other sources before you make your final commitment.

Making Your Decision

When you have completed your shopping you should then compare the offerings of each store. A process similar to that used in the software evaluation matrix (Table 1) might be helpful in making certain that you are comparing "apples to apples." A point system will provide you with a quantitative way to evaluate the many elements of your specification and help lead you to the right selection.

As you make your final decision, don't forget to consider warranties, service policies and availability, training provisions, and your evaluation of how well the store and the salesperson will support you after the sale. These considerations may well be the "tie-breaker" and one of the most important long-term considerations in your decision.

A Final Word

The acquisition process defined in this guide may seem complex. However, it is important to consider it in the context of the impact of a poor computer selection decision. Many computers go unused because the wrong decisions were made. Others operate at only partial capacity because of an error in the definition of requirements. Still other computer systems become a source of aggravation rather than a tool in improving your personal or professional performance because the system was purchased from the wrong source. Again, careful consideration of the process discussed here will help you make better computer selection decisions.

End User Computer Selection Projects

1. Imagine a possible computer application of computers for a ca-

reer you are considering. Go through the steps identified in the Computer System Specification Road Map (Figure 1) and prepare a set of specifications for this application.

2. This book suggests that you can use a variety of computer publications as sources to assist you in comparing computer products. Visit your library or buy a computer magazine and look up several comparison articles on a type of software package you might want to use. Prepare a software evaluation matrix similar to the one in Table 1 comparing two alternative packages.

3. Visit a computer store, or "shop" in computer magazines for two different computer systems. Identify the features and capabilities of each system. Evaluate the two systems and the two sources in terms of cost and other factors. Prepare a hardware specification checklist similar to Table 2. Make a brief report to the class explaining your analysis and selection of one of the computer systems and sources.

PART IV

Applications and Issues

We are about to look at applications and issues in end user and organizational computing from the point of view of the computer user. We will examine application development by both users and IS specialists and survey a variety of computer applications in the work place, including business, management, manufacturing, engineering, design, health care, and government. We will wrap up by considering computer crime and security, and exploring the effect of computers on society, including the vital issues of privacy, health, and ethics.

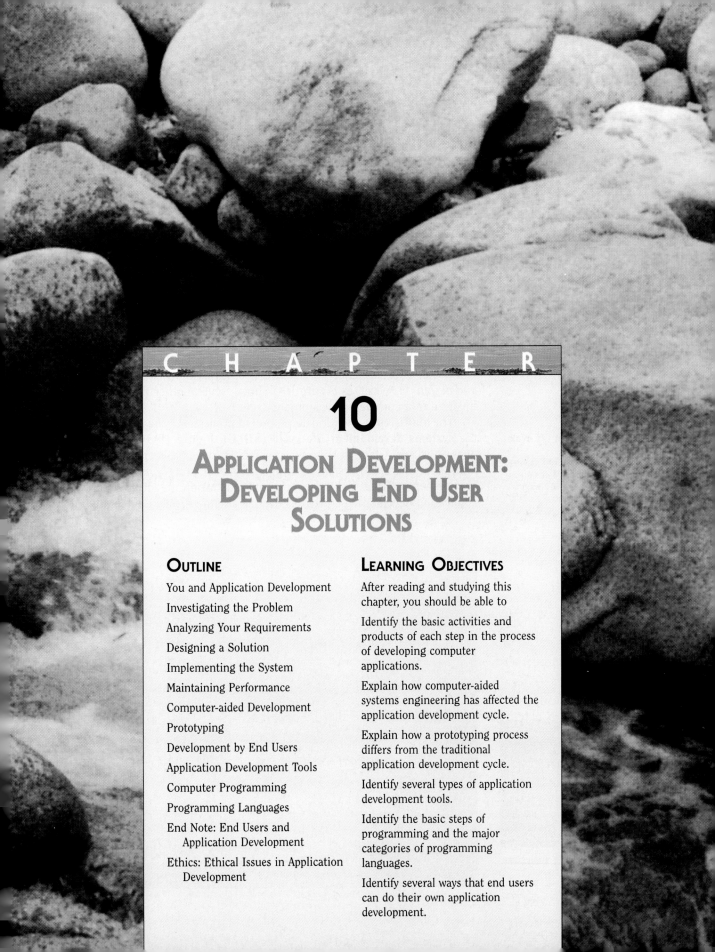

CHAPTER

10

APPLICATION DEVELOPMENT: DEVELOPING END USER SOLUTIONS

OUTLINE

LEARNING OBJECTIVES

After reading and studying this chapter, you should be able to

Identify the basic activities and products of each step in the process of developing computer applications.

Explain how computer-aided systems engineering has affected the application development cycle.

Explain how a prototyping process differs from the traditional application development cycle.

Identify several types of application development tools.

Identify the basic steps of programming and the major categories of programming languages.

Identify several ways that end users can do their own application development.

You and Application Development

Imagine that you are director of patient services at a hospital. The hospital administrator asks you to find a better way to use computers to supply vital patient information to doctors and nurses. How would you react to such a request? Is there a systematic way to help you develop a computer-based solution to the problem your administrator has presented to you? There is. It's a problem-solving process called *application development*. See Figure 10-1.

The Application Development Cycle

The development of computer-based solutions to end users' problems is traditionally called **systems development,** but increasingly is called **application development.** That's because computer-based information systems *(computer applications)* are usually conceived, designed, and implemented using a systematic development process. The goal of this process is to develop effective solutions to end users' problems. End users and IS specialists typically *design* information systems based on an *analysis* of the information requirements of end users. Thus, a major part of this process is known as *systems analysis and design*. However, as Figure 10-1 shows, several other major activities are involved in a complete development cycle.

The multistep application development process or cycle is frequently called the **systems development life cycle (SDLC).** Figure 10-2 summarizes what goes on in each stage of this cycle, which includes the steps of (1) *investigation,* (2) *analysis,* (3) *design,* (4) *implementation,* and (5) *maintenance.* However, remember that this is a conceptual illustration. In actual practice, most application development activities overlap and are highly related and interde-

systems development
Developing or improving information systems by a process of investigation, analysis, design, implementation, and maintenance.

application development
Developing computer applications for end users by a systems development process.

systems development life cycle (SDLC)
A multistep development process or cycle that includes (1) investigation, (2) analysis, (3) design, (4) implementation, and (5) maintenance activities.

Figure 10-1
Application development is a multistep problem-solving process or cycle.

End users and systems analysts work together to develop computer-based soutions.

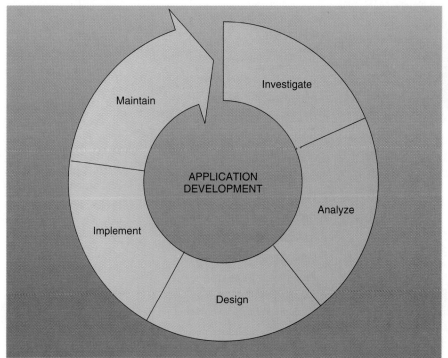

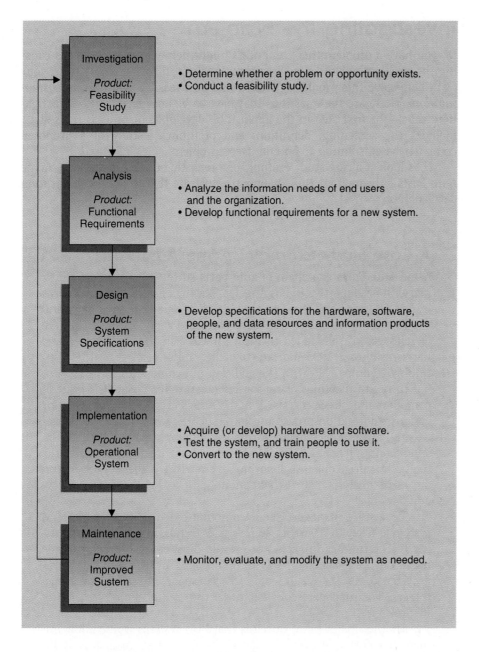

Figure 10-2

Each step of traditional application development results in a product that is used in the next step of the cycle.

The figure shows the following steps:

Investigation
Product: Feasibility Study
• Determine whether a problem or opportunity exists.
• Conduct a feasibility study.

Analysis
Product: Functional Requirements
• Analyze the information needs of end users and the organization.
• Develop functional requirements for a new system.

Design
Product: System Specifications
• Develop specifications for the hardware, software, people, and data resources and information products of the new system.

Implementation
Product: Operational System
• Acquire (or develop) hardware and software.
• Test the system, and train people to use it.
• Convert to the new system.

Maintenance
Product: Improved Sustem
• Monitor, evaluate, and modify the system as needed.

pendent. For example, you may cycle back at any time to repeat previous activities in order to modify and improve a system you are building. Therefore, several activities can occur at the same time, and parts of a project can be at different stages of a developmental cycle.

You should also realize that computer-based developments such as *computer-aided systems engineering (CASE)* and *prototyping* methods are automating and changing some of the activities of the systems development cycle. As you will see later in this chapter, these developments are improving the quality of application development and making it easier for IS professionals, while enabling more end users to develop their own systems.

Investigating the Problem

Do you have a problem that computers might help you solve? What is causing the problem? Would a new or improved way to use computers in your work help solve this problem? What would be a feasible *information system solution?* These are the questions that have to be answered in the **investigation** stage—the first step in the application development process. This stage includes the screening, definition, and preliminary study of a proposed computer-based solution to an end user's problem.

investigation
The screening, definition, and preliminary study of a proposed information system solution to an end user problem.

Let's look at a case study example of a realistic business situation—Acme Auto Parts—throughout this chapter to illustrate the process of application development.

A Case Study Example: Acme Auto Parts

Acme Auto Parts is a chain of auto parts stores in Southern California, with headquarters in Los Angeles. The firm has grown to 14 stores in just 10 years, and it offers a wide variety of automotive parts and accessories. Sales and profits have increased each year, but the rate of sales growth has failed to meet forecasts in the last three years. Early results for 1995 indicate that the rate of sales growth is continuing to drop, even with the addition of two new stores in 1994.

In recent meetings of corporate and store managers, the issue of computer use has been raised. Acme Auto Parts uses computers for various information processing jobs, such as sales transactions processing, analysis of sales performance, employee payroll processing, and accounting applications. However, sales transactions are still written up by salespeople. Also, corporate and store managers depend on daily sales analysis reports that contain information that is always several days old.

Most store managers see a computer-based point-of-sale (POS) system as a key to reversing Acme's sales trends. They believe that using POS terminals in each store would drastically shorten the time needed by a salesperson to write up a sale. This would not only improve customer service, it would free salespeople to sell to more customers. The managers consider these the "selling floor" benefits of POS systems.

Another major point raised is that POS systems would allow immediate information to be made available to store managers at PC workstations connected into the company's telecommunications network. This would provide the capability for information on sales performance to be tailored to each manager's information needs. Currently, store managers have to depend on daily sales analysis reports that use the same report format. Too much of a manager's time is being used to generate sales performance information not provided by the system. Store managers complain they don't have enough time to plan and support sales efforts unless they make decisions without enough information.

Feasibility Studies

Many end user problems arise when existing systems cannot produce documents or reports on time, adequately process the quantity of transactions that occur, or deliver information in an easy-to-use form for managerial decision making. Since the process of developing computer-based solutions to such problems can be costly, the investigation stage may include a preliminary study called a **feasibility study.** This study investigates the information needs of end users, defines the problems they are having, and estimates the costs and benefits of a proposed use of computers.

Typically, you would use a variety of methods to collect data for analysis in a feasibility study. Some examples are:

- Interviews with employees and managers
- Questionnaires to appropriate end users
- Personal observations or involvement in business operations
- Examination of documents and reports

feasibility study
An investigation that identifies the information needs of end users and estimates the costs and benefits of a proposed use of computers.

The Feasibility of a Solution

Once you come up with an idea for a proposed solution, you should evaluate it in terms of its organizational, economic, technical, and operational feasibility. **Organizational feasibility** focuses on how well a proposed solution supports the objectives of an organization. A proposal that does not directly contribute to meeting an organization's objectives will typically not be funded. **Economic feasibility** is concerned with whether expected cost savings, increased revenues, or other types of benefits will exceed the costs of developing and implementing a proposed solution. If a proposal cannot cover its development costs, it won't be approved unless mandated by other considerations, such as government regulations. **Technical feasibility** means that reliable hardware and software capable of meeting the requirements of a proposed solution can be acquired or developed. Finally, **operational feasibility** means that the requirements of end users, managers, customers, government agencies, and others are being met by a proposed computer-based solution. For instance, if a new POS system is too difficult to use and does not provide enough help displays, salespeople will avoid using it. Thus, it would fail to show operational feasibility.

The findings of a feasibility study are usually formalized in a written report that you would submit to the management of the organization. Typically, the report will explain if there is a feasible and desirable way to use computers to solve an end user's information problem. Only if management would approve the recommendations of the feasibility study would you begin the *analysis* stage of the development process.

organizational feasibility
How well a proposed information system supports an organization's objectives.

economic feasibility
Whether expected cost savings, increased revenue, increased profits, and reductions in required investments exceed the costs of developing and operating a proposed system.

technical feasibility
Whether reliable hardware and software capable of meeting the needs of a proposed system can be acquired or developed by an organization in the required time.

operational feasibility
The willingness and ability of management, employees, customers, and suppliers to operate, use, and support a proposed system.

Acme Auto Parts: POS Feasibility

A group of store managers and systems analysts from the information services department of Acme Auto Parts were commissioned to conduct a feasibility study of the POS options facing the firm. The sys-
(continued on following page)

(continued from previous page)
tems analysts made personal observations of the sales processing system in action and interviewed managers, salespeople, and other employees. Based on a preliminary analysis of user requirements, the systems analysts proposed a new sales processing system. This new system features a telecommunications network of point-of-sale (POS) terminals and management workstations. Table 10-1 outlines several examples of feasibility factors that were determined for the new point-of-sale system at Acme Auto Parts. After reviewing the feasibility study, the top management of the company gave the go-ahead for the development of the new POS system.

Analyzing Your Requirements

Whether you want to develop a new application quickly or are involved in a long-term project, you or a systems analyst will need to perform several analytical activities, commonly called **systems analysis.** Systems analysis is an in-depth study of end user information requirements that is needed before the design of a computer-based solution can be completed. This traditionally involves studying:

- The information needs of an organization and its end users, such as a retail store and its salespeople
- The characteristics of any information systems already being used, such as a POS (point-of-sale) system
- The new capabilities required to meet the information needs of end users, such as faster checkout of customers

systems analysis
Analyzing in detail the information needs of an organization and its end users, the characteristics of any present information system, and the capabilities required to meet the needs of end users.

**Table 10-1
Examples of Ways to Measure the Feasibility of a Proposed POS System for Acme Auto Parts**

Organizational Feasibility	Economic Feasibility
How well the proposed system fits the store's image	Savings in checkout costs
	Increased sales revenue
	Decreased investment in inventory
	Increased profits
Technical Feasibility	**Operational Feasibility**
Capability, reliability, and availability of POS hardware and software	Acceptance of salespeople
	Store management support
	Customer acceptance

- When a customer wants to buy an auto part, a salesclerk writes up a sales order form. Recorded on this form is customer data, such as name, address, and account number, and product data, such as name, product number, and price. A copy of the sales order form is given to the customer as a receipt.
- Sales order forms are sent at the end of each day to the information services department. The next day they are entered into the computer system by data entry clerks using video terminals and stored on the mainframe computer's magnetic disk units.
- These daily sales transactions are used by a sales processing program to update a sales master file to reflect the sales for the day.
- Sales processing also involves the use of a sales analysis program to produce sales analysis reports that tell store managers the trends in sales for various types of auto parts.

**Table 10-2
Analysis of the Present
Sales Processing Activities
at Acme Auto Parts**

The analysis stage begins as a more thorough continuation of the feasibility study you did in the previous investigation stage. First, you need to study any information systems that are currently being used. This helps you gain a better understanding of the resources, activities, and information needs of end users. For example, you need to analyze how such systems use hardware, software, and people resources to convert data resources, such as data from business transactions, into information products, such as reports and video displays. You should also document how input, processing, output, storage, and control activities are accomplished in the present system as well as the timing, volume, frequencies, and quality of such activities. Then, in the design stage, you can specify what the resources, products, and activities *should be* in the system you are designing. See Table 10-2.

After a current system is documented, you can concentrate on possible improvements that can be made to better meet your information needs. Your main goal should be to identify what should be done, not how to do it. Interaction you may have with systems analysts should help you identify the specific information needs you and other end users have.

Functional Requirements

You should work with systems analysts to discover what type of information end users require, what its format, volume and frequency should be, and what response times are required. Then they can help you determine the capabilities required for each information processing activity (input, processing, output, storage, and control) to meet those information needs. Finally, systems analysts can help you state these capabilities as **functional requirements.** Functional requirements are end user information requirements that are not tied to the hardware, software, and people resources that are being used or might be used in the future. This is left to the design stage to determine. For example, Table 10-3 lists some of the functional requirements developed for the user interface and the processing, storage, and control activities of a point-of-sale information system at Acme Auto Parts.

functional requirements
End user and other required information system capabilities such as user interface, processing, storage, and control requirements.

**Table 10-3
Examples Of Functional
Requirements For A POS
System For Acme Auto
Parts**

User Interface Requirements	Automatic entry of product data and easy-to-use data entry screens for salespeople
Processing Requirements	Fast, automatic calculation of sales totals and sales taxes
Storage Requirements	Fast retrieval and update of data from product, pricing, and customer databases
Control Requirements	Signals for data entry errors and easy-to-read receipts for customers

Designing A Solution

The analysis stage describes *what* a computer-based system should do to meet your information needs. The design stage specifies *how* the system will accomplish this objective. One helpful way to accomplish the design stage is emphasized by the saying, "Design output, then files, then input." This means you should first consider what outputs (displays, reports, documents) you want your system to produce. Then you should consider what types of data you will need to store in files or databases, that can be processed to give you the output you want. Finally, you can decide how to enter or capture the data the systems will need using methods such as paper forms, keyboarding, optical scanning, and so on. Table 10-4 presents a design overview of the proposed POS system for Acme Auto Parts.

Another good way to look at **systems design** is illustrated in Figure 10-3. In this framework, the design stage consists of three design activities: user interface, data, and process design. These design activities will result in *system specifications* for the user interface methods, database structures, and processing that will be included in your new application.

systems design
Includes user interface, data, and process design activities that produce system specifications to satisfy the functional requirements developed in the analysis stage.

**Table 10-4
Design Overview of the
New POS System at Acme
Auto Parts**

- When a customer wishes to buy an auto part, the salesclerk enters customer and product data using an online POS terminal. The POS terminal has a keyboard for data entry and a video screen for display of input data, as well as data entry menus, prompts, and messages. POS terminals are connected in a telecommunications network to the store's mainframe computer, which uses a comprehensive sales transaction processing program.

- The POS terminal prints out a sales receipt for the customer that contains customer and product data and serves as a record of the transaction.

- The POS terminal transmits sales transaction data to the store's mainframe computer. This immediately updates the sales records in the company's database, which is stored on magnetic disk units.

- The computer performs sales analyses using the updated sales records in the company database. Afterward, sales performance information is available to corporate and store managers in a variety of report formats at their management workstations.

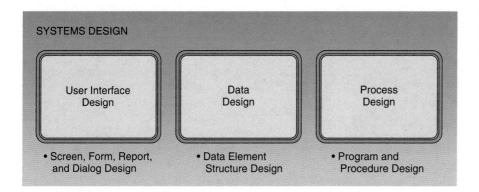

Figure 10-3
System design consists of designing user interfaces, data, and processes.

User Interface Design

In user interface design, end users and systems analysts are concerned with designing the interactions between end users and computer systems. Thus, you should concentrate on methods of input and output. Many times, user interface design is a *prototyping* process where working models or *prototypes* of user interface methods are designed and modified with end users' feedback. This results in detailed specifications for information products such as display screens, interactive user/computer dialogues, audio responses, forms, documents, and reports.

Data Design

In data design, end users and analysts focus on the design of the structure of databases and files to be used by a proposed computer-based system. For ex-

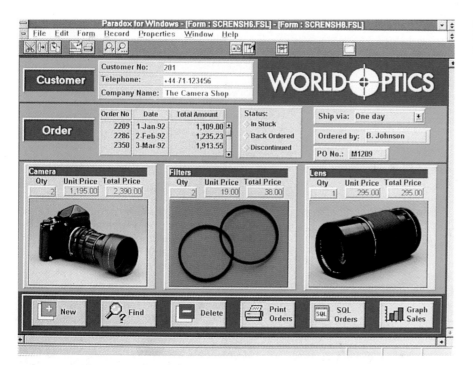

Customer sales data are entered through a customer display data entry screen.

ample, in data design, you should try to identify the *attributes* or characteristics of the *entities* (people, places, things, events) about which information needs to be maintained and the *relationships* these entities have to each other. As we saw in Chapter 6, this results in a *data dictionary* containing detailed descriptions of the *data elements* (databases, files, records, and so on) that need to be maintained by the proposed system.

Process Design

Process design results in the design of programs and procedures needed by a proposed computer-based system. Analysts and end users concentrate on developing specifications for the programs that will be purchased as software packages or developed by custom programming. This produces the detailed program specifications and procedures needed to meet the functional requirements that were established in the analysis stage.

System Specifications

So you see, system design is the detailed design of user interface methods and products, database structures, and processing and control procedures. Hardware, software, and personnel specifications are also developed. Systems analysts work with you so they can use your knowledge of your work activities

Table 10-5
Examples of System Specifications for a POS System at Acme Auto Parts

User Interface Specifications	Use hand-held optical scanning wands to automatically capture product data on bar-coded tags. Use data entry screens with key data highlighted for better readability.
Database Specifications	Develop databases that use a relational structure to organize access to all necessary customer and merchandise data.
Software Specifications	Develop or acquire a sales processing program that can accept entry of optically scanned bar codes, retrieve necessary product data, and compute sales amounts in less than 0.5 seconds. Acquire a relational database management package to manage stored databases.
Hardware Specifications	Install POS terminals at each checkout station connected to a system of networked microcomputers in each store that are also connected to the corporate headquarters network.
Personnel Specifications	All hardware and software must be operable by regular store personnel. IS personnel should be available for hardware and software maintenance as needed.

REAL-WORLD EXAMPLE

Garber Travel: Making Dumb Terminals Smart

Garber Travel is a Boston-based international travel agency with 67 offices. Garber ranks in the top 20 in business volume among the 36,000 travel agencies in the United States. For example, they issue up to 8,000 airline tickets per week. Of their $150 million in annual business, $110 million is from air travel. Garber also has more than 600 IBM PS/2 microcomputers tied into the worldwide SABRE electronic reservation system from American Airlines. Yet Garber managers thought they were not getting enough out of their investment in computers.

So they did something about it. Garber developed new uses for the PS/2s used by each travel agent as terminals to make reservations through the SABRE system. Rock Blanco, vice-president of information systems, says: "Agents had no place to store, query, or use information. They were keeping information on Rolodexes or study pads. Here you had this wonderful PS/2 on your desk and it was still acting like a dumb terminal." So Blanco developed an integrated system of useful applications for Garber's agents. He installed a local area network of powerful PS/2s in Boston, purchased spreadsheet and office automation software packages that could run on the LAN, and installed fax circuit boards in a PS/2 in each office. Now all 600 agency PS/2s can access the LAN to use its software and databases.

Installing the new system has dramatically changed the way Garber agents operate. Everything they need is integrated through their terminals. Without leaving their desks or exiting SABRE, agents can look up a schedule, download it into a letter or expense report, and fax it to a customer. They can split the screen, checking airline schedules on one half and running a spreadsheet on the other. The client does not even need to call for reservations; these too can be handled by fax.

1. Why was Garber Travel unsatisfied with its use of computers?

2. How did it develop the new system for its agents?

and their knowledge of computing systems to specify the design of a new or improved computer-based system. This results in the final product of the design stage, the **system specifications.** Table 10-5 outlines several specifications for the new POS system at Acme Auto Parts.

system specifications
Specifications for the hardware, software, facilities, personnel, databases, and the user interface of a proposed information system.

Quick Quiz

1. The development of new computer-based solutions to end user problems is called _____.

2. The _____ is a multistep cycle of investigations, analysis, design, implementation and maintenance activities.

3. The _____ is a preliminary study to investigate the feasibility of a proposed new computer application.

4. The _____ stage is an in-depth study of end user information requirements.

5. The _____ stage produces systems specifications through user interface, data and process design.

Answers: 1. application development   2. systems development life cycle   3. feasibility study   4. systems analysis   5. systems design

Implementing the System

implementation
The stage of systems development in which hardware and software are acquired, developed, and installed, the system is tested and documented, people are trained to operate and use the system, and an organization converts to the use of a newly developed system.

Once a proposed information system has been designed, it needs to be implemented. The **implementation** stage involves hardware and software acquisition, testing of programs and procedures, and a variety of installation activities. It also involves the education and training of the end users who will operate the new system. You will find that implementation can be a difficult process. However, it is a vital stage in assuring the success of any newly developed system. Even a well-designed system will fail if it is not properly implemented. Table 10-6 outlines some of the activities of the implementation stage at Acme Auto Parts.

Note: Refer to "Viewpoint: A Guide to Computer Selection" beginning on page 307 for a guide to the steps you should take in evaluating and selecting hardware and software.

Build or Buy

In the implementation step, you develop or purchase programs based on software specifications developed in the design stage. At this point you must decide whether to develop software in-house (custom software) or purchase a software package. You should evaluate the cost of developing programs yourself, or with in-house programmers, versus the cost and features provided by a software package. Frequently, buying an economical software package that meets your design requirements makes sense instead of developing the program yourself.

Although software packages can be modified to some extent, most of the time you must be willing to work within the capabilities and constraints imposed by a package. The advantages of purchasing software packages is that they can usually be implemented faster, have been thoroughly tested, and are less expensive to acquire. The biggest advantage of building the software in-house is that it can be customized to fit the exact requirements of end users. It can also be modified later to reflect changing needs and could even be sold

Table 10-6
Activities of the
Implementation Stage at
Acme Auto Parts

Acquisition	Evaluate and acquire POS terminals and POS software packages
Software development	Develop custom POS programs or modify POS software packages
Training	Educate and train store personnel in the operations of the POS system
Testing	Test and make necessary corrections to the software and hardware of the new system
Conversion	Convert from the use of the present sales system to the operation of the new POS system

later to other organizations similar to yours. However, this alternative usually takes much longer to accomplish. It also may be riskier, because there is no guarantee that the programs you develop in-house will work better than the software packages you can buy and test.

Testing

Implementation requires *testing* a newly developed system. This involves testing hardware devices, *debugging* computer programs, and testing information processing procedures. Programs are tested for *bugs* (errors) using test data. Testing attempts to simulate all conditions that may arise during processing. In good programming practice, programs are subdivided into levels of *modules* to assist their development, testing, and maintenance. Program testing usually proceeds from higher to lower levels of program modules until an entire program is tested as a unit. The program is then tested along with other related programs in a final *systems test* to be sure that the entire system works together.

Conversion

Before you can begin to use a new computer-based system, a **conversion** process is usually necessary. The procedures, equipment, input/output methods, and databases of an old information system must be changed to the requirements of a new system. Even the organizational structure and the duties of employees may have to be changed to accommodate the new system. So conversion is an important process. The four major forms of conversion are the parallel, pilot, phased, and direct cutover approaches. See Figure 10-4.

> **conversion**
> The process in which the hardware, software, people, and data resources of an old information system must be changed to the requirements of a new information system. This usually involves a parallel, phased, pilot, or plunge conversion process from the old to the new system.

The Parallel Approach

Conversions can be done on a *parallel* basis, where you operate both the old and the new systems for a time, until you finally switch completely over to the new system. During this time the operations and results of both systems are compared and evaluated. Errors can be identified and corrected, and the operating problems can be solved before the old system is abandoned. This approach offers more safety; however, it can also be costly, since you operate two systems during the conversion period.

The Phased Approach

In the phased approach, a conversion is conducted in steps or increments. For example, instead of implementing an entire system at once, you implement a system gradually, one subsystem at a time. Or only a few departments, branch offices, or other locations at a time may be converted to a new application until the entire organization is using the new system. Thus, the phased conversion is much less disruptive to an organization.

The Pilot Approach

In the pilot approach, a conversion is accomplished at a single department or location. This approach gives you a test site in which the effects of any errors will be restricted to a single part of the organization. The new system can be tried out at this site until you feel it can be implemented throughout the organization.

The Direct Cutover Approach

In the *direct cutover* or *plunge* conversion, you switch over to the new

Figure 10-4
These are four ways to convert to a new system.

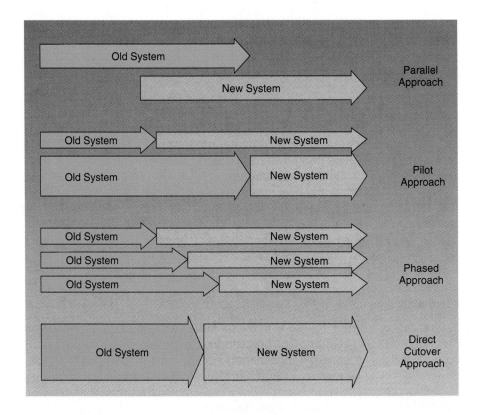

information system and abandon the old system all at once, typically at the end of the month, quarter, or year. This method of implementation requires rigorous testing since there is no fall-back position. It is most appropriate for simple, straightforward conversions or where the other strategies are too costly or too complicated.

Maintaining Performance

maintenance
The monitoring, evaluating, and modifying of a system to make desirable or necessary improvements.

The **maintenance** stage involves monitoring, evaluating, and modifying a system to make desirable or necessary improvements. This might include a *post-implementation review* process where you review a newly implemented system to ensure that it meets the development objectives established for it. Errors in the development or use of a system can also be identified and corrected by periodic *audits,* in which you or IS professionals review a system's performance. The maintenance stage also includes making changes to a system due to changes that occur within an organization or its environment, for example, a change in state or federal tax laws. This usually requires changes to the tax computations in the payroll and tax-accounting systems of an organization.

Computer-aided Development

Major changes are occurring in the application development process. That's because the traditional systems development life cycle process has often been too inflexible, time consuming, and expensive for many organizations. In many cases, end user requirements are defined too early in the process. Then end users are "locked out" of the process until the system is implemented. Also, the backlog of unfilled end user requests for new computer-based systems has grown from two to five years in many companies.

Computer-aided Software Engineering

Many organizations are using a computer-aided approach to speed up and improve the application development process. A variety of software packages for application development are now available for systems analysts, programmers, and end users. **Computer-aided software engineering (CASE)** involves using software packages, called CASE tools, to perform many of the activities of the systems development life cycle.

CASE tools include software packages to do a variety of application development activities. This includes business planning, project evaluation and management, user interface design, database design, and software development. For example, systems analysts can use CASE tools for developing user interface products such as data entry screens or management reports. CASE tools also help automate the drawing of flow charts and other diagrams and the creation of data dictionaries.

CASE packages provide computer-based tools for both the *front end* (planning, analysis, and design) and the *back end* (implementation and maintenance) of the application development cycle. Integrated CASE tools (called I-CASE) are now available that can be used in all of the stages of systems development. Other CASE tools support *backward engineering,* that is, they help

computer-aided software engineering (CASE)
Using software packages to perform some of the activities of the systems development life cycle.

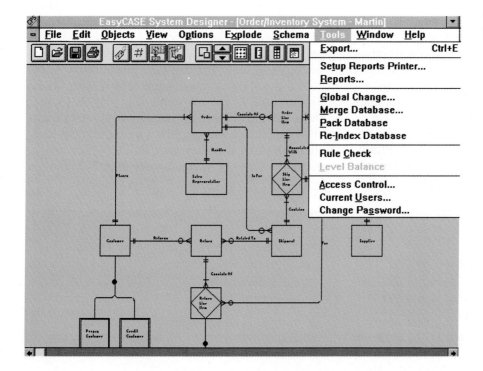

This CASE software package features pull-down menus.

analyze the logic of program codes for old applications and convert them into more efficient programs.

Many CASE tools now include an expanded data dictionary component known as a **system repository.** It serves as a special database or *repository* that documents design features that systems analysts generate with other system development tools. For instance, they can start using the repository to document their investigation and analysis activities and continue to use it to record the design of databases and the user interface. Finally, they can use the repository to help ensure proper implementation and maintenance by recording all changes to a system.

system repository
A special database and software to document design features that systems analysts generate with other systems development tools.

Prototyping

Microcomputers and a variety of CASE and other software packages allow the rapid development and testing of working models, or **prototypes,** of new applications. This takes place in an interactive process, typically involving both systems analysts and end users, known as **prototyping.** Prototyping improves the development process and makes it faster and easier for systems analysts. It also opens up the applications development process to end users. Prototyping is thus changing the roles of end users and IS specialists in application development.

prototype
A working model of part or all of an information system including tentative versions of user input and output, databases, control methods, and processing routines.

prototyping
The rapid development and testing of working models, or prototypes, of an information system in an interactive, iterative process typically involving both systems analysts and end users.

The Prototyping Process

Prototyping is a fast and *iterative* (repetitive) application development process. Large and complex transaction processing systems may still require using the traditional system development approach, but parts of such systems can frequently be prototyped. You or a systems analyst can develop a prototype of a computer-based system quickly, using a variety of application development packages. The prototype system is then repeatedly refined until it is acceptable to you. See Figure 10-5.

To do prototyping, you need to use CASE tools, database management systems, or other software packages. Prototyping can take many forms. At the low end, a prototype may be a mock-up of screens and reports with little if any actual functionality for later use. At the other end, it is possible to build a prototype that can be enhanced and become the actual operational system.

End users with sufficient experience with application development packages can do prototyping themselves. Or they can work with a systems analyst to develop a prototype system in a series of interactive sessions. For example,

Figure 10-5
Application development can use a prototyping approach.

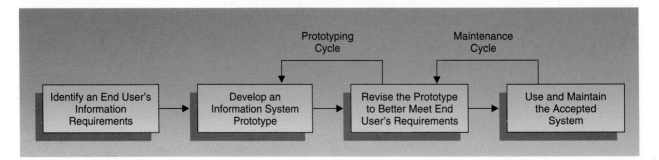

	Prototyping Cycle		Maintenance Cycle	
Identify an End User's Information Requirements	→	Develop an Information System Prototype	→	Revise the Prototype to Better Meet End User's Requirements	→	Use and Maintain the Accepted System

they could develop prototypes of management reports or data-entry screens such as the one illustrated in the photograph below. The prototype is usually modified several times until an end user finds it acceptable. Any programs not directly produced by a program generator can then be coded using conventional programming methods.

Development by End Users

In a traditional application development cycle, your role as an end user is similar to that of a customer or a client. Typically, you will make a request for a new or improved system, answer questions about your specific information needs and information processing problems, and provide background information on your existing information systems.

Systems analysts and other IS professionals work with you to determine the cause of your information system problem. They try to define the nature of your problem to make it as precise as possible. The systems analysts will then analyze and suggest several alternative solutions. When you approve their recommendation of the best alternative, it is designed, constructed, and implemented.

End User Development

However, many end users can now develop new or improved ways to perform their jobs without the direct involvement of IS professionals. The application development capabilities built into several types of end user software packages have made it easier for them to develop their own computer-based solutions. For example, you can use an electronic spreadsheet package as a tool to develop a way to easily analyze weekly sales results for the sales managers in a company. Or you could use a database management package to design data-entry displays to help sales clerks enter sales data, or to develop monthly sales analysis reports needed by district sales managers.

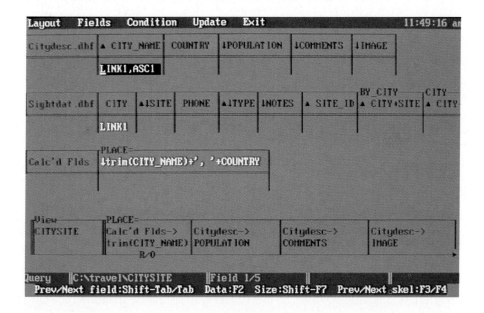

Here is an example of a prototype data entry screen.

REAL-WORLD EXAMPLE

Hospital of Saint Raphael: Curing Paper Clot

Imagine nurses spending 25 percent of their day doing paperwork. That's what they typically do, according to Debbie Salerni, director of surgical critical-care nursing at the Hospital of Saint Raphael in New Haven, Connecticut. She says: "A nurse will write down little bits of information on any scrap of paper he or she can find." Then at the end of the day, the nurse must spend time sorting through these bits of data and enter them into logs for every patient.

However, Saint Raphael's has cured this paper clot. The hospital formed an evaluation team consisting of Donald Meyers, vice president of the medical support and information group, two nurses including Salerni, a pharmacist, a radiologist, a lab technician, and a business office staffer. After five years of study and evaluation, Saint Raphael's has installed a computerized patient care information system equalled by only 10 to 15 percent of other U.S. hospitals. The system relies on a network of 5 Data General minicomputers, 50 personal computers, and 650 dumb terminals, spread throughout all 491 patient rooms as well as nurses' stations and other offices. Saint Raphael's system uses the Uticare patient care software package to automate all patient records and record keeping. "What I liked best about Uticare was that it's at the bedside," says Salerni. "That way, you have immediate access to what's happening to the patient." Vice-president Meyers likes the built-in backup provided by 5 minicomputers and the security of electronically coded terminal keys and passwords, which limit access to vital patient records.

1. Why do you think it took five years of study to develop Saint Raphael's patient care system?

2. What system features do Salerni and Meyers like best? Which ones would you choose? Explain.

In end user development, IS professionals play a consulting role while you do your own application development. Typically, a staff of user consultants may be available to help you and other end users with your application development efforts. For instance, a *user services* department or *information*

Several types of software packages are available for end user development.

center may provide assistance for both mainframe and microcomputer applications development. This may include training in the use of application packages, selection of hardware and software, assistance in gaining access to organization databases, and, of course, assistance in analysis, design, and programming.

Levels of End User Development

End users can be their own analysts, designers, and programmers for many types of applications. However, end user development can vary substantially. At the low end of the spectrum, end users may merely follow a hierarchy of menus and make selections from predefined reporting formats. At the upper end, some end users can develop programs in a procedural language that is a part of a database management or spreadsheet package. Some end users are extremely knowledgeable about particular software packages, such as Lotus 1-2-3, dBASE, or WordPerfect. These knowledgeable end users, sometimes called "power users," are those you might consult when you want to do more complex jobs using software packages.

Problems with End User Development

Several problems can arise when end users develop their own applications. Many end users are not properly trained in computer-based problem-solving techniques. Thus it is difficult for them to apply computers to solve the unique problems of their own work activities. End user programming is frequently criticized for poor program structure, control methods, documentation, and testing. For example, many instances of incorrect spreadsheet macros developed by end users have been reported. So as we will see in Chapter 11, end users must be properly trained and managed if end user development is to be successful.

Quick Quiz

1. The _____ stage involves buying hardware and software, testing, training, and other activities.
2. The _____ process involves parallel, pilot, phased, or direct cutover approaches to implementing a new system.
3. Using software packages to perform many of the activities of the application development process is called _____.
4. A _____ process involves the rapid development and testing of working models of new computer-based systems.
5. In _____, end users develop new or improved ways to perform their jobs with computers.

Answers: 1. implementation 2. conversion 3. computer-aided software engineering 4. prototyping 5. end user development

Application Development Tools

The steps of application development involve the use of a variety of tools. Most of them take the form of diagrams and other graphic representations. That's

Table 10-7
Examples of Application
Development Tools

System Feature	Examples
System Components and Flows	System flowcharts and data flow diagrams
User Interface	Input/output layout forms and screens
Data Attributes and Relationships	Data dictionaries and entity-relationship diagrams
Detailed System Processes	Structure charts, pseudocode, and program flowcharts

because they are easier to understand than long narrative descriptions of a system. Good graphic tools can represent the major activities and resources of a system while showing various modules and levels of detail when needed. Many of these tools can be used in several stages of application development— as analytical tools, design tools, and documentation methods. For example, you could use system flowcharts or data flow diagrams to (1) *analyze* an existing system, (2) express the *design* of a new system, and (3) provide the *documentation* for the implementation and maintenance of a newly developed system.

Figure 10-6
These are some of the symbols that can be used in system flowcharts.

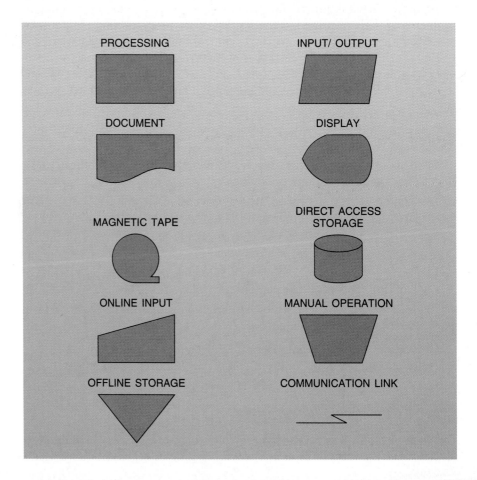

Table 10-7 outlines some of the major types of tools used for application development. Notice that the tools can be grouped into four categories based on features each typically documents: (1) the components and flows of a system, (2) the user interface, (3) data attributes and relationships, and (4) detailed system processes.

For example, *system flowcharts* are typically used to show the flow of information processing activities as data are processed by people and computers. *Data flow diagrams* use a few simple symbols to illustrate data flow among external entities (such as people or organizations), processing activities, and data storage elements. *Layout forms and screens* are used to design the formats of input/output documents, reports, and displays.

A System Flowchart Example

Figure 10-6 illustrates some common system flowchart symbols. Figure 10-7 shows how they are used in a system flowchart to illustrate the flow of data media and the information processing procedures in the proposed sales processing system for Acme Auto Parts. Note how the system flowchart pictures a data-entry terminal, magnetic disk storage, and several printed reports produced by this system. This is called a *physical design* because the hardware devices and media that will be used in the new system are specified.

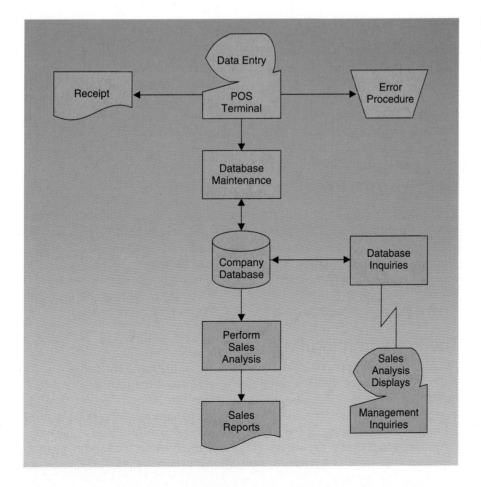

Figure 10-7
This is a system flowchart of the new sales processing system for Acme Auto Parts.

Figure 10-8
Data flow diagrams use these four basic types of symbols.

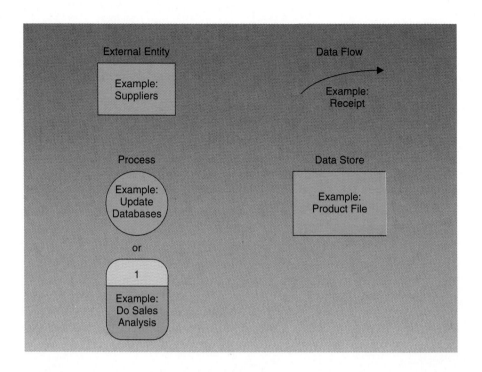

data flow diagram (DFD)
A graphic diagramming tool that uses a few simple symbols to illustrate the flow of data among external entities, processing activities, and data storage elements.

A Data Flow Diagram Example

A **data flow diagram (DFD)** can help you identify the flow of data in a system *logically,* that is, without specifying the media or hardware involved. DFDs can be drawn in increasing levels of detail, starting with a summary high-level view and proceeding to more detailed lower-level views. Figure 10-8 illustrates the four basic symbols used in data flow diagrams. Figure 10-9 shows how a data flow diagram can be used to portray the flow of data in the new sales processing system for Acme Auto Parts.

Computer Programming

As we mentioned earlier, one of the important decisions in application development is deciding whether to buy a software package or develop a custom program. **Computer programming** is the process of developing custom programs or software packages using a variety of programming languages and other programming tools. A detailed discussion of computer programming is beyond the scope of this text. However, as a computer-literate end user, you should understand some basic facts about the programming process.

computer programming
The process of developing sets of instructions (computer programs) for end user applications using a variety of programming languages or other programming tools.

The Programming Process

Programming is a process of developing a set of instructions (called a computer program) that direct a computer to perform the information processing tasks you want accomplished. This process can be quite simple or quite complex, depending on the tasks. Developing programs for complex tasks must typically be done as part of the application development process we have discussed in this chapter. The design stage can result in detailed *software specifications* that serve as a guide for professional programmers. CASE packages

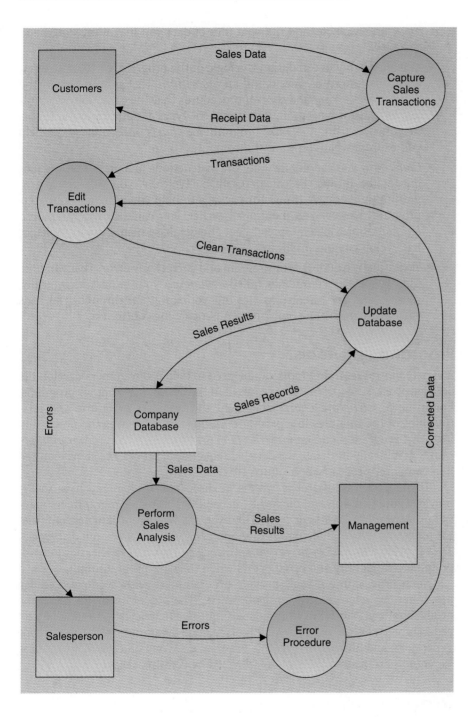

Figure 10-9
This data flow diagram illustrates the flow of data in a new sales processing system for Acme Auto Parts.

can also be used to automate the development of much of the computer instructions that make up a custom program.

However, as an end user, there is a simpler way to understand the process of programming. Basically, programming is a *problem-solving* process that creates a software solution. It consists of the following steps:

- *Analyze:* Define what you want the program to do. For example, you should determine (1) what forms of *output* you need, (2) what types of *input* are available, and (3) what files of data you may want *stored* and accessed.

- *Design:* Then you can design the logic of the program. In computer science, it's known as developing an *algorithm.* That is, you design the detailed *processing* and *control* procedures that the computer must follow to transform program inputs into the types of output you want. This may involve using tools like program *flowcharts* or *pseudocode* to help you express what you want the computer to do.
- *Code:* Now you can finally write the instructions in a programming language like BASIC, Pascal, or COBOL. Typically, you will use a programming language translator package to help you write and edit your program. However, as mentioned earlier, you can also use the *macro languages* provided by spreadsheet and database management packages to develop custom programs.
- *Test:* Finally, you test your program and correct any errors that you find. This process is commonly called *debugging* your program. Typically, most errors are revealed as you test your program through trial runs with test data. Then your program is ready for you to use.

Programming Tools

programming tools
Diagramming techniques and software packages that provide editing and diagnostic capabilities and other support facilities to assist the programming process.

A variety of **programming tools** can be used to help programmers develop the detailed processing instructions required in the design of computer programs. For instance, *structure charts* document the purpose, structure, and relationships of the modules in a program. *Pseudocode* expresses the processing logic of a program module in a series of short phrases. Finally, *program flowcharts* graphically illustrate the detailed sequence of processing steps required in a computer program. See Figure 10-10.

The language translator programs we discussed in Chapter 3 have always provided some editing and diagnostic capabilities to help programmers identify programming errors, or *bugs.* However, many current language translator programs now include powerful graphics-oriented *editors* and *debuggers.* They provide a *graphical programmer interface* that makes it easier for programmers to identify and avoid errors while they are programming.

Such programming tools provide programmers with a computer-aided programming *environment* or *workbench.* Their goal is to decrease the drudgery of programming while increasing the efficiency and productivity of programmers. Other programming tools include diagramming packages, code generators, and libraries of reusable program code and objects. Many of these same tools are part of the *tool kit* provided by CASE packages.

Programming Languages

To properly understand programming and the programs you use, you need to understand some basic facts about programming languages. You should know the categories of the programming languages that programmers use to develop the sets of instructions that constitute a computer program. Many different programming languages have been developed, each with its own unique *syntax,* that is, vocabulary, punctuation, and grammatical rules. The four major categories of programming languages are shown in Figure 10-11.

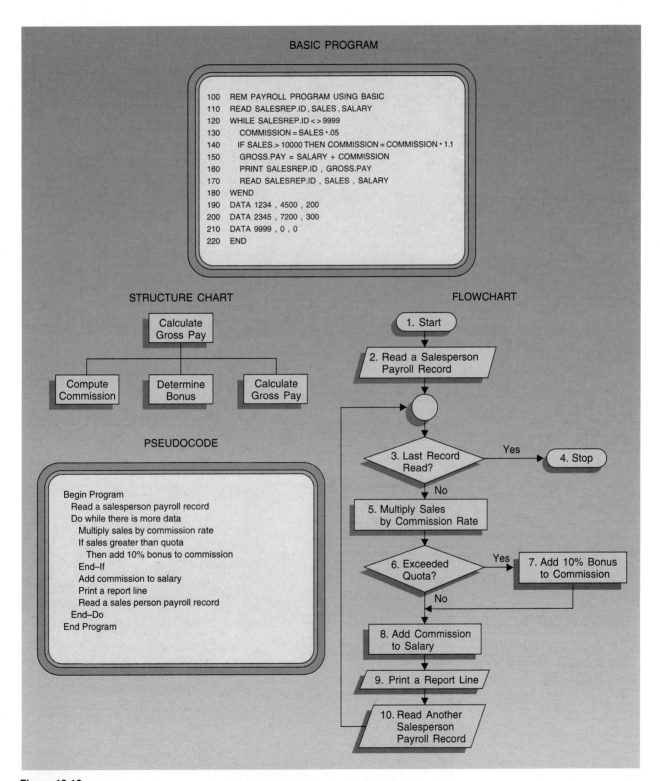

BASIC PROGRAM

```
100   REM PAYROLL PROGRAM USING BASIC
110   READ SALESREP.ID , SALES , SALARY
120   WHILE SALESREP.ID < > 9999
130       COMMISSION = SALES * .05
140       IF SALES.> 10000 THEN COMMISSION = COMMISSION * 1.1
150       GROSS.PAY = SALARY + COMMISSION
160       PRINT SALESREP.ID , GROSS.PAY
170       READ SALESREP.ID , SALES , SALARY
180   WEND
190   DATA 1234 , 4500 , 200
200   DATA 2345 , 7200 , 300
210   DATA 9999 , 0 , 0
220   END
```

STRUCTURE CHART

FLOWCHART

```
            Calculate
            Gross Pay
                |
    +-----------+-----------+
    |           |           |
Compute     Determine   Calculate
Commission    Bonus     Gross Pay
```

1. Start

2. Read a Salesperson Payroll Record

3. Last Record Read? →Yes→ 4. Stop

No

5. Multiply Sales by Commission Rate

6. Exceeded Quota? →Yes→ 7. Add 10% Bonus to Commission

No

8. Add Commission to Salary

9. Print a Report Line

10. Read Another Salesperson Payroll Record

PSEUDOCODE

Begin Program
  Read a salesperson payroll record
  Do while there is more data
    Multiply sales by commission rate
    If sales greater than quota
      Then add 10% bonus to commission
    End–If
    Add commission to salary
    Print a report line
    Read a sales person payroll record
  End–Do
End Program

Figure 10-10
These are examples of the structure chart, flowchart, and pseudocode for a simple BASIC payroll program.

Figure 10-11
These are the four major types of programming languages.

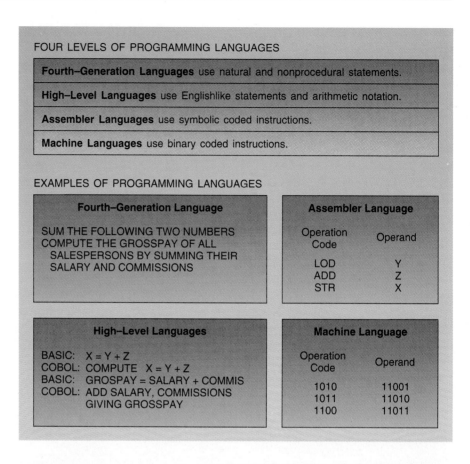

FOUR LEVELS OF PROGRAMMING LANGUAGES

Fourth–Generation Languages use natural and nonprocedural statements.

High–Level Languages use Englishlike statements and arithmetic notation.

Assembler Languages use symbolic coded instructions.

Machine Languages use binary coded instructions.

EXAMPLES OF PROGRAMMING LANGUAGES

Fourth–Generation Language

SUM THE FOLLOWING TWO NUMBERS
COMPUTE THE GROSSPAY OF ALL
  SALESPERSONS BY SUMMING THEIR
  SALARY AND COMMISSIONS

Assembler Language

Operation Code	Operand
LOD	Y
ADD	Z
STR	X

High–Level Languages

BASIC: X = Y + Z
COBOL: COMPUTE X = Y + Z
BASIC: GROSPAY = SALARY + COMMIS
COBOL: ADD SALARY, COMMISSIONS
          GIVING GROSSPAY

Machine Language

Operation Code	Operand
1010	11001
1011	11010
1100	11011

Toolkits are a common feature of new programming packages like DBKit by NeXT.

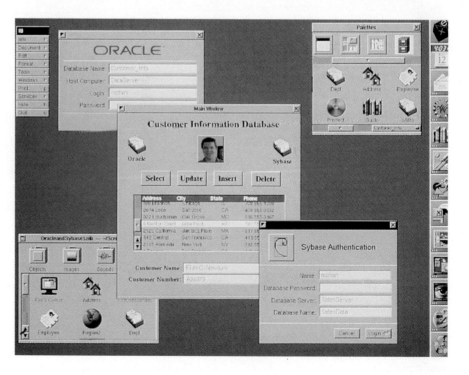

Machine Languages

Machine languages are the most basic level of programming languages. Program instructions must be written using *binary codes* unique to each computer. Machine language programmers must write long series of detailed instructions to accomplish even simple processing tasks. For example, programming in machine language requires specifying the memory locations for every instruction and item of data used. Instructions must be included for every switch and indicator in the CPU that is used by the program. These requirements make machine language programming a difficult and error-prone task.

A machine language program to add two numbers together in the CPU of a computer and store the result might take the form shown in the bottom portion of Figure 10-11. Like many computer instructions, these instructions consist of an *operation code,* which specifies what is to be done, and an *operand,* which specifies the address of data or device to be operated upon.

machine language
A programming language that uses binary codes unique to each type of computer.

Assembler Languages

Assembler languages are the next level of programming languages. They were developed to reduce the difficulties of writing machine language programs. The use of assembler languages requires *the use of language translator* programs called *assemblers,* which were discussed in Chapter 3. An assembler program converts the instructions of assembler languages into machine instructions. Assembler languages are frequently called *symbolic languages* because alphabetic abbreviations and other symbols are used to represent operation codes, storage locations, and data elements. For instance, the computation $X = Y + Z$ in an assembler language program might take the form shown in Figure 10-11.

assembler language
A programming language that utilizes symbols to represent operation codes and storage locations.

High Level Languages

High-level languages are also known as *compiler languages.* The instructions or *statements* of high-level languages resemble human sentences or mathematical equations. Therefore, many end users and most *application programmers* use high-level languages like BASIC, COBOL, or Pascal when developing application programs. If you want to learn how to program a computer, this is the type of programming language you may have to learn.

Each high-level language statement is called a *macro instruction.* That's because it generates several machine instructions when translated into machine language by translator programs called *compilers* or *interpreters.* For example, the computation $X = Y + Z$ would be programmed in the high-level languages of BASIC and COBOL as shown in Figure 10-11. Then it would be translated into machine language codes before being executed by a computer. Figure 10-11 also illustrates how close to the English language high-level language statements can be.

high-level language
A programming language that uses statements closely resembling human language or mathematical notation to describe the problem to be solved or the procedure to be used.

Fourth-Generation Languages

Some programming languages are called fourth-generation languages (4GLs) to differentiate them from machine languages (first generation), assembler languages (second generation), and high-level languages (third generation). Most fourth-generation languages are **nonprocedural languages** that encour-

nonprocedural language
A programming language that allows users and professional programmers to specify the results they want without specifying how to solve the problem.

age you to specify the *results* you want and let the computer determine the sequence of instructions that will accomplish those results. So, end users and programmers no longer have to spend a lot of time developing the sequence of instructions the computer must follow to achieve a result. Thus, fourth-generation languages simplify the programming process. See Figure 10-11.

natural language
A programming language that is very close to human language.

Some 4GLs use **natural languages** that are very close to English or other human languages. Their language translator programs use artificial intelligence (AI) techniques to translate a 4GL program into machine language. Natural programming languages are thus as easy to use as ordinary conversation. You should also realize that many types of software have fourth-generation language capabilities. For example, the query languages and report generators of database management packages are popular types of 4GLs.

Object-Oriented Languages

object-oriented programming (OOP)
Developing programs that create and use objects (consisting of data and actions to be performed on the data).

Object-oriented programming (OOP) languages are also humorously called OOPS (object-oriented programming systems). They have become an important new tool in software development. While most other programming languages separate data elements from the procedures or actions that will be performed on them, OOP languages tie them together into *objects*. Thus, an *object* consists of data and the actions that can be performed on the data. For instance, an object could be data about an employee and all the operations (such as payroll calculations) that might be performed on the data. Or an object could be data in graphic form, such as an icon in a video display, plus the display actions that might be used on it.

Object-oriented languages like Visual Basic and C++ are easier to use and more efficient for programming the graphical user interfaces required by many applications. Once objects are programmed, they are reusable. Programmers

NextStep is an object-oriented programming package.

or end users can construct data-entry displays for a new program by assembling standard objects such as windows, bars, buttons, and icons. Thus, the use of object-oriented languages for user interface programming is growing significantly. The photograph on page 346 shows a display of an object-oriented programming language.

Comparing Languages

Assembler languages are still widely used by developers of system and application software packages, so most computer manufacturers provide an assembler language that reflects the unique machine language *instruction set* of a particular CPU or microprocessor. This feature is particularly desirable to some *systems programmers* because it provides them with greater flexibility in designing a program for a particular line of computers. They can then produce more *efficient* software, that is, programs that require a minimum of instructions, storage, and CPU time to perform a specific processing assignment.

A high-level language is obviously easier to learn and understand than an assembler language. Also, high-level languages have less rigid rules, forms, and syntaxes, so the potential for error is reduced. Unlike assembler languages, most high-level languages are *machine-independent,* that is, they can be used on many different brands of computers. Therefore, programs written in a high-level language do not have to be completely reprogrammed if you change to a new computer. However, since high-level language programs are less efficient, they take longer to translate and execute than assembler programs. Table 10-8 highlights some of the major high-level languages in use today.

**Table 10-8
Highlights of Popular
High-Level Languages**

Ada	Developed for the U.S. Department of Defense to replace COBOL and FORTRAN. It resembles an extension of Pascal. Named after Augusta Ada Byron, who is considered the world's first computer programmer.
ALGOL	ALGOrithmic Language. An international algebraic language designed primarily for scientific and mathematical applications; widely used in Europe.
APL	A Programming Language. A mathematically oriented language that uses a concise symbolic notation designed for efficient interactive programming.
BASIC	Beginner's All-purpose Symbolic Instruction Code. A simple programming language widely used for end user programming.
C	A structured language that resembles a machine-independent assembler language. Popular for system software programming and development of packages.
COBOL	Common Business Oriented Language. The most widely used programming language for business applications. Designed as an English-like language for business data processing.
FORTRAN	FORmula TRANslation. The most widely used programming language for scientific and engineering applications.
Pascal	A popular language named after Blaise Pascal. Designed specifically to incorporate structured programming concepts.
PL/1	Programming Language/1. A general-purpose language that combines features of COBOL, FORTRAN, and ALGOL.
RPG	Report Program Generator. A problem-oriented language that generates reports and performs other data processing tasks.

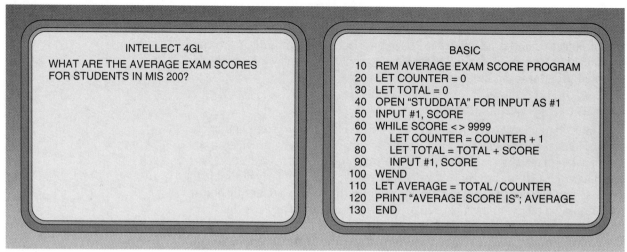

```
INTELLECT 4GL

WHAT ARE THE AVERAGE EXAM SCORES
FOR STUDENTS IN MIS 200?
```

```
                        BASIC
 10   REM AVERAGE EXAM SCORE PROGRAM
 20   LET COUNTER = 0
 30   LET TOTAL = 0
 40   OPEN "STUDDATA" FOR INPUT AS #1
 50   INPUT #1, SCORE
 60   WHILE SCORE < > 9999
 70      LET COUNTER = COUNTER + 1
 80      LET TOTAL = TOTAL + SCORE
 90      INPUT #1, SCORE
100   WEND
110   LET AVERAGE = TOTAL / COUNTER
120   PRINT "AVERAGE SCORE IS"; AVERAGE
130   END
```

Figure 10-12
Fourth-generation languages are
easier to use than third-generation
languages like BASIC.

Note that the most widely used languages include COBOL for business application programs, BASIC for microcomputer end users, and FORTRAN for scientific and engineering applications.

The ease of use of fourth-generation languages is their outstanding feature. However, this is usually gained at the expense of some loss in flexibility. For instance, it may be difficult to override some of the prespecified formats or procedures of 4GLs. Also, the machine language code generated by a program developed by a 4GL is frequently much less efficient (in processing speed and amount of storage capacity needed) than a program written in a language like BASIC. See Figure 10-12.

Quick Quiz

1. System flowcharts and data flow diagrams are important graphic _____ tools.

2. Custom computer programs are developed in a _____ process of analysis, design, coding, and testing activities.

3. Pseudocode, program flowcharts, and programming editors are examples of _____.

4. The major types of _____ include machine, assembler, high-level, fourth generation, and object-oriented.

5. Ada, BASIC, COBOL, Pascal, and FORTRAN are examples of _____.

Answers   1. application development   2. computer programming   3. programming tools   4. programming languages   5. high-level languages

End Note: End Users and Application Development

In this chapter, you have seen that developing computer solutions to end users' problems is not an easy task. Quick fixes are always possible, of course, but a

REAL-WORLD EXAMPLE

Sun Hydraulics:
Programming in Visual Basic

At Sun Hydraulics Corporation, Windows programmer Chris Barlow is applying Visual Basic to his company's custom-computing needs. His three-person team has been using the object-oriented programming language for two and a half years, developing Windows applications for this Sarasota, Florida-based maker of hydraulic valves. They started off with a database access application they call CatNav. Sales support employees navigate through the company's product catalog with it. "We liked that way of providing an easy Windows application where someone could type in a selection and find a product," Barlow says. "But we found that a lot of people use a word processor, and that's pretty much what they live in. They aren't all that interested in using other programs."

In only a few hours of Visual Basic programming, his team added a CatNav icon to The Microsoft Word For Windows toolbar so that users could access the product catalog from their word processing programs. Now users type a product code in Word, hit the CatNav icon, and the information they need appears in their Word document. Says Barlow: "We now think of our information systems as groups of mini applications that use only one little part of all the data that we can make available to users. I'd say Visual Basic is about ten times faster to develop in than any other language I've worked with, including C, FORTRAN AND COBOL."

1. How did Chris Barlow use Visual Basic to make computing easier for Sun Hydraulics' end users?

2. What are some of the benefits of using object-oriented programming languages like Visual Basic?

more organized process of application development will probably give you better results. That's why many organizations use a systems development life cycle, in which you investigate, analyze, design, implement, and maintain applications of computers to jobs that need to be done.

This application development process is not cast in stone, however. There are many variations in actual practice. And developments like computer-aided systems engineering (CASE) and prototyping use computers to help improve the process, make it faster and easier for IS professionals, and involve end users more heavily in developing their own applications. So rather than spend a long time trying to develop a perfect system, IS professionals can use CASE tools and prototyping to quickly develop and repeatedly improve working models of a system with a lot of feedback from end users.

We have also seen that you and other end users can be your own analysts, designers, and programmers for many types of applications. End user development can be as simple as using menus or entering commands, or as complex as doing your own programming. You can use a variety of application development tools and software packages to develop your own software solutions to get things done in whatever career you plan to enter. However, once again, you first need to be a computer-literate end user. Hopefully, with the help of this chapter, and most importantly, with some hands-on experience in using software packages, you can begin to develop your own computer solutions.

E T H I C S

Ethical Issues in Application Development

One of the important ethical issues in application development concerns the question of who owns software. The programmer who developed it? The company the programmer works for? The customer who buys the program? The answer, as in many other ethical issues, is hazy and depends on the circumstances involved.

A software package is considered to be *intellectual property* and is protected by copyright law, just like a movie video. Many software packages come shrink-wrapped, with a copyright statement and a *licensing agreement* prominently displayed on the package.

Do you *own* the software you buy? Probably not! Most software packages are licensed, not purchased. You agree to the software's licensing agreement the moment you break the shrinkwrap on the package. It says that the software publisher retains the right of ownership, so you can NOT do anything you want with it. For example, the *fair use* clause of the agreement usually allows you to make a copy of the software but forbids you to make multiple copies, copies for others, or copies for resale. That's why unauthorized copying of software is called *software piracy,* which we discuss in Chapter 3.

Even if you develop a program yourself, you may not own it. If you develop it for a company that employs you, it may belong to that company. Many companies ask their employees to sign agreements requiring that all software developed during the term of employment belongs to the company. Even without such agreements, many companies have battled successfully to retain the rights to software their employees develop.

Of course, even if you buy a widely used software package, you have few guarantees of quality, except for the reputation and goodwill of the software developer. Does a software developer who owns the software you license have any liability if the program does not work properly or damages your work when you use it? That's another hotly debated question. Most software licensing agreements have disclaimers, which state that they are not responsible for errors or damages. Figure 10-13 is a tongue-in-cheek example that won a prize in a contest run by Abacus magazine.[1]

What Do You Think?

Who should own a software package? Who should be liable if a software package doesn't work properly? What are the ethical responsibilities of software developers to their customers and employees? What do you think?

---

[1]John Shore, "Why I Never Met a Programmer I Could Trust," in Roy Dejoi et al., *Ethical Issues in Information Systems* (Boston, MA: Boyd and Fraser, 1991), p. 98.

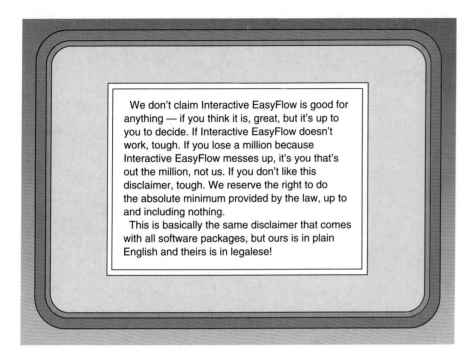

Figure 10-13
This humorous example drama-tizes the perils of software liability disclaimers.

We don't claim Interactive EasyFlow is good for anything — if you think it is, great, but it's up to you to decide. If Interactive EasyFlow doesn't work, tough. If you lose a million because Interactive EasyFlow messes up, it's you that's out the million, not us. If you don't like this disclaimer, tough. We reserve the right to do the absolute minimum provided by the law, up to and including nothing.

This is basically the same disclaimer that comes with all software packages, but ours is in plain English and theirs is in legalese!

Summary

The Application Development Cycle   Developing a new computer application is a process in which you conceive, design, and implement computer-based solutions to end user problems. Figure 10-2 summarizes the stages, activities, and products of the systems development cycle.

CASE and Prototyping   Computer-aided software engineering (CASE) tools and other software packages are widely used to automate parts of the application development process. Prototyping is an application development process that promotes an iterative, interactive process to develop prototypes of user interfaces and other application components.

Tools of Application Development   A variety of graphics methods and software packages are used as application development tools. System flowcharts and data flow diagrams are examples of graphics tools. Computer-aided tools include CASE packages and other software packages that have application development capabilities.

End User Development   End users can now develop new or improved ways to use computers to do their jobs. They can use several types of software packages to develop new ways to analyze and process data or produce the reports and other information products they need. IS professionals play a consulting role to help end users develop their own applications.

Programming and Programming Languages   Programming is the process of developing a computer program. It is a problem-solving process in which you analyze, design, code, and test software solutions to an end user problem. The four levels of programming languages are machine languages, assembler languages, high-level languages, and fourth-generation languages.

High-level languages such as BASIC and COBOL are the most widely used programming languages for business applications. However, natural, nonprocedural fourth-generation languages and object-oriented languages are also widely used.

Key Terms and Concepts

application development	natural language
assembler language	nonprocedural language
computer-aided software	object-oriented language
engineering	operational feasibility
computer programming	organizational feasibility
conversion alternatives	programming languages
economic feasibility	programming tools
end user development	prototyping
feasibility study	system repository
fourth-generation language	system specifications
functional requirements	systems analysis
high-level language	systems design
implementation stage	systems development life cycle
investigation stage	technical feasibility
machine language	tools of application development
maintenance stage	

Review Quiz

True/False

_____ 1. Application development is a problem-solving process to conceive, design, and implement computer applications.

_____ 2. The systems development life cycle is a multistage cycle for developing and maintaining new information systems.

_____ 3. Analysis is the first stage of application development.

_____ 4. If cost savings of a proposed application exceed its initial cost, it has technical feasibility.

_____ 5. If customers will have trouble using a proposed system, it has operational feasibility.

_____ 6. In the analysis stage, you study the information needs of end users and any information systems presently used.

_____ 7. In the design stage, you develop specifications for the user interface, data, and processes of a proposed application.

_____ 8. The maintenance stage involves acquiring hardware and software, testing a proposed system, and training people to use it.

_____ 9. The implementation stage involves monitoring, evaluating, and changing a system.

_____ 10. CASE (computer-aided software engineering) involves using software packages to computerize many application development activities.

Multiple Choice

_____ 1. A programming language that uses instructions in the form of binary codes of ones and zeros is
- a. an assembler language.
- b. a high-level language.
- c. a machine language.
- d. a fourth-generation language.

_____ 2. A programming language that uses instructions consisting of symbols representing operation codes and storage locations is
- a. an assembler language.
- b. a high-level language.
- c. a machine language.
- d. a fourth-generation language.

_____ 3. A programming language like BASIC, COBOL, or Pascal is
- a. an assembler language.
- b. a high-level language.
- c. a machine language.
- d. a fourth-generation language.

_____ 4. A programming language that might take the form of query languages and report generators is
- a. an assembler language.
- b. a high-level language.
- c. a machine language.
- d. a fourth-generation language.

_____ 5. Programming languages that tie together data and the actions that will be performed on the data are called
- a. high-level.
- b. fourth generation.
- c. object oriented.
- d. natural.

_____ 6. End user development can include
- a. menu-using development.
- b. command-using development.
- c. user programming.
- d. all of the above.

_____ 7. Defining what you want your program to do is
- a. analysis.
- b. design.
- c. coding.
- d. testing.

_____ 8. Developing the processing logic of a program is
- a. analysis.
- b. design.
- c. coding.
- d. testing.

_____ 9. Converting to a new system in stages is
- a. parallel conversion.

       b. phased conversion.

       c. pilot conversion.

       d. direct cutover.

_____ 10. Converting to a new system using a test site is

       a. parallel conversion.

       b. phased conversion.

       c. pilot conversion.

       d. direct cutover.

Fill-in

1. In _____, end users can develop their own ways of using computers to help them do their jobs.

2. An interactive and iterative process of application development is called _____.

3. Several _____ can be used to help you analyze, design, and document applications you are developing.

4. A _____ shows you the flow of information processing procedures in an application.

5. A _____ shows you the logical flow of data in an application without specifying the media or equipment involved.

6. You would use _____ packages to do computer-aided application development.

7. A _____ is a database of descriptions of the design features of an organization's computer-based systems.

8. There are parallel, phased, pilot, or direct cutover _____ approaches for installing a new computer application in an organization.

9. Finding and removing errors in programs during testing is known as _____.

10. In _____ conversion, both the new and old systems are operated until all managers agree to switch completely to a new system.

Questions for Thought and Discussion

1. Suppose you decide to use a personal computer to do a job you have never done before. Could the application development process discussed in this chapter help you? Why or why not?

2. How are computers automating the application development process?

3. How is a prototyping process different from the traditional application development cycle?

4. What major trends are occurring in programming languages? What impact do they have on end users and programmers?

5. How is end user development different from traditional application development? What variations of end user development are possible?

6. Refer to the Real-World Example of Garber Travel in the chapter. Why didn't the SABRE system provide the applications that travel agents needed?

7. Can end users do their own programming? What programming languages or software packages can they use?

8. Refer to the Real-World Example of Sun Hydraulics in the chapter. Is there really a need for end users to do their own programming? Why can't they just use prewritten software packages?

9. In the Real-World Example of the Hospital of Saint Raphael, what end user development activities or issues do you recognize?

10. Assume you could do application development as an end user at school or work. What jobs would you computerize or improve? What software packages would you use? What would you have to show for your efforts when you were done? Make a brief report to the class.

Review Quiz Answers

True/False: **1.** T **2.** T **3.** F **4.** F **5.** F **6.** T **7.** T **8.** F **9.** F **10.** T

Multiple Choice: **1.** c **2.** a **3.** b **4.** d **5.** c **6.** d **7.** a **8.** b **9.** b **10.** c

Fill-in: **1.** end user development **2.** prototyping **3.** application development tools **4.** system flowchart **5.** data flow diagram **6.** CASE **7.** system repository **8.** conversion **9.** debugging **10.** parallel

CHAPTER

11

COMPUTERS AT WORK: AUTOMATING THE WORKPLACE

OUTLINE

LEARNING OBJECTIVES

After reading and studying this chapter, you should be able to

Outline the purpose of several major computer applications in business, accounting, manufacturing, engineering and design, health care, and government.

Discuss how several types of management information systems support decision making by managers.

Identify several ways that organizations manage the computing activities of their end users and IS professionals.

You and Computers in the Workplace

Computers are automating the workplace. You can see the pervasive impact of computers in everything from office automation to factory automation, from computer-aided design to management information systems, and computerized accounting to computer-based health care. Some of these applications, such as office automation and decision support, were discussed in Chapters 4 and 5. In this chapter, we will discuss key applications of computers in business, management, accounting, manufacturing, engineering and design, health care, and government. This should give you a broad view of the use of computers in the workplace.

As a computer-literate end user, you should understand the major ways computers are used in the workplace. Then you should try to gain specific knowledge about how computers are used in a field you are interested in, such as business, government, engineering, health care, and so on. For instance, if you are planning a career in health services, you should have a *specific* understanding of how computers affect a particular *health profession (health management,* for example) or a *particular health industry* (hospital health care, for example) that is directly related to your career objectives. So, if you are planning a career in hospital management, you should have a basic understanding of how computers are used in health services, and how computers support the health care activities of hospitals and other health organizations.

You should also realize that the use of computers in the workplace has to be managed. This is true whether it's your individual computing efforts, those of other end users in offices, departments, and work groups, or the centralized computing operations of a large organization. For example, costs can get out of hand because computer hardware and software are expensive to acquire and maintain, and IS personnel are highly paid professionals. Most computer-based information systems are also too important to an organization's success to be left unmanaged. So in this chapter, we will also look briefly at how end users and organizations manage their computing efforts.

Computers in Business

Computers are used in business in thousands of ways. However, Table 11-1 illustrates how major applications of computers can be grouped into five business function categories. This should give you an idea of the importance of computer applications in business. Computers play a major role in supporting the business functions of accounting, marketing, production operations, finance, and human resource management. As an example, computer-based information systems can provide a business with:

- Accounting information about its assets and liabilities
- Marketing information about its sales performance and trends
- Financial information concerning its financing costs and investment returns
- Production information analyzing its raw material requirements and worker productivity
- Human resource management information concerning employee compensation and professional development

Table 11-1
Overview of Computer
Applications in Business

Accounting
Computers are used for legal and business recordkeeping and to produce financial statements, forecasts, budgets, and financial reports for management.

Marketing
Computers support the distribution and sale of products and services through such applications as advertising and promotion analysis, market research, sales forecasting, and sales analysis.

Production/Operations
Computers help produce goods and services and manage the operations of organizations through applications such as computer-aided manufacturing, process control, robotics, and inventory control.

Finance
Computers help find sources of financing and evaluate the financial impact of proposed projects through such applications as financial forecasting, capital budgeting, and cash management.

Human Resource Management
Computers support the recruitment, compensation, and professional development of employees through applications such as personnel recordkeeping, compensation analysis, and personnel requirements forecasting.

Transaction Processing Systems

One of the most common but important applications of computers is transaction processing. **Transaction processing systems** process data resulting from the occurrence of business and other transactions. *Transactions* are events such as sales, purchases, deposits, withdrawals, refunds, and payments. Think, for example, of the data generated whenever a business sells you something on credit. Data about you, the product you purchased, the salesperson, store, and so on must be captured and processed. This in turn causes additional transactions, such as credit checks, customer billing, and inventory changes, which generate even more data. Thus, transaction processing systems are needed to capture and process such data, or most organizations could not continue to operate.

Computers and telecommunications networks make **online transaction processing** possible. That is, they allow organizations to immediately capture and process data generated by a variety of business transactions, so they can improve the efficiency and quality of business operations and customer service. Data about each transaction can be captured by online point-of-sale (POS) terminals as it is generated, and transmitted from many remote sites to the organization's computer systems for immediate processing. This is called *online* or *realtime* processing. For instance, customer and inventory files can be updated immediately and sales evaluated and reported to management as soon as they occur.

On the other hand, data about transactions can be accumulated into batches at remote sites, stored on magnetic disk or tape devices, and transmitted periodically to a central computer for processing at a later time. This procedure is known as batch processing. Thus, telecommunications networks allow business offices, banks, retail stores, and distribution centers to mini-

transaction processing system
An information system that processes data arising from business and other transactions.

online transaction processing
Using online terminals for the immediate capture and processing of data as it is generated by a variety of business transactions.

An online transaction processing system may provide a customer order status display.

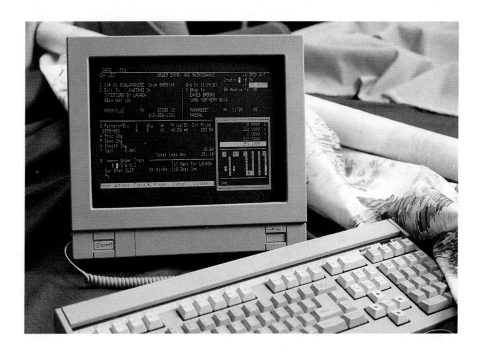

mize the manual entry of data, and expedite transaction processing. This cuts costs, reduces errors, and improves customer service.

Most online transaction processing systems allow authorized employees to make inquiries and receive immediate responses about information stored in departmental and corporate databases. This can provide up-to-date information for business operations and decision making by managers. Employees can receive immediate responses at their workstations when they check on the status of a sales order, the balance in an account, the amount of products in inventory, or the current market price of a company's stock.

Electronic Data Interchange

electronic data interchange (EDI)
The electronic transmission of source documents between the computers of different organizations.

The cutting edge of online transaction processing is called **electronic data interchange,** or **EDI.** This involves the electronic transmission of business transaction documents over telecommunications networks among the computers of *trading partners,* that is, organizations and their customers and suppliers. EDI replaces the exchange of paper *transaction documents* (such as purchase orders, invoices, requests for quotations, and shipping notices) with electronic versions that are transmitted using standard document formats. Thus, EDI is an example of the almost complete automation of the data-entry process, since transaction data is transmitted over telecommunications links directly between computers, without paper documents or human intervention. See Figure 11-1.

Benefits of EDI

EDI eliminates the printing, mailing, checking, and handling by employees of numerous multiple copy forms of business documents. Also, since standard formats are used, the delays caused by mail or telephone communication be-

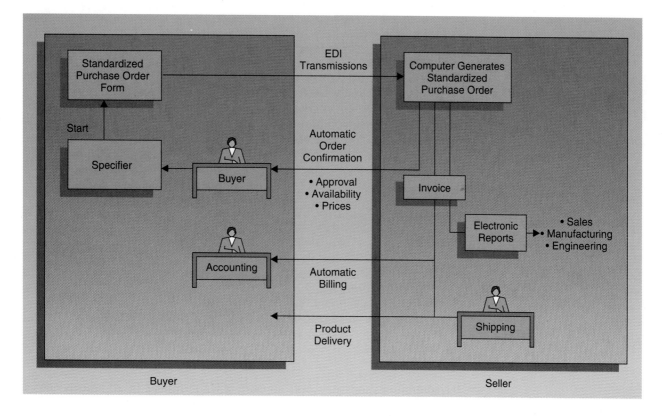

Figure 11-1
An EDI system can automatically generate a purchase order.

tween businesses to verify what a document means are drastically reduced. So EDI eliminates both paper forms and human involvement. Some of the benefits that result are reductions in paper, postage, and labor costs; faster flow of transactions; reduction in errors; increases in productivity; reductions in inventory levels; and better customer service. As an example, RCA expects the cost of processing a purchase order to drop from $50 to $4, and it is estimated that EDI saves about $200 per automobile in the auto industry.

However, EDI is more than a way to increase efficiency, cut costs, and provide better service. EDI has become a prime example of *strategic information systems (SIS),* since it builds strategic relationships between a firm and its customers and suppliers. In many industries, EDI has become an absolute business requirement. General Motors has made EDI a requirement for its 20,000 suppliers, while the U.S. Department of Defense requires EDI for all of its thousands of suppliers. Experts predict that by 1995 one-third of all business documents will involve EDI. Thus, EDI promises to revolutionize data entry in transaction processing while promoting strategic relationships between many organizations.

Electronic Funds Transfer

Electronic funds transfer (EFT) systems are an important application of computers in the banking and retailing industries. EFT systems use computers and telecommunications networks to electronically capture and process money and credit transfers between organizations and their customers. Bank

electronic funds transfer (EFT)
Banking and payment systems that transfer funds electronically instead of using cash or paper documents such as checks.

REAL-WORLD EXAMPLE

Dillard Department Stores: EDI or Out

Imagine being the owner of a small business that makes expensive leather gloves for upscale specialty shops and department stores. Imagine your panic when one of your largest customers, Dillard Department Stores, says that it will stop buying your gloves unless you use electronic data interchange (EDI) for all business transactions with them. If you didn't even own a computer, much less know exactly how EDI works, your panic would be quite justified.

Well that's what happened to Fownes Brothers Co., a small glove manufacturer, and many of the more than 800 Dillard suppliers a few years ago. So Mike Beniameninovitz, Fownes' data processing manager, bought a PC system that included a data communications modem and EDI software, the ESPII package from Foretell Corporation. Total cost was $7,000. Buster Brown Apparel, on the other hand, never panicked. "We were ready for EDI," says John Keener, MIS director, "this made us go." Buster Brown's cost was in the $10,000 range to install an EDI capability on its existing PCs. EDI coordinator Larry Reines of Nina Footwear says EDI is "a necessity—all the majors are going to be doing this."

1. Why do you think Dillard Department Stores gave its suppliers an EDI ultimatum?

2. What problems can you foresee in installing an EDI capability into a small business?

telecommunications networks support teller terminals in all branch offices and automated teller machines at locations throughout a city or region, so you can do your banking electronically and conveniently. Also supported are *pay-by-phone* services, which allow you to use a telephone as a computer terminal to electronically pay bills. Telecommunications networks also connect POS (point-of-sale) terminals in retail stores to bank EFT systems, so you can make payments electronically from your checking account for purchases you make.

Computers in Management

Computing power and information resources are now readily available to most managers. Advances in microcomputer systems, software packages, telecommunications, database management, and office automation have made this possible. Many managers can now have computer-based information systems more tailored to their information needs. Surveys now show that significant computer use has even spread from lower and middle managers to senior management.

So computers are a vital component of information systems designed to provide information needed for effective decision making by managers. These **management information systems (MIS)** are needed by all types of managers, especially given the increased complexity and rate of change in today's business world. Let's look at a few examples.

A manager of a retail clothing store needs information about product merchandise levels, sales, and fashion trends. A bank manager needs information about consumer loans and savings deposits. A factory supervisor needs information outlining daily production requirements and worker job assignments.

management information system (MIS)
An information system that provides information to support managerial decision making. More specifically, an information reporting system, executive information system, or decision support system.

Managers rely on management information systems to provide information for decision making.

An office manager requires information concerning staff appointments, meetings, and secretarial work loads. A top executive needs competitive information to plan and control the strategic performance of a corporation.

Thus, management information systems must be able to give managers a variety of information products to support their decision-making responsibilities. Providing such information is not a simple task. For example, the information requirements of management depend heavily on the activities of managers at three major levels: (1) *strategic management,* (2) *tactical management,* and (3) *operational management.* These levels are similar to the traditional management levels of top management, middle management, and operating, or supervisory, management.

At the strategic management level, top executives require more unscheduled reports, forecasts, and external intelligence to support their planning and policy-making responsibilities. Managers at the operational management level, on the other hand, require more regular internal reports containing detailed current data to support their control of day-to-day operations. See Figure 11-2.

Therefore, several types of management information systems are needed to provide information in a variety of ways to meet the diverse information needs of managers. For example, in Chapter 5, we discussed **decision support systems (DSS),** which are computer-based modeling systems that support decision making. DSS allows managers to use spreadsheet packages or other software to do what-if analysis or other types of analytical modeling. This lets managers explore their decision-making alternatives in an interactive, hands-on process. In this chapter, let's look at two other types of MIS: information reporting systems and executive information systems.

decision support system (DSS)
An information system that allows managers to explore decision alternatives in an interactive, hands-on process.

Figure 11-2
Management information systems provide information for three levels of management.

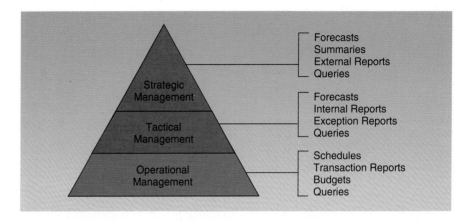

Strategic Management — Forecasts / Summaries / External Reports / Queries

Tactical Management — Forecasts / Internal Reports / Exception Reports / Queries

Operational Management — Schedules / Transaction Reports / Budgets / Queries

Quick Quiz

1. Computer applications in _____ can be grouped into the accounting, marketing, finance, production/operations, and human resource management categories.

2. An _____ system immediately captures and processes data arising from the occurrence of business or other transactions.

3. The computer-to-computer exchange of business transaction documents between trading partners is _____.

4. An automated teller machine network is an example of an _____ system.

5. A decision support system is a _____ that uses computer-based modeling to support decision making by managers.

Answers: 1. business   2. online transaction processing
3. electronic data interchange   4. electronic funds transfer
5. management information system

Information Reporting Systems

information reporting system
An information system that produces prespecified reports, displays, and responses on a periodic, exception, or demand basis.

Information reporting systems are the original type of management information system. They produce information products that support many of the day-to-day decision-making needs of management. Reports, displays, and responses produced by such systems provide information that managers have asked for to meet their information needs. Such predefined information products can satisfy the information needs of many managers. For example, a sales manager may rely heavily on sales analysis reports to evaluate differences in performance among salespeople who sell the same types of products to the same types of customers. Most sales managers have a good idea of the kinds of information about sales results they will need in order to manage sales performance effectively. So those are the kinds of things they want to see information about in a sales analysis report.

A Periodic Scheduled Report, available each month, gives information to managers about sales for each product.

An Exception Report lists only delinquent accounts. It is produced automatically whenever more than 10 percent of customers are delinquent.

SALES BY PRODUCT REPORT
MONTH ENDING 03/31/--

Product	Sold This Month	Gross Profit	Profit Percent
Aluminum	2,810.39	281.64	10
Brass	1,317.42	180.37	14
Copper	7,110.93	575.45	8
Steel	8,446.16	554.63	7

DELINQUENT ACCOUNTS REPORT

Customer Name	Balance	Credit Line
Anderson Co.	3815.35	3000.00
Acme Intl.	4296.25	4000.00
Granger Corp.	2542.13	2000.00
Smith Corp.	1842.36	1500.00
Young Co.	3265.25	3000.00

A Demand Report is produced whenever a manager wants to know information about the current status of purchases made from vendors.

PURCHASE ANALYSIS BY VENDOR

Vendor's Name	Amount This Month	Returns Year to Date	Net Amount Year to Date
Ace Machine Co.	1325.36		3526.25
Acme Tool Co.			1854.35
Alan Abrasive Co.	456.25		1625.30
American Alloys Co.		85.63	5261.25
Angus Machine Co.			956.25
Apex Metal Co.			845.24
Argus Corp.	3256.12	213.25	11564.25

Figure 11-3
Managers can receive reports on a periodic, exeption, or demand basis.

Reporting Alternatives

How do managers want and need their information? Do they prefer periodic scheduled reports or a quick response on demand? Or reports whenever an exceptional condition occurs? These are some of the reporting choices facing managers. They know that information reporting systems can produce information to suit their timing and form preferences. For instance, they can have information in the form of video displays or paper reports, using either text data or presentation graphics. Or they can have reports periodically, on an exception basis, or whenever they want to access their own computer systems. See Figure 11-3.

periodic scheduled report
Providing information to managers using a prespecified format designed to provide information on a regularly scheduled basis.

exception reports
Reports produced only when exceptional conditions occur, or reports produced periodically that contain information only about exceptional conditions.

demand reporting
Information provided whenever a manager or end user demands it.

executive information system (EIS)
An information system designed to provide strategic information tailored to the needs of top management.

The oldest form of management reporting is the **periodic scheduled report.** For example, a manager may receive weekly sales analysis reports and monthly financial statements. This form of providing information to managers uses a *prespecified* format, that is, managers receive information on a regular basis in a form they have specified.

Exception reports are another popular form of information reporting. For example, a credit manager may receive a report only if and when customers exceed their credit limits. Such exception reporting promotes *management by exception,* instead of overwhelming managers with detailed periodic reports.

Finally, many managers can now get information whenever they want it through **demand reporting.** For example, query languages and report generators allow managers to get immediate responses or reports displayed at their computer workstations. They do not have to wait for periodic reports to arrive.

Executive Information Systems

Executive information systems (EIS) are computer-based systems that are tailored to the strategic decision-making needs of top management. They have become so popular in the last few years that their use is growing rapidly in lower levels of management. Though initially designed to meet the needs of top management, these easy-to-use MIS are thus spreading into the ranks of middle managers.

The goal of executive information systems is to provide top management with immediate and easy access to information about their *critical success factors,* that is, those key factors that are critical to accomplishing their organization's strategic objectives. For instance, the executives of a chain of department stores would probably consider such factors as their sales per salesperson and their ability to move merchandise quickly as keys to their survival and success.

Executive information systems provide executives with key information.

REAL-WORLD EXAMPLE

Alverno Administrative Services:
An EIS for Everyone

Tricia Myton is a product manager of financial systems at Alverno Administrative Services, a computing center for nine hospitals and seven nursing homes in the Midwest. Tricia doesn't like the sound of "executive information system" (EIS). She says it makes it seem that such systems are only for executives, which leaves out too many people who need to use an EIS. Myton says she prefers to call the EIS package from the SAS Institute, which Alverno uses, a "business information system."

The SAS system can be accessed by personal computers or terminals connected to their mainframe. This EIS will be used by more than 400 people. This means all managers from department heads or higher will be able to use the system for management reporting. Myton says that top executives do need information from the EIS, but many other managers also need quick, easy access to information. For example, Alverno is developing a module for its cardiac unit that will include database inquiry, report generation, and a text and graphics display. The EIS will also allow users to move a cursor to a point on a graph and "drill down" for data represented by the graphic display.

1. Why doesn't Tricia Myton like the term *executive information system?* Do you agree with her? Explain.

2. Does Alverno's SAS system sound like an EIS? Explain.

Executive information systems are easy to operate and understand. Response time is immediate, and graphics displays are used extensively. Most EIS rely heavily on telecommunications links to access both internal and external databases. This allows an EIS to provide both company and competitive information about the status and trends of key factors chosen by a company's top executives.

Thus, executive information systems attempt to meet the special information needs of top management that are not provided by other forms of MIS. Software packages that support EIS on mainframe, minicomputer, and microcomputer systems are now available. They provide top executives with graphics-based exception reporting and trend analysis of key factors. They also let executives quickly "drill down" to lower levels of detailed information if they wish. The photograph on page 366 illustrates how an EIS package provides interactive graphics displays to top executives.

Computers in Accounting

Out of all the possible applications of computers, several basic accounting applications stand out. You will find that computers are used for these applications in both large and small businesses and many other types of organizations. Thus, accounting systems are one of the most widely found applications of computers at most computer-using organizations.

Computer-based accounting systems record and report the flow of funds through an organization. They emphasize legal and historical recordkeeping and the production of accurate financial statements and management reports.

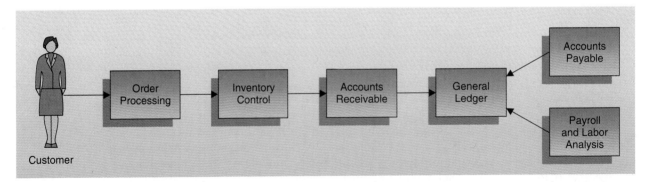

Figure 11-4
Accounting applications are inter-related systems.

Typically, accounting software packages include modules for applications such as order processing, inventory control, accounts receivable, accounts payable, payroll, and general ledger. Many accounting packages also focus on the planning and control of business operations. They emphasize cost accounting reports, the development of financial budgets, and reports comparing actual to forecasted performance. Figure 11-4 illustrates how important accounting systems are related to each other. Let's briefly review each of them.

Order Processing

order processing
Systems that process customer orders and produce invoices (bills) for customers and the data needed to analyze sales.

Order processing is an important accounting system. It processes customer orders and produces invoices (bills) for customers and the data needed to analyze sales. It also may keep track of the status of customer orders until goods are delivered. Computer-based order processing thus provides a fast and accurate method of recording and screening customer orders and sales transactions. It also provides inventory control systems with information on accepted orders that can be filled as quickly as possible.

Inventory Control

inventory control
Systems that process data reflecting changes to items in inventory.

Inventory control systems process data reflecting changes to items in inventory. Once data about customer orders is received from an order processing system, an inventory control system records changes to inventory levels and prepares shipping documents. Then it may notify managers about items that need reordering and provide them with a variety of inventory status reports. Computer-based inventory control thus helps a business provide high-quality service to customers while minimizing investment in inventory and inventory carrying costs.

Accounts Receivable

accounts receivable
Systems that keep records of amounts owed by customers and payments received from them.

Accounts receivable systems keep track of amounts owed by customers. They also keep track of purchases made and payments received from customers. Accounts receivable systems stimulate prompt customer payment by preparing accurate and timely monthly statements to credit customers. They provide managers with reports to help them control the amount of credit given and the amount of money that must be collected from customers.

Accounts Payable

Accounts payable systems keep track of data concerning purchases from suppliers and payments made to them. They prepare checks to pay outstanding invoices and produce cash management reports. Accounts payable systems help assure prompt and accurate payment of suppliers. They also provide tight financial control over all cash disbursements of the business. Therefore, they can provide managers with reports that analyze payments, expenses, purchases, employee expense accounts, and cash requirements.

accounts payable
Systems that keep track of data concerning purchases from suppliers and payments made to them.

Payroll

A **payroll** system produces paychecks for employees and other documents such as earning statements and payroll reports. A payroll system helps a business make prompt and accurate payments to its employees, as well as produce reports to management, employees, and government agencies concerning earnings, taxes, and other deductions. It may also produce reports analyzing labor costs and productivity.

payroll
A system that produces paychecks for employees and other documents such as earning statements and payroll reports.

General Ledger

General ledger is the accounting application that consolidates the financial records of a business. That is, it consolidates data received from accounts receivable, accounts payable, payroll, and other accounting systems. At the end of each accounting period, it "closes the books" by producing financial statements that show the revenue, expenses, and profit or loss of a business (the *income statement*), its assets and liabilities (the *balance sheet*), and other financial and managerial reports. A general ledger system helps a business

general ledger
Consolidates data received from other accounting systems and produces financial statements that disclose the performance of a business during that accounting period.

MYOB is an example of a general ledger package.

This bank of monitors displays the status of various components of an industrial process control system.

accomplish these important accounting tasks in an accurate and timely manner.

Computers in Manufacturing

computer-integrated manufacturing (CIM)
An overall concept stressing that the goals of computer use in factory automation should be to simplify, automate, and integrate production processes and other aspects of manufacturing.

The modern factory has become as computerized a workplace as today's electronic office, as *factory automation* rivals *office automation* in its use of computers. **Computer-integrated manufacturing (CIM)** stresses simplifying, automating, and integrating factory resources, environments, and functions with computers, robots, and telecommunications networks. A major thrust of CIM is **computer-aided manufacturing (CAM),** which is the use of computers to directly assist the manufacturing process. CAM is accomplished by using computers to control a physical process (process control), a machine tool (machine control), and humanlike machines (robotics). Let's take a brief look at each of these technologies in this section.

computer-aided manufacturing (CAM)
The use of computers to automate the production process and operations of a manufacturing plant.

Process Control

process control
The use of a computer to control an ongoing industrial process.

Process control is the use of computers to control an ongoing physical process. For example, process control computers control manufacturing processes in petroleum refineries, cement plants, steel mills, chemical plants, food product manufacturing plants, pulp and paper mills, and electric power plants, to name a few instances. Many process control computers are special-purpose minicomputer systems that rely on sensing devices to measure chemical, temperature, or pressure changes. These measurements are converted to digital form and relayed back to the process control computer.

Process control computers use software that analyzes the data generated by an ongoing production process and compares it to standards or forecasts of required results. The computer system uses control devices that can directly control the process by adjusting thermostats, valves, switches, and so on. Computers also produce messages and displays about the status of the process, so human operators can take appropriate control measures.

Machine Control

Computers are frequently used to control the actions of machine tools used in the production process. This is called **machine control** or *numerical control*. Computer software converts product design data and machining instructions into commands that control the actions of machine tools. This may involve the use of special-purpose microcomputers called *programmable logic controllers (PLCs)*. These devices operate one or more machines according to the directions of a numerical control program. Personal computers are used to develop and install numerical control programs in PLCs and analyze the

machine control
Automatic control of a machine process by a computer.

Robots are commonly used in the manufacturing of automobiles.

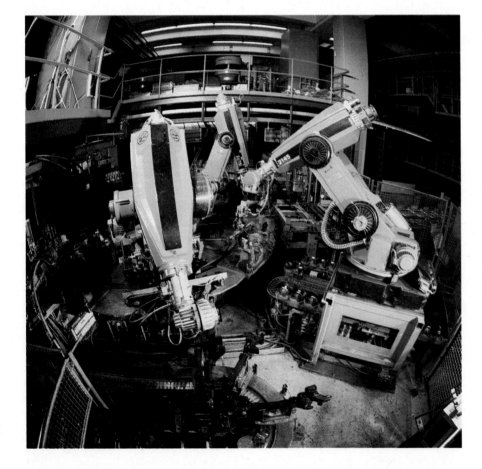

production data furnished by the PLCs. This helps engineers fine-tune the performance of machine tools.

Robotics

robotics
The technology of building and using machines (robots) with computer intelligence and some human-like physical capabilities.

Advances in machine control and artificial intelligence have led to the development of humanlike machines or *robots*. **Robotics** is the technology of building and employing machines with computer intelligence and some computer-controlled humanlike physical capabilities (dexterity, movement, vision, and so on). Of course, many robots are simple programmable machines whose output takes the form of one or more mechanical motions. However, robotics for manufacturing applications has now become a major area of research and development efforts in the field of artificial intelligence.

In manufacturing, robots are considered to be "steel-collar" workers. They help factories increase productivity and cut costs, and are particularly valuable for hazardous areas or work activities. Robots follow programs loaded into their special-purpose microcomputers. Input is received from visual and/or tactile sensors, processed by the microcomputer, and translated into movements of the robot. This typically involves moving its arms and hands to pick up and load items or perform some other work assignment such as painting, drilling, or welding. Robots are becoming more important in manufacturing because of improvements in their visual, tactile, and navigational capabilities.

computer-aided engineering (CAE)
The use of computers to simulate and evaluate models of product designs and production processes developed using computer-aided design methods.

computer-aided design (CAD)
Using computer graphics in engineering, architecture, and other fields for the interactive design of products and structures.

Computers in Engineering and Design

Computers have revolutionized how engineers and designers design products, structures, and production processes. For example, manufacturing engineers use **computer-aided engineering (CAE)** to simulate and evaluate electronic models of product designs and manufacturing processes. Engineers and designers develop such designs using **computer-aided design (CAD)** methods. Powerful *engineering workstations* with enhanced graphics and computational capabilities are used to analyze and design products and manufacturing facilities.

Computer-aided design packages and engineering workstations are the software and hardware resources that are automating many engineering and design activities. Engineers use these high-powered workstations for the design and testing of products, facilities, and processes. Input is by light pen, graphics pad, or keyboard, with the CAD package refining an engineer's initial drawings. Output is in two- or three-dimensional graphics that can be rotated to display all sides of the object being designed. For example, an engineer can zoom in for close-up views of a specific part and even make parts of the product appear to move as they would in normal operation. The design can then be converted into a finished mathematical model of the product. This is used as the basis for production specifications and machine tool programs.

Typically, products are designed according to specifications determined in cooperation with the design efforts of marketing research and product design specialists. One of the final outputs of this design process is the *bill of materials* (specification of all required materials) used in producing a product. Engineers also use computers to develop and evaluate standards for product

Engineers use powerful workstations to design products, structures, and production processes.

The image on screen represents a computer-aided design of a rotary engine.

quality as part of the *quality assurance* function, which stresses the production of high-quality products. Engineers must then use computers to design the production processes needed to manufacture the products they design. Using computers to perform the necessary analysis and design is known as *computer-aided process planning (CAPP)*.

Computer graphics are used to design building interiors.

Other CAD Applications

Computer-aided design is not limited to the engineering profession. Designers in many other fields make heavy use of CAD techniques. Thus, designers in the clothing and publishing industries, architects, and specialists in interior design use CAD extensively.

For example, clothing designers use CAD to design the shape, detail, and color of clothes to produce patterns for specific articles of clothing. Data about these design features can be stored on a computer's magnetic disk for later use. Designers can retrieve the patterns and other details of clothing and easily make design changes. The finished design can then be used by computer-controlled cutting machines that follow the electronic patterns to automatically cut the fabric needed to produce clothing.

Architects and interior designers also make extensive use of computer-aided design packages. Many architects no longer build scale models and draw blueprints of buildings they are designing. Instead, they enter data describing tentative specifications for a structure. This produces a computerized model just as engineers do when designing products. Architects then manipulate and modify the model to refine their design. They can rotate the design to produce views from different angles, or take a simulated walk through a building to display views of the different rooms in the structure. The computer can then produce blueprints for the finished design.

Interior designers can use an architect's electronic specifications for the rooms in a building as a starting point. Or they can start from scratch to build their own electronic models of room designs. Interior designers can use CAD software or the draw and paint programs found in many computer graphics packages. They can develop an electronic design that includes room dividers, furniture, carpeting, wall hangings, window treatments, room accessories, and other design elements. Colors and other features can be changed quickly to experiment with various combinations until the designer is satisfied with the finished design.

Quick Quiz

1. An _____ system can provide reports periodically, on an exception basis, or on demand.

2. An _____ system provides top executives with easy access to information about key factors of an organization's performance.

3. Popular computer applications in _____ include order processing, inventory control, accounts receivable, accounts payable, general ledger, and payroll.

4. Process control and robotics are examples of important computer applications in _____.

5. Computer-aided design is an example of an important computer application in _____.

Answers: 1. information reporting 2. executive information
3. accounting 4. manufacturing 5. engineering

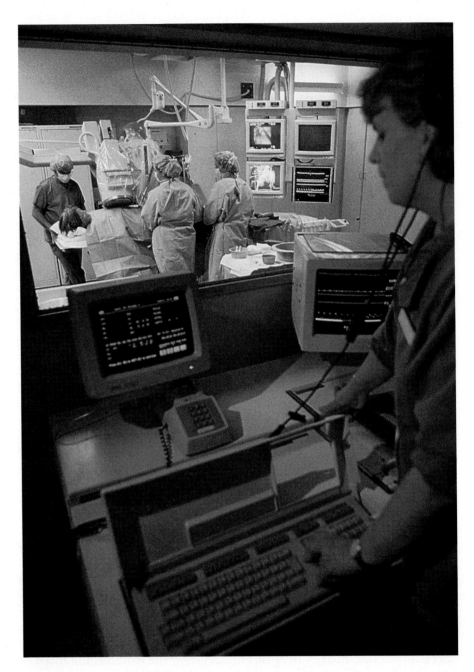

Patient monitoring systems monitor a patient's vital signs during surgery.

Computers in Health Care

Computers now play a major role in almost all areas of the health services industry. Hospitals, clinics, and doctors' offices have become automated workplaces for millions of health professionals. If you are thinking of a career in the health professions, whether as a doctor, a nurse, a therapist, or a health technician, using computers will become a commonplace activity in your work. Let's take a brief look at a few important examples.

Computers have many uses in health care. They range from the routine recordkeeping of patient accounting to vital applications in medical diagnosis and patient monitoring. Computers can contribute to high medical costs when used in sophisticated diagnostic machines, but they can also help control costs by supporting efficient use of scarce medical resources. For example, **patient accounting** systems can monitor the occupancy of hospital rooms, keep the medical charts of patients updated, and maintain an up-to-date record of a patient's account that reflects charges for medical supplies, doctors' visits, drugs administered, and lab tests completed.

Patient monitoring systems are used in intensive care units to monitor the vital signs of critically ill patients. As an example, sensors that measure brain activity, breathing, and heartbeat continually monitor a patient's status. The monitor sounds an alarm if a drastic change occurs, so health professionals can administer life-saving techniques. Such systems are also used in operating rooms during surgery. They help keep surgeons and anesthesiologists aware of important changes in a patient's vital signs during the course of an operation.

Medical Imaging

Computers also play a vital role in the diagnosis of an illness. In Chapter 5, we mentioned the use of artificial intelligence techniques and *expert systems,* such as Mycin, in which computers provide the advice of many experts to a physician in diagnosing an illness. More widely used are computerized **medical imaging** machines, which have become invaluable tools for medical diagnosis. CAT (computer tomography) scanners, ultrasound scanners, and MRI (magnetic resonance imaging) scanners, for example, are much more capable than traditional x-ray machines in diagnosing many forms of illness. They are also much less invasive and dangerous than exploratory surgery or other medical procedures.

CAT scanners send x-rays through the body at different angles. A computer then combines these images into horizontal "slices" of the human body that can be stacked to show three-dimensional images of its sections. Ultrasound scanners use low-frequency sound waves to take "radar" images of the body from different angles. These are recombined by a computer to form images for diagnosis. This technique is much safer and less costly than some other diagnostic methods. MRI scanners use a magnetic field from a large electromagnet that surrounds the patient and radio frequencies to create three-dimensional images. Because MRI can show the movement of blood or chemicals through parts of the body, it is an invaluable diagnostic tool.

Computers in Government

The use of computers by government agencies is as widespread and pervasive as in the workplaces of the private sector. Thus, if you plan to work for a local, state, or federal agency, you will see computers used for everything from office automation to law enforcement, from military defense systems to engineering and scientific research, from tax collection to the space program. Let's take a brief look at a few major applications.

patient accounting
A system of maintaining up-to-date records of a patient's medical treatment and charges.

patient monitoring
A system of monitoring the vital signs of critically ill patients.

medical imaging
The use of x-ray, ultrasound, and electromagnetic technologies to create images of the internal parts of the body for diagnostic purposes.

Many cities use computers to co-ordinate police, fire, and emergency services. This is a 911 computer control center.

State and Local Government

State and local governments are big users of computers. Local government agencies use computers for routine accounting applications such as utility billing and property tax collections, as well as vital emergency services such as police and fire protection. For example, many cities and counties now use a computer-based 911 system to dispatch and coordinate police, fire department, and emergency personnel and equipment in response to emergencies. Many police, fire, and emergency vehicles are also equipped with small computers or computer terminals. This allows police officers to check a driver's license and auto registration in seconds for outstanding arrest warrants or stolen vehicle reports.

Many state government agencies are so large that they each have their own large-scale computer operations. For example, you will find that state welfare departments, highway patrols, motor vehicle departments, legislatures, court systems, and executive branches all have information systems departments, complete with their own computer centers and telecommunications networks. State computers do everything from processing tax returns and motor vehicle registrations, tracking down wanted criminals and stolen property, to preparing a variety of social benefit checks, scheduling court dates, and managing legislative sessions.

Federal Government

If you go to work for the federal government, you will work for the largest user of computers in the world! For instance, the Internal Revenue Service (IRS) is the largest computer user in the federal government. It processes more than 100 million tax returns a year. The IRS even allows qualified taxpayers and accountants to file tax returns electronically by connecting their computers into the IRS's network. Another example is the Federal Bureau of

Members of Congress have immediate access to the *Congressional Record* through their office computers.

Investigation, which uses a computer network called the National Crime Information System (NCIS) to help its agents and other police agencies locate wanted criminals and collect crime data.

The U.S. Congress relies on computer systems to help senators and representatives cast votes and to examine and track the progress of legislative bills. The congressional computer network includes terminals in members' offices and on the House floor. Members also use the network extensively for electronic mail. The system is open to reporters, lobbyists, and others who wish to keep tabs on the status of legislation and the voting records of members. Even the White House has a sizable computer center, though it is dwarfed by the huge computer operations of large federal agencies such as the Department of Health and Human Services, the Justice Department, the Food and Drug Administration, the Federal Aviation Administration, and so on.

Of course, the U.S. Department of Defense relies heavily on computers. Computers are used for the basic accounting applications needed to pay millions of military men and women and keep track of huge inventories of military vehicles, parts, and supplies. Naturally, computers are a vital component of sophisticated computer-based defense and weapons systems. However, the sophistication of military defense systems is more than matched by the complexity of the computer systems and networks of the U.S. space program. The National Aeronautics and Space Administration (NASA) uses a vast telecommunications network with computer sites around the world to coordinate communications between land-based computers and the computers onboard space shuttles and other spacecraft.

Managing End User Computing

Even experienced computer users need help occasionally. Whether it's learning how to use a new software package, fixing a malfunctioning printer, or developing a new way to use computers, end users need support. That's why organizations try to support and maintain the computing efforts of their end users. Many organizations have an end user support function called *user*

Computer terminals at the Johnson Space Center help Mission Control personnel track spacecraft.

REAL-WORLD EXAMPLE

Ropes & Gray and Corporate Software: End User Help Skills

The best end user help desk staffers are usually not super techno-weenies, networking gurus, or programming wizards. In fact, technical proficiency is not even among the top five most sought-after help desk skills. Instead, help desk managers say they are more concerned with how a candidate communicates and handles stress. "Customer skills and motivation are more important than technical skills," says David Gregson, manager of the user support group at Ropes & Gray, a large Boston law firm. "You can train people in technology, but you can't teach great customer service." During job interviews, Gregson gives candidates real-life scenarios and asks them to respond. "I look for laid-back, easygoing people. You don't want the loner, and you don't want the coder. You want the bubbly person."

Corporate Software, Inc., a software reseller in Canton, Massachusetts, also offers help desk support to corporate customers. "What we're looking for are obvious communication skills," says Margaret Mansfield, a consultant in Corporate Software's support group. The company also gives applicants a brief quiz over the phone to measure their command of basic PC, DOS, Windows, and Macintosh know-how. One of the more difficult skills to find is "the ability to step through a problem logically," Mansfield says. "It's not necessary that a person know the inside of every operating environment. We want people who know they don't know everything but can go through steps to find an answer in a couple of minutes."

1. Do you agree with these firms on the types of skills they want their help desk staffers to have? Why or why not?

2. Would you like to work on a help desk or be an end user consultant? Why or why not?

services. This may include a department known as an *information center* to provide assistance to end users. Or individual departments in an organization may have their own end user support specialists instead of using an information center.

Most organizations also develop policies and procedures concerning hardware and software acquisition and application development by end users. For example, guidelines regulating the cost and types of hardware and software that end user departments can purchase are common. In this way, an organization can avoid supporting too many types of hardware and software and assure compatibility among its computing resources. Application development guidelines encourage end users to develop efficient, well-documented applications. They stress the design of built-in controls, so end user applications do not threaten the security of an organization's databases. Therefore, many organizations hire user consultants to help end users develop applications that meet such standards.

Information Centers

An **information center** is a department or group that provides hardware, software, and people support to end users in an organization. It is typically part of an organization's centralized computer services department. However, large

information center
A support facility for the end users of an organization. End users are provided with hardware, software, and people support provided by user consultants.

Information center consultants assist end users in many organizations.

end user departments may have their own information centers. Most information centers offer three basic types of support:

- *Hardware support* is provided for end users who need it. The information center may loan end users microcomputers, advanced graphic terminals, color laser printers, and plotters for their short-term use.
- *Software support* is provided by offering software training sessions and the temporary use of new or specialized software packages. End user instruction in a variety of popular application programs is also common.
- *People support* is provided by a staff of end user consultants. These in-house consultants act as systems analysts, programmers, and other specialists to train end users in the proper use of hardware and software and help them apply computers to their work activities.

Table 11-2 summarizes many of the services provided by information centers. As you can see, most of them deal with end user education and training, assistance with application development, and the evaluation and sharing of hardware and software. Information centers typically offer training programs for new employees on the operation of hardware devices and software pack-

Table 11-2
Examples of Information Center Services

Computer literacy education
Training on hardware and software
Hardware/software sharing
Application development consulting
Help center and hotline telephone
Evaluating new hardware and software
Setting standards for hardware and software
Security standards and audits
Maintenance of PC equipment

ages, and create user liaison positions or "help desks" that end users can call for assistance. These services are the responsibility of specialists with titles such as *user consultant, technical specialist, business analyst,* or *account executive.* They perform a vital role by troubleshooting problems, directing training efforts, and helping end users with application development.

Managing Organizational Computing

If you are going to work in a large organization, chances are you will have to deal with people who work for a centralized computing department. Many organizations still rely on a specialized department to manage the delivery of computing services to their users. This *computer services* or **information services department** is staffed with a variety of information systems professionals and managers, some of whom we described in Chapter 2. For example, the IS function may be led by an executive vice-president called the chief information officer (CIO) and managers for systems development, programming, computer operations, user services, telecommunications, and so on. See Table 11-3.

An information services department performs three basic functions: (1) application development, (2) operations, and (3) technical services. The organization chart shown in Figure 11-5 shows how each of these areas is organized. Let's look briefly at how they are managed.

information services department
A department within an organization that is responsible for developing, operating, and managing computer-based information services.

Managing Application Development

Managing the application development efforts of an organization is a major responsibility. It requires overseeing the activities of systems analysts, programmers, and end users working on a variety of development projects. Each application development project is an attempt to design new ways to use computers to benefit end users in an organization. However, such projects must

---

Chief Information Officer
Oversees all the information technology for a firm, including information processing, telecommunications, and office systems. Concentrates on long-term planning and strategy.

Manager of Information Services
Plans and directs the activities of the entire information services organization.

Manager of Systems Development
Directs the activities of systems development personnel and projects.

Operations Manager
Manages an organization's central computing facilities and the production of all information processing jobs.

Network Administrator
Manages local area and wide area networks. Monitors and evaluates telecommunications processors, network control software, and network usage.

**Table 11-3
Management Positions in
Information Services**

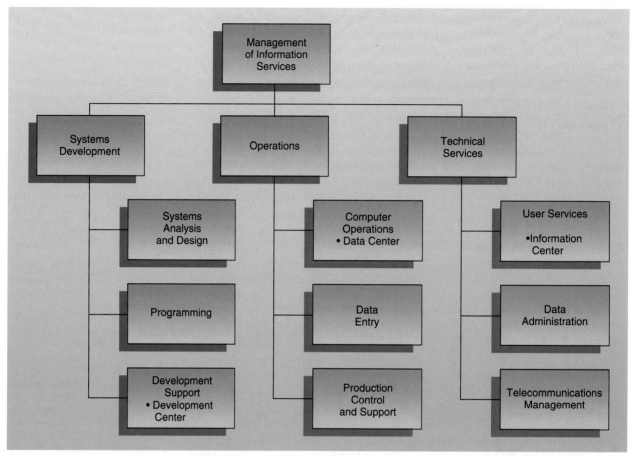

Figure 11-5
An information services department is organized to support application development, operations, and technical services activities

development center
A systems development group that serves as consultant to the IS professionals of an organization.

be carefully planned and monitored to be sure that they properly use hardware, software, people, and data resources and meet their design objectives.

In addition, many systems development groups have established **development centers.** These are staffed with specialists who act as consultants to the professional programmers and systems analysts in their organizations. Their role is to evaluate computer-aided systems engineering (CASE) methods and help information systems specialists use them to improve their application development efforts. Development centers thus play a supporting role to IS developers similar to that provided to end users by information centers.

Managing Computer Operations

data center
An organizational unit that uses centralized computing resources to perform computer services for an organization. Also known as a computer center.

Obviously, the operations of the **data centers** (computer centers) of an organization must be managed. This is true whether the centers rely on mainframes, minicomputers, or networked microcomputer systems for computer processing of end user jobs. For example, the activities of *data entry operators* who key transactions data into a computer system must be managed to ensure proper entry of data into the organization's computer systems and databases. Likewise, the work of *computer operators,* who operate large computer systems, also needs to be planned and supervised to assure timely and efficient processing of end user jobs.

Some of the management activities of data center operations are now being automated. *System performance monitors* are software packages that can help a data center "manage itself." That is, they monitor the processing of computer jobs in the data center, gather statistics on computer use, and develop schedules to make data center activities more efficient. In some cases, this leads to "lights out" data centers, which can continue to operate unattended after normal business hours.

Managing Technical Services

Managing organizational computing involves more than managing applications development and computer operations. Several other more technical or specialized activities must also be managed. One important example is *data administration*. This involves developing policies and procedures that regulate how data is collected, stored, and disseminated in an organization. Data administrators treat data as a valuable common resource that all end users can share as long as its quality and confidentiality is protected.

Another example is managing an organization's telecommunications networks. *Network administrators* typically manage the operation of wide area and local area telecommunications networks. They monitor and evaluate telecommunications processors (such as network servers), network control software (such as network operating systems), and other network hardware and software resources to assure proper service to network end users.

The screens on the left are displaying operating statistics provided by a system performance monitor for the mainframe system on the right.

E T H I C S

Ethical Issues in the Automated Workplace

As we have seen throughout this text, there are many ethical issues in the automated workplace. For example, in other chapters, we have discussed the ethical responsibilities of end users and IS professionals, the unauthorized monitoring of electronic mail, equal access to computers on the job, and the rights of programmers to their work. However, one of the most explosive ethical issues in the automated workplace is **computer monitoring.** That is, computers are being used to monitor the productivity and behavior of millions of employees while they work.

What's wrong with that, you may ask? Can't employers collect productivity data about their employees to increase the efficiency and quality of service? Here's one answer: Monitoring isn't simply the benign use of computers to collect data. It is different in three important ways: It monitors not just the work, but the worker; it measures work in real time; and it is constant. It effectively provides a permanent time study not simply to gather data, but to pace and discipline the workforce.[1]

What are some examples of computer monitoring in the workplace? Consider the thousands of airline reservation agents who work for the major airline companies. When you call to make a reservation, the agent is timed on the exact seconds he or she takes per caller, the time between calls, and the number and length of breaks taken. Sometimes, your conversation may also be monitored. The following are two more examples:

The maids at the hotel where you are staying at are probably monitored. Your maid punches a code in the phone when she enters and leaves your room, providing a detailed log of her speed and a record of her movements for the entire day.

And don't get sick, because nurses are monitored. They carry boxes on their belts that track the amount of time used for each procedure with a patient. So don't be surprised if they lack bedside manner.[2]

Computer monitoring has been criticized as an invasion of the privacy of employees. In some cases, workers do not know that they are being monitored. In others, they don't know how the information is being used. Besides privacy rights, the right of due process may be compromised by the improper use of collected data to make personnel decisions. The stress that computer monitoring places on those who must work under constant electronic surveillance has also been blamed for damaging the health of monitored workers. Finally, computer monitoring has been blamed for robbing workers of the dignity

(continued on next page)

(continued on next page)

computer monitoring
Using computers to monitor the productivity and behavior of employees while they work.

(continued from previous page)
of their work, creating an "electronic sweatshop" where workers are forced to work at a frantic pace under poor working conditions.

These are some of the criticisms arising from the use of computers to increase worker productivity through computer monitoring. In the meantime, lawsuits by monitored workers against employers are rising fast, with jury awards to workers in the hundreds of thousands of dollars. The Privacy for Consumers and Workers Act is making its way through both houses of Congress. This proposed law would regulate computer monitoring, protecting the workers' right to know and right to privacy.

What Do You Think?
What do you think of computer monitoring? Would you like to have your work activities constantly monitored by a computer system? Is computer monitoring ethical? Should it be legally regulated or abolished? What do you think?

---

[1] Karen Nussbaum, "Computer Monitoring: A Threat to the Right to Privacy?," in Roy De-Joie et al., *Ethical Issues in Information Systems* (Boston: Boyd & Fraser. 1991), pp. 136–137.
[2]Ibid.

Quick Quiz

1. Patient account and patient monitoring are examples of computer applications in _____.
2. Computerized _____ applications includes the use of ultrasound and magnetic resonance imaging (MRI) scanners.
3. Voting systems, tax processing systems, and military defense systems are examples of computer applications in _____.
4. An _____ is a support group for end user computing in many organizations.
5. The three basic functions of an _____ department are application development, computer operations, and technical services.

Answers: 1. health care   2. medical imaging   3. government
4. information center   5. information services

End Note: Managing Computers at Work

This chapter has given you a glimpse at the many important uses of computers in the workplace you may soon be entering. We hope you now realize how important it is to be a computer-literate end user in the computer-based fields and professions we have described. Whether you plan to be a professional or a technician, a manager or an entrepreneur, you can be more productive, more successful, and even more creative if you learn how computers are used and how to use them in your future occupation.

This chapter has also shown you how end user and organizational computing are managed. How does this affect you? As a prospective end user, it means that there will probably be information centers and user services specialists available to you to help you use computers more efficiently and effectively to get your job done. For example, you might be able to call a user services help desk to talk to an IS professional about a computing problem. Or have an information center specialist show you how to use a new software package. Or have a data center representative explain how you can get better service from your company's computing operation.

What if you are thinking of a career in information systems? Then you should realize that dealing with end users will probably be your biggest assignment. For instance, as a user consultant, software developer, or systems analyst, you will be working with end users to develop new or improved applications of computers. Hopefully, you should be able to count on support from development center consultants to help you learn new ways of developing better applications for end users. Other technical specialists should also be available in specialties like telecommunications and data administration to help you develop better solutions to end user problems.

Finally, as a prospective end user, you should realize that you will be held responsible for managing your own computing efforts. That's because being computer literate means knowing enough to use your computing resources to effectively do your job and meet the goals of the organization you work for. So that's why many end users, work groups, and departments are taking the initiative to manage their own computing efforts. That's why the managers of many end user departments are being held responsible for the computing efforts of their departments. Managing the computing efforts of an organization is no longer just a job for the manager of a central information services department. If you become a manager or own your own business, managing computing will be one of your major responsibilities.

Summary

Computers in Business   Computers help people in business perform the basic business functions of accounting, marketing, production/operations, finance, and human resource management. Transaction processing systems that process data from business transactions are vital to the daily operation of businesses and other organizations. Online transaction processing systems, such as electronic data interchange (EDI) and electronic funds transfer (EFT), process transactions data instantly to improve business operations and customer service.

Computers in Management   Computers help managers through management information systems that provide information for effective decision making. This includes information reporting systems, which provide prespecified information needed by managers on demand, according to a schedule, or on an exception basis. Executive information systems are easy-to-use management information systems that are tailored to the strategic information needs of top management.

Computers in Accounting   Several basic accounting systems exist in both large and small computer-using organizations. These applications help an organization keep track of its business activities and produce accurate financial statements and reports. They are order processing, inventory control, accounts receivable, accounts payable, payroll, and general ledger.

Computers in Manufacturing   Computer-integrated manufacturing stresses simplifying, automating, and integrating factory resources, environments, and functions with computers, robots, and telecommunications networks. Computer-aided manufacturing allows computers to automate many of the activities needed to produce products of all kinds. For example, computers are used to manufacture the products in a factory by directly controlling a physical process (process control), a machine tool (machine control), or a machine with some humanlike capabilities (robot).

Computers in Engineering and Design   Engineers use computer-aided engineering to simulate and evaluate electronic models of product designs and manufacturing processes that they develop using computer-aided design (CAD) methods. Clothing designers use CAD to design electronic patterns for clothing that can be used by automatic cutting machines. Architects use CAD to design all types of structures, and interior designers use graphics programs to design building interiors.

Computers in Health Care   Computers play a major role in the health services industry, ranging from patient accounting and monitoring systems to expert systems and medical imaging machines. Examples include computer tomography scanners, ultrasound scanners, and magnetic resonance scanners, which provide invaluable tools for medical diagnosis.

Computers in Government   Local, state, and federal government agencies are big users of computers. Typical computer uses for cities and counties include utility billing, tax collection, and police and fire protection. State agencies have large computer operations for applications such as processing motor vehicle registrations, preparing benefit checks, and assisting state courts and legislatures. Federal government agencies depend heavily on computers to process tax returns, assist criminal investigations, and help manage congressional activities, while the military and the space program depend on large, complex computer networks.

Managing Computing   Organizations support and manage the computing efforts of their end users. This frequently takes the form of information centers that provide hardware, software, and in-house consultants to support end users. Organization-wide computing is provided and managed by an information services function. This includes management of applications development, computer operations, and a variety of technical services. As an end user, you should take advantage of the end user services provided by your organization, but realize that you must manage your own computing efforts.

Key Terms and Concepts

accounting applications
business function applications
computer-aided design
computer-aided engineering
computer-aided manufacturing
computers in government
demand reporting
electronic data interchange
electronic funds transfer
exception reporting
information center
information reporting systems

information services department
machine control
management information systems
managing end user computing
medical imaging
online transaction processing
patient accounting
patient monitoring
periodic reporting
process control
robotics
transaction processing systems

Review Quiz

True/False

_____ 1. Management information systems include information reporting and executive information systems to provide information for various levels of management.

_____ 2. Decision support systems provide information for managers in a variety of structured formats.

_____ 3. Computer-integrated manufacturing stresses simplifying, automating, and integrating factory resources, environments, and functions.

_____ 4. Computer-aided manufacturing includes manufacturing process control, machine control, and robotics.

_____ 5. Computer-aided design is used by engineers, architects, interior and clothing designers and other designers of products, structures, and spaces.

_____ 6. Medical imaging applications include patient accounting and monitoring.

_____ 7. Computer use in business includes marketing, production/operations, accounting, finance, and human resource management applications.

_____ 8. In a data center, user consultants help end users manage their own computing efforts.

_____ 9. Accounting applications include inventory control, accounts payable, payroll, and general ledger.

_____ 10. An information services department provides applications development, computer operations, and technical computing services for an organization.

Multiple Choice

_____ 1. Electronic transmission of transaction documents among companies is called

     a. electronic funds transfer.
     b. electronic data interchange.
     c. online processing.
     d. transaction processing.

_____ 2. Electronic transfer of money and credit transactions is called

     a. electronic funds transfer.
     b. electronic data interchange.
     c. online processing.
     d. transaction processing.

_____ 3. The processing of data resulting from business transactions is called

     a. electronic funds transfer.
     b. electronic data interchange.
     c. online processing.
     d. transaction processing.

_____ 4. Processing transaction data immediately after it is captured is called

     a. electronic funds transfer.
     b. electronic data interchange.
     c. online processing.
     d. transaction processing.

_____ 5. Information provided on a scheduled basis is called

     a. demand reporting.
     b. exception reporting.
     c. periodic reporting.
     d. model reporting.

_____ 6. Information provided on a selective basis is called

     a. demand reporting.
     b. exception reporting.
     c. periodic reporting.
     d. model reporting.

_____ 7. Information provided whenever you want it is called

     a. demand reporting.
     b. exception reporting.
     c. periodic reporting.
     d. model reporting.

_____ 8. Medical imaging scanners utilize

     a. computer tomography.
     b. ultrasound.
     c. magnetic resonance.
     d. all of the above.

_____ 9. The health care application that uses sensors to measure the vital signs of critically ill patients is

a. patient accounting.
b. patient diagnostics.
c. patient monitoring.
d. medical imaging.

_____ 10. The largest user of computers in the world is

a. IBM.
b. the space program.
c. the federal government.
d. the defense department.

Fill-in

1. Using computers to control a petroleum refinery is known as _____.
2. Using computers to control machine tools is known as _____.
3. Computerized devices that can take over some production activities from human workers are called _____.
4. The _____ application processes orders received from customers.
5. The _____ application records changes in inventory.
6. The _____ application keeps track of amounts owed by customers.
7. The _____ application keeps track of purchases from suppliers.
8. The _____ application produces employee paychecks and earnings statements.
9. Producing the financial statements of the firm is the job of the _____ application.
10. An _____ provides hardware, software, and people resources to support end user computing.

Questions for Thought and Discussion

1. How are computers used in various areas of business? Give several examples.
2. How can management information systems support the decision-making needs of top executives, middle management, and operating managers?
3. Refer to the Real-World Example of Alverno Administrative Services in the chapter. Should the features of executive information systems be available to all end users?
4. Will computer-aided manufacturing and robotics lead to factories without human workers? Why or why not?
5. How important is computer-aided design to engineers, architects, clothing designers, and interior designers? Give several examples to justify your answer.
6. How important are computers for patient care and medical diagnosis in modern health services? Defend your answer.

7. You interested in a career in local, state, or federal government? Explain several ways you would probably use computers in your work.

8. Refer to the Real-World Example of Ropes & Gray and corporate software in the chapter. What would be your choices for the top five help desk skills? Explain your choices.

9. Refer to the Real-World Example of Dillard Department Stores in the chapter. In what ways besides EDI can department stores and other retail stores use computers?

10. How does your college or university manage end user and organizational computing? Talk to an IS professional who works at your school. Make a brief report to the class.

Review Quiz Answers

True/False: **1.** T **2.** F **3.** T **4.** T **5.** T **6.** F **7.** T **8.** F **9.** T **10.** T

Multiple Choice: **1.** b **2.** a **3.** d **4.** c **5.** c **6.** b **7.** a **8.** d **9.** c **10.** c

Fill-in: **1.** process control **2.** machine control **3.** robots **4.** order processing **5.** inventory control **6.** accounts receivable **7.** accounts payable **8.** payroll **9.** general ledger **10.** information center

CHAPTER

12

COMPUTER CHALLENGES: SECURITY AND SOCIETAL ISSUES

LEARNING OBJECTIVES

After reading and studying this chapter, you should be able to

Identify several major types of computer crime.

Outline several types of controls that can be used to assure the computer security of end users and organizations.

Discuss several major beneficial and adverse effects of computers on society.

Identify several privacy and health concerns arising from the use of computers.

You and the Challenge of Computers

information revolution
The dramatic growth and impact of computer-based information systems on our ability to analyze and communicate information in society.

As we have seen in this text, using computers presents many challenges to end users. Computers present us with powerful and valuable resources that we must learn to manage wisely. We really are in the midst of an **information revolution.** The widespread use of computers has greatly magnified our ability to analyze, compute, and communicate in our workplaces and throughout many facets of our lives. This has had a variety of impacts on our information society. Computers have been a tremendous boon to society, but as we have seen, they also have had several detrimental effects.

In this chapter, you will see both sides of the impact that computers can have on our information society. We will discuss both illegal acts with computers—computer crime—and methods used to protect computer resources from such acts—computer security. Then we will discuss both the beneficial and adverse effects of computer use including health, privacy, and other important issues. This should help show you some of the ways that you and other end users can respond to the challenges posed by computers in our information society.

Computer Crime

As a computer-literate end user, you should know what computer crime is, who commits such crimes, and how to protect yourself against it. Criminal activity involving computers is a growing threat. It thus presents a major challenge to the security of computer-based systems for all end users and organizations.

Why are computer-based information systems so vulnerable to computer crime? Part of the problem is the increased dependence on computers in our society. The widespread distribution of computer power through interconnected networks of computers has significantly increased the potential for computer crime. Even the proliferation of microcomputers in business, government, and education has provided new opportunities for computer crime.

No one knows the full extent of computer crime. That's because most computer crimes are "inside jobs," that is, done by employees of a business or government agency. So many organizations don't report or prosecute the individuals responsible for computer crimes against them. They fear the loss of public confidence that might result if the crimes are revealed. Organizations also fear that other criminals might try to duplicate a computer crime if its details were known. But estimates of the cost of damages or theft due to computer crime range in the billions of dollars each year. Thus computer crime is a serious threat to many organizations and hurts their customers and the public as well. See Table 12-1.

Computer Crime Laws

One way to understand computer crime is to see how current laws define it. The Data Processing Management Association (DPMA) has a good definition of computer crime in its model computer crime law. Basically, it says computer crime involves:

Year	Crime	Estimated Cost
1988	Cornell virus	$186 million
1988	Union Bank of Switzerland	$54 Million
1986–88	U.S. telephone access fraud	$125 million
1984	Volkswagen AG	$428 million
1982	Toronto Board of Education Credit Union	$7.8 million
1982	Saxon Industries	$53 million
1981	Wells Fargo	$21 million

Table 12-1
Costs of Some of the
Largest Computer Crimes

- The unauthorized use, duplication, alteration, or destruction of hardware, software, or data resources.
- Using or conspiring to use computer resources to commit an illegal act.

A good example of a computer crime law is the Federal Computer Fraud and Abuse Act. This federal law says that computer crime involves the access of computers used by the federal government or operating in interstate or foreign commerce (1) with intent to defraud, (2) resulting in more than a $1,000 loss, or (3) to gain access to certain medical computer systems. Buying and selling or publishing computer passwords is also prohibited. Penalties for violations of this law are severe. They include up to 5 years in prison for a first offense, 10 years for a second offense, and 20 years for three or more offenses. Fines can range up to $250,000 or twice the value of stolen data.

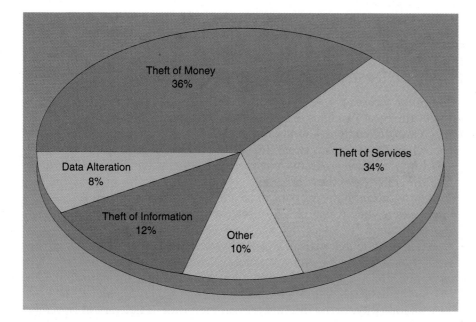

Figure 12-1
These are the major forms of computer crime.

Figure 12-1 illustrates basic types of computer crime. Notice that computer crime typically involves theft of money or services, theft or destruction of data and software, and unauthorized or illegal access to computer or data resources. Let's take a look at a few examples.

Theft of Money and Services

Money Theft

Of course, many computer crimes involve the theft of money. Such crimes almost always involve the fraudulent alteration of computer files. Then computer criminals can conceal their theft of money from a computer-using organization or swindle money from others based on falsified computer records. Famous examples are the Volkswagen AG case of 1984 and the Equity Funding case of 1973. In the first instance, a group of company executives altered computerized accounting files so they could secretly steal more than $400 million from Volkswagen. In the second case, the criminals were con artists who used a large insurance company's computers to produce thousands of falsified insurance policies with a face value exceeding $2 billion. These were then used to swindle investors out of $600 million they invested for stock in a fictitious company.

Service Theft

Unauthorized use of your computer system resources by someone else is called service theft. This type of crime is quite common. For example, any unauthorized use of a company-owned microcomputer by an employee, whether it is to do private consulting, to compute personal finances, or to play computer games, would be service theft. Obviously, most cases aren't reported by the employees involved.

One reported example is the case of a county employee convicted of theft under New York State's criminal code for unauthorized use of a county computer system. Another New York case involved a university computer system. The manager of the computer center and his assistant used the school's computer to provide services to businesses for fees that they pocketed.

Theft or Destruction of Data or Software

Computer Viruses

computer virus
Program code that copies its annoying or destructive program routines into the computer systems of anyone who accesses the computer systems that have used the program, or anyone who uses copies of data or programs taken from such computers.

One of the most insidious examples of this type of computer crime involves the creation of **computer viruses** or *worms*. Virus is the more popular term, but technically, a virus is program code that cannot work without being inserted into another program. A *worm* is a distinct program that can run by itself. In either case, these programs copy their destructive or annoying routines into the computer systems of anyone who accesses the "infected" computers where they reside or who uses copies of magnetic disks taken from such computers.

Thus, a computer virus or worm can spread its destruction among many users. The contents of memory, hard disks, and other storage devices can be wiped out. Copy routines in these programs are used to spread the virus and destroy the data and software of many computer users. A good example was the contamination of the Internet telecommunications network in November

COMPUTER VIRUS CONTAMINATION ACROSS THE UNITED STATES

Infected Areas

The Arpanet communications network provided a vehicle for spreading the virus. Some computers at universities, companies, and military research facilities received and spread the virulent program, eventually forcing hundreds of users off the network. Some of the major links in the network are shown below.

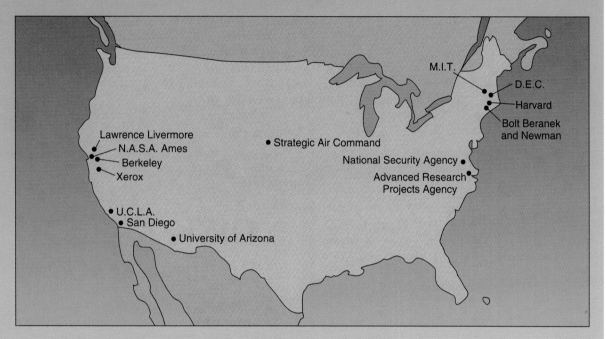

How the Infection Spread

1. Virus program is written by a computer science graduate student at Cornell and designed to secretly spread to other companies.

2. The Arpanet (Advanced Research Projects Agency Network) communications network, which connects military and civilian computers, is infected.

3. The virus spreads throughout the network by mailing itself to other computers and by masquerading as a legitimate user.

4. By continually copying itself, the virus forces the host computer to dedicate all of its computing power to the new illegitimate files. The effect is to shut or slow down the computer.

5. The virus begins to send itself to other computers it has not already infected and is supposed to skip the ones where it already resides. A programming mistake causes one out of every 10 infected computers to accept it again, tying up even more computing power.

6. Users disconnect from the network to delete the virus and the files it has created and try to destroy any traces it might have left behind.

7. Users, fearing they will be reinfected, remain off–line as investigators try to sterilize the network and eliminate the virus.

Figure 12-2
The Internet network was infected with a virus that disabled more than 6,000 computers.

1988. The computer virus was developed by a graduate student at Cornell. Its constant replications of itself overwhelmed the memory capacity of more than 6,000 infected computers in the network. Cost in computer time lost and cleanup efforts exceeded $100 million. Thus the Cornell virus is a classic example of the disruptive and destructive potential of computer viruses. See Figure 12-2.

A virus usually copies itself into the files of a computer's operating systems. Then it spreads to main memory and copies itself onto the computer's hard disk and any inserted floppy disks. It spreads to other computers through telecommunications links or floppy disks from infected computers. There are hundreds of known computer viruses. Figure 12-3 identifies a few of the viruses often found at infected computer sites.

Computer viruses typically enter a computer system through illegal or borrowed copies of software or through network links to other computer systems. Copies of software downloaded from electronic bulletin boards can be another source of viruses. So you see, you should avoid using software from questionable sources without checking for viruses. *Vaccine* programs are available that can help you diagnose and remove computer viruses from infected files on your hard disk or in a network.

Figure 12-3
Computer viruses can damage
your system in a variety of ways.

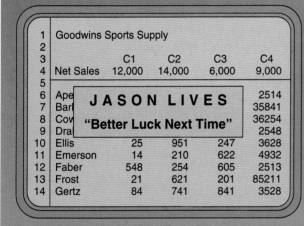

Friday 13th Virus. Alias "Black Friday." Erases programs when you try to run them.

Disk Killer Virus. Alias "Ogre." Causes unexpected formatting of your hard disk.

Datacrime Virus. Adds garbage to files and reformats disk.

AirCop Virus. Alias "Red State." Attacks boot sector on non–write–protected diskettes.

Vaccine programs remove computer viruses.

Software Piracy

Unauthorized copying of software is called software piracy. It's a problem whose ethical impact was discussed in Chapter 3. Software copying is really a form of software theft. Software is protected by the Computer Software Piracy and Counterfeiting Amendment to the Federal Copyright Act. Several major cases involving the unauthorized copying of software by large corporate users or competing software companies have been widely reported. These include lawsuits by the Software Publishers Association, an industry association of major software developers, against major corporations allowing unauthorized copying of their programs. Software companies such as Lotus Development Corporation have won lawsuits against several of their competitors. This involved companies that were marketing software *clones* that copy the "look and feel" of Lotus 1-2-3 and other popular software packages.

As we mentioned in Chapter 10, software is intellectual property that is protected by copyright and licensing agreements. The many restrictions of software copyrights and licensing agreements have led to a variety of legal alternatives. For example, many organizations sign **site licensing** contracts that allow them to make copies of a software package for use by employees at a particular location or in a particular department.

Another alternative is *shareware,* in which free copies of software are distributed by their developers. Shareware developers encourage you to make copies of such programs to share with others. They hope you and your friends might eventually buy a copy of the software, so that you can get full documentation and updated versions of the package. You can also get other free software, known as *public domain* software, that is not copyrighted. However,

site licensing
Contracts that allow an organization to make copies of a software package for use by employees at a particular location or in a particular department.

such software has no guarantees of quality, and, like other free software you get, it should be inspected as a possible carrier of computer viruses.

Data Alteration and Theft

Sometimes people use computers to steal or make illegal changes to data. Altering data not only damages its value but may lead to other crimes. For instance, an employee of the University of Southern California was convicted of taking payments from students and changing their grades in return. Several reported schemes have involved alteration or theft of credit information. Stolen credit information can then be sold to fraudulently qualify people for credit. Changes made to computerized motor vehicles records have helped criminals steal cars whose records were altered. Other examples have involved malicious replacement of data in files with obscene or nonsensical information.

Unauthorized or Illegal Access

Hacking

In computerese, a person who is an obsessive user of computers is called a *hacker*. However, the unauthorized access and use of computer systems is also frequently called *hacking*. Sometimes illegal hackers steal vital information or damage data or programs. Other times a hacker only commits "electronic breaking and entering." Here the hacker is an intruder who gets access to computer systems, reads some files, but neither steals nor damages anything. This computerized snooping is common in many computer crime cases that are prosecuted. In California, a court found that the computer crime law prohibiting malicious access to a computer system applied to any user gaining unauthorized access to another's computer systems.

International Issues

Computer-based systems can violate international laws and regulations. An example is the use of telecommunications networks by the computer based systems of multinational corporations to transfer data among their far-flung locations. This has been challenged by many nations as violating their national sovereignty. Information systems that cross national borders generate *transborder data flows* that may violate tariff, taxation, privacy, or labor regulations of host countries. This has been a major point of controversy among the European Community and other nations. As the use of computers and telecommunications in global networks continues to grow, such international issues have become a major management concern of any company that does business in the international marketplace.

Quick Quiz

1. Three major forms of computer crime include the theft of money, information, and _____.

2. Computer programs that copy destructive or annoying routines are called _____.

3. Unauthorized copying of software is called _____.

**Carnegie Mellon and Rice Universities:
Hacking on the Internet**

The Computer Emergency Response Team (CERT) at Carnegie Mellon University advised users to batten down the hatches in the face of a rash of password thefts and other breaches of security discovered in Unix-based computers on the Internet. "CERT has observed a dramatic increase in reports of intruders monitoring the network traffic," the U.S. Department of Defense-sponsored group said in an advisory sent over the Internet. "Systems of some service providers have been compromised...[and] intruders have captured access to information for tens of thousands of systems across the Internet."

A spokesman for CERT declined to identify organizations affected, but *The Washington Post* reported that Rice University in Houston had replaced 3,000 passwords and taken other safeguards after being hit by an intruder. Officials at Rice could not be reached for comment. CERT said intruders gain access to systems, install a "Trojan Horse" program to catch passwords and then install a "back door" program to access later. It said any computer allowing access for remote login, telnet, or file transfer is at risk. It advised users at those sites to immediately change passwords for any network-accessed accounts.

1. What types of computer crime appear to have been committed by Internet intruders?

2. What do you think can be done to protect the Internet and other networks from such crimes?

4. Many organizations sign _____ contracts that allow them to legally make copies for their employees or other end users.

5. Unauthorized access and use of computer systems is frequently called _____.

Answers: 1. services 2. computer viruses or worms 3. software piracy 4. site licenses 5. hacking

Computer Security and Controls

It should be obvious that computer crime and computer criminals present a major security challenge to both end users and IS professionals. However, don't forget that computer-based information systems are vulnerable to other threats as well. For example, honest mistakes made by end users and IS specialists and natural disasters can threaten the accuracy, integrity, and safety of computer-based systems. Therefore, computer security must involve security measures and control methods that protect end users and organizations from the results of computer crime, human error, or other destruction of their computing resources. See Figure 12-4.

Have computers made it harder to detect some types of errors and fraud? Yes. Manual and mechanical information systems use paper documents and other media that can be visually checked. Several persons are usually involved in such systems, so cross-checking procedures are easily performed. These characteristics make it easier to detect errors and fraud.

Figure 12-4
Three levels of controls are needed to provide computer security.

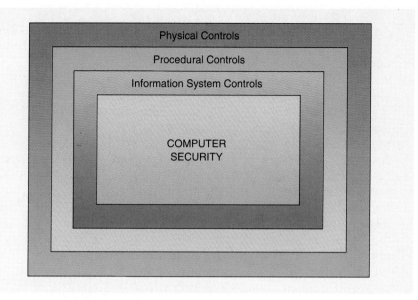

Computer-based information systems, on the other hand, rely on the CPU's electronic circuits and media such as magnetic disks for most of their information processing activities. Incorrect or unauthorized changes to information processing procedures and the contents of databases is harder to detect. In addition, a small number of IS professionals may control processing activities that are critical to the survival of the organization. Therefore, the ability to detect errors and fraud can be reduced by computerization. This makes developing effective control methods an important factor in the design of computer-based systems.

So all computer-based systems need to be protected by a variety of controls to assure their quality and security. Effective controls provide *quality assurance* for end users and organizations. That is, they can make a computer-based system more free of errors and fraud and able to provide information products of higher quality than manual types of information processing. This increased security and quality can help reduce the potential negative impact and increase the positive impact that computer-based systems can have on end users, their organizations, and society in general.

Information System Controls

First of all, control methods need to be designed for the basic activities of information systems. That is, **information system controls** must be developed to monitor and maintain the quality and security of the input, processing, output, and storage activities of a computer-based system. For example, controls must be developed to ensure proper data entry, processing techniques, storage methods, and information products. See Figure 12-5.

information system controls
Controls that monitor and maintain the quality and security of the input, processing, output, and storage activities of a computer-based information system.

Input Controls

In Chapter 1, we used the phrase *garbage in, garbage out*. It emphasizes why controls are needed for the proper entry of data into a computer system. Data-

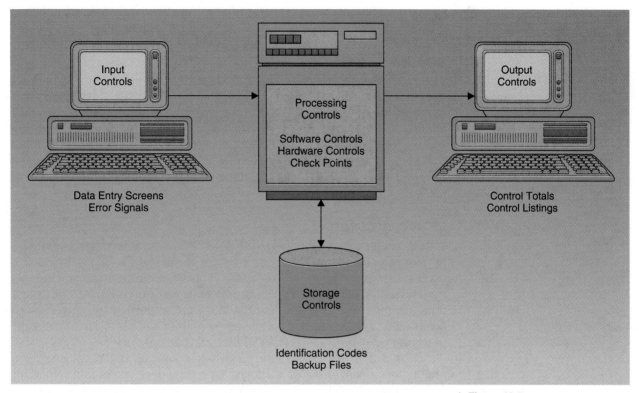

Figure 12-5
Controls are needed for input, processing, output, and storage activities.

entry software can identify incorrect or improper input data as it is entered into a computer system. It can check for, and reject, invalid codes, data fields, and transactions before they are entered into a computer system.

Computers can also calculate and monitor **control totals.** A *record count* is a control total that consists of counting the total number of input records and comparing this total to the number of records the computer counts at other stages of processing. If the totals do not match, the computer will alert you that a mistake has been made.

control totals
Using a total of data items (such as a count of records processed) that can be computed and compared several times during processing to assure consistency in information processing activities.

Processing Controls

Once you enter data correctly into a computer system, it must be processed properly. Processing controls are designed to identify errors in arithmetic calculations and logical operations. They are also used to ensure that data are not lost or do not go unprocessed.

For example, a typical processing control is the establishment of *checkpoints* during the processing of a program. Checkpoints are intermediate points within a program being processed where intermediate totals are calculated, "dumps" of data are recorded on magnetic tape or disk, or messages are displayed on the status of processing. Checkpoints minimize the effect of processing errors or failures, since processing can be restarted from the last checkpoint, rather than from the beginning of the program. They also help build an **audit trail.** That is, they build a trail of recorded checkpoints that

audit trail
The presence of media and procedures that allow a transaction to be traced through all states of information processing, beginning with its appearance on a source document and ending with its transformation into information output.

allows transactions being processed to be traced through the steps of their processing.

Output Controls

The quality of information products produced by your computer system needs to be assured. Output controls are developed to ensure that information products are correct and complete and are transmitted to authorized end users in a timely manner. For example, control totals on output can be compared with control totals generated during input. Control listings can also be produced that provide a detailed record of documents and reports produced. And identification codes can be required to limit displays of sensitive information to authorized end users.

Storage Controls

Your data files and databases are valuable resources. So your data resources have to be protected from unauthorized or accidental use. Typically, a computer's operating system or a *security monitor* package protects databases from unauthorized use or processing accidents. Account codes, passwords, and other identification codes are used to allow access only to authorized users. A catalog of authorized users enables a computer system to identify eligible users and determine which types of files or databases they can access.

Backup files are another form of storage control. As an end user, you might store floppy disks or magnetic tape cartridges containing important files at home, as well as at work. Organizations may store duplicate files of data away from the computer center, sometimes in special storage vaults in remote locations. Some organizations use duplicate files that are updated by telecommunication links. Files can also be protected by *file retention* measures. For example, if current files are destroyed, the files from previous periods can be used to reconstruct new files. Usually, several *generations* of files are kept for control purposes.

Procedural Controls

procedural controls
End user procedures or organizational policies designed to maintain the integrity of computing operations.

A variety of **procedural controls** are needed to assure computer security. Procedural controls are end user procedures or organizational policies designed to maintain the integrity of computing operations. For example, your department may have a policy that requires you to make a backup copy of your hard disk's contents each night before you leave work. Or an organization may establish a production control section to monitor the progress of information processing jobs, data-entry activities, and the quality of output.

disaster recovery
Developing contingency plans and procedures to help an organization recover from a disaster to its computing facilities.

Disaster recovery procedures are another example. We know that natural and manmade disasters do happen. Hurricanes, earthquakes, fires, floods, power failures, criminal and terrorist acts, and human error can all severely damage an organization's computing resources. This can put the health of the organization itself at risk. Many organizations, like airlines and banks, are crippled by even a few hours' loss of computing power. Others could only survive a few days without computing facilities. That's why organizations do contingency planning, develop disaster recovery procedures, and formalize them in *disaster recovery plans*. They specify what employees will participate in disaster recovery, what their duties will be, what hardware, software, and facilities will be used, and the priority of applications that will be processed.

Physical Controls

Computers—from your own PC to the largest mainframe—need protection. That's why they need physical controls. Computers are subject to such hazards as accidents, natural disasters, unauthorized use, sabotage, vandalism, industrial espionage, destruction, and theft of resources. Therefore **physical controls** must be developed to protect computer centers and individual computers from loss or destruction.

Providing maximum security and disaster protection from computers requires many types of controls. For instance, only authorized personnel may be allowed access to a computer center through such techniques as identification badges for information services personnel, electronic door locks, burglar alarms, security police, closed-circuit TV, and other detection systems. Computer centers may also be protected from disaster by such safeguards as fire detection and extinguishing systems; fireproof storage vaults for the protection of files; emergency power systems; electromagnetic shielding; and temperature, humidity, and dust control. Even access to a PC can be controlled by a key lock system for turning it on.

Biometric controls are an exciting development in physical controls. They provide security by using devices that measure unique physical traits. This includes voice verification, fingerprints, hand geometry, signature dynamics, keystroke analysis, retina scanning, face recognition, and genetic pattern analysis. Biometric control devices use special-purpose sensors to measure and digitize a *biometric profile* of an individual's fingerprints, voice, or other physical traits. The digitized signals are processed and compared to a previously processed personal profile stored on a magnetic disk. If the profiles match, that person is allowed entry into a computer facility or given access to other system resources.

physical controls
Security measures to protect the physical facilities of computer centers and end user computers from loss or destruction.

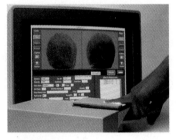

Fingerprints are used as a biometric control.

biometric controls
Security measures that check a person's unique physical traits such as voice verification or fingerprints.

End Users and Computer Security

Many organizations are realizing that computer applications developed by their end users can perform extremely important functions. That is, many end users are involved in much more than personal productivity, decision support, or database management. Instead, their computer use involves activities that are critical to the success and survival or their organization. Thus, such end user computing activity results in *organization-critical* end user applications.

Table 12-2 outlines examples of controls that could be established for critical end user applications. Business firms and other organizations are trying

Comply with all software licensing agreements
Guard all data and applications from unauthorized use and access
Regularly back up data and store it in secure locations
Protect PC equipment from damage and theft
Test applications thoroughly, to be sure they perform as intended
Arrange for disaster recovery
Screen for viruses on a routine basis
Apply security measures when communicating with other systems
Document applications for future users

Table 12-2
Controls for End User Applications

to protect themselves from the havoc that errors, fraud, destruction, and other hazards could cause to these critical applications and thus to the organization itself. Most of the controls involved are standard practice in applications developed by professional systems analysts. However, such controls are often ignored when end users develop their own applications.

So designing effective computer controls has now become a vitally important assignment for many end users. They must learn to work with systems analysts and IS security specialists to develop many of the control methods we have just discussed. Together, end users and IS professionals can build, operate, and maintain secure systems. Only then can computer security be a realizable goal.

Quick Quiz

1. Counting the number of records processed is an example of an information system control known as a _____.
2. A _____ package is designed to protect a computer system from unauthorized use.
3. Helping an organization recover from damage to its computer systems by accidents or natural disasters is known as _____.
4. Devices that measure one or more unique physical traits to provide computer security are called _____.
5. Requiring employees to back up computer files and screen for computer viruses on a regular basis are examples of _____.

Answers: 1. control total   2. security monitor   3. disaster recovery   4. biometric controls   5. end user controls

Computers and Society

As a computer-literate end user, you should understand that computers have both beneficial and adverse effects on society. For example, computerizing a factory production process may have an *adverse* effect of a decrease in the number and type of factory jobs. However, it may have the *beneficial* effect of providing consumers with products of better quality at lower cost.

Understanding societal issues of computers helps end users plan and control the development and use of computer-based systems. Then they can help assure the survival and success of their organizations in our dynamic society. So this section analyzes some of the major societal impacts of computers. This includes the use of computers to solve human and social problems such as crime and pollution and other societal effects of computers as illustrated in Figure 12-6.

Computer Solutions for Society

Computers can be used for the good of society. Computers can solve human and social problems through societal applications such as medical diagnosis, computer-assisted instruction, governmental program planning, environmental quality control, and law enforcement. Let's look at some examples:

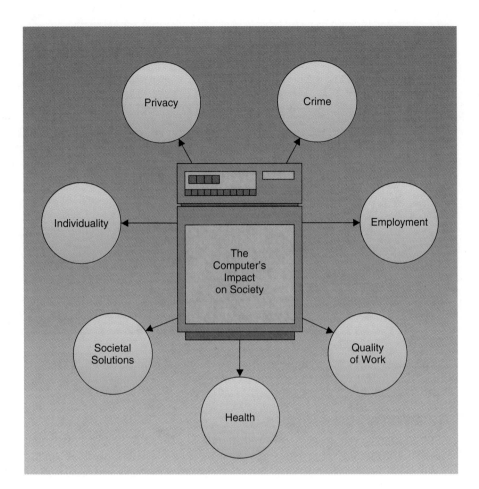

Figure 12-6
Computers have had a major impact on society.

- Computers can heal. They can help diagnose an illness, prescribe necessary treatment, and monitor the progress of hospital patients.
- Computers can teach. Computer-assisted instruction (CAI) can allow a computer to serve as "tutor," especially if it is designed to tailor instruction to the needs of a particular student.
- Computers can fight crime. A variety of law enforcement applications allow police to identify and respond quickly to evidences of criminal activity.
- Computers can fight pollution. They monitor the level of pollution in the air and in bodies of water to detect the sources of pollution, and to issue early warnings when dangerous levels are reached.
- Computers can control urban sprawl. They are used for program planning by many government agencies in such areas as urban planning, population density and land use studies, highway planning, and urban transit studies.
- Computers can reduce unemployment. They are being used in regional and national job placement systems to help match unemployed persons with available jobs.

This computer provides prenatal monitoring through ultrasound techniques.

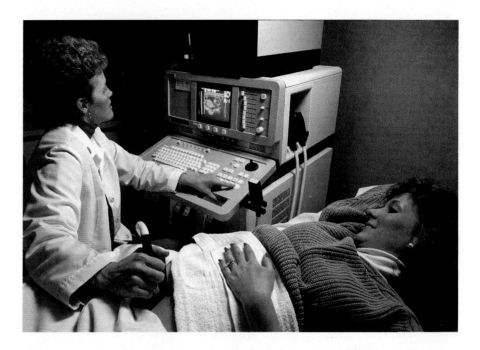

These and many other applications illustrate that computer-based systems can be used to help solve the problems of society.

Computers and Employment

Computers have created new jobs and increased productivity, but computers have also eliminated some types of jobs. For example, computers automate jobs formerly performed by many clerical and factory workers and create other jobs in their place. Also, many jobs created by computers require different types of skills and education than do the jobs they eliminate. That leads to *job displacement.* For example, factory automation has significantly upgraded the minimum skills needed to be a factory worker in many industries. For these jobs, a general high school education is no longer adequate. So untrained workers are displaced from their jobs and may become unemployed unless they can be retrained for these new, more demanding positions.

However, don't forget that the computer industry has created many new job opportunities for the manufacture, sale, and maintenance of computer hardware and software and for a variety of other computer services. Many new jobs, such as systems analysts, programmers, analysts, and end user consultants, have been created in computer-using organizations. Also, many new jobs have been created in industries that provide services to firms in the computer industry and to other industries that are heavily dependent on computers, such as those involved in space exploration and microelectronics.

Computers and Individuality

Computers have been criticized for creating inflexible, impersonal systems that depersonalize human activities. For instance, it is more efficient for many computer-based systems to deal with an individual as a number than as a name. Thus you may feel a loss of identity if you seem to be treated as "just another number" by a computer-based system.

Horror stories that describe how inflexible and uncaring computer-based systems can be are another common example. They don't seem responsive when it comes to rectifying their own mistakes. Some systems seem to be designed to eliminate any human intervention in problem situations. You or someone you know has probably had such experiences. Over and over again we hear about computerized customer billing systems that demand payment and send warning notices to customers whose accounts have already been paid.

However, it's a fact that computer-based systems can be designed to include human factors that minimize depersonalization. The development of "user friendly" computer-based systems has thus become a major goal of system designers. The photograph below is an example of how a software package can include features that provide you with a pleasing, easy-to-use graphical-user interface. The widespread use of microcomputers has helped accelerate the development of user-friendly software for end users.

Computers and Work

Computers have eliminated many monotonous or obnoxious tasks in the office and the factory. Furthermore, computers have helped increase the number of more pleasant, challenging, and interesting job assignments. For example, computers have upgraded the skill level of secretarial work in many offices. They have created more challenging and interesting tasks involving word processing, desktop publishing, electronic mail, and electronic office management. Thus, computers have upgraded the quality of work because they can improve the quality of working conditions and the content of work activities.

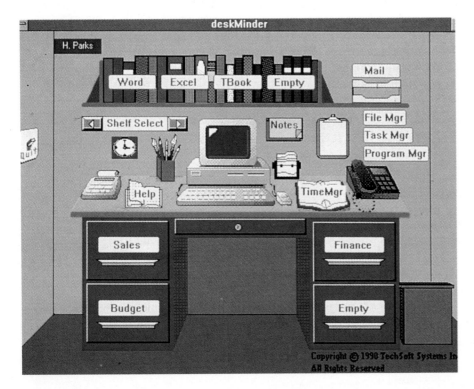

Human factors can be included in the design of user-friendly applications software.

REAL-WORLD EXAMPLE

Citicorp: The Case for Computer Monitoring

Imagine what it would be like to be an employee of Citicorp's accounts payable department. That's the department responsible for processing the invoices (bills) Citicorp receives from its suppliers. You and your fellow departmental employees authorize millions of dollars of checks in payment of these bills when they are due. How does Citicorp assure itself that dishonest employees don't authorize payment of fraudulent checks to fictitious companies that end up in their own pockets? Through computer monitoring, that's how.

What Citicorp does is use expert systems and behavioral profiles based on data taken from sampling the use of computers by everyone in its accounts payable department and any other depart-ment viewed as having a high risk from fraudulent activity. Says Ben Flaherty, Citicorp's manager of corporate security: "We are using artificial intelligence to come up with security software. . . to set up a profile." For example, the software remembers what time of the week or month an employee should be paying invoices and which suppliers should be involved. Citicorp informs employees that they are being monitored, since it sees such warnings as a deterrent. Says Flaherty, "We find it well within our interest to publicize it a lot."

1. How is computer monitoring used at Citicorp?

2. Would you agree to having your work activities monitored by such systems? Explain.

On the other hand, computers have created jobs that are very repetitive and routine. Data entry is a good example, though automated methods of data entry such as optical scanning are replacing many manual data-entry methods. As we discussed in Chapter 11, computers can also create an "electronic sweatshop" work environment. That is, computers are being used to monitor and increase worker productivity in some industries. Data-entry clerks and telephone operators may have the number of keystrokes or calls per hour monitored by the computer systems they were using. So, since computers are a key component of automation, they must take some responsibility for automated operations that require people to "work like machines."

Privacy Issues

Computer systems can collect, store, and retrieve information quickly and easily. This is an important benefit of computer-based systems. However, the computer's power to store and retrieve information can adversely affect your right to privacy. Confidential information on you and other individuals contained in centralized computer databases by credit bureaus, government agencies, and private business firms can be misused. For instance, the unauthorized used of your credit history can invade your privacy. Errors in such data files can seriously hurt your credit standing or reputation and those of other consumers.

Such crimes were possible before computers became commonplace. However, the speed and power of computers interconnected by telecommunications networks to electronic databases greatly increases the potential for invasions of privacy. Nationwide computer-based systems of corporations, credit bureaus, and government agencies contain large databases of personal information. This substantially increases the potential for the misuse of computer-stored information.

Privacy Threats

Several major threats to privacy are forms of computer crime we have discussed previously, such as the fraudulent alteration of computer-based credit histories, student records, and accounting files that computer criminals use to steal from or swindle their victims. Other privacy threats involve unauthorized use or mistakes in **computer matching** of personal data.

For example, you have probably heard the news reports of individuals who were accused, arrested or jailed due to erroneous computer matching of their personal information with the profiles or characteristics of suspected criminals. Another potential threat is the use of Social Security numbers to match the computerized records of individuals in government files. For instance, government agencies do computer matching to try to identify tax evaders, welfare cheats, draft registration avoiders, and student loan delinquents. Though legitimate, errors in such matching can seriously harm the individuals involved. Unauthorized matching of computerized information about you gleaned from purchases you make with credit cards is another example of a common threat to individual privacy.

computer matching
Using computers to match data about individuals in a variety of databases as the basis for identifying them as criminal suspects, business prospects, or for other purposes.

Privacy Laws

Several laws have been established in the United States to counter such threats to privacy. For example, the Fair Credit Reporting Act regulates how credit bureaus issue credit reports and allows you to inspect your credit files for accuracy. The Freedom of Information Act gives you the right to inspect information about you held in the databases of many government agencies. It also allows individuals and organizations to request disclosure of other government information based on the public's right to know.

The Federal Privacy Act strictly regulates the collection and use of personal data by government agencies. Exceptions are law enforcement investigative files, classified files, and civil service files. This law says that you have the right to inspect your personal records, make copies, and correct or remove erroneous or misleading information. Agencies must also inform you of the reasons for requesting personal information from you. Federal agencies must retain personal data records only if it is relevant and necessary to accomplish a legal purpose. They must also annually disclose the types of personal data files they maintain and cannot disclose personal information to any other individual or agency except under certain strict conditions. Finally, federal agencies must "establish appropriate *administrative, technical,* and *physical* safeguards to ensure the security and confidentiality of records."

More recently, the Electronic Communications Privacy Act, the Computer Fraud and Abuse Act, and the Computer Security Act were established. A major goal of these federal laws is to protect the privacy of computer-based files and telecommunications. For example, they prohibit intercepting data communications messages, stealing or destroying data, or trespassing in federal-related computer systems. Such laws recognize the serious threat to privacy of computer crime and the vulnerability of telecommunications networks.

Along with other federal laws, they also stress the importance of developing appropriate control methods in computer-based systems. They emphasize that effective controls are necessary to protect the security of end user and organizational databases in business and government.

Health Issues

Using computers may be dangerous to your health! That's the message that thousands of computer users are reporting. They see their heavy use of computers as causing health problems such as job stress, damaged arm and neck muscles, eye strain, radiation exposure, and even death by computer-caused accidents. What are the potential threats to your health caused by computers? Let's briefly review some of the major health issues in computing, and close with a look at some possible solutions.

Job Stress

In Chapter 11 and earlier in this section, we discussed the computer's impact on the workplace. Computers are being used to monitor the performance and productivity of data-entry operators and other networked computer users. This **computer monitoring** of workers and the *electronic sweatshop* environment it creates is blamed as a major cause of computer-related job stress. For example, some companies use computer networks to continually count the number of keystrokes per hour and errors made by each worker. Then they pay workers based on the number of correct keystrokes processed per hour.

computer monitoring
Using computers to supervise productivity and behavior of employees.

Managers who use computer monitoring defend it as providing an objective and unbiased way to measure performance. They feel that using statistics from computer monitoring allows them to objectively supervise, improve and reward worker productivity. Workers, unions, and some government officials criticize computer monitoring and computer piecework payment as putting too much stress on employees who must work with computers all day. This can lead to further health problems, as workers are forced to "work like machines" at fast paced, monotonous, and repetitive job tasks.

Muscle/Skeletal Strain

Muscle/skeletal strain is one of the major health problems in computing. People who must work at personal computers or video display terminals (VDTs) in fast-paced, repetitive jobs can suffer from a variety of painful conditions known as *cumulative trauma disorder* or *repetitive strain disorder*. Their fingers, wrists, arms, neck, and back can become so weak and painful that they cannot work. Some computer workers suffer from *carpal tunnel syndrome,* a painful, crippling ailment of the hand and wrist that typically requires surgery to cure.

Muscle/skeletal strain can thus cause strained muscles, back pain, nerve damage, and other ailments. The constant repetition of keystrokes for long periods of time while seated at a VDT or personal computer is one obvious cause of this health problem. So many employees are demanding, and many managers are recommending, changes in the workplace. Installing workstations that take health factors into account and providing more variety in job tasks for computer workers top the list of suggested improvements.

Other Health Problems

Eye Strain

The use of microcomputer video monitors has made computer output very attractive and convenient. However, prolonged viewing of video displays causes eye strain in employees who must do this all day. This is especially true of data-entry operators and word processing specialists who must continually switch from looking at paper documents to their video screens. The glare of some video screens, along with poor resolution and contrast and flickering displays, are other causes of eye strain.

Radiation

Computer video displays can cause a health problem considerably more serious than eye strain. Radiation caused by the *cathode ray tubes (CRTs)* that produce most video displays is the health concern on the minds of many people. Like your home TV set, both color and monochrome CRTs produce an electromagnetic field. This may cause harmful radiation to employees who work too close for too long in front of video monitors. Reports of problems by pregnant workers include miscarriages and fetal deformities for those with long exposure to CRTs at work. While several studies have failed to find conclusive evidence concerning this problem, several organizations recommend that women workers minimize their use of CRTs during pregnancy. Hopefully, the replacement of CRTs with new display technologies like LCDs (liquid crystal displays) will significantly lessen this problem.

Accidents

Computers control machines that have accidentally harmed or killed factory workers and other persons. For instance, industrial robots have inadvertently injured or killed workers in several factories in Japan and the United States. Computer-controlled radiation machines used for medical treatment are another example. Software errors have resulted in harmful or fatal amounts of radiation to patients at several hospitals. This problem is expected to become more serious as the number of robots and other computer-controlled machines continues to increase.

Ergonomic Solutions

Some of the solutions to the health problems discussed in this chapter can be found in the science of **ergonomics,** sometimes called *human factors engineering.* The goal of ergonomics is to design healthy work environments that are safe, comfortable, and pleasant for people to work in, thus increasing their morale and productivity. Ergonomics thus encompasses the healthy design of the workplace, workstations, computers, and other machines, and even software packages.

ergonomics
The science and technology emphasizing the design of safe, comfortable, and pleasant work environments and human-operated machines such as computers.

For example, Figure 12-7 shows the specifications for an ergonomically designed computer workstation. The design recommends proper heights and distances for a comfortable and safe workstation. Other ergonomic factors might include a detachable keyboard, tilting and swiveling video monitor, and an adjustable chair.

Other health issues we have raised have more to do with *job design* than workplace design. For example, policies are needed that provide for work

Figure 12-7
An ergonomically designed work-station should be safe and comfortable.

breaks every few hours from heavy VDT use and limit the CRT exposure of pregnant workers. Ergonomic job design should also include providing more variety in job tasks for workers who spend most of their workdays at computer workstations.

 Quick Quiz

1. Computer-based systems should include _____ factors in their design to avoid creating inflexible, difficult systems.

2. In computer _____ , personal data is matched with other types of data in computer databases.

3. Many _____ laws have been enacted to legally protect the privacy of consumers and employees.

4. Using computers to monitor employee job performance is known as computer _____ .

5. Safe, comfortable, and pleasant work environments and tools such as computers are the goals of _____ design.

Answers: 1. human 2. matching 3. privacy 4. monitoring
5. ergonomic

End Note: End Users and Computer Challenges

In this chapter we have surveyed both the beneficial and adverse effects of computers on society. You should have seen that computers can be used ille-

REAL-WORLD EXAMPLE

University of California at Los Angeles:
Virus Attack

It all started at about 3 o'clock on an otherwise quiet Wednesday afternoon. Barry Gerber, administrative director of Social Sciences Computing at the University of California at Los Angeles, tells the story:

Mike Franks, a member of our staff, rushed in to report that things seemed to be falling apart on the network in one of the computer labs. The end of the academic quarter was nearing, and the lab was packed. Nearly 70 student users were logged into the lab from inside and outside. Users couldn't run certain software. Some couldn't even log in. Many reported receiving the NetWare operating system's maddening "network error—abort, retry" message.

Based on past experience and the error message, I suspected a cable break or a failure in the network operating system. I ran Novell's FCONSOLE diagnostic program to see how we were doing on server memory and disk and LAN I/O. I couldn't find anything out of the ordinary. Meanwhile, we started getting calls from another lab. Users there reported similar experiences. It was starting to look like a disaster of major proportions. At this point, I suggested that all users log off the server, then we could bring it down and back up. It had been running for 136 days. Maybe it just needed a good memory flushing. That didn't help. After that, we shut down the labs.

Then George Bing, another member of my staff, started searching for viruses using the SCAN virus detector program. George soon reported that he'd found the Jerusalem virus on the server that provides most of the services to the lab. NetWare's own LOGIN program was infected. That, of course, was why people couldn't log in. It also was the likely source of those network errors. Soon all the resources of our staff were turned to tracking down the virus. We found it in two diagnostic programs I'd run. It was starting to look like I was the culprit, until we found the virus in WordPerfect's WP.EXE program file on the LAN. We soon realized that most of the damage had been done by our staff when they logged in with supervisors' rights from lab machines which had become infected by students who brought in their own infected programs on floppy disks.

By 8 p.m., things were back to normal. We had to replace a number of infected files with copies from other servers or from our tape backups. Our encounter with the Jerusalem virus cost us about 25 person-hours. It also seriously disrupted the lives of a couple hundred of the students who use our labs. However, the experience taught us that we have little to fear, if we're careful. We now make it a practice to check our local disks with SCAN before logging into the network, and we don't log in with supervisors' rights from lab machines unless we absolutely must.

1. How were the computer labs at UCLA infected with computer virus? How did it spread?

2. What damage was done, what security measures were used, and what lessons were learned?

gally for criminal activity or can be used to help solve the problems of society. You have also seen how end users and IS professionals can develop a variety of information system, procedural, and physical controls to help protect the security and quality of computer-based systems. We have also discussed how computers can have both good and bad effects on employment, individuality, the workplace, and the right to privacy. Finally, we have discussed a variety of issues relating to the impact on our health of the use of computers in the modern workplace.

E T H I C S

Ethical Issues in Computing

Throughout this text, we have dealt with issues in **computer ethics** such as computer crime, privacy issues, and a variety of abuses of computer power. Therefore, you should now be better able to recognize whether a computer-based situation is ethical or unethical or has no ethical dimension. Let's look at five typical scenarios and see if you can answer some simple questions about their ethical content.

Situation 1: The silent manager. A programming department manager discovers that one of his programmers and another from the inventory control department are involved in a corporate plan to defraud company stockholders by inflating company assets. The programs in question passed his quality assurance testing because they were identified as simulation and test files. Eventually, the fraud was discovered and the perpetrators were prosecuted. The programming manager—who is responsible for all applications programming throughout the company, but who had told no one of the scheme—was identified as an unindicted conspirator.

Situation 2: The bare-bones system. A programming analyst at a large retailer is charged with project responsibility for building a customer billing and credit system. During the project, money runs out. The programming analyst had continually warned management about impending problems but was told to keep going and finish the development of a bare-bones system as quickly and cheaply as possible. To meet this directive, several key features, including safeguards, error detection, and correction, had to be left out until later versions. After a difficult and costly conversion to the new system, a great many unfixable problems arose, including wrong and unreadable billings and credit statements. Customers were outraged, fraud increased, company profits fell, and the project leader was blamed for it all.

Situation 3: The nosy security manager. The information security manager at a large company also acted as administrator of a huge electronic mail network. During his regular monitoring of mail, the manager discovered personal messages about football bets, sexual encounters, and other nonbusiness matters. Printed listings of the messages were regularly given to the company's human resources director and corporate security director. In some cases, managers punished employees, using the messages as evidence. Employees became angry, charging their privacy rights on E-mail were the same as on the company's telephone or interoffice mail system.

Situation 4: All work, no play. The manager of research at a computer company explicitly told workers that anyone found playing games on company computers would be subject to dismissal. On a random inspection, a computer game was discovered in the files of a programmer, who was then punished.

(continued on following page)

(continued from previous page)

Situation 5: It's not our job. A software professional was charged with developing control software for part of a large system. The job looked straightforward and trouble-free. To work, the software required input from other units in the system. The developer then read an article by a noted software specialist and was convinced that input from the other units could not be trusted. So he decided that neither the software he was designing nor the unit his company was providing would do the job they were supposed to. He showed his supervisor the article and explained his concerns but was told only to worry about his group's part of the project.

What Do You Think?

Situation 1: Was the manager unethical in not responding to evidence of wrongdoing?

Situation 2: Was it unethical for the project leader to order the system into production prematurely?

Situation 3: Was it ethical for the information security manager to monitor E-mail and inform management of personal use?

Situation 4: Was it ethical for the manager to prohibit the use of computer games in employee files?

Situation 5: Was it ethical for the developer to continue working on the project?

What Do the Experts Think?

A panel of 27 IS professionals, ethical philosophers, and attorneys were asked by SRI International to evaluate these scenarios. Here are their answers.

Situation 1: *unethical: 23; not unethical: 1; no ethics issue: 0.*

Situation 2: *unethical: 24; not unethical: 0; no ethics issue: 0.*

Situation 3: *unethical: 22; not unethical: 2; no ethics issue: 0.*

Situation 4: *unethical: 7; not unethical: 5; no ethics issue: 13.*

Situation 5: *unethical: 12; not unethical: 7; no ethics issue: 1.*

Source: Adapted from Glenn Rifkin, "The Ethics Gap," *Computerworld,* October 14, 1991, p. 85.

It should now be obvious to you that many of the adverse effects of computers on society are caused by people or organizations who are not accepting their ethical responsibilities in either the design or use of computer-based systems. Like other powerful tools, computers possess great potential for good or ill. This is especially true as our information society continues to become more dependent on them. So you and every end user can help assure the use of computers for the good of society by accepting your responsibility for the proper control and beneficial use of computers.

You can respond to the challenges posed by computers by acting as a socially responsible end user. Then you will

- Act with integrity in your development and use of computer-based systems.
- Strive to increase your computer competency.
- Set high standards for computing performance.
- Accept responsibility for the results of your computing.
- Use computers to advance the general welfare of other end users, your organization, and society.

Summary

Computer Crime   Computer crime is a growing threat to society. Such crimes use computers for illegal purposes or involve the theft, alteration, destruction, or unauthorized use of hardware, software, or data resources. Computer viruses and worms that reproduce themselves throughout networked computer systems also pose a major threat. Several major laws have been enacted to counter computer crime, including the Computer Fraud and Abuse Act.

Computer Security and Controls   Controls are needed that ensure the security and quality of the computing activities and resources of an organization and its end users. Such controls attempt to minimize errors, computer crime, and destruction in computer-based systems. Controls can be grouped into the three major categories of information system controls, procedural controls, and physical controls.

Computers and Society   Computers have had a major impact on society. Societal computer solutions provide a direct beneficial effect to society when they are used to solve human and social problems. Computers have had both beneficial and detrimental effects on employment, individuality, and the quality of work.

Privacy and Health Issues   Computers pose a potential threat to the privacy and health of individuals. Databases of personal information held by businesses, credit bureaus, and government agencies are subject to unauthorized access and use that can seriously damage individual privacy rights. Several federal laws exist to protect the privacy of computer databases. Computer-based systems can also seriously affect the health of workers through job stress, muscle/skeletal strain, eye strain, radiation from CRTs, and accidents with robots and computer-controlled machines. The ergonomic design of workstations and the work environment can help improve the health and safety of computer workers.

Key Terms and Concepts

audit trail
biometric controls
computer crime
computer virus
computers and health
computers and privacy

control totals
disaster recovery
ergonomics
ethical end user computing
hacking

Review Quiz

True/False

_____ 1. The goal of computer security is to ensure the quality, integrity, and safety of computer system activities and resources.

_____ 2. Control totals are an example of a physical control.

_____ 3. Fire and access detection systems are examples of procedural controls.

_____ 4. Computers may cause job stress, muscle and eye strain, and radiation exposure.

_____ 5. Employees may have to retrain or transfer because of computers.

_____ 6. A computer virus can be eradicated by turning off your computer.

_____ 7. Personal information in computer-accessible databases is invulnerable to unauthorized access.

_____ 8. Computer monitoring involves surveillance of worker activities.

_____ 9. Human factors design includes giving people a variety of choices when using computers.

_____ 10. End users acting with integrity and competence in their work are practicing ethical computing.

Multiple Choice

_____ 1. A data-entry screen that helps you properly enter data into a computer screen is an example of

    a. an input control.
    b. a processing control.
    c. an output control.
    d. a storage control.

_____ 2. Checkpoints in a program are an example of

    a. an input control.
    b. a processing control.
    c. an output control.
    d. a storage control.

_____ 3. Backup files are an example of

    a. an input control.
    b. a processing control.
    c. an output control.
    d. a storage control.

_____ 4. Control listings are an example of

a. an input control.
b. a processing control.
c. an output control.
d. a storage control.

_____ 5. Unauthorized use of your computer resources by someone else is an example of

a. money theft.
b. service theft.
c. software piracy.
d. data theft.

_____ 6. An "electronic sweatshop" work environment can be created by

a. computer viruses.
b. computer matching.
c. computer monitoring.
d. computer analysis.

_____ 7. Comparing the Social Security numbers of individuals in various computerized files is called

a. computer viruses.
b. computer matching.
c. computer monitoring.
d. computer analysis.

_____ 8. Health issues in computing may include

a. job stress.
b. muscle strain.
c. eye strain.
d. all of the above.

_____ 9. The possible radiation hazard in computing is attributed to

a. CRTs.
b. LCDs.
c. laser printers.
d. optical scanners.

_____ 10. Ergonomic solutions to computer health issues include safe, comfortable, and healthy

a. workstations.
b. work environments.
c. work procedures.
d. all of the above.

Fill-in

1. Computerized monitoring of environmental quality is an example of _____.

2. Fraudulent transfer of funds by computers is an example of _____.

3. Electronic breaking and entering into a computer system is called _____.

4. A(n) _____ is a program that makes copies of itself into other computers and destroys their data and programs.

5. Computer monitoring of workers may create a stressful _____ environment.

6. Voice verification, handprint analysis, and retina scanning are examples of _____ controls.

7. The goal of _____ is a computerized workplace that is safe, comfortable, and easy to use.

8. Comparing Social Security numbers of individual records in several databases is known as _____.

9. Requiring end users to make backup copies of their hard disks each night is an example of _____ controls.

10. A(n) _____ allows you to check what happened to a transaction during its stages of processing.

Questions for Thought and Discussion

1. Is it a crime for employees to use their companies' computers to write personal letters or play computer games during their lunch hours? Why or why not?

2. Suppose a computer-literate student found a loophole in a university's student information system and used it to read other student's records. Would this be ethical? Should this student notify someone about the loophole? Explain your reasoning.

3. Suppose a student needs to use an expensive software package to complete class assignments. Is it ethical for the student to make a copy of the package provided in the school's computer lab, so she or he can use it at home, even if the software clearly forbids unauthorized use? Explain your reasoning.

4. Refer to the Real-World Example on Carnegie-Mellon and Rice Universities in the chapter. Do you think the Internet computer systems and networks involved could have been better protected against such intrusions? Explain.

5. What are some specific ways that you and other end users can protect your computer system resources? Be sure to mention the role of procedural, physical, and information system controls in your answer.

6. Refer to the Real-World Example of Citicorp in the chapter. Are its detection systems an example of improper computer monitoring of workers? Explain.

7. What are some specific ways you can protect your computer system from errors, computer crime, computer viruses, and accidents? Explain.

8. Refer to the Real-World Example of the University of California at Los Angeles. Do you think students deliberately infected the system with a virus? Why or why not?

9. What are some societal solutions of computers? Give several examples of the good things that computers can do in society.

10. What are some concerns you have about the use of computers after reading this chapter? For example, are you concerned about computer crime, computer viruses, computer job displacement, computer monitoring of

workers, or computer health hazards? Do additional research on your areas of concern at your library. Make a brief report to the class.

Review Quiz Answers

True/False: 1. T 2. F 3. F 4. T 5. T 6. F 7. F 8. T 9. T 10. T

Multiple Choice: 1. a 2. b 3. d 4. c 5. b 6. c 7. b 8. d 9. a 10. d

Multiple Choice: 1. societal solutions of computers 2. computer crime 3. hacking 4. computer virus 5. work 6. biometric 7. ergonomics 8. computer matching 9. procedural 10. audit trail

V I E W P O I N T

COMPUTERS PAST AND FUTURE

TRENDS IN COMPUTING

As a computer-literate end user, you should be prepared for future computing developments. That's why it is important to understand the major trends that have developed in each stage or **generation** of computing. The first generation of computers began in the early 1950s, the second generation in the late 1950s, the third generation in the mid-1960s, while the fourth generation began in the early 1970s and continues to the present time. A fifth generation of computers is expected to arrive during the 1990s.

Volumes could be written on the past, present, and future of computers. Instead, this brief essay provides you with a summary of the origins and generations of computing. It should give you an overview of significant historical developments in computing, as well as the trends expected to continue into your future.

The Origins of Computing Machines

Manual Computing

Early humans used their fingers, stones, and sticks as computing devices. Babylonians wrote on clay tablets while ancient Egyptians developed written records on paper made of papyrus.

The earliest form of manual calculating device is the *abacus*. The abacus was used for thousands of years in many civilizations. It is still used in China as a calculator.

Machine Computing

The first machinery to perform arithmetic operations were developed in seventeenth-century Europe. Blaise Pascal of France is credited with developing the *adding machine* and Gottfried von Liebnitz of Germany developed the *calculating machine*. However, these and other early mechanical data processing devices were not reliable machines. It took the next two centuries of experimentation before a practical, working computing machine was developed.

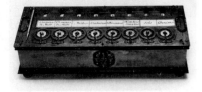

Electromechanical Computing

Electromechanical punched card machines were developed by Joseph Jacquard of France during the eighteenth century. Originally designed to control textile weaving equipment, they were later used for data processing by the statistician, Dr. Herman Hollerith, of the U.S. Census Bureau in the 1880s. This machine processed data recorded by holes punched in paper cards. Dr. Hollerith eventually started the Tabulating Machine Company to manufacture punched card machines. International Business Machines Corporation (IBM) is a descendant of that firm.

By the 1930s, improved punched card machines "read" data from punched cards when electrical impulses were generated by the action of metal brushes making contact through the holes in the punched cards. These "automatic data processing" (ADP) machines were used in business and government until the late 1950s when they became obsolete by the development of computers.

Computer Pioneers

The Origin of Modern Computers

Charles Babbage designed and partially built a steam-driven mechanical calculator called the "difference engine" that is considered to be the first proposed concept of the modern computer. His model was designed to accept punched card input, automatically perform any arithmetic operation in any sequence under the direction of a mechanically stored program of instructions, and produce either punched card or printed output.

Babbage had designed the first *general-purpose, stored pro-*

THE LATE MR. BABBAGE.

gram digital computer. However, the concept would have to wait for over 100 years for the development of electrical and electronic components before it could be built.

Lady Augusta Ada Byron, Countess of Lovelace, daughter of Lord Byron the English poet, recorded and analyzed many of Babbage's ideas. She is considered by some to be the world's first computer programmer. **Ada,** a programming language, is named in her honor.

Electromechanical Computers

Almost 100 years later a pioneering period began in which Babbage's ideas were further developed. Vannevar Bush of MIT built a large-scale electromechanical analog computer in 1925, which measured changes in voltage to compute approximate answers to mechanical problems. In 1941, Konrad Zuse of Germany built an electromechanical digital com-

puter called the Z3 that used electrical switches (relays) to perform its computations. The Z3 was a digital computer in that it performed computations on numbers (digits), and thus its calculations were as precise as the data it was given.

Howard Aiken of Harvard University, with support of IBM, developed the first large-scale electro-mechanical digital computer in 1944. The Automatic Sequence Controlled Calculator, nicknamed MARK I, used electrical relays instead of mechanical gears.

Electronic Computers

The first working model of an electronic digital computer was built by John Atanasoff of Iowa State University in 1942. The ABC (Atanasoff-Berry Computer) used vacuum tubes instead of electrical relays to carry out its computations.

The first operational electronic digital computer, the ENIAC (Electronic Numerical Integrator and Calculator), developed by John Mauchly and J. P. Eckert of the

University of Pennsylvania in 1946, weighed over 30 tons and utilized over 18,000 vacuum tubes. It was controlled by external switches that had to be changed for each new series of computations.

The first stored-program electron computer was the Electronic Delayed Storage Automatic Computer (EDSAC), developed under the direction of M. V. Wilkes of Cambridge University, England, in 1949. EDSAC and several other early electronic computers were based on the concepts of Charles Babbage and those advanced in 1945 by John von Neumann of the Institute for Advance Study at Princeton University. Von Neumann proposed the *stored-program* concept, where the operating instructions, or programs of computers, are stored in a high-speed internal storage unit or *memory*.

Von Neumann also proposed that both data and instructions be represented internally by the *binary* number system (which uses only the two digits 0 and 1).

The First Three Generations—The Technical Highlights

First Generation

The UNIVAC I (Univeral Automatic Computer), the first general-purpose electronic digital computer to be commercially available, marks the beginning of the first generation of computers.

- The first Univac was installed at the U.S. Census Bureau in 1951. It used vacuum tubes for its circuitry and memory and magnetic tape as an input and output medium.

- The IBM 650, an intermediate-size computer designed for both business and scientific applications, used a magnetic drum memory and punched cards for input and output.

- Unlike the special purpose, one-of-a-kind machines of earlier years, general-purpose, first generation computers were duplicated. Forty-eight UNIVAC Is and almost 2,000 IBM 650s were built. These machines were quite large and their hundreds or thousands of vacuum tubes generated enormous amounts of heat.

Second Generation
New developments in 1959 marked the beginning of the next generation of computers.

- Vacuum tubes were replaced by **transistors** and other *solid-state, semiconductor* devices. Transistorized circuits were much smaller, generated little heat, were less expensive, and

required less power than vacuum tubes.

- Tiny *magnetic cores* were used for the computer's memory, or internal storage. Removable *magnetic disk packs* were introduced, and magnetic tape emerged as the major input, output, and additional storage medium for large computer installations.

Third Generation
The IBM System 360 series of computers marked the arrival of the third generation in 1964.

- **Integrated circuits** in which all the elements of a complex elec-

tronic circuit are contained on a small *silicon chip* replaced transistorized circuitry.

- *Time sharing,* where many users at different terminals share the same computer, emerged. *Data communications* networks and the ability to process several programs simultaneously (*multiprogramming*) also marked the third generation.

- Software increased in importance as a means to more efficiently use computers. *Operating system* programs were developed to supervise computer processing. High-level programming languages such as FORTRAN and COBOL greatly simplified computer programming by more closely resembling natural language or standard mathematical notations.

- **Application software packages** for end users proliferated as the number of independent software companies grew. This resulted from the discontinuation of *bundling* software and hardware in 1969 by IBM and other manufacturers. Hard-

ware and software started to be sold separately.

- The first **minicomputer,** the PDP-8, appeared on the market in 1965 from the Digital Equipment Corporation.

The Fourth Generation

We are now near the end of the fourth generation of computing. It began in the 1970s and continues to the present time.

Microelectronic Computing

- Thousands of electronic circuits were placed on tiny chips of silicon in LSI (large-scale integration) semiconductor circuit technology for use as *logic* and *memory* chips. *Semiconductor memory chips* began to replace the *magnetic core* memories of earlier computers.

- In 1971, the Intel 4004 became the first commercially available **microprocessor.** All of the circuitry for the main processing unit was placed on a single chip. Three years later Intel had developed the 8080 microprocessor used in the first commercially available **microcomputer system,** the Altair 8800, which appeared on the market in 1975.

- Microcomputer sales and uses did not grow dramatically until the development of the Apple II by Steve Jobs and Steve Wozniak in 1978 and the IBM Personal Computer in 1981.

- By the mid-1980s, millions of microcomputer systems were used in homes, schools, and businesses.

- Main memory capacity of fourth-generation computers increased dramatically over the early second-generation computers. The old, medium-size IBM 1401 had a memory of only 4,000 to

16,000 character positions of storage. Now, even microcomputers have memories ranging from hundreds of thousands to millions of storage positions. The cost of such memory has dropped from about $2 per character to only a fraction of a cent per character of storage.

- Microminiaturization significantly reduced cost, size, and power requirements and increased processing speeds. Speeds in the billionths of a second and in millions of instructions per second are now common. The processing power of third-generation computers that once cost hundreds of thousands of dollars can now be purchased for only a few thousand dollars in the fourth-generation.

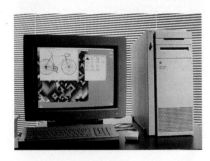

User-Friendly Computing

- The increased use of *direct input/output* devices provided a more natural *user interface*. Keyboards were joined with the electronic mouse, trackball, light pens, touch screens, and optical scanning wands for easy entering of data and instructions. Direct output of information through video displays of text and graphics and audio

(voice) response devices also became commonplace.

- The software trend toward easy-to-use graphical user interfaces (GUIs) was led by the Apple Macintosh beginning in 1984 and Microsoft Windows in 1988.

- Easy-to-use *productivity software* packages for microcomputers, led by the VisiCalc *electronic spreadsheet* and Word Star *word processing* packages developed in 1979, and the dBASE II *database management* package and the Lotus 1-2-3 spreadsheet package developed in 1982, contributed to the purchase of millions of soft-

ware packages by microcomputer users.

The Fifth Generation: The Future

As Table 1 illustrates, several major trends that began in past generations continue to develop today, leading into a fifth generation of computing that began in the 1990s and will continue into the next century.

Intelligent Computers

Intelligent computers with the ability to think, see, feel, listen, and talk are the goal of the fifth generation. These computers will depend on *parallel processing* computer architecture instead of the serial processing of most current computers. Thus, data and instructions will be processed many at a time instead of one at a time. The development of intelligent computers is one of the major goals of the science of *artificial intelligence (AI)*.

Table 1
Key Trends in Computing: First to Fifth Generations

	First Generation	Second Generation	Third Generation	Fourth Generation	Fifth Generation
Size (typical computers)	Room Size	Closet size	Desk-size micrcomputer	Typewriter-size minicomputer	Credit card-size micro?
Circuitry	Vacuum tubes	Transistors	Integrated semi-conductor circuits	Large-scale integrated (LSI) semiconductor circuits	Very large-scale integrated (VLSI) superconductor circuits?
Density (circuits per component)	One	Hundreds	Thousands	Hundreds of thousands	Millions?
Speed (instructions/second)	Hundreds	Thousands	Millions	Tens of millions	Billions?
Reliability (failure of circuits)	Hours	Days	Weeks	Months	Years?
Memory (capacity in characters)	Thousands	Tens of thousands	Hundreds of thousands	Millions	Billions?
Cost (per million instructions)	$10	$1.00	$.10	$.001	$.0001?

Conversational Computing

Expect the acceleration of the trend toward new modes of computer communication with direct input of data and instructions through voice and visual input

coupled with voice and visual output. In the future, most end users will only have to talk and listen to a computer to get things done.

Circuitry

Hardware costs and sizes will continue to decrease steadily. VLSI (very large-scale integration) technology will allow hundreds of thousands, even millions, of circuit elements to be placed on a microelectronic chip. This should accelerate the development of *superconductor* circuit materials that do not need super cold temperatures to dramatically increase the speed of electronic circuits.

Optical and Bionic Computers

Also making their appearance are *optical computers* that use *photonic,* or optoelectronic, circuits rather than electronic circuits. They process data using pulses of laser light instead of electronic

pulses, and they operate near the speed of light. Even farther into the future are extremely small, fast, and powerful *biocomputers* grown from organic materials using individual cells as circuits.

Software

Computer software will continue to grow in its ease of use and versatility. Software will help us converse with computers in natural human languages. Programs will become integrated and multipurpose for easy use by nontechnical end users. Expert-system features will be built into many software packages to make them more powerful and easy to use.

Virtual Reality

Computer generated artificial realities may eventually emerge as the ultimate user interface. End uses will then communicate with computers simply by being there, behaving as if the simulated environment were real. *Virtual reality, cyberspace,* and *artificial reality* are all terms used to describe multisensory devices that allow users to effectively enter abstract spaces—to "pass through the looking glass,"—into an experience where the physical computer and viewer do not exist. You will most likely enter virtual environments for entertainment, but futurists see applications in the workplace and classroom as the next step.

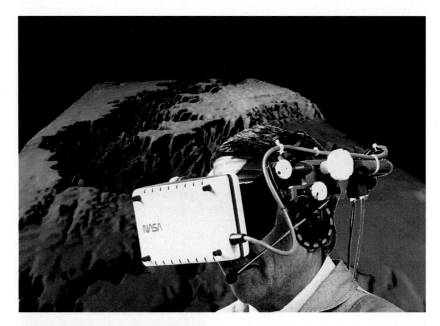

The Computing Society

Everyday use of computer-based systems will increase dramatically in many areas. *Smart products* with microcomputer intelligence, *electronic funds transfer* systems in banking, *point-of-sale* systems in retailing, *robotics* in manufacturing, *computer-assisted instruction* systems in education, *telecommuting* systems for in-home work activities, and *videotext* systems for electronic shopping, banking, and information services in the home will all become commonplace. Our society as a whole will become even more reliant on computers as we enter the twenty-first century. The goal of this text has been to prepare you for that moment. Happy computing!

APPENDIX

Computer Codes and Number Systems

In Chapters 1 and 7, we introduced the concepts of the binary number system and binary codes used in all modern computers. In this appendix, we will discuss them in more detail for those students who want to delve deeper into the codes and number systems used by most modern computers.

The Binary Number System

By now you know that data is represented in a computer by either the presence or absence of electronic or other signals in its circuitry or in the media it uses. This is called a **binary**, or two state, representation of data, since only two possible states or conditions are possible. For example, electronic circuits can be either in a conducting (ON) or nonconducting (OFF) state, while media such as magnetic disks represent data with magnetized spots whose magnetic fields can have two different directions or *polarities*.

So the **binary number system** (which has only two symbols, 0 and 1) is the basis for representing data in computers. For example, in a computer's electronic circuits, the conducting (ON) state represents a 1 and the nonconducting (OFF) state represents a 0. This means that a computer performs all of its operations by manipulating groups of zeroes and ones (bits) that represent data through the use of various binary-based computer codes.

Since the binary number system has only two symbols, 0 and 1, it is said to have a *base* of two. The familiar decimal system has a base of 10 since it uses 10 symbols (0 through 9). The binary symbol 0 or 1 is commonly called a **bit**, which is a contraction of the term *binary digit*. In the binary number system, all numbers are expressed as groups of binary digits *(bits)*, that is, as groups of zeroes and ones.

Conversion from Binary to Decimal

Just as in the decimal or any other number system, the value of a binary number depends on the postion or *place* of each digit in a grouping of binary digits. Figure A-1 shows how you can determine the decimal value of binary

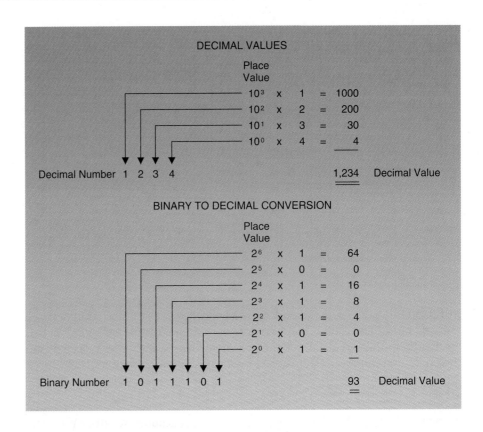

numbers. Values are based on the right-to-left position values, for example $(2^3, 2^3, 2^1, 2^0)$. Therefore, the rightmost position has a value of 1 (2^0); the next position to the left has a value of 2 (2^1); the next position a value of 4 (2^2); the next, 8 (2^3); the next, 16 (2^4); and so forth.

Thus, the decimal value of any binary number consists of adding together the values of each position in which there is a binary one digit and ignoring those positions that contain a binary *zero* digit. Table A-1 gives you a simple illustration of how you can convert from the binary number system to decimal values.

Binary Arithmetic

Arithmetic in the binary number system is like arithmetic in the decimal system—there are just less digits to worry about. For example, look at the following examples of binary addition and subtraction:

Binary Addition	**Binary Subtraction**
1011101	1011101
+1011	−1011
1101000	1010000

Notice that in these examples, you carry a one or borrow a one from the next position just as you do in decimal arithmetic. Notice especially that in binary arithmetic, 1 + 1 = 10! Since 1 is the highest number in the binary number

Table A-1
How the Binary Number System
Represents Decimal Values

Binary Position Values							
2^6	2^5	2^4	2^3	2^2	2^1	2^0	Examples of Equivalent Decimal Numbers
64	32	16	8	4	2	1	
Binary Numbers							
0	0	0	0	0	0	0	0
0	0	0	0	0	0	1	1
0	0	0	0	0	1	0	2
0	0	0	0	0	1	1	3
0	0	0	0	1	0	0	4
0	0	0	0	1	0	1	5
0	0	0	0	1	1	0	6
0	0	0	0	1	1	1	7
0	0	0	1	0	0	0	8
0	0	0	1	0	0	1	9
0	0	0	1	0	1	0	10
0	0	0	1	1	1	1	15
0	0	1	0	0	0	0	16
0	0	1	0	0	0	1	17
0	0	1	1	1	1	1	31
0	1	0	0	0	0	0	32
0	1	0	0	0	0	1	33
0	1	1	1	1	1	1	63
1	0	0	0	0	0	0	64
1	0	0	0	0	0	1	65

system, you must place a 0 at first position and carry a 1 to the next position. That's why a 10 is the binary equivalent of the decimal number 2. Other binary arithmetic operations such as multiplication and division are also similar to the way those operations are accomplished in the decimal number system.

The Hexadecimal Number System

The binary number system has the disadvantage of requiring a large number of bits to express a given number value. The hexadecimal number system, which has a base of 16, can replace the long *string* of ones and zeros that make up a binary number. This is also helpful in simplifying computer codes based on the binary number system, as we will see shortly. For example, several popular computer codes use eight bit positions to represent a character. The hexadecimal equivalent would need only two positions to represent the

Table A-2
Examples of Equivalents of Decimal Numbers in Binary and Hexadecimal Number Systems

Decimal	Binary	Hexadecimal
0	0	0
1	1	1
2	10	2
3	11	3
4	100	4
5	101	5
6	110	6
7	111	7
8	1000	8
9	1001	9
10	1010	A
11	1011	B
12	1100	C
13	1101	D
14	1110	E
15	1111	F
16	10000	10
17	10001	11
18	10010	12
19	10011	13
20	10100	14

same character. This makes it easier for professional programmers to decipher displays or printouts *(memory dumps)* of the data or instruction contents of primary storage.

Table A-2 shows examples of the binary and hexadecimal equivalents of the decimal numbers 0 through 20. Using the relationships in this table, you should be able to determine that the decimal number 21 would be expressed by the binary number 10101 and the hexadecimal number 15, and so on.

Computer Codes

Computers use several binary-based codes that use groups of bits to represent each character of data. These codes make the job of communicating with a computer easier and more efficient than using long "strings" of binary digits. You can consider them as shorthand methods of expressing binary numbers within a computer.

Table A-3 shows examples of the two popular computer codes. The most widely used code is the **American Standard Code for Information Interchange (ASCII)** (pronounced *as-key)*. It's standard form is a 7-bit code, but it is now widely used in its "extended" form (Extended ASCII), an 8-bit code that can represent 256 different characters. ASCII is used by most microcomputers and minicomputers, as well as by many larger computers. It has been adopted as a standard code by national and international standards organizations. Table A-3 also illustrates another computer code, the **Extended Binary Coded Decimal Interchange Code (EBCDIC)** (pronounced eb-si-dick). It is an 8-bit code that is used by IBM and other mini and mainframe computers.

Symbol	ASCII	EBCDIC	Symbol	ASCII	EBCDIC	Symbol	ASCII	EBCDIC
(space)	00100000	01000000	?	00111111	00110111	^	01011110	
!	00100001	01011010	@	01000000	01111100	—	01011111	
"	00100010	01111111	A	01000001	11000001	a	01100001	10000001
#	00100011	01111011	B	01000010	11000010	b	01100010	10000010
$	00100100	01011011	C	01000011	11000011	c	01100010	10000010
%	00100101	01101100	D	01000100	11000100	d	01100100	10000100
&	00100110	01010000	E	01000101	11000101	e	01100101	10000101
'	00100111	01111101	F	01000110	11000110	f	01100110	10000110
(	00101000	01001101	G	01000111	11000111	g	01100111	10000111
)	00101001	01011101	H	01001000	11001000	h	01101000	10001000
*	00101010	01011100	I	01001001	11001001	i	01101001	10001001
+	00101011	01001110	J	01001010	11010001	j	01101010	10010001
,	00101100	01101011	K	01001011	11010010	k	01101011	10010010
-	00101101	01100000	L	01001100	11010011	l	01101100	10010011
.	00101110	01001011	M	01001101	11010100	m	01101101	10010100
/	00101111	01100001	N	01001110	11010101	n	01101110	10010101
0	00110000	11110000	O	01001111	11010110	o	01101111	10010110
1	00110001	11110001	P	01010000	11010111	p	01110000	10010111
2	00110010	11110010	Q	01010001	11011000	q	01110001	10011000
3	00110011	11110011	R	01010010	11011001	r	01110010	10011001
4	00110100	11110100	S	01010011	11100010	s	01110011	10100010
5	00110101	11110101	T	01010100	11100011	t	01110100	10100011
6	00110110	11110110	U	01010101	11100100	u	01110101	10100100
7	00110111	11110111	V	01010110	11100101	v	01110110	10100101
8	00111000	11111000	W	01010111	11100110	w	01110111	10100110
9	00111001	11111001	X	01011000	11100111	x	01111000	10100111
:	00111010	01111010	Y	01011001	11101000	y	01111001	10101000
;	00111011	01011110	Z	01011010	11101001	z	01111010	10101001
<	00111100	01001100	[	01011011	01001010	{	01111011	
=	00111101	01111110	\	01011100		}	01111101	
>	00111110	01101110	]	01011101	01011010			

Table A-3
**Examples of Extended ASCII
and EBCDIC Computer Codes**

Note: Missing EBCDIC codes indicate
symbols not represented in the EBCDIC
coding system.

Glossary for End Users

Ada A programming language named after Augusta Ada Byron, considered the world's first computer programmer. Developed for the U.S. Department of Defense as a standard high-order language.

ad hoc inquiries Unique, unscheduled, situation-specific information requests.

ALGOL: ALGOrithmic Language An international procedure-oriented language that is widely used in Europe. Like FORTRAN, it was designed primarily for scientific-mathematical applications.

algorithm A set of well-defined rules or processes for the solution of a problem in a finite number of steps.

analog computer A computer that operates on data by measuring changes in continuous physical variables such as voltage, resistance, and rotation. Contrast with *digital computer*.

analytical modeling Interactive use of computer-based mathematical models to explore decision alternatives using what-if analysis, goal-seeking analysis, and optimization analysis.

APL: A Programming Language A mathematically oriented language originated by Kenneth E. Iverson of IBM. Realtime and iterative versions of APL are used by many time-sharing systems.

application generator A software package that supports the development of an application through an interactive terminal dialogue, where the programmer/analyst defines screens, reports, computations, and data structures.

application software Programs that specify the information processing activities required for the completion of specific tasks of computer users. Examples are electronic spreadsheet and word processing programs or inventory or payroll programs.

application-specific programs Application software packages that support specific applications of end users in business, science and engineering, and other areas.

application development See *systems development*.

arithmetic-logic unit (ALU) The unit of a computing system containing the circuits that perform arithmetic and logical operations.

artificial intelligence (AI) A science and technology whose goal is to develop computers that can think, as well as see, hear, walk, talk, and feel. A major thrust is the development of computer functions normally associated with human intelligence, for example, reasoning, learning, and problem solving. Major areas of AI research and development include cognitive science, computer science, robotics, and natural language applications.

ASCII: American Standard Code for Information Interchange A standard code used for information interchange among data processing systems, communication systems, and associated equipment.

assembler A computer program that translates an assembler language into machine language.

assembler language A programming language that utilizes symbols to represent operation codes and storage locations.

asynchronous In data transmission, involving the use of start and stop bits with each character to indicate the beginning and end of the character being transmitted.

audio-response unit An output device of a computer system whose output consists of the spoken word. Also called a voice synthesizer.

audit trail The presence of media and procedures that allow a transaction to be traced through all states of information processing, beginning with its appearance on a source document and ending with its transformation into information on a final output document.

automatic teller machine (ATM) A special-purpose transaction terminal used to provide remote banking services.

auxiliary storage Storage that supplements the primary storage of the computer. Same as *secondary storage*.

background processing The automatic execution of lower-priority computer programs when higher-priority programs are not using the resources of the computer system. Contrast with *foreground processing*.

bar codes Vertical marks or bars placed on merchandise tags or packaging that can be sensed and read by optical character-reading devises. The width and combination of vertical lines are used to represent data.

BASIC: Beginner's All-purpose Symbolic Instruction Code A programming language developed at Dartmouth College that is popular for microcomputer and time-sharing systems.

batch processing A category of data processing in which data is accumulated into "batches" and processed periodically. Contrast with *realtime processing*.

baud A unit of measurement used to specify data transmission speeds. It is a unit of signaling speed equal to the number of discrete conditions or signal events per second. In many data communications applications it represents one bit per second.

binary Pertaining to characteristic or property in which there are two possibilities, or pertaining to the number system that utilizes a base of two.

bit A contraction of "binary digit." It can have the value of 0 or 1.

block A grouping of continuous data records or other data elements that are handled as a unit.

bootstrap A technique in which the first few instructions of a program are sufficient to bring the rest of itself into the computer from an input device.

branch A transfer of control from one instruction to another that is not part of the normal sequential execution of the instructions of a computer program.

buffer Temporary storage used to compensate for a difference in rate of flow of data, or time of occurrence of events, when transmitting data from one device to another.

bug A mistake or malfunction.

bulletin board system (BBS) A service of personal computer networks in which electronic messages, data files, or programs can be stored for other subscribers to read or copy.

bundling The inclusion of software, maintenance, training, and other products or services in the price of a computer system.

bus A set of conducting paths for movement of data and instructions that interconnects the various components of the CPU.

byte A sequence of adjacent binary digits operated on as a unit and usually shorter than a computer word. In many computer systems, a byte is a grouping of eight bits that can represent one alphabetic or special character.

C A low-level structured programming language developed by AT&T-Bell Laboratories. It resembles a machine-independent assembler language and is popular for software package development.

cache memory A high-speed temporary storage area in the CPU for storing parts of a program or during processing.

cathode ray tube (CRT)   An electronic vacuum tube (television picture tube) that displays the output of a computer system.

CD-ROM   An optical disk technology for microcomputers featuring compact disks with a storage capacity of over 500 megabytes.

cellular radio   A radio communications technology that divides a metropolitan area into a honeycomb of cells to greatly increase the number of frequencies and thus the users that can take advantage of mobile phone service.

central processing unit (CPU)   The unit of a computer system that includes the circuits that control the interpretation and execution of instructions. In many computer systems, the CPU includes an arithmetic-logic unit and the control unit.

channel   A path along which signals can be sent. Also, a small special-purpose processor that controls the movement of data between the CPU and input/output devices.

charge-coupled device (CCD)   A slower serial access form of semiconductor memory that uses a silicon crystal's own structure to store data.

check bit   A binary check digit; for example, a parity bit.

check digit   A digit in a data field that is utilized to check for errors or loss of characters in the data field as a result of data transfer operations.

check point   A place in a program where a check or a recording of data for restart purposes is performed.

chief information officer   A senior management position that oversees all information technology for a firm, concentrating on long-range information system planning and strategy.

client/server network   A computing environment where end user workstations (clients) are connected to micro- or mini-LAN servers and possibly to mainframe *superservers*.

clock   A device that generates periodic signals utilized to control the timing of a computer. Also, a register whose contents change at regular intervals in such a way as to measure time.

coaxial cable   A sturdy copper or aluminum wire wrapped with spacers to insulate and protect it. Groups of coaxial cables may also be bundled together in a bigger cable for ease of installation.

COBOL: Common Business Oriented Language   A widely used business data processing programming language.

CODASYL: COnference on DAta SYstems Languages   The group of representatives of users and computer manufacturers who developed and maintain the COBOL language.

code   Computer instructions.

common carrier   An organization that supplies communications services to other organizations and to the public as authorized by government agencies.

communications satellite   Earth satellites placed in stationary orbits above the equator that serve as relay stations for communications signals transmitted from earth stations.

compiler   A program that translates a high-level programming language into a machine language program.

computer   A device that has the ability to accept data, internally store and execute a program of instructions, perform mathematical, logical, and manipulative operations on data, and report the results.

computer-aided design (CAD)   The use of computers and advanced graphics hardware and software to provide interactive design assistance for engineering and architectural design.

computer-aided engineering   The use of computers to simulate, analyze, and evaluate models of product designs and production processes developed using computer-aided design methods.

computer-aided manufacturing (CAM)   The use of computers to automate the production process and operations of a manufacturing plant. Also called factory automation.

computer-aided software engineering (CASE)   Same as computer-aided systems engineering, but emphasizing the importance of software development.

computer-aided systems engineering (CASE)   Using software packages to accomplish and automate many of the activities of information systems development, including software development or programming.

computer application   The use of a computer to solve a specific problem or to accomplish a particular job for an end user. For example, common business computer applications include sales order processing, inventory control, and payroll.

computer-assisted instruction (CAI)   The use of computers to provide drills, practice exercises, and tutorial sequences to students.

computer-based information system   An information system that uses computer hardware and software to perform its information processing activities.

computer crime   Criminal actions accomplished through the use of computer systems, especially with intent to defraud, destroy, or make unauthorized use of computer system resources.

computer ethics   A system of principles governing the legal, professional, social, and moral responsibilities of computer specialists and end users.

computer generations   Major stages in the historical development of computing.

computer graphics   Using computer generated images to analyze and interpret data, present information, and do computer-aided design and art.

computer-integrated manufacturing (CIM)   An overall concept stressing that the goals of computer use in factory automation should be to simplify, automate, and integrate production processes and other aspects of manufacturing.

computer program   A series of instructions or statements, in a form acceptable to a computer, prepared in order to achieve a certain result.

computer system   Computer hardware as a system of input, processing, output, storage, and control components. Thus a computer system consists of input and output devices, primary and secondary storage devices, the central processing unit, the control unit within the CPU, and other peripheral devices.

computer terminal   Any input/output device connected by telecommunications links to a computer.

computer virus or worm   Program code that copies its annoying or destructive program routines into the computer systems of anyone who accesses computer systems that have used the program, or anyone who uses copies of data or programs taken from such computers. This spreads the destruction of data and programs among many computer users. Technically, a *virus* will not run unaided, but must be inserted into another program, while a *worm* is a distinct program that can run unaided.

concentrator   A special-purpose computer that accepts information from many terminals using slow-speed lines and transmits data to a main computer system over a high-speed line.

connectivity   The degree to which hardware, software, and databases can be easily linked together in a telecommunications network.

control   The systems component that evaluates feedback to determine whether the system is moving toward the achievement of its goal and then makes any necessary adjustments to the input and processing components of the system to ensure that proper output is produced.

control listing A detailed report that describes each transaction occurring during a period.

control unit A subunit of the central processing unit that controls and directs the operations of the computer system. The control unit retrieves computer instructions in proper sequence, interprets each instruction, and then directs the other parts of the computer system in their implementation.

conversion The process in which the hardware, software, people, and data resources of an old information system must be converted to the requirements of a new information system. This usually involves a parallel, phased, pilot, or plunge conversation process from the old to the new system.

cooperative processing Allows the various types of computers in a distributed processing network to share the processing of parts of an end user's application.

counter A devise such as a register or storage location used to represent the number of occurrences of an event.

cursor A movable point of light displayed on most video display screens to assist the user in the input of data.

data Facts or observations about physical phenomena or business transactions. More specifically, data are objective measurements of the characteristics of *entities* such as people, places, things, and events.

data bank A comprehensive collection of libraries of data.

database A collection of logically related records or files. A database consolidates many records previously stored in separate files so that a common pool of data records serves many applications.

database administration A data resource management function that includes responsibility for developing and maintaining the organization's data dictionary, designing and monitoring the performance of databases, and enforcing standards for database use and security.

database administrator A specialist responsible for maintaining standards for the development, maintenance, and security of an organization's databases.

database management approach An approach to the storage and processing of data in which independent files are consolidated into a common pool or database of records available to different application programs and end users for processing and data retrieval.

database management system (DBMS) A set of computer programs that controls the creation, maintenance, and utilization of the databases of an organization.

data center An organizational unit that uses centralized computing resources to perform information processing activities for an organization. Also known as a computer center.

data communications See *telecommunications.*

data dictionary A software module and database containing descriptions and definitions concerning the structure, data elements, interrelationships, and other characteristics of an organization's databases.

data entry The process of converting data into a form suitable for entry into a computer system.

data flow diagrams A graphic diagramming tool that uses a few simple symbols to illustrate the flow of data among external entities, processing activities, and data storage elements.

data processing The execution of a systematic sequence of operations performed upon data to transform it into information.

debug To detect, locate, and remove errors from a program or malfunctions from a computer.

decision support system (DSS) An information system that utilizes decision models, a database, and a decision maker's own insights in an ad hoc, interactive analytical modeling process to reach a decision.

demand reports and responses Information provided whenever a manager or end user demands it.

desk-top accessory package A software package that provides features such as a calculator, note pad, alarm clock, phone directory, and appointment book that is available as a pop-up window on a computer display screen at the touch of a key.

desktop publishing The use of microcomputers, laser printers, and page-makeup software to produce a variety of printed materials, formerly done only by professional printers.

development centers Systems development consultant groups formed to serve as consultants to the professional programmers and systems analysts of an organization to improve their application development efforts.

digital computer A computer that operates on digital data by performing arithmetic and logical operations on the data. Contrast with *analog computer.*

digitizer A device that is used to convert drawings and other graphic images on paper or other materials into digital data that is entered into a computer system.

direct access A method of storage where each storage position has a unique address and can be individually accessed in approximately the same period of time without having to search through storage positions.

direct-access storage device (DASD) A storage device that can directly access data to be stored or retrieved, for example, a magnetic disk unit.

direct input/output Devices such as terminals that allow data to be input into a computer system or output from the computer system without the use of machine-readable media.

disk pack A removable unit containing several magnetic disks that can be mounted on a magnetic disk storage unit.

distributed processing A form of decentralization of information processing made possible by a network of computers dispersed throughout an organization.

document (1) A medium on which data has been recorded for human use , such as a report or invoice. (2) In word processing a generic term for text material such as letters, memos, reports, and so on.

documentation A collection of documents or information that describes a computer program, information system, or required data processing operations.

downtime The time interval during which a device is malfunctioning or inoperative.

dump To copy the contents of all or part of a storage devise, usually from an internal device, onto an external storage device.

duplex In communications, pertaining to a simultaneous two-way independent transmission in both directions.

EBCDIC: Extended Binary Coded Decimal Interchange Code An eight-bit code that is widely used by mainframe computers.

echo check A method of checking the accuracy of transmission of data in which the received data are returned to the sending device for comparison with the original data.

economic feasibility Whether expected costs savings, increased revenue, increased profits, and reductions in required investment exceed the costs of developing and operating a proposed system.

EDI: Electronic Data Interchange The electronic transmission of source documents between the computers of different organizations.

edit To modify the form or format of data, for example, to insert or delete characters such as page numbers or decimal points.

EFT: Electronic Funds Transfer The development of banking and payment systems that transfer funds electronically instead of using cash or paper documents such as checks.

electronic data processing (EDP) The use of electronic computers to process data automatically.

electronic document management An image-processing technology in which an electronic document may consist of digitized voice notes and electronic graphics images, as well as digitized images of traditional documents.

electronic mail The transmission, storage, and distribution of text material in electronic form over communications networks.

electronic meeting systems (EMS) The use of video and audio communications to allow conferences and meetings to be held with participants who may be geographically dispersed or may be present in the same room. This may take the form of group decision support systems, teleconferencing, or other methods.

electronic spreadsheet package An application program used as a computerized tool for analysis, planning, and modeling that allows users to enter and manipulate data into an electronic worksheet of rows and columns.

emulation To imitate one system with another so that the imitating system accepts the same data, executes the same programs, and achieves the same results as the imitated system.

encryption To scramble data or convert it, prior to transmission, to a secret code that masks the meaning of the data to unauthorized recipients. Similar to enciphering.

end user Anyone who uses an information system or the information it produces.

ergonomics The science and technology emphasizing the safety, comfort, and ease of use of human-operated machines such as computers. The goal of ergonomics is to produce systems that are user friendly, that is, safe, comfortable, and easy to use. Ergonomics is also called human factors engineering.

exception reports Reports produced only when exceptional conditions occur, or reports produced periodically that contain information only about exceptional conditions.

executive information system An information system that provides strategic information tailored to the needs of top management.

expert system A computer-based information system that uses its knowledge about a specific complex application area to act as an expert consultant to users. The system consists of a knowledge base and software modules that perform inferences on the knowledge and communicates answers to a user's questions.

facsimile The transmission of images and their reconstruction and duplication on some form of paper at a receiving station.

fault-tolerant computer systems Computers with multiple central processors, peripherals, and system software that are able to continue operations even when there is a major hardware or software failure.

feasibility study A preliminary study that investigates the information needs of end users and the objectives, constraints, basic resource requirements, cost/benefits, and feasibility of proposed projects.

feedback (1) Data or information concerning the components and operations of a system. (2) The use of part of the output of a system as input to the system.

fiber optics The technology that uses cables consisting of very thin filaments of glass fibers that can conduct the light generated by lasers at frequencies that approach the speed of light.

field A data element that consists of a grouping of characters that describes a particular attribute of an enitity, for example, the name field or salary field of an employee.

fifth-generation The next generation of computing, which will provide computers that will be able to see, hear, talk, and think. This would depend on major advances in parallel processing, user input/output methods, and artificial intelligence.

file A collection of related data records treated as a unit. Sometimes called a data set.

file maintenance The activity of keeping a file up to date by adding, changing, or deleting data.

file processing Utilizing a file for data processing activities such as file maintenance, information retrieval, or report generation.

firmware The use of microprogrammed read-only memory circuits in place of "hardwired" logic circuitry. See also *microprogramming*.

flip-flop A circuit or device containing active elements, capable of assuming either one or two states at a given time. Synonymous with toggle.

floating-point Pertaining to a number representation system in which each number is represented by two sets of digits. One set represents the significant digits or fixed-point "base" of the number, while the other set of digits represents the "exponent," which indicates the precision of the number.

floppy disk A small plastic disk coated with iron oxide that resembles a small phonograph record enclosed in a protective envelope. It is a widely used form of magnetic disk media that provides a direct access storage capability for microcomputer systems.

flowchart A graphical representation in which symbols are used to represent operations, data, flow, logic, equipment, and so on. A program flowchart illustrates the structure and sequence of operations of a program, while a system flowchart illustrates the components and flows of information systems.

foreground processing The automatic execution of the computer programs that have been designed to preempt the use of computing facilities. Contrast with *background processing*.

format The arrangement of data on a medium.

FORTRAN: FORmula TRANslation A high-level programming language widely utilized to develop computer programs that perform mathematical computations for scientific, engineering, and selected business applications.

fourth-generation languages (4GL) Programming languages that are easier to use than high-level languages like BASIC, COBOL, or FORTRAN. They are also known as nonprocedural, natural, or very high-level languages.

front-end processor Typically a smaller, general-purpose computer that is dedicated to handling data communications control functions in a communications network, thus relieving the host computer of these functions.

functional requirements The information system capabilities required to meet the information needs of end users.

fuzzy logic systems Computer-based systems that can learn to process data that are incomplete or only partially correct, that is, *fuzzy data*. Such systems can learn to solve unstructured problems with incomplete knowledge, as humans do.

general-purpose application programs Programs that can perform information processing jobs for users from all application areas. For example, word processing programs, electronic spreadsheet programs, and graphics programs can be used by individuals for home, education, business, scientific, and many other purposes.

general-purpose computer   A computer that is designed to handle a wide variety of problems. Contrast with *special-purpose computer.*

generate   A computer program that performs a generating function.

gigabyte   A billion bytes. More accurately, 2 to the 30th power, or 1,073,741,824 in decimal notation.

GIGO   A contraction of "Garbage In, Garbage Out," which emphasizes that information systems will produce erroneous and invalid output when provided with erroneous and invalid input data or instructions.

goal-seeking analysis   Making repeated changes to selected variables until a chosen variable reaches a target value.

graphical-user interface   A software interface that relies on icons, bars, buttons, boxes, and other images to initiate tasks for users.

graphics   Pertaining to symbolic input or output from a computer system, such as lines, curves, and geometric shapes, using video display units or graphics plotters and printers.

graphics pen and tablet   A device that allows an end user to draw or trace material placed on a pressure-sensitive tablet and have it digitized and captured by the computer and displayed on its video screen.

graphics software   A program that helps users generate graphics displays.

group decision support system (GDSS)   A decision support system that provides support for decision making by groups of people.

groupware   Software packages that support work activities by members of a work group whose workstations are interconnected by a local area network.

hacking   (1) Obsessive use of a computer. (2) The unauthorized access and use of computer systems.

handshaking   Exchange of predetermined signals when a connection is established between two communications terminals.

hard copy   A data medium or data record that has a degree of permanence and that can be read by people or machine.

hardware   (1) Machines and media. (2) Physical equipment, as opposed to computer programs or methods of use. (3) Mechanical, magnetic, electrical, electronic, or optical devices. Contrast with *software.*

hash total   The sum of numbers in a data field that are not normally added, such as account numbers or other identification numbers. It is utilized as a control total, especially during input/output operations of batch processing systems.

header label   A machine-readable record at the beginning of a file containing data for file identification and control.

heuristic   Pertaining to exploratory methods of problem solving in which solutions are discovered by evaluation of the progress made toward the final result. It is an exploratory trial-and-error approach guided by rules of thumb. Opposite of algorithmic.

hexadecimal   Pertaining to the number system with a base of 16. Synonymous with sexadecimal.

hierarchical data structure   A logical data structure in which the relationships between records form a hierarchy or tree structure. The relationships among records are one-to-many, since each data element is related only to one element above it.

high-level language   A programming language that utilizes macro instructions and statements that closely resemble human language or mathematical notation to describe the problem to be solved or the procedure to be used. Also called a computer language.

HIPO chart (Hierarchy + Input/Processing/Output)   Also known as an IPO chart. A design and documentation tool of structured programming utilized to record input/processing/output details of hierarchical program modules.

hollerith   Pertaining to a type of code or punched card utilizing 12 rows per column and usually 80 columns per card. Named after Herman Hollerith, who originated punched card data processing.

host computer   Typically a larger central computer that performs the major data processing tasks in a computer network.

hypermedia   Documents that contain multiple forms of media, including text, graphics, video and sound, which can be interactively searched like hypertext.

hypertext   A methodology for the construction and interactive use of text material in which a body of text in electronic form is indexed in a variety of ways so that it can be quickly searched by a reader.

icon   A small figure on a video display that looks like a familiar office or other device such as a file folder (for storing a file), a wastebasket (for deleting a file), or a calculator (for switching to a calculator mode).

image processing   A computer-based technology that allows end users to electronically capture, store, process, and retrieve images that may include numeric data, text, handwriting, graphics, documents, and photographs. Image processing makes heavy use of optical scanning and optical disk technologies.

impact printers   Printers that form images on paper through the pressing of a printing element and an inked ribbon or roller against the face of a sheet of paper.

index   An ordered reference list of the contents of a file or document together with keys or reference notations for identification or location of those contents.

index sequential   A method of data organization in which records are organized in sequential order and also referenced by an index. When utilized with direct access file devices, it is known as index sequential accesss method or ISAM.

inference engine   The software component of an expert system that processes the rules and facts related to a specific problem and makes associations and inferences resulting in recommended courses of action.

information   Data placed in a meaningful and useful context for an end user.

information center   A support facility for the end users of an organization. It allows users to learn to develop their own application programs and to accomplish their own information processing tasks. End users are provided with hardware support, software support, and people support (trained user consultants).

information float   The time when a document is in transit between the sender and receiver, and thus unavailable for any action or response.

information processing   A concept that covers both the traditional concept of processing numeric and alphabetic data, and the processing of text, images, and voices. It emphasizes that the production of information products for users should be the focus of processing activities.

information quality   The degree to which information has content, form, and time characteristics that give it value to specific end users.

information reporting system   A management information system that produces prespecified reports, displays, and responses on a periodic, exception, or demand basis.

information resource management (IRM)   A management concept that views data, information, and computer resources (computer hardware, software, and personnel) as valuable organizational resources that should be efficiently, economically, and effectively managed for the benefit of the entire organization.

information retrieval The methods and procedures for recovering specific information from stored data.

information system (IS) A set of people, procedures, and resources that collects, transforms, and disseminates information in an organization. Also, a system that accepts data resources as input and processes them into information products as output.

information system resources People, hardware, software, and data are the resources of an information system.

information system specialist A person whose occupation is related to the providing of information system services; for example, a system analyst, programmer, or computer operator.

information systems development See *systems development*.

information systems planning A formal planning process that develops plans for developing and managing information systems to support the goals of the organization. This includes strategic, tactical, and operational planning activities.

information technology (IT) Hardware, software, telecomunications, database management, and other information processing technologies used in computer-based information systems.

input Pertaining to a device, process, or channel involved in the insertion of data into a data processing system. Opposite of *output*.

input/output (I/O) Pertaining to either input or output, or both.

inquiry processing Computer processing that supports the realtime interrogation of online files and databases by end users.

instruction A grouping of characters that specifies the computer operation to be performed.

integrated circuit A complex microelectronic circuit consisting of interconnected circuit elements that cannot be disassembled because they are placed on or within a "continuous substrate" such as a silicon chip.

integrated packages Software that combines the ability to do several general-purpose applications (such as word processing, electronic spreadsheet, and graphics) into one program.

intelligent terminal A terminal with the capabilities of a microcomputer which can thus perform many data processing and other functions without accessing a larger computer.

interactive processing A type of realtime processing in which users can interact with a computer on a realtime basis.

interactive video Computer-based systems that integrate image processing with text, audio, and video processing technologies, which makes possible interactive multimedia presentations.

interface A shared boundary, such as the boundary between two systems. For example, the boundary between a computer and its peripheral devices.

interpreter A computer program that translates and executes each source language statement before translating and executing the next one.

interrupt A condition that causes an interruption in a processing operation during which another task is performed. At the conclusion of this new assignment, control may be transferred back to the point where the original processing operation was interrupted or to other tasks with a higher priority.

iterative Pertaining to the repeated execution of a series of steps.

job A specified group of tasks prescribed as a unit of work for a computer.

job control language (JCL) A language for communication with the operating system of a computer to identify a job and describe its requirements.

joystick A small lever set in a box used to move the cursor on the computer's display screen.

K An abbreviation for the prefix "kilo," which is 1,000 in decimal notation. When referring to storage capacity it is equivalent to 2 to the 10th power, or 1,024 in decimal notation.

keys One or more fields within a data record that are used to identify it or control its use.

keyboarding Using the keyboard of a microcomputer or computer terminal.

key-to-disk Data entry using a keyboard device to record data directly onto a magnetic disk.

knowledge base A collection of knowledge about a subject in a variety of forms, such as facts and rules of inference, frames, and objects.

knowledge base information system An information system that adds a knowledge base to the database and other components found in other types of computer-based information systems.

knowledge engineer A specialist who works with experts to capture the knowledge they possess in order to develop a knowledge base for expert systems and other knowledge-based systems.

knowledge workers People whose primary work activities include creating, using, and distributing information.

label One or more characters used to identify a statement or an item of data in a computer program or the contents of a data file.

language translator program A program that converts the programming language instructions in a computer program into machine language code. Major types include assemblers, compilers, and interpreters.

large scale integration (LSI) A method of constructing electronic circuits in which thousands of circuits can be placed on a single semiconductor chip.

layout forms and screens Tools that are used to construct the formats and generic content of input/output media and methods for the user interface, such as display screens and reports.

light pen A photoelectric device that allows data to be entered or altered on the face of a video display terminal.

line printer A device that prints all the characters of a line as a unit.

liquid crystal displays (LCDs) Electronic visual displays that form characters by applying an electrical charge to selected silicon crystals.

local area network (LAN) A communications network that typically connects computers, terminals, and other computerized devices within a limited physical area such as an office, building, manufacturing plant, or other worksite.

logical data elements Data elements that are independent of the physical data media on which they are recorded.

LOGO An interactive graphical language used as a tool for learning a variety of concepts (color, direction, letters, words, sounds, and so on) as well as learning to program and use the computer. Forms and figures are used (sprites and turtles) that a child learns to move around on the screen to accomplish tasks.

loop A sequence of instructions in a computer program that is executed repeatedly until a terminal condition prevails.

machine cycle The timing of a basic CPU operation as determined by a fixed number of electrical pulses emitted by the CPU's timing circuitry or internal clock.

machine language A programming language where instructions are expressed in the binary code of the computer.

macro instruction An instruction in a source language that is equivalent to a specified sequence of machine instructions.

magnetic bubble An electromagnetic storage device that stores and moves data magnetically as tiny magnetic spots that look like bubbles under a microscope as they float on the surface of a special type of semiconductor chip.

magnetic core Tiny rings composed of iron oxide and other materials strung on wires that provide electrical current to magnetize the cores. Data is represented by the direction of the magnetic field of groups of cores. Widely used as the primary storage media in second- and third-generation computer systems.

magnetic disks A flat circular plate with a magnetic surface on which data can be stored by selective magnetization of portions of the curved surface.

magnetic drum A circular cylinder with a magnetic surface on which data can be stored by selective magnetization of portions of the curved surface.

magnetic ink An ink that contains particles of iron oxide that can be magnetized and detected by magnetic sensors.

magnetic ink character recognition (MICR) The machine recognition of characters printed with magnetic ink. Primarily used for check processing by the banking industry.

magnetic tape A plastic tape with a magnetic surface on which data can be stored by selective magnetization of portions of the surface.

mag stripe card A plastic wallet-sized card with a strip of magnetic tape on one surface; widely used for credit/debit cards.

mainframe A larger-size computer system, typically with a seperate central processing unit, as distinguished from microcomputer and minicomputer systems.

management information system (MIS) An information system that provides information to support managerial decision making. More specifically, an information reporting system, executive information system, or decision support system.

manual data processing (1) Data processing requiring continual human operation and intervention that utilizes simple data processing tools such as paper forms, pencils, and filing cabinets. (2) All data processing that is not automatic, even if it utilizes machines such as typewriters and calculators.

mark-sensing The electrical sensing of manually recorded conductive marks on a nonconductive surface.

mass storage Secondary storage devices with extra large storage capacities such as magnetic or optical disks.

master file A data file containing relatively permanent information, which is utilized as an authoritative reference and is usually updated periodically. Contrast with *transaction file*.

mathematical model A mathematical representation of a process, device, or concept.

media All tangible objects on which data are recorded.

megabyte A million bytes. More accurately, 2 to the 20th power, or 1,048,576 in decimal notation.

memory Same as *storage*.

menu A displayed list of items (usually the names of alternative applications, files, or activities) from which an end user makes a selection.

menu driven A characteristic of interactive computing systems that provides menu displays and operator prompting to assist an end user in performing a particular job.

microcomputer The smallest major category of computers—used as personal computers (PCs), end-user workstations, technical workstations, network servers, and so on. They range in size from portable hand-held units to desktop and floor standing models.

micrographics The use of microfilm, microfiche, and other microforms to record data in greatly reduced form.

microprocessor A microcomputer central processing unit (CPU) on a chip, without input/output or primary storage capabilities in most types.

microprogram A small set of elementary control instructions called microinstructions or microcode.

microprogramming The use of software (microprograms) to perform the functions of hardware (electronic control circuitry). Microprograms stored in a read-only storage module of the control unit interpret the machine language instructions of a computer program and decode them into elementary microinstructures, which are then executed.

microsecond A millionth of a second.

millisecond A thousandth of a second.

minicomputer A small (for example, the size of a desk) electronic, digital, stored-program, general-purpose computer.

model base An organized collection of conceptual, mathematical, and logical models that express business relationships, computational routines, or analytical techniques. Such models are stored in the form of programs and programs subroutines, command files and spread sheets.

modem (MOdulator-DEModulator) A device that converts the digital signals from input/output devices into appropriate frequencies at a transmission terminal and converts them back into digital signals at a receiving terminal.

monitor Software or hardware that observes, supervises, controls, or verifies the operations of a system.

mouse A small device that is electronically connected to a computer and is moved by hand on a flat surface in order to move the cursor in a video screen in the same direction. Buttons on the mouse allow users to issue commands and make responses or selections.

multiplex To interleave or simultaneously transmit two or more messages on a single channel.

multiplexer An electronic device that allows a single communications channel to carry simultaneous data transmission from many terminals.

multiprocessing Pertaining to the simultaneous execution of two or more instructions by a computer or computer network.

multiprocessor computer systems Computer systems that use multiple processors for their processing functions. This includes the use of support microprocessors, multiple CPUs, or a parallel processor design.

multiprogramming Pertaining to the concurrent execution of two or more programs by a computer by interleaving their execution.

multitasking The concurrent use of the same computer to accomplish several different information processing tasks. Each task may require the use of a different program, or the concurrent use of the same copy of a program by several users.

nanosecond A billionth of a second.

natural language A programming language that is very close to human language. Also called very high-level language.

network An interconnected system of computers, terminals, and communications channels and devices.

network architecture A master plan designed to promote an open, simple, flexible, and efficient telecommunications environment through the use of standard protocols, standard communications hardware and software interfaces, and the design of a standard multilevel telecommunications interface between end users and computer systems.

network data structure A logical data structure that allows many-to-many relationships among data records. It allows entry into a database at multiple points, because any data element or record can be related to many other data elements.

neural networks Massively parallel neurocomputer systems whose architecture is based on the human brain's mesh-like neuron structure. Such networks can process many pieces of information simultaneously, and can learn to recognize patterns and program themselves to solve related problems on their own.

node A terminal point in a communications network.

nonimpact printers Printers that use specially treated paper that form characters by laser, thermal (heat), electrostatic, or electrochemical processes.

nonprocedural languages Programming languages that allow users and professional programmers to specify the results they want without specifying how to solve the problem.

numerical control Automatic control of a machine process by a computer that makes use of numerical data, generally introduced as the operation is in process. Also called machine control.

object A data element that includes both data and the methods or processes that act on that data.

object-based knowledge Knowledge represented as a network of objects.

object-oriented language An object-oriented programming (OOP) language used to develop programs that create and use objects to perform information processing tasks.

object program A compiled or assembled program composed of executable machine instructions. Contrast with *source program*.

octal Pertaining to the number representation system with a base of eight.

OEM: Original Equipment Manufacturer A firm that manufactures and sells computers by assembling components produced by other hardware manufacturers.

office automation (OA) The use of computer-based information systems that collect, process, store, and transmit electronic messages, documents, and other forms of office communications among individuals, work groups, and organizations.

office management systems Office automation systems that integrate a variety of computer-based support services, including desktop accessories, electronic mail, and electronic task management.

offline Pertaining to equipment or devices not under control of the central processing unit.

online Pertaining to equipment or devices under control of the central processing system.

online transaction processing (OLTP) A realtime transaction processing system.

operand That which is operated upon. That part of a computer instruction that is identified by the address part of the instruction.

operating environment package Software packages or modules that add a graphics-based interface between end users, the operating system, and their application programs and may also provide a multitasking capability.

operating system The main control program of a computer system. It controls the operations of a computer by communicating with end

users, managing hardware resources and files, supervising the accomplishment of tasks, and providing other support services.

operation code A code that represents specific operations to be performed upon the operands in a computer instruction.

operational feasibility The willingness and ability of management, employees, customers, and suppliers to operate, use, and support a proposed system.

optical character recognition (OCR) The machine identification of printed characters through the use of light-sensitive devices.

optical disks A secondary storage medium using laser technology to read tiny spots on a plastic disk. The disks are currently capable of storing billions of characters of information.

optical scanner A device that optically scans characters or images and generates their digital representations.

optimization analysis Finding an optimum value for selected variables in a mathematical model, given certain constraints.

organizational feasibility How well a proposed information system supports the objectives of an organization's strategic plan for information systems.

output Pertaining to a device, process, or channel involved with the transfer of data or information out of an information processing system.

overlapped processing Pertaining to the ability of a computer system to increase the utilization of its central processing unit by overlapping input/output and processing operations.

packet A group of data control information in a specified format that is transmitted as an entity.

packet switching A data transmission process that transmits addressed packets such that a channel is occupied only for the duration of transmission of the packet.

page A segment of a program or data, usually of fixed length.

paging A process that automatically and continually transfers pages of programs and data between primary storage and direct-access storage devices. It provides computers with multiprogramming and virtual memory capabilities.

parallel processing Executing many instructions at the same time, that is, in parallel. Performed by advanced computers using many instruction processors organized in clusters or networks.

parity bit A check bit appended to an array on binary digits to make the sum of all the binary digits, including the check bit, always odd or always even.

Pascal A high-level, general-purpose, structured programming language named after Blaise Pascal. It was developed by Niklaus Wirth of Zurich in 1968.

pen-based computers Tablet-style microcomputers that recognize handwriting or hand drawing done by a pen-shaped device on their pressure sensitive display screens.

performance monitor A software package that monitors the processing of computer system jobs, helps develop a planned schedule of computer operations that can optimize computer system performance, and produces detailed statistics that are used for computer system capacity planning and control.

periodic reports Providing information to managers using a prespecified format designed to provide information on a regularly scheduled basis.

peripheral devices In a computer system, any unit of equipment, distinct from the central processing unit, that provides the system with input, output, or additional storage capabilities.

personal information manager (PIM) A software package that helps end users store, organize, and retrieve text and numerical data in the form of notes, lists, memos, and a variety of other forms.

picosecond A trillionth of a second.

PILOT: Programmed Inquiry, Learning or Teaching A special-purpose language designed to develop CAI (computer-aided instruction) programs.

PL/1: Programming Language 1 A procedure-oriented, high-level, general-purpose programming language designed to combine the features of COBOL, FORTRAN, and ALGOL.

plasma display Output devices that generate a visual display with electrically charged particles of gas trapped between glass plates.

plotter A hard-copy output device produces drawings and graphical displays on paper or other materials.

pointer A data element associated with an index, a record, or other set of data that contains the address of a related record.

pointing devices Devices that allow end users to issue commands or make choices by moving a cursor on the screen display.

point-of-sale (POS) terminal A computer terminal used in retail stores that serves the function of a cash register as well as collecting sales data and performing other data processing functions.

port (1) Electronic circuitry that provides a connection point between the CPU and input/output devices. (2) A connection point for a communications line on a CPU or other front-end device.

private branch exchange (PBX) A switching device that serves as an interface between the many telephone lines within a work area and the local telephone company's main telephone lines or trunks. Computerized PBXs can handle the switching of both voice and data in the local area networks that are needed in such locations.

procedure-oriented language A programming language designed for the convenient expression of procedures used in the solution of a wide class of problems.

procedures Sets of instructions used by people to complete a task.

process control The use of a computer to control an ongoing physical process such as petrochemical production.

process design The design of the programs and procedures needed by a proposed information system, including detailed program specifications and procedures.

processor A hardware device or software system capable of performing operations upon data.

program A set of instructions that cause a computer to perform a particular task.

programmer A person mainly involved in designing, writing, and testing computer programs.

programming language A language used to develop the instructions in computer programs.

programming tools Software packages or modules that provide editing and diagnostic capabilities and other support facilities to assist the programming process.

prompt Messages that assist the user in performing a particular job. This would include error messages, correction suggestions, questions, and other messages that guide an end user.

protocol A set of rules and procedures for the control of communications in a communications network.

prototype A working model. In particular, a working model of an information system that includes tentative versions of user input and output, databases and files, control methods, and processing routines.

prototyping The rapid development and testing of working models, or prototypes, of new information system applications in an interactive, iterative process involving both systems analysts and end users.

pseudocode An informal design language of structured programming that expresses the processing logic of a program module in ordinary human-language phrases.

punched card A card punched with a pattern of holes to represent data.

punched tape A tape on which a pattern of holes or cuts is used to represent data.

query language A high-level, human-like language provided by a database management system that enables users to easily extract data and information from a database.

queue (1) A waiting line formed by items in a system waiting for service. (2) To arrange in or form a queue.

random access Same as *direct access*.

random-access memory (RAM) One of the basic types of semiconductor memory used for temporary storage of data or programs during processing. Each memory position can be directly sensed (read) or changed (write) in the same length of time, irrespective of its location on the storage medium.

read-only memory (ROM) A basic type of semiconductor memory used for permanent storage. Can only be read, not "written," that is, changed. Variations are Programmable Read Only Memory (PROM) and Erasable Programmable Read Only Memory (EPROM).

realtime Pertaining to the performance of data processing during the actual time a business or physical process transpires, in order that results of the data processing can be used in supporting the completion of the process.

realtime processing Data processing in which data is processed immediately rather than periodically. Also called online processing. Contrast with *batch processing*.

record A collection of related data fields treated as a unit.

reduced instruction set computer (RISC) A CPU architecture that optimizes processing speed by the use of a smaller number of basic machine instructions than traditional CPU designs.

redundancy In information processing, the repetition of part or all of a message to increase the chance that the correct information will be understood by the recipient.

registers A device capable of storing a specified amount of data such as one word.

relational data structure A logical data structure in which all data elements within the database are viewed as being stored in the form of simple tables. DBMS packages based on the relational model can link data elements from various tables as long as the tables share common data elements.

remote access Pertaining to communication with the data processing facility by one or more stations that are distant from that facility.

remote job entry (RJE) Entering jobs into a batch processing system from a remote facility.

report generator A feature of database management system packages that allows an end user to quickly specify a report format for the display of information retrieved from a database.

reprographics Copying and duplicating technology and methods.

resource management An operating system function that controls the use of computer system resources such as primary storage, secondary storage, CPU processing time, and input/output devices by other system software and application software packages.

robotics   The technology of building machines (robots) with computer intelligence and humanlike physical capabilities.

routines   An ordered set of instructions that may have some general or frequent use.

RPG: Report Program Generator   A problem-oriented language that utilizes a generator to construct programs that produce reports and perform other data processing tasks.

secondary storage   Storage that supplements the primary storage of a computer. Synonymous with *auxiliary storage*.

sector   A subdivision of a track on a magnetic disk surface.

security monitor   A software package that monitors the use of a computer system and protects its resources from unauthorized use, fraud, and vandalism.

semiconductor memory   Microelectronic storage circuitry etched on tiny chips of silicon or other semiconducting material. The primary storage of most modern computers consists of microelectronic semiconductor memory chips for random-access memory (RAM) and read-only memory (ROM).

sequential access   A sequential method of storing and retrieving data from a file. Contrast with *random access*.

sequential data organization   Organizing logical data elements according to a prescribed sequence.

serial   Pertaining to the sequential or consecutive occurrence of two or more related activities in a single device or channel.

server   A computer that supports telecommunications in a local area network, as well as the sharing of peripheral devices, software, and databases among the workstations in the network.

service bureau   A firm offering computer and data processing services. Also called a computer service center.

smart products   Industrial and consumer products, with "intelligence" provided by built-in microcomputers or microprocessors that significantly improve the performance and capabilities of such products.

software   Computer programs and procedures concerned with the operation of an information system. Contrast with *hardware*.

software package   A computer program supplied by computer manufacturers, independent software companies, or other computer users. Also known as canned programs, proprietary software, or packaged programs.

solid state   Pertaining to devices such as transistors and diodes whose operation depends on the control of electric or magnetic phenomena in solid materials.

source data automation   The use of automated methods of data entry that attempt to reduce or eliminate many of the activities, people, and data media required by traditional data-entry methods.

source document   A document that is the original formal record of a transaction, such as a purchase order or a sales invoice.

source program   A computer program written in a language that is subject to a translation process. Contrast with *object program*.

special-purpose computer   A computer that is designed to handle a restricted class of problems. Contrast with *general-purpose computer*.

spooling   Simultaneous peripheral operation online. Storing input data from low-speed devices temporarily on high-speed secondary storage units, which can be quickly accessed by the CPU. Also, writing output data at high speeds onto magnetic tape or disk units from which it can be transferred to slow-speed devices such as a printer.

storage   Pertaining to a device into which data can be entered, with which it can be held, and from which it can be retrieved at a later time.

strategic information systems   Information systems that provide a firm with competitive products and services that give it a strategic advantage over its competitors in the marketplace.

structure chart   A design and documentation technique to show the purpose and relationships of the various modules in a program.

structured programming   A programming methodology that uses a top-down program design and a limited number of control structures in a program to create highly structured modules of program code.

structured query language (SQL)   A query language that is becoming a standard for advanced database management system packages. A query's basic form is SELECT . . . FROM . . . WHERE.

subroutine   A routine that can be part of another program routine.

subsystem   A system that is a component of a larger system.

supercomputer   A special category of large computer systems that are the most powerful available. They are designed to solve massive computational problems.

superconductor   Materials that can conduct electricity with almost no resistence. This allows the development of extremely fast and small electronic circuits. Formerly only possible at super cold temperatures near absolute zero. Recent developments promise superconducting materials near room temperature.

switch   (1) A device or programming technique for making a selection. (2) A computer that controls message switching among the computers and terminals in a telecommunications network.

synchronous   A characteristic in which each event, or the performance of any basic operation, is constrained to start on, and usually to keep in step with, signals from a timing clock. Contrast with *asynchronous*.

system   (1) A group of interrelated or interacting elements forming a unified whole. (2) A group of interrelated components working together toward a common goal by accepting input and producing output in an organized transformation process.

system flowchart   A graphic diagramming tool used to show the flow of information processing activities as data are processed by the people and devices in an information system.

system software   Programs that control and support operations of a computer system. System software includes a variety of programs such as operating systems, database management systems, communications control programs, service and utility programs, and programming language translators.

system specifications   The product of the systems design stage. It consists of specifications for the hardware, software, facilities, personnel, databases, and the user interface of a proposed information system.

system support programs   Programs that support the operations, management, and users of a computer system by providing a variety of support services. Examples are system utilities and performance monitors.

systems analysis   (1) Analyzing in detail the components and requirements of a system. (2) Analyzing in detail the information needs of an organization, the characteristics and components of presently utilized information systems, and the functional requirements of proposed information systems.

systems design   Deciding how a proposed information system will meet the information needs of end users. Includes user interface, data, and process design activities that produce system specifications to satisfy the system requirements developed in the systems analysis stage.

systems development (1) Conceiving, designing, and implementing a system. (2) Developing information systems by process of investigation, analysis, design, implementation, and maintenance. Also called the systems development life cycle (SDLC), information systems development, or application development.

systems development tools Graphical, textual, and computer-aided tools and techniques that are used to help analyze, design, and document the development of an information system. They are typically used to represent (1) the components and flows of a system, (2) the user interface, (3) data attributes and relationships, and (4) detailed system processes.

systems implementation The stage of systems development in which hardware and software are acquired, developed, and installed, the system is tested and documented, people are trained to operate and use the system, and an organization converts to the use of a newly developed system.

systems investigation The screening, selection, and preliminary study of a proposed information system solution to a business problem.

systems maintenance The monitoring, evaluating, and modifying of a system to make desirable or necessary improvements.

technical feasibility Whether reliable hardware and software capable of meeting the needs of a proposed system can be acquired or developed by an organization in the required time.

telecommunications Pertaining to the transmission of signals over long distances, including not only data communications but also the transmission of images and voices using radio, television, and other communications technologies.

telecommunications channel The part of a telecommunications network that connects the message source with the message receiver. It includes the physical equipment used to connect one location to another for the purpose of transmitting and receiving information.

telecommunications controller A data communications interface device (frequently a special-purpose mini or microcomputer) that can control a telecommunications network containing many terminals.

telecommunications control program A computer program that controls and supports the communications between the computers and terminals in a telecommunications network.

telecommunications monitors Computer programs that control and support the communications between the computers and terminals in a telecommunications network.

telecommunications processors Multiplexers, concentrators, communications controllers, and cluster controllers that allow a communications channel to carry simultaneous data transmissions from many terminals. They may also perform error monitoring, diagnostics and correction, modulation-demodulation, data compression, data coding and decoding, message switching, port contention, buffer storage, and serving as an interface to satellite and other communications networks.

telecommuting The use of telecommunications to replace commuting to work from one's home.

teleconferencing The use of video communications to allow business conferences to be held with participants who are scattered across a country, continent, or the world.

telephone tag The process that occurs when two people who wish to contact each other by telephone, repeatedly miss each other's phone calls.

teleprocessing Using telecommunications for computer-based information processing.

terabyte One trillion bytes. More accurately, 2 to the 40th power, or 1,009,511,627,776 in decimal notation.

terminal Any input/output device that uses telecommunication networks to transmit or receive data.

text data Words, phrases, sentences, and paragraphs used in documents and other forms of communication.

throughput The total amount of useful work performed by a data processing system during a given period of time.

time sharing Providing computer services to many users simultaneously while providing rapid responses to each.

top-down design A methodology of structured programming in which a program is organized into functional modules, with the programmer designing the main module first and then the lower-level modules.

touch-sensitive screen An input device that accepts data input by the placement of a finger on or close to the CRT screen.

track The portion of a moving storage medium, such as a drum, tape, or disk, that is accessible to a given reading-head position.

trackball A rollerball device set in a case used to move the cursor on a computer's display screen.

transaction An event that occurs as part of doing business, such as a sale, purchase, deposit, withdrawal, refund, transfer, payment, and so on.

transaction document A document that is produced as part of a business transaction, for example, a purchase order, paycheck, sales receipt, or customer invoice.

transaction file A data file containing relatively transient data to be processed in combination with a master file. Contrast with *master file.*

transaction processing system An information system that processes data arising from the occurrence of business transactions.

transaction terminals Terminals used in banks, retail stores, factories, and other worksites that are used to capture transaction data at its point of origin. Examples are point-of-sale (POS) terminals and automated teller machines (ATMs).

turnaround document Output of a computer system (such as customer invoices and statements) that is designed to be returned to the organization as machine-readable input.

turnaround time The elapsed time between submission of a job to a computing center and the return of the results.

turnkey systems Computer systems where all of the hardware, software, and systems development needed by a user are provided.

unbundling The separate pricing of hardware, software, and other related services.

universal product code (UPC) A standard identification code using bar coding, printed on products that can be read by the optical supermarket scanners of the grocery industry.

user friendly A characteristic of human-operated equipment and systems that makes them safe, comfortable, and easy to use.

user interface The part of an operating system or other program that allows users to communicate with it to load programs, access files, and accomplish other computing tasks.

user interface design Designing the interactions between end users and computer systems, including input/output methods and the conversion of data between human-readable and machine-readable forms.

utility program A standard set of routines that assists in the operation of a computer system by performing some frequently required process such as copying, sorting, or merging.

value-added carriers   Third-party vendors who lease telecommunications lines from common carriers and offer a variety of telecommunications services to customers.

videotex   An interactive information service provided over phone lines or cable TV channels.

virtual memory   The use of secondary storage devices as an extension of the primary storage of a computer, thus giving the appearance of a larger main memory than actually exists.

virtual reality   The use of multisensory human/computer interfaces that enable human users to experience computer-simulated objects, entities, spaces, and "worlds" as if they actually existed.

VLSI: Very Large-Scale Integration   Semiconductor chips containing hundreds of thousands of circuits.

voice mail   A variation of electronic mail where digitized voice messages rather than electronic text are accepted, stored, and transmitted.

voice recognition   Direct conversion of spoken data into electronic form suitable for entry into a computer system. Also called voice data entry.

volatile memory   Memory (such as electronic semiconductor memory) that loses its contents when electrical power is interrupted.

wand   A hand-held optical character recognition device used for data entry by many transaction terminals.

what-if analysis   Observing how changes to selected variables effect other variables in a mathematical model.

wide area network (WAN)   A data communications network covering a large geographic area.

window   One section of a computer's multiple section display screen, each of which can have a different display.

word   (1) A string of characters considered as a unit. (2) An ordered set of bits (usually larger than a byte) handled as a unit by the central processing unit.

word processing   The automation of the transformation of ideas and information into a readable form of communication. It involves the use of computers to manipulate text data in order to produce office communications in the form of documents.

work group computing   End user computing in a work group environment in which members of a work group may use a local area network to share software and databases to accomplish group assignments.

workstation   A computer terminal or micro- or minicomputer system designed to support the work of one person. Also, a high-powered computer to support the work of professionals in engineering, science, and other areas that require extensive computing power and graphics capabilities.

Credits

Part and Chapter Opening Photos

Part 1 © Tony Stone/Worldwide. **Part II** © Jed Share/Westlight. **Part III** © Butch Gemin; inset Motorola. **Part IV** J. Nettis/H. Armstrong Roberts. **Chapter 1** © Tony Stone/Worldwide. **Chapter 2** Butch Gemin; inset Larry Mulvehill/Science Source/Photo Researchers. **Chapter 3** © David Brownell/The Image Bank. **Chapter 4** © Darrell Jones/All Stock. **Chapter 5** T. del Amo/H. Armstrong Roberts. **Chapter 6** © 1994 Steven Lunetta/StockUp. **Chapter 7** © Nancy Brown/The Image Bank. **Chapter 8** © Michael Salas/The Image Bank. **Chapter 9** © Barros & Barros/The Image Bank. **Chapter 10** © Grant Faint/The Image Bank. **Chapter 11** © Steve Smith/Westlight. **Chapter 12** © Jim Pickerell/Tony Stone Images, Inc.

Text Photos

Page 8 *(top left)* © Robert A. Herko/The Image Bank; *(top right)* Courtesy of Apple Computers; *(center and bottom)* Courtesy of International Business Machines Corporation. **11** *(top left and top center)* Courtesy of International Business Machines Corporation; *(top right)* © Steve Niedorf/The Image Bank; *(right)* © Weinberg-Clark/The Image Bank. **12** © Bill Varie/The Image Bank. **16** *(top)* © Steven Lunetta/StockUp; *(left)* Courtesy of NASA. **17** © Barrow & Barros/The Image Bank. **18** AICorporation. **20** Courtesy of Cray Computers. **22** *(top and bottom)* Courtesy of International Business Machines Corporation. **25** © Lou Jones/The Image Bank. **41** © Jeff Smith/The Image Bank. **42** Courtesy of GRiD Systems Corporation. **47** © Reid Rahn. **49** © Bill Varie/The Image Bank. **50** © Maria Taglienti/The Image Bank. **60** *(top left)* Martin Marietta Corporation; *(top right)* Jon Feingersch/NASD; *(bottom)* Courtesy of Canon USA, Inc. **61** *(top left)* Jay Freis/The Image Bank; *(top right)* DuPont Corporation; *(center)* Image courtesy of Silicon Graphics, Inc./Korea Electric Power Corporations "ENERTOPIA", Angel; *(bottom left)* Gregory I Ieisler/The Image Bank; *(bottom right)* H&R Block. **70** Microsoft{reg} Corporation. **71** Courtesy of International Business Machines Corporation. **75** Microsoft{reg} Corporation. **76** Courtesy of International Business Machines Corporation. **79** Microsoft{reg} Corporation. **80** Courtesy of International Business Machines Corporation. **83** SunSoft. **85** Fractal Design Corporation. **89** *(top)* Courtesy of International Business Machines Corporation; *(bottom)* Novell. **100** John Madere/Reproduced with permission of AT&T. **103, 104** WordPerfect v6.0 for Windows, © 1991–93 WordPerfect Corporation. All Rights Reserved. Used with permission. **105** Microsoft{reg} Corporation. **107** WordPerfect v6.0 for Windows, © 1991–93 WordPerfect Corporation. All Rights Reserved. Used with permission. **108** Que Software. **110** *(top)* John Greenleigh/Apple Computer; *(bottom)* ClickArt courtesy T/Maker Company. **111** Quark. **112** Copyright Truevision, Inc. **113** *(top)* Lotus Development Corporation; *(bottom)* Stephen Derr/The Image Bank. **114** *(top)* Courtesy of International Business Machines Corporation; *(bottom)* WindowsDraw courtesy Micrografx. **116** Lotus Development Corporation. **118** Arni Katz/Stock South. **119** *(top)* Joseph Nettis/Photo Researchers; *(bottom)* Courtesy of International Business Machines Corporation. **121** Channel Computing. **122** Ascend, Courtesy of Franklin Quest, Salt Lake City, Utah. **132** *(top and bottom)* Courtesy of International Business Machines Corporation. **136** Courtesy of Lotus Development Corporation. **142, 144** Microsoft{reg} Corporation. **146** Courtesy of International Business Machines Corporation. **147** Quattro Pro by Borland International. **149** Lotus Development Corporation. **150** Microsoft{reg} Corporation. **152** Charles River Analytics. **153** © 1991 Keith Bardin. **154** Courtesy of EXSYS, Inc., Albuquerque, NM. **164** *(top)* Paradox, Courtesy of Borland International; *(bottom)* dBASE IV, Courtesy of Borland International. **166** *(top and bottom)* Courtesy of Borland International. **171** First choice by Spinnaker Software. **183** *(top and bottom)* Courtesy of Software Products International. **185** Contact Software. **188, 189** Courtesy of International Business Machines Corporation. **200** *(top left)* Silicon Graphics; *(top right)* Courtesy Wacom Technology; *(bottom left)* 3D Models by Jim Ludtke © 1991 MTV Networks; *(bottom right)* Courtesy Silicon Graphics. **201** *(top)* Image courtesy of Silicon Graphics, Inc./Designer/Director: Joel Hynec, First Light, Inc. Animation: Kleiser-Walczak Construction Co. © 1993; *(left)* David Parker/Science Photo Library/Photo Researchers; *(right)* Image provided courtesy Silicon Graphics/Art Associates. **202** *(left)* © ModaCAD, Inc. 1992; *(center)* Courtesy of International Business Machines Corporation; *(bottom)* Cray Research, Inc. **203** *(top)* Courtesy of Analogic Corporation; *(bottom)* Courtesy of Gold Disk. **209** Courtesy of Motorola. **210** Jay Brousseau/The Image Bank. **211** Courtesy of Motorola. **212** *(top)* Peter Grumann/The Image Bank; *(bottom)* Larry Keenan Associates/The Image Bank. **215** *(top left)* Courtesy of Apple Computers/John Greenleigh; *(top right)* Courtesy of Dell Computer Corp.; *(bottom left)* Courtesy of Compaq Computers; *(bottom right)* Courtesy of Texas Instruments. **217** *(top and bottom)* Courtesy of International Business Machines Corporation. **219** Courtesy of Digital Equipment Corporation. **220** Courtesy of International Business Machines Corporation. **222** *(top)* Image Courtesy of Silicon Graphics, Inc./Screen image Courtesy of Sony Corporation/Alias; *(bottom)* Photo courtesy of the Home Shopping Network. **240** Courtesy of International Business Machines Corporation. **241** *(bottom)* Courtesy Logitec Corporation. **242** Wacom Technology Corporation. **243** GRiD Systems Corporation. **244** *(left)* Image courtesy of Silicon Graphics, Inc.; *(right)* Courtesy of International Business Machines Corporation. **245** *(left)* Courtesy of International Business Machines Corporation; *(right)* Courtesy of Apple Computer, Inc./photo by John Greenleigh. **246** Zeva Oelbaum/Peter Arnold. **250** Courtesy of International Business Machines Corporation. **252** Courtesy of Logitec Corporation. **254** *(far left)* Antonio Rosario/The Image Bank; *(center left)* Lou Jones/The Image Bank; *(center right)* Ken Cooper/The Image Bank; *(far right)* Walter Bibikow/The Image Bank. **257** Courtesy Exabyte. **258** Gregory Heisler/The Image Bank. **260** Courtesy of Apple Computer, Inc./photo by Frank Proyr. **273** Courtesy Sprint International. **282** *(top)* T. J. Florian/Rainbow; *(bottom)* NASA. **283** Jim Newberry. **284** The Teleport Family of Modems Courtesy of Global Village Communication, Inc. **285** AT&T Archives. **286** Developed by FutureSoft, Inc. **287** Courtesy of International Business Machines Corporation. **290** *(top)* Lotus Development Corporation. **292** *(top)* Prodigy. **308** *(top)* Richard Mack; *(bottom)* Courtesy of International Business Machines Corporation. **310** *(top)* Kano Photography; *(bottom)* Jack Deutsch/Innervisions. **312, 314** Lee Gregory. **315** Courtesy CompUSA Inc. **320** Tim Davis/Photo Researchers. **327** Courtesy of Borland International. **333** Courtesy of Evergreen CASE Tools. **335, 336** Courtesy of Borland International. **344, 346** Courtesy of NeXT Computer, Inc. **360** © Joel Gordon. **363** Courtesy of International Business Machines Corporation. **366** Courtesy of IRI Software. **369** Teleware. **370** Paul Shambroom/Photo Researchers. **371** H. R. Bramaz/Peter Arnold. **372** Steve Dunwell/The Image Bank. **373** *(top)* Greenlar/The Image Words; *(bottom)* Image courtesy of Silicon Graphics, Inc. Sigma Design, Inc. **375** Alvis Upitis/The Image Bank. **377** Stan Wolenski. **378** *(top)* Lee Gregory; *(bottom)* NASA.

380 © Jay Freis/The Image Bank. **383** © Steve Smith/Westlight. **399** Courtesy Central Point Software. **405** EDS Corporation. **408** © Charles Gupton/Tony Stone Images, Inc. **409** Courtesy of TechSoft Systems, Inc. **424** *(top left)* Masaaki Hiraga/Photonica; *(bottom left)* The Computer Museum; *(top right)* The Bettmann Archive; *(bottom right)* Bill Pierce/Rainbow. **425** *(top)* The Computer Museum; *(bottom)* Courtesy of International Business Machines Corporation. **426** *(top)* Unisys Corporation; *(center)* The Computer Museum; *(bottom)* Courtesy of Digital Equipment Corporation, Corporate Photo Library. **427** *(left)* Dan McCoy/Rainbow; *(top right and bottom right)* The Computer Museum. **428** *(top)* Tim Davis/Science Source/Photo Researchers; *(bottom left)* Laura Dwight/Peter Arnold; *(bottom right)* Courtesy NCR Corporation. **429** AT&T Archives. **430** *(top)* NASA; *(bottom)* NCR Corporation.

Index